Social History of Western Civilization

Volume I

THIRD EDITION

Social History of Western Civilization

Volume I

Readings from the Ancient World to the Seventeenth Century

THIRD EDITION

RICHARD M. GOLDEN

University of North Texas

St. Martin's Press   New York

Manager, publishing services: Emily Berleth
Project management: Richard Steins
Production supervisor: Melissa Kaprelian
Cover design: Richard Emery Design, Inc.
Cover art: Detail from Pieter Bruegel the Elder, *The Harvesters (July)*.
     Copyright ©1988
     The Metropolitan Museum of Art, Rogers Fund, 1919. (19.164)

For information, write:
St. Martin's Press, Inc.
175 Fifth Avenue
New York, NY 10010

ISBN: 0-312-09645-3

Acknowledgments
It is a violation of the law to reproduce these selections by any means whatsoever without the written permission of the copyright holder.

"Formation of Western Attitudes toward Women." Vern L. Bullough, Brenda Shelton, and Sarah Slavin, from *The Subordinate Sex: A History of Attitudes Toward Women*. Athens, Georgia: University of Georgia Press, 1988. Copyright © 1988 by the University of Georgia Press. Reprinted by permission.

"Slavery in the Ancient Near East." Isaac Mendelsohn. From *Biblical Archaeologist*, volume 9, December 1946, pages 74–88. Reprinted with permission.

"Afterlife: Ancient Israel's Changing Vision of the World Beyond." Bernhard Lang, first appeared in *Bible Review*, February 1988, pages 12, 14–23. Reprinted with permission of the Biblical Archeological Society, 4710 41st Street, NW, Washington, D.C., 20016.

"Religious and Social Order in Ancient Egypt." John Baines. Reprinted from Byron E. Shafer, ed.: *Religion in Ancient Egypt: Gods, Myths, and Personal Practice*. Copyright © 1991 by Cornell University Press. Used by permission of the publisher, Cornell University Press.

Acknowledgments and copyrights are continued at the back of the book on pages 322–323, which constitute an extension of the copyright page.

Preface

Social History of Western Civilization, Third Edition, is a two-volume reader for Western Civilization courses. The essays in each volume deal with social history because I believe that the most original and significant work of the past two decades has been in this area and because Western Civilization textbooks tend to slight social history in favor of the more traditional political, intellectual, and cultural history, though this bias is slowly changing. In the twenty years that I have taught Western Civilization, I have used many books, texts, and readers designed specifically for introductory courses. I decided to compile this anthology because I perceived that other collections generally failed to retain student interest. My students found many of the essays in these other books boring, often because the selections assumed a degree of background knowledge that a typical student does not possess. To make this reader better suited to students, I have attempted to include essays that are both important and readable. This has not been an easy task, for many significant history articles, which have been written solely for specialists, are, unfortunately, simply too difficult for college undergraduates. I have gone through hundreds of articles searching for the few that are challenging, fascinating, important, and readable. To further enhance the readability of the selected articles, I have translated foreign words and identified individuals and terms that students might not recognize. All footnotes are therefore my own unless otherwise indicated. I, for one, do not understand why anthologies intended for college students do not routinely translate foreign expressions, phrases, and book titles and, moreover, seem to take for granted that students will be familiar with Tertullian, Gustavus Adolphus, or Pearl Buck, to mention some examples.

A Western Civilization reader cannot be all things to all instructors and students, but I have consciously tried to make these two volumes useful for as many Western Civilization courses as possible, despite the widely varying ways in which such courses are taught. The readings in these volumes cover many geographical areas and a broad range of topics in social history. Some historians argue that Western civilization began with the Greeks, but I have included in Volume One a section on the Ancient Near East for the courses that begin there. Both volumes contain material on the seventeenth century; indeed, Volume Two includes in its first selections some material that precedes the seventeenth century. This chronological overlap is intentional because Western Civilization courses break differently according to the policies of instructors and institutions.

To show how the articles in *Social History of Western Civilization* may be used in most Western Civilization courses, there is a correlation chart at the beginning of each volume that relates each essay to a relevant chapter in the major Western Civilization textbooks currently on the market. Though the textbooks do not always offer discrete discussions on all the subjects covered in the essays, they touch upon many of the subjects. As for the others, students will at least be able to place the articles in a historical context by reading the standard history of the period in the relevant textbook chapter, thereby gaining fresh insight into that historical period.

I have also provided introductions to the major periods in history for each volume as well as an introduction to each selection where I have asked pertinent questions in order to guide students through the essays and to encourage them to think about the problems and issues the authors of these essays raise. These introductions do not contain summaries and so may not be substituted for the reading of the selections.

The preparation of this reader was more time-consuming than I had originally thought possible. There always seemed to be somewhere a more attractive article on every topic. This was true for all of the editions. In the third edition, I have changed approximately one quarter of the essays, substitutions based on my own searching and conversations over the past three years with historians around the country who adopted *Social History of Western Civilization* for their classes. Many people also suggested essays to me, critiqued what I wrote, and helped in other ways as well. I thank Ove Anderson, Jay Crawford, Fara Driver, Phillip Garland, Laurie Glover, Tully Hunter, and Laurie McDowell. Especially generous with their time and comments were Philip Adler, Kathryn Babayan, William Beik, Robert Bireley, Richard Bulliet, Caroline Walker Bynum, Elizabeth D. Carney, Edward Coomes, Suzanne A. Desan, Lawrence Estaville, Hilda Golden, Leonard Greenspoon, Alan Grubb, Christopher Guthrie, Sarah Hanley, George Huppert, Thomas Kuehn, Charles Lippy, Donald McKale, Steven Marks, Victor Matthews, John A. Mears, William Murnane, David Nicholas, Thomas F. X. Noble, D. G. Paz, James Sack, Carol Thomas, and Roy Vice. The editorial staff at St. Martin's Press has been tolerant of my lapses, supportive throughout, and wonderfully professional.

I would also like to thank the following individuals who reviewed or responded to questionnaires for this edition for St. Martin's Press: Steven D. Cooley, University of Dayton; Charles T. Evans, Northern Virginia Community College; Anita Guerrini, University of California; Christopher E. Gutherie, Tarleton State University; Sarah Hanley, University of Iowa; Benjamin Hudson, Penn State University; Jonathan Katz, Oregon State University; Donna T. McCaffrey, Providence College; Maureen Melody, Oakton Community College; Kathryn E. Meyer, Washington State University; Lohr E. Miller, Auburn University; Gerald M. Schnabel, Bemidji State University; Paul Teverow, Missouri Southern State College; Sara W. Tucker, Washburn University of Topeka; and Lindsay Wilson, Colby College.

Contents

Topical Table of Contents

Correlation Chart for Western Civilization Texts and Volume I of Social History of Western Civilization

	Vern L. Bullough et al., *Formation of Western Attitudes toward Women*	Isaac Mendelsohn, *Slavery in the Ancient Near East*	Bernhard Lang, *Afterlife: Ancient Israel's Changing Vision of the World Beyond*	John Baines, *Religious and Social Order in Ancient Egypt*	William J. Baker, *Organized Greek Games*	W. K. Lacey, *Marriage and the Family in Athens*
Winks et al., *A History of Civilization*, 8/e (1992)	1	1	1	1	2	2
Willis, *Western Civilization: A Brief Introduction* (1987)	1	1	1	1	2	2
Willis, *Western Civilization*, 4/e (1985)	1	1	1	1	2	2
Wallbank et al., *Civilization Past and Present*, 7/e (1992)	1	1	1	1	2	2
Sullivan, Sherman, Harrison, *A Short History of Western Civilization*, 8/e (1994)	1,2,3	1,2,3	2	1,2	5	5
Spielvogel, *Western Civilization*, 2/e (1994)	1	1	2	1	3	3
Perry et al., *Western Civilization: Ideas, Politics & Society*, 4/e (1992)	1	1	2	1	3	3
Perry, *Western Civilization: A Brief History*, 2/e (1993)	1	1	2	1	3	3
Palmer & Colton, *A History of the Modern World*, 7/e (1992)					1	1
Noble et al., *Western Civilization: The Continuing Experiment* (1994)	1	1	1	1	3	3
McNeill, *History of Western Civilization*, 6/e (1986)	I-A	I-A	I, A-5	I, A-3	II, A-3	II, A-4
McKay, Hill, Buckler, *A History of Western Society*, 5/e (1995)	1,2	1,2	2	1,2	3	3
Lerner et al., *Western Civilizations*, 12/e (1993)	2, 3	2	4	3	5	5
Kishlansky et al., *The Unfinished Legacy* (1993)	1	1	1	1	2	3
Kishlansky et al., *Civilization in the West* (1991)	1	1	1	1	2	3
Kagan, Ozment, Turner, *The Western Heritage*, 4/e (1991)	1	1	1	1	2	3
Hunt et al., *The Challenge of the West* (1995)	1	1	1	1	2	3
Greaves, Zaller, Roberts, *Civilizations of the West* (1992)	1	1	1	1	3	2
Greer, *A Brief History of the Western World*, 6/e (1992)	1	1	1	1	2	2
Goff et al., *A Survey of Western Civilization* (1987)	1	1	1	1	2	2
Esler, *The Western World* (1994)	1	1	1	1	2	3
Darst, *Western Civilization to 1648* (1990)	2	2	2	2	3	4
Chodorow, Knox, Schirokauer, Strayer & Gatzke, *The Mainstream of Civilization*, 5/e (1989)	1	1	1	1	2	2
Chambers et al., *The Western Experience*, 6/e (1995)	1	1	1	1	2	2
Bouchard, *Life and Society in the West* (1988)	1	1	1	1	2	2
Blackburn, *Western Civilization* (1991)	1	1	2, 3	1	3	3

	K. J. Dover, Classical Greek Attitudes to Sexual Behavior	P. A. Brunt, The Roman Mob	Suzanne Dixon, Roman Marriage	Mary R. Lefkowitz, The Motivations for St. Perpetua's Martyrdom	Georges Duby, Rural Economy and Country Life in the Medieval West	David Herlihy, Medieval Children	David Nicholas, Vendetta and Civil Disorder in Late Medieval Ghent
Winks et al., *A History of Civilization*, 8/e (1992)	2	3	3	4	5	7	10
Willis, *Western Civilization: A Brief Introduction* (1987)	2	3	3	4	5	6	7
Willis, *Western Civilization*, 4/e (1985)	2	4	4	5	7	8	10
Wallbank et al., *Civilization Past and Present*, 7/e (1992)	2	3	3	5	9	11	11
Sullivan, Sherman, Harrison, *A Short History of Western Civilization*, 8/e (1994)	5	9,10	10	12	17,18	9	14
Spielvogel, *Western Civilization*, 2/e (1994)	3	5	6	6	9	8, 10	12
Perry et al., *Western Civilization: Ideas, Politics & Society*, 4/e (1992)	3	6	7	8	9	9,10	12
Perry, *Western Civilization: A Brief History*, 2/e (1993)	3	4	4	5	6	6,7	7
Palmer & Colton, *A History of the Modern World*, 7/e (1992)	1	1	1	1	3	3	5
Noble et al., *Western Civilization: The Continuing Experiment* (1994)	3	6	6	6	8	11	12
McNeill, *History of Western Civilization*, 6/e (1986)	II, A-4	II-C	II-C, II-D	II, D-2	II, B-1	III, B-2	III, B-3
McKay, Hill, Buckler, *A History of Western Society*, 5/e (1995)	3	5	6	6	10	10	12
Lerner et al., *Western Civilizations*, 12/e (1993)	5	7	7	8	10	10, 12	12
Kishlansky et al., *The Unfinished Legacy* (1993)	3	4	5	5	7	8	8
Kishlansky et al., *Civilization in the West* (1991)	3	5	5	6	8,9	9	10
Kagan, Ozment, Turner, *The Western Heritage*, 4/e (1991)	3	4,5	5	5	6,8	8	9
Hunt et al., *The Challenge of the West* (1995)	3	5,6	5,6	6	8	10	13
Greaves, Zaller, Roberts, *Civilizations of the West* (1992)	2	4	4	4	7	7	9
Greer, *A Brief History of the Western World*, 6/e (1992)	2	3	3,8	4	5	18	23
Goff et al., *A Survey of Western Civilization* (1987)	3	7	7,8	9	12	5,6	7
Esler, *The Western World* (1994)	3	5	6	6	7	9	11
Darst, *Western Civilization to 1648* (1990)	4	5	6	7	9	12	12
Chodorow, Knox, Schirokauer, Strayer & Gatzke, *The Mainstream of Civilization*, 5/e (1989)	2	3	4	4	9	10	12
Chambers et al., *The Western Experience*, 6/e (1995)	3	4	5	5	6	9	11
Bouchard, *Life and Society in the West* (1988)	2	3	3	3	4,6	4,6, 9	9
Blackburn, *Western Civilization* (1991)	3	5	5	5	7	8,9	9

Title																										
J. Russell Major, "Bastard Feudalism" and the Kiss: Changing Social Mores in Late Medieval and Early Modern France	9	10	11	12	16	11	7	23	9	13	10	8	10	12	12	12	III, B-3	12	8,13	7	12	14	11	10	7	10
Georges Vigarello, Concepts of Cleanliness: The Water That Infiltrated	11		13	14	21	14	9	31	14	11,12,13		14	15,16	III, C-1	15	13	9	15	17,19	15	8	15				
David Herlihy, The Family in Renaissance Italy	10	10	12	13	18	13	8	25	10	14	10	9	11	13	13	14	III, B-3	12	6	8	13	16	12	11	7	11
M. E. Combs-Schilling, The Effects of the Black Death on North Africa and Europe	9	9	11	12	12,19	11	7	23	9	13	9	8	10	12	12	12	III, B-3	12	5	7	12	14	11	10	7	10
Norman Roth, The Jews of Spain and the Expulsion of 1492	10	10	14	11	21	12,13	9	27	14	14	10	10	12	13	13	III, B-3	13	8	9	16	13,14	11	10	9	10	
Alfred W. Crosby, Jr., The Early History of Syphilis: A Reappraisal	10	10	14	15	19	14,17	12	28	14	14	10	10	12	15	15	III, C-1	15	11	9	15	15,18	16	13	9	14	
Merry Wiesner, Nuns, Wives, and Mothers: Women and the Reformation in Germany	11		13	14	20	14	11	29	15	11	11	14	14	14,15	III, C-1	16	9	8	14	14,17	13	12	8	12		
Mary Elizabeth Perry, "Lost Women" in Early Modern Seville: The Politics of Prostitution	11		14	15	19	17	12	28	15	11,12	14	12	14	16	15	III, C-1	15	13	9	16	15,18	16	13	9	13	
Joseph Klaits, Sexual Politics and Religious Reform in the Witch Hunts	11		16	15	21	15	11	29	16	14	14	12	15	15	15	III, C-1	15	28,32	10	15	15,18	13	10	8	15	
Natalie Z. Davis, The Rites of Violence: Religious Riot in Sixteenth-Century France	11		15	15	21	14	13	30	16	12	15	13	15	15	15	III, C-1	15	15	9	16	15,18	17	12,8 15	9	13	
Wendy Gibson, Birth and Childhood in Seventeenth-Century France	11		16	15	22	15	14	31	16	13	16	13	16	16	16	III, C-1	16	21	9	16	15,19	17	15	12	15	
Michael MacDonald, Insanity in Early Modern England	11		16	15	24	15	14	31	16,13,17	16	13	16	16	16	III, C-2	16	34	9	17	15,21	17	15	11	15		

Introduction

The social history of Western civilization seeks to include the complete fabric of human experience. Such comprehensiveness, like the quest for historical objectivity or the search for truth, is impossible to achieve. Nevertheless, the desire to learn about the totality of life differentiates social history from other subject areas such as military, intellectual, religious, cultural, diplomatic, biographical, economic, or art history. The social historian looks at groups or masses of people, at conditions that affected populations in everyday life. In part, this approach has been a reaction against biographies and the study of prominent people, usually military, political, or religious leaders, that dominated historical writing during the nineteenth century and the first half of the twentieth century. This history of elites ignores the vast majority of people and so implies that ordinary lives are unimportant. Hence, "history from the bottom up" seeks to rediscover previously neglected populations and lifestyles. But, ironically, social history, the history of aggregates, has sometimes become a history without names, that is, without the mention of individuals. Is it necessary to refer to anyone by name in discussing the agricultural system of the early Middle Ages or the effects of epidemics on human communities? On the other hand, discovering those "nameless" people and more intimate details constitutes the very humanness of history.

Though contemporary problems should not be the sole criterion for a historian's choice of a topic, the subjects that form the backbone of social history still exist today, though in different forms. In other words, the social history of ancient civilizations or the Middle Ages is intrinsically of interest to us as citizens of the twentieth century because it is often relevant, though it must be emphasized that relevance is not a goal of the social historian. Rather, awareness of concerns in present society has often led to investigations of similar problems in the past. Thus, primary topics in social history, all of which are discussed in this volume, include the family, marriage, children, death, disease, sports, violence, crime, women, persecution, food, sexuality, the environment, social behavior, religion, insanity, and the daily lives of various social groups. People in the past seem very different from us in Western civilization today; they thought and behaved in ways that appear alien to us, for the principles by which they ordered their universe are contrary to ours. The faceless masses, whom social historians are now beginning to see, fascinate precisely because they dealt with many of our problems—sex, for example—and our institutions—such as the family—in ways that from our vantage point seem superstitious, exotic, and neurotic. To appreciate social history, one must understand, not judge, and one must try to immerse oneself in the period studied and in the mentality of the people. The German poet Heinrich Heine said, "If one has no heart, one cannot write for the masses." To study the lives of the masses in history likewise requires heart; as the selections in this book reveal, the vast majority of people in past societies lived short, unhealthy lives, punctuated more often than not by violence, brutality, and exploitation. The study of social history needs empathy, the ability to place oneself in the hearts and minds of ordinary people in the past.

Social History of Western Civilization

Volume I

THIRD EDITION

I

ANCIENT NEAR EAST

Where did Western civilization begin? Some argue that it began with the Greeks because they were so like us: They thought in terms of history, they reflected on the human predicament, and they questioned all areas of life. The Greeks invented history, drama, and philosophy and so were the first to tackle in a systematic way the perennial major questions basic to humanity: What are goodness, truth, beauty, justice, love? The Greeks were also the first to study nature as an autonomous and distinct entity, without reference to outside, supernatural forces. In history, science, and philosophy, the Greeks parted company with the earlier civilizations of the ancient Near East.

But a cogent argument could be made to include the ancient Near East in Western civilization. The cultures in what is today known as the Middle East, extending from Egypt to Iran, contributed writing, the alphabet, iron, astronomy, elements of common mathematics, agriculture, monumental architecture, cities, codes of law, and, with the Hebrews, a religion of ethical monotheism. All these influenced Graeco-Roman civilization, and thus our own.

Filling the universe with exotic gods, the minds of most Near Eastern people seem alien to us. In social life and personal relationships, nevertheless, they bear affinities with the Western cultures that followed them. Slavery, for example, was a feature of every ancient society, dying out in the modern West only in 1865 and in the Middle East in the 1970s. The belief in the inferiority of women and even in their relative equality could be found in the Near East. Echoes of these convictions are heard in rancorous debates in the twentieth century. Some attitudes toward children and education appear quite familiar to us, though others seem grotesque, if not inhuman.

Hebrew culture was not different from other cultures in its imperialism and in its unification of life around religion. The Hebrew religion was unusual—after all, it is the only ancient Near Eastern religion that has survived to our own day. Although there may be theological reasons for the continuation of Judaism, its penetration of every aspect of life certainly contributed to its longevity. Slavery, childrearing, and diet all bore the imprint of Hebraic religion.

The following selections on the ancient Near East address fundamental topics in the social history of Western civilization. They identify common as well as dissimilar features among Near Eastern civilizations. At the same time, they provide comparisons with conditions of life in later cultures.

Formation of Western Attitudes toward Women

VERN L. BULLOUGH,
BRENDA SHELTON, and SARAH SLAVIN

In order to understand later attitudes toward women in Western civilization, Vern L. Bullough, Brenda Shelton, and Sarah Slavin investigate and compare the role of women in Mesopotamia and ancient Egypt.

The inhabitants of the Tigris-Euphrates river valley, whether Sumerians, Babylonians, or Assyrians, treated women as property rather than as persons. What implications did this have for marriage, the treatment of adultery, and the lives of female slaves? That we know the names of only a few Mesopotamian women suggests the tight grip of male dominance; women were rarely able to distinguish themselves as individuals. Law codes indicated the very real subordination of women, and religion, always a cultural phenomenon, likewise preached female inferiority.

Women fared better in Egypt, though certainly there was no pretence of equality. But at least Egyptian women had greater standing in law than their Mesopotamian counterparts. What legal rights did Egyptian women have? Do you agree with Bullough's reasons for the comparatively higher status of women in Egypt? The most famous Egyptian woman, besides Cleopatra, was Hatshepsut, who reigned for approximately twenty years. How did her gender affect her rule? Her experience shows clearly an ingrained negative attitude toward women that would continue through Western civilization. Societies did not permit women to be warriors, for the military was a means to power. The only power attributed to women, other than that of mother, was the ability—or so men thought—to trap, delude, and steer men away from the right path.

The cradle of civilization, or at least of Western civilization, was the river valleys of the Near East (sometimes called the Middle East), particularly in the area extending from modern Egypt to modern Iraq. Attitudes formed in these areas were incorporated into Jewish, Greek, and later Western Roman and Christian attitudes. . . .

It has been said that man's vision of the gods reflects his own vision of himself and his activities. If there is any merit to this statement it seems clear that the inhabitants of the Tigris-Euphrates Valley quite early held man to be superior to woman, and in fact relegated her to being a kind of property. There are hints that in the beginning of Sumerian society women had a much higher status than in the heyday of Sumerian culture. Tiamat, a mother goddess, was a dominant figure, and it was her body that was used to form the earth and the heavens after she was killed by Enlil (called Marduk in the Babylonian versions and Asshur in the Assyrian ones). The blood of Tiamat's consort, Kingu, served to form individual humans. This death of a female goddess and her replacement by a dominant male figure is a common theme in the mythology of many peoples. The meanings of this matricide are unclear, and all we can say for certain is that by the time the Babylonian theology was organized into the form in which it has come down to us, the mother goddess was clearly subordinate to male gods.

The names and positions of the gods changed during different periods of Mesopotamian civilization as differing peoples achieved dominance. There were hundreds of deities but there were two major triads of gods: Anu, Enlil, and Ea; Sin, Shamash, and Ishtar. Over and above them was another god, Marduk or Asshur. The only female in the group was Ishtar, or in Sumerian, Inanna, goddess of war and of love. Like humans, the gods had wives and families, court servants, soldiers, and other retainers. Ishtar, however, remained unmarried. Her lovers were legion, but these unhappy men usually paid dearly for her sexual favors. She was identified with the planet Venus, the morning and evening star, and could arouse the amorous instinct in man, although she also had the power of causing brothers who were on good terms to quarrel among themselves and friends to forget friendship. If she perchance withdrew her influence, "The bull refuses to cover the cow, the ass no longer approaches the she-ass, in the street the man no longer approaches the maidservant." Part of her difficulty was that she did not really know her place. In the poem translated as *Enki and World Order* the god Enki (whose powers are similar to Ea's) assigned the gods various tasks. Ishtar, however, felt left out and complained to Enki. Her complaint applies to woman in general: "Me, the woman, why did you treat differently?/ Me, the holy Inanna, where are my powers?" She was given various tasks as a result, but because she was an unmarried and erotic figure it was no wonder that sacred prostitution formed part of her cult. When she descended to earth she was accompanied by courtesans and prostitutes. The implication might well be . . . that woman was to be either wife and mother or an unmarried professional, a prostitute.

The mere presence of Ishtar, or Inanna, in the heavenly triad is probably striking evidence of the great strength of the forces of nature, which were so deeply rooted in primitive society. She represented the blending of several different characters into one, most obviously the lady of love and the lady of battles, although these different aspects of her powers were worshiped at different places. If Ishtar chose to favor a mere mortal, he could gain fame and riches, and she was much sought after. Sargon, the Akkadian conquerer who lived toward the end of the third millennium B.C., felt himself to be under the protection of Ishtar and believed it was through her influence that he became king. . . .

If the place of women in official mythology was somewhat circumscribed, it was even more so in actual life. Our chief source of information about actual conditions is the various law codes. These might be regarded as the official male view of women since they are essentially male social constructs.... Formal law codes are known from Ur-Nammu of the third dynasty of Ur [c. 2050 B.C.] and Lipit Ishtar of Isin [c. 1870 B.C.]. Neither of these codes is preserved completely and their great importance to us lies in the influence they had on later laws. In the Semitic dialects the first law code was that of the town of Eshnunna, dating from about 1800 B.C. The best known, however, was that of Hammurabi (c. 1700 B.C.), which contained about 250 laws. Later from the Assyrian scribes there exists another legal corpus dating from 1100 B.C., which has a long section on women and marriage.

Women legally were property. They were neither to be seen nor heard. Monogamy was the normal way of life, but monogamy meant something different for the man than for the woman. A wife who slept with another man was an adulteress but a man could not only visit prostitutes but in practice also took secondary wives as concubines. Rich men and royalty often had more than one legal wife. Women were always under the control of a male. Until the time of her marriage a girl remained under the protection of her father, who was free to settle her in marriage exactly as he thought fit. Once married she was under the control of her husband. During the marriage ceremony a free woman assumed the veil that she wore from then on outside her home. In fact the veil was the mark of a free woman, and anyone who met a slave or courtesan wearing a veil had the duty of denouncing her. A concubine could only wear a veil on those occasions when she accompanied the legal wife out of doors. It was an offence for a woman to have any dealings in business or to speak to a man who was not a near relation.

Some scholars have argued that the earliest form of marriage required the bridegroom to purchase his bride, emphasizing even further the woman as property....

The economic dependence of the woman upon the male was reinforced by the various provisions allowing her to remarry. In cases where a woman's husband was taken captive and he had not left enough for her to eat, she could live with another man as his wife. If her husband returned, though, she was to go back to him. Any children by the temporary husband remained with him. If, however, the absence of her husband was malicious, motivated by a "hatred of king and country," he had no further claim upon his wife if she took a second husband. Women could also hold property. An unmarried daughter, for example, could be given either a dowry, a share of her father's property, or the usufruct, the right to the profits from the land. She was free to dispose of her dowry as she wished, but in other cases her property rights upon her death reverted to her brothers, except under special conditions.

The purpose of marriage was by law procreation, not companionship. The wife's first duty was to raise her children and a sterile marriage was grounds for divorce. The wife who gave birth to children, particularly to sons, was accorded special protection. The man who divorced the mother of his sons or took another wife was committing a culpable act. Her childbearing responsibilities were emphasized by penalties to anyone injuring a woman sufficiently to cause a miscarriage and also by statutes against abortion.

Adultery was not a sin against morality but a trespass against the husband's property. A husband had freedom to fornicate, while a wife could be put to death for doing the same thing. Free women were inviolable and guarded; a man who gave employment to a married woman not closely related to him was in difficulty. A man caught fornicating with an adulterous woman could be castrated or put to death, while the woman could be executed or have her nose cut off. Offenses with unmarried free women were treated differently from those with married women because there was no husband. If the offender had a wife, she was taken from him and given to her father for prostitution and the offender was compelled to marry the woman who was his victim. If he had no wife, he had to pay a sum of money to the woman's father as well as marry her, although the father might accept money and refuse to give him his daughter. In any case, the payment was for damaging property, lessening the value of the woman. If a man could prove by oath that an unmarried woman gave herself to him, he was not compelled to surrender his own wife, although he still had to pay a sum of money for the damage he had caused. If a married woman was seized by a man in a street or public place and, in spite of her efforts to defend herself, was violated, she was regarded as innocent. If, however, she was acting as a prostitute either in a temple brothel or in the street, the man could be convicted of engaging in an adulterous relationship only if he was shown to have had guilty knowledge.

These laws applied to freewomen. There were other women, particularly slaves. A slave had no human personality but instead was real property. If she was injured, it was her master and not she herself who was entitled to compensation. A female slave was under obligation to give her purchaser not only her labor but also herself, without any counter obligation on his part. He could in fact turn her over to prostitution. Even when she became the purchaser's concubine and had children by him, she still remained a slave liable to be sold. At her owner's death, however, she and her children received liberty. If a female slave was bought by a married woman either as her servant or as a concubine for her husband (as in the case of a childless woman), she remained the property of the wife. A male slave could, with his master's consent, marry a freewoman, and even if she lacked a dowry, she and her children would still remain free. If she brought a dowry, she could keep it, but any increase from investment was split with her husband's master. There were also temple slaves who were not confined to the temple but worked in the towns and hired out to private employers. Their legal status was harsher than that of ordinary slaves since they had no hope of adoption, while their children automatically became the property of the gods. Children and wives of freemen were different from slaves, but the father still had almost total control. He could deposit his children with creditors, and apparently also his wife, although she could not be kept for more than four years....

Specific laws dealt with women as tavernkeepers, priestesses, and prostitutes, occupations in which women could act outside conjugal or paternal authority. In general, however, the law failed to recognize women as persons. For example, a woman could be careless with animals just as a man could, but the law only refers to men. As far as priestesses and prostitutes were concerned, there were various kinds of both. At the head of the priestesses was the Entu, the wife of the gods, or the "lady [who is] a deity." They were of very high standing and the kings could make their daughters Entu of a god. They were expected to remain virgins, although they might eventually take husbands, perhaps after menopause. A second class of priestesses was the Naditu, who were lower in rank but who were also not expected to have children. The Hammurabic code had several provisions attempting to ensure the rights of a priestess to dowry and other shares of her father's goods. Apparently their conduct was rigidly circumscribed since any priestess who went to a tavern to drink could be put to death. Prostitutes seem to have been quite common and there was a considerable variety of harlots and hierodules.[1] ...

With such a male-oriented society, few women emerged as real individuals in the history of the Mesopotamian civilizations....

...It was only through their sons that women in the Mesopotamian civilizations seem to have had any influence at all. Even the wives of the king were not important enough to be regarded as queens since the use of the term was restricted to goddesses or to women who served in positions of power. The chief wife instead was usually called "she of the palace," and she lived along with the concubines and other wives in a harem guarded by eunuchs. Their way of life was carefully regulated by royal edicts, although in the last period of the Assyrian kingdom the influence of the king's wife and mother was somewhat greater than before.

Other than a few exceptional royal wives, only a handful of women managed to break through into the pages of history. There is an isolated reference to a woman physician at the palace in an Old Babylonian text, and we can assume that women attended other women in childbirth, but there is no further reference. The professional physician was usually a male. Women were also generally illiterate if only because in this period reading and writing were restricted to a professional class of scribes who underwent long training. Poetry, however, is a preliterate form of literature, and one of the most remarkable poets, in fact one of the few we know by name, was a woman, Enheduanna. She was the daughter of Sargon, whose administration marked the fusion of Semitic and Sumerian culture. As part of this fusion the Sumerian Inanna and the Akkadian Ishtar came together, and in this process Enheduanna played an important role, at least

[1] Temple slaves.

if her identification is correct. She was a high priestess of the moon god, the first of a long line of royal holders of this office, and in this capacity she wrote a poem usually entitled "The Exaltation of Inanna." Her poetry served as a model for much subsequent hymnography and her influence was so great that she later seems to have been regarded as a god herself.... Most of the cuneiform literature from the area is anonymous, or at best pseudonymous, so how many other women poets there were must remain unknown. The attitudes expressed about women in most of the poetry tend to indicate that they had male authors.

In one of the great classics of Mesopotamian literature, the Gilgamesh epic, it seems obvious that woman's duty was to keep man calm and peaceful. In the beginning of the account Gilgamesh was oppressing the city of Erech, taking the son from the father, the maiden from her lover. The people complained to the gods, who created a rival, Enkidu, from clay to deal with Gilgamesh. Enkidu was a wild man whose whole body was covered with hair, who knew neither people nor country. When the existence of Enkidu was reported to Gilgamesh he sent forth a temple harlot to ensnare the wild man: "Let her strip off her garment; let her lay open her comeliness;/ He will see her, he will draw nigh to her...." Then with his innocence lost he could be more effectively handled by Gilgamesh.

> *The prostitute untied her loin-cloth and opened her legs,*
> *and he took possession of her comeliness:*
> *She used no restraint but accepted his ardour,*
> *She put aside her robe and he lay upon her.*
> *She used on him, the savage, a woman's wiles,*
> *His passion responded to her.*
> *For six days and seven nights Enkidu approached and*
> *coupled with the prostitute.*
> *After he was sated with her charms,*
> *He set his face toward his game.*
> *[But] when the gazelles saw him, Enkidu, they ran away;*
> *The game of the steppe fled from his presence.*
> *Enkidu tried to hasten [after them, but] his body was*
> *[as if it were] bound.*
> *His knees failed him who tried to run after his game.*
> *Enkidu had become weak, his speed was not as before.*
> *But he had intelligence, wide was his understanding.*

...The legend suggests that woman was designed to ensnare a man, to weaken him, to prevent him from realizing his full potentiality. In this forerunner of the stereotype of Eve, woman was both a source of pleasure and yet a delusion....

Woman, nonetheless, was designed to be at the side of man, and as a proverb stated, "a house without an owner is like a woman without a husband." The ideal wife was both passionate and able to bear sons: "May [the goddess] Inanna cause a hot-limbed wife to lie down for you; / May she bestow upon you broad-armed sons; / May she seek out for you a place of happiness." Even a good wife was a burden and responsibility: "The man who does not support either a wife or a child, / His nose has not borne a leash." Or in a more hostile vein: "As the saying goes: 'Were not my wife in the cemetery, and were not also my mother in the river, I should die of hunger.'" Women, as well as men, enjoyed sex. "Conceiving is nice," but "being pregnant is irksome." It was also recognized that the "penis of the unfaithful husband" was no better "than the vulva of the unfaithful wife," but in most things a woman was discriminated against. "A rebellious male may be permitted a reconciliation; / A rebellious female will be dragged in the mud." Obviously women were regarded as a mixed blessing, and it was thought best that they be kept in their place.

Life in Mesopotamia was harsh and unpredictable. There were floods, famine, scorching heat, and cloudbursts, and always the danger of invasions. It might well be that in such a society the strong man was admired while the weak woman was regarded as a liability but necessary because of her childbearing abilities. Inevitably the male was forced to assert himself, to man the armies, to do the fighting, to keep his womenfolk in subordination. Is this an adequate explanation for male dominance? The difficulty with such a thesis is that these same attitudes are found in other cultures where environmental conditions are quite different. Nonetheless environment might have had some influence, since the place of women in Egyptian society seems to be quite different from that of Mesopotamian society.

. . . Most recent studies would not regard Egypt as a matriarchal society, but all would agree that the status of women was probably higher there than in Mesopotamia and that women had the right to own and transmit property. . . .

Part of the difficulty with reconstructing the real status of women in Egypt is that we lack the kind of comprehensive law codes present in ancient Mesopotamian society. We do, however, have numerous legal documents, particularly from the time of the Persians and the Greeks who occupied Egypt in the last half of the first millennium B.C. From these it would appear that women had the right to own property, to buy, sell, and testify in court. . . . [I]t is apparent that women not only enjoyed full equality to own property but also could go about their transactions in the same manner as men. Moreover, they were allowed to regain the property they brought with them as dowry if their marriage broke up. If, however, the woman had committed adultery, no such guarantee existed. Women were listed as taxpayers, and they could also sue. Apparently a woman did not need a guardian to be able to execute legal acts, nor did it matter whether she was married or not. A daughter, at least in the Ptolemaic period, was entitled to equal succession in the estate of her father. Women could acquire wealth or property through their parents or husbands or purchase it. A wife was entitled to a third of her husband's possessions after his death, whereas the other two-thirds had to be divided among the children and sisters and brothers of the testator. If a husband desired his wife to receive more, he had the right to donate it to her before he died.

The comparative economic independence of women may have given them greater freedom than in Mesopotamia. . . . Such independence must have been limited to the upper levels of society. The ordinary peasant, whether male or female, lacked many possessions, and the slave was even lower on the scale. Nevertheless, women of all classes were recognized as important, as is evidenced by the numerous goddesses. Particularly important were the triads of gods composed of a man, woman, and child, almost always a son. . . .

Since goddesses were so important it would seem to follow that royal women would also be important, if only because the pharaoh's first wife was the consort of a god. Inevitably, too, she became the "mother of the god" who would be the successor to her husband. At all periods in Egyptian society the queens were the first ladies of the land, and originally the tombs of some were as big and as elaborate as those of the kings. . . .

. . . [I]t was not until the eighteenth dynasty (c. 1570–1305) that the Egyptian queen achieved her highest prestige. The most influential of all was Hatshepsut (c. 1486–1468), who stole the throne from her young nephew and stepson, Thutmose III, and wielded the scepter for about twenty years. Hatshepsut, however, ruled as a king and not as a queen, an indication of the difficulties women had in ruling. The reigning monarch of Egypt had to be male: the titles, laudatory inscriptions, and ceremonies were all designed for men and were so deeply rooted in tradition and dogma that it was easier for a woman to adapt herself to fit the titles than to change the titles to fit her sex. Inevitably her reign is somewhat confusing since she is shown both in a man's kilt (and body) wearing the king's crown and artificial beard, and as a woman with feminine dress and queen's crown. She also has two tombs, one in her capacity as queen and one as king, the latter being larger. When she died or was driven from the throne by her nephew, Thutmose III, he destroyed almost anything Hatshepsut had ever touched, and even tried to obliterate all inscriptions which referred to her. Though Hatshepsut must have been a strong-willed woman, one of her great difficulties seems to have been her inability to lead an army. She recorded no military conquests or campaigns; her great pride was in the internal development of Egypt. Some would say she lacked military exploits because she may have been a leader of a peace party opposed to expansion. Actually there is nothing in a woman's biological makeup that would prevent her from being a soldier or general, in fact; many women disguised themselves as males to serve in the American Civil War, but women almost without exception were not trained as soldiers. In the past, when kings had to lead their armies, this discrimination might have prevented more women from being rulers. Hatshepsut obviously was supported by the bureaucracy of the state, but civil powers can be diffused. In a military crisis, however, power must be centralized into the hands of one person, and though a woman might appoint a male to act as commander, there is little to stop him from turning against her, particularly if he has the loyalty of the troops. It might well be that Thutmose III used his military ability to regain the throne, since he either deliberately introduced military imperialism or was forced to expand in order to defend his country's borders.

Hatshepsut was not the only woman to sit on the throne. There were at least three others, although only as regents for their sons.... Women continued to exercise considerable influence down to the time of Cleopatra.[2] ... Though Cleopatra was Greek rather than Egyptian, her importance emphasizes the continuing influence of women in Egyptian affairs, whether foreign or native.

The relative importance of the queen mother was no indication that the king was restricted to one wife. Concubines and harems were common, but such women seldom appeared in public. The size of the harem probably varied and at times reached remarkable numbers. Ramses II (1290–1224 B.C.), for example, had at least seventy-nine sons and fifty-nine daughters. The members of the royal harem lived apart from the rest of the court. Employees of the harem were not eunuchs, as in Mesopotamia, but included normal men, many of them married, as well as numerous women. In general the harem women were chosen by the pharaoh either for political reasons or for their great beauty. It was through this last procedure that many nonroyal women gained admission and some became queens. There were also a number of women of foreign birth. Inevitably there were conspiracies in the harem as various wives tried to maneuver their sons into key positions. When women were not in the harem for political reasons, their chief purpose was to amuse their lord. They were instructed in dancing and singing and other arts designed to arouse and delight the male. Some of the richer Egyptians also had harems and concubines, but as a general rule Egyptians practiced monogamy if only because economic factors worked against polygamy. The husband could dismiss his wife if he wished to remarry or if his wife ceased to please him, but he had to return her dowry and give other forms of settlement. Women had no such freedom.

Like most societies, Egypt practiced a double standard. Concubinage existed but not polyandry. Maidservants belonged to their owner and adultery for the male was not considered a sin. Prostitution was widespread.... If a married woman committed adultery, however, she could be deprived of her property and be subject to punishment. We have two folktales from the Middle and New Kingdom of women committing adultery: in the first the woman was burned to death; in the second her husband killed her and threw her corpse to the hounds. In other folktales women appeared as very

[2]69–30 B.C.

sexual creatures, willing to betray their husbands, use various kinds of tricks, and do other things in order to get the men who attracted them physically into bed....

...Instead of evidence of female promiscuity, such tales might only be male-oriented pornography, designed to arouse the male. By emphasis on female sexual desire, however, female insubordination might also be encouraged. Thus to reassert their control men emphasized clitoridectomies, allowing unlimited pleasure for the male but only limited temptation for females to be insubordinate. We also know that before this time the Egyptian woman was seldom pictured in any negative way in the literature. She was always portrayed as the faithful caring wife, the princess with many suitors, or the mistress praised by songs and poems. Motherhood was her revered function. Not to have children was a terrible and lamentable situation, and mother and children were depicted at all times in Egyptian tombs and pictures.

Women seldom appeared in public life although some women did hold public offices. There are records of a woman director of a dining hall, a manageress of a wig workshop, a headmistress of singers, a female supervisor of a house of weavers, and numerous mistresses of royal harems or superintendents of houses. In later Egyptian history wives of eminent persons or members of old noble families also were allowed to use honorary official titles. We know of at least one woman scribe who belonged to the household of a thirteenth-dynasty queen, and it is possible some queens and princesses knew how to write. Most women, even of the upper classes, could not. Women could also serve in the temples, and priestesses were recruited not only from the royal house, the civil services, or clergy, but also from the working class. Generally women served as musicians or dancers in the temple, although some might have become high priestesses.

Egyptians also believed that males rather than females were the key to procreation, and the male phallus was often portrayed. The female sex organs were not usually depicted in ancient Egypt. There was, however, a widespread belief that a women might succumb to hysteria if the womb remained barren long after puberty....

The extant literature seems to be from the hands of males, and it reflects the various attitudes of men toward women. Ptah Hotep, the semi-legendary sage of the Old Kingdom who lived in the third millennium B.C., said: "If you are a man of note, found for yourself a household, and love your wife at home, as it beseems. Fill her belly, clothe her back; unguent is the remedy for her limbs. Gladden her heart, so long as she lives; she is a goodly field for her lord [that is, she will produce children if you cultivate her]. But hold her back from getting the mastery. [Remember that] her eye is her stormwind, and her vulva and mouth are her strength." Though wives were good if kept in their place, care should be exercised in their choice.... Women were also dangerous: "If you would prolong friendship in a house to which you have admittance, as master, or as brother, or as friend, into whatsoever place you enter, beware of approaching the women. It is not good in the place where this is done. Men are made fools by their gleaming limbs of carnelian. A trifle, a little, the likeness of a dream, and death comes as the end of knowing her." . . . Motherhood was especially revered. "Double the bread that thou givest to thy mother, and carry her as she carried [thee]. When thou wast born after thy months, she carried thee yet again about her neck, and for three years her breast was in thy mouth. She was not disgusted at thy dung, she was not disgusted and said not: 'What do I?' She put thee to school, when though hadst been taught to write, and daily she stood there [at the schoolhouse] . . . with bread and beer from her house." When a man married he should keep the example of his mother in front of him. "When thou art a young man and takest to thee a wife and art settled in thine house, keep before thee how thy mother gave birth to thee, and how she brought thee up further in all manner of ways. May she not do thee harm nor lift up her hands to the Gods and may he not hear her cry." . . .

Women, in general, however, were a snare and a delusion. "Go not after a woman, in order that she may not steal thine heart away." In particular beware "of a strange woman, one that is not known in her city. Wink not at her . . . have no carnal knowledge of her. She is a deep water whose twisting men know not. A woman that is far from her husband, 'I am fair,' she saith to thee every day, when she hath no witnesses."

Yet a woman could also be a delight.

. . .

Lovely are her eyes when she glances,
Sweet are her lips when she speaks,
　and her words are never too many!
Her neck is long, and her nipple is radiant,
　and her hair is deep sapphire.
Her arms surpass the brilliance of gold,
　and her fingers are like lotus blossoms.
Her buttocks curve down languidly from her trim belly,
　and her thighs are her beauties.
Her bearing is regal as she walks upon the earth—
　she causes every male neck to turn and look at her.
Yes, she has captivated my heart in her embrace!
In joy indeed is he who embraces all of her—
　he is the very prince of lusty youths!

. . .

In sum, the Egyptian woman had a relatively pleasant life and we do not need to resort to questionable generalizations like that of primitive matriarchy in order to explain it. Her somewhat higher status than that of the Mesopotamian woman still did not mean that she was considered equal to men. Women were clearly subordinate, and compared to men's, their lives were circumscribed. It might well be that the very passivity of living in Egypt, owing to the great fertility of the soil and to the regularity of life, lent less emphasis to war and to the making of war. Women worked in the fields along with the men in ancient times, as they do now, although their assigned functions differed. Even the fact that women appeared as rulers does not mean that they had equality, since all apparently exercised their power in the name of a son or took a male name. It is also worthy of comment that most of the women rulers appeared at the end of a dynasty, apparently striving to keep the family in power either because their sons were young or their husbands were enfeebled. Hatshepsut, of course, was an exception. Some Egyptian women worked outside of their homes, but the professions were not open to them nor were any of the crafts, except the traditionally feminine ones. They were not priests, nor were they carpenters, sculptors, or scribes. Woman's place was in the home, and it was as mothers that they had their greatest influence. If Egypt is the example of the power that women had under what some have called a matriarchy, their status in times past must never have been very high....

Slavery in the Ancient Near East

ISAAC MENDELSOHN

For people in antiquity, a society without slaves was virtually inconceivable. The trade in slaves linked cultures in the ancient Near East, as did the shared belief in the necessity and virtue of slavery. That belief was as widespread then as the feeling today that slavery is morally wrong.

Mendelsohn first discusses various ways—war, sale, and indebtedness—in which one could become a slave in the ancient Near East. War was endemic in that period; individuals and entire populations could suddenly lose their freedom. Omnipresent poverty was the cause of the sale of minors and the sale of oneself as well as the reason for people falling into debt and hence into slavery. Such a precarious existence for ancient Near Eastern peoples! Terrorized by vengeful and sometimes fickle gods, they received no relief from the sociopolitical world. Invading armies routinely crisscrossed the countryside from present-day Iraq to Israel. Enormous disparities in wealth, poor weather, and erratic harvests help explain the plunge into slavery for those whose lifelong poverty became destitution. How did slavery affect family relationships in these conditions?

Second, Mendelsohn analyzes the legal status of slaves, how they were treated by various law codes, particularly that of Hammurabi in Babylonia and the Bible. Were there significant differences between the Hebrew Bible and Hammurabi's Code concerning the regulation of slavery? Is there reason to believe that slaves were treated as the laws specified? How could a slave become free? Would slaves always desire liberty?

Third, in explaining the economic role of slavery, Mendelsohn shows that institution to be even more nuanced. Not only did slavery differ from culture to culture, but also according to the economic function of the slaves. Slaves worked for governments, temples, and private individuals, most often in agriculture or in industry. Historians of slavery are always drawn to the question of whether or not slavery was economically beneficial.

Finally, Mendelsohn looks at the attitude of religion toward slavery. Because religion is a product of culture, we should not be surprised to learn that Near Eastern religions accepted slavery as part of the natural order of things. But were there any seeds in religion that would later germinate to produce moral outrage against one person's owning another person?

The earliest Sumerian terms for male and female slaves are the composite signs *nita + kur* "male of a foreign country," and *nunus + kur* "female of a foreign country," indicating that the first humans to be enslaved in Ancient Babylonia were captive foreigners. That prisoners of war, spared on the battle field, were reduced to slavery is amply attested in the annals of the long history of the Ancient Near East. The Hammurabi Code[1] took this universal practice of the enslavement of war captives for granted and decreed that (1) a captive state official should be ransomed, in case he had no resources of his own, by his city temple or by the state, and (2) that a woman whose husband was taken prisoner may re-marry in case she had no means to support herself and her children. The Late Assyrian annals repeatedly mention large numbers of war captives "from the four corners of the world" who were dragged to Assyria and were compelled to perform forced labor. The small city-states of Syria in the middle of the second millennium B.C. employed the same procedure with regard to their war prisoners. In a war between the cities of Carchemish and Ugarit in which the former was victorious, many prisoners were taken. The king of Ugarit then requested the king of Carchemish to free one of the captives, offering him one hundred shekels as ransom. In answer to this request the king of Carchemish pointed out that he had already sold many prisoners for forty shekels a piece and that he could not be expected to free a high ranking captive for the small sum offered. The Tell el-Amarna letters (14th century B.C.)[2] tell us of war captives being sent as "gifts" by Syrian and Palestinian princes to their Egyptian overlords. The Old Testament tells us that in their conquest of Palestine the Israelites enslaved many of their Canaanite enemies.

No sooner was this practice of enslaving foreigners established than it was carried over and applied to natives themselves. Man became a commodity

---

[1] Main collection of law in Mesopotamia, named after the Babylonian king of the eighteenth century B.C.

[2] Correspondence uncovered at Tell el-Amarna in Egypt between Egyptian pharaohs and Syro-Palestinian rulers.

and the total exploitation of his physical strength served as a new source of profit. Although captives of war and imported foreign slaves made up a substantial part of the slave population of the Ancient Near East, the bulk of the Babylonian, Assyrian, Canaanite, and Hebrew slaves originally came from the ranks of the free-born native population. The native-born slaves were recruited from the following three sources: sale of minors by their parents, voluntary self-sale by adults, and enslavement of defaulting debtors.

Poor parents who were either unable to support their children or were in need of money sold their offspring in the market. These sales were transacted in two ways: (1) unconditional sale; that is, the parent(s) handed the child over to the buyer and in return received the purchase price "in full," and (2) conditional sale or sale-adoption; that is, the parent(s) received the price and the sold minor was adopted by the purchaser. We have documentary evidence showing that the practice of the sale of minors was in use throughout the history of Babylonia and Assyria. Our evidence from Syria and Palestine, however, is very inadequate. Still, there are enough references to prove that this practice was also prevalent there. The Tell el-Amarna letters tell us that some people were forced to sell their children in order to procure food. From the Old Testament we learn that parents sold their daughters into conditional slavery (Ex. 21:7–11); that creditors seized the children of their deceased debtors (II Kings 4:1); and that debt-ridden farmers were forced to hand over their sons and daughters as slaves (Nehemiah 5:5).

The evidence of the existence of the second method of sale, namely, the sale of young girls into conditional slavery, comes from Nuzi[3] and Palestine. Nuzian and Hebrew parents often sold their daughters with the condition that the purchaser give them into marriage when the girls will have reached puberty. In Nuzi this type of sale was drawn up in the form of a fictitious adoption. The general scheme of a Nuzian sale-adoption contract runs as follows: (1) Preamble: Contract of daughtership and daughter-in-lawship. A has given his daughter B "into daughtership and daughter-in-lawship" to C. (2) Conditions: After [B has] reached puberty C shall give B into marriage either to a free-born man or to a slave. (The free-born man may be the purchaser himself, one of his sons, or a stranger "in the gate." In case the girl is given into marriage to one of her purchaser's slaves, she must remain in her owner's house as long as she lives.) (3) Price: The sum paid by the purchaser to the girl's father. The condition that the girl be married was fundamental. Fathers took the precaution to safeguard for their daughters a continuous marital status by inserting in the sale document a special clause (in case the condition was that the girl be married to a slave) to the effect that should her first slave-husband die, her master would give her into marriage to another one of his slaves. In some documents provisions are made for four husbands and in one for as many

---

[3]Nuzi was a city in Assyria.

as eleven: "If ten of her husbands have died, in that case to an eleventh into wife-hood she shall be given."

This Nuzian practice had its parallel in Palestine. A section of the earliest Old Testament slave legislation, that of Exodus 21:7–11 reads:

> If a man sells his daughter to be an *amah* ("handmaid, female slave"), she shall not leave as the slaves do (i.e., in the seventh year). If her master dislikes her, although he had appointed her (as wife) for himself, then shall he let her be redeemed; to sell her (as a wife) to a stranger he shall have no power for he has dealt deceitfully with her. But if he has appointed her for his son, he shall treat her in the manner of daughters. If he takes to himself another (wife), he shall not diminish her food, her clothing, and her conjugal rights. If he does not do these three (things) to her, then she shall go out free without compensation. . . .

In view of the Nuzian practice, this Biblical law represents a fragment of a series of enactments which originally dealt with all cases of conditional sales of young girls. The section before us deals, to use the Nuzian terminology, with a "daughtership and daughter-in-lawship" sale. The conditions as set forth in this case are: (1) that the master himself marry the girl (hence the prohibition of treating her like a slave woman or selling her into marriage to a stranger); (2) in case he refuses, after she had reached puberty, to abide by the stipulation in the contract on the ground that the girl now does not find favor in his eyes, he may take recourse to one of the following alternatives: (a) he may let her be redeemed, (b) he may give her as wife to one of his sons, or (c) he may retain her as his concubine. Should he refuse, however, to comply with any of these alternatives open to him; then, as a penalty for breach of contract, "she shall go out free without compensation." . . .

Poverty or debt drove people to sell their children first and then themselves into slavery. In the absence of any state or community help for those driven from the soil by war, famine, or economic misfortune, a man or woman had only one recourse to save himself from starvation, and that was self-sale into slavery. Voluntary self-sale was a common phenomenon especially among strangers. From Nuzi we possess a number of documents relating to self-enslavement. These documents concern themselves mostly with the Habiru,[4] who not being able to find employment entered "of their own free will," singly or with their families, into the state of servitude. The term "servitude" is here used advisedly in preference to "slavery," because legally most of the Habiru self-sale cases in Nuzi differ fundamentally from the self-sale documents of Babylonia. In Babylonia the person who sold himself received his purchase price and as a result he became a slave, the property of another man. But in Nuzi no purchase price is paid to those who "sell themselves." The Habiru enter voluntarily into the state of servitude in exchange for food, clothing,

---

[4]Possible ancestors of the Hebrews.

and shelter.... These Habiru then, retain some kind of legal personality for in some documents it is expressly stated that only after desertion will they "be sold for a price," that is, be reduced to slavery.

Of all the ancient law codes, the Old Testament alone mentions the case of self-sale or voluntary slavery. Ex. 21:2–6 and Deut. 15:16–17 deal with the case of a Hebrew debtor-slave who refuses "to go out" after his six year term of service has been completed because he loves his master, his wife, and his children. The law provides that such a man (who prefers slavery with economic security to freedom with economic insecurity) shall have his ear bored through and shall remain a slave "forever." Leviticus 25:39–54 deals with a free Hebrew who, because of poverty, is forced to sell himself. In this case, the law provides that such a man, regardless of the fact that he had sold himself for ever, shall be freed in the year of the jubilee.

Although slaves were recruited from various indigenous and foreign sources, the basic source of supply for the ever mounting number of slaves in the Ancient Near East was the native defaulting debtor. Insolvency could be the result of many causes, such as drought, war, etc., against which the individual was powerless to act, but one of the chief factors leading to the foreclosure of property and man was unquestionably the exorbitant interest rate charged on loans. The average rate of interest in Ancient Babylonia was 20–25% on silver and 33 1/3% on grain. Assyria had no fixed or average rate. In Late Assyria the usurer had a free hand in determining the rate of interest. Interest on money varied from 20% to as high as 80% per annum. In addition to this general type there were two other kinds of loans current in Babylonia and Assyria. These were loans granted without interest by the temples and the landlords to their tenant-farmer and loans on which interest was charged only after the date of maturity. In the latter case the interest was enormous. In Babylonia the double of the principal, that is, 100% was charged; in Neo-Babylonia[5] we find 40% and also 100%; and in Late Assyria 100% and even 141% was charged. In Nuzi the average interest rate seems to have been 50% "till after the harvest." There is no information in the Old Testament as to the rate of interest charged in Palestine. From the injunction against the taking of interest from a fellow Hebrew we may infer that a higher interest rate was charged and that Palestine was no exception to the rule.

The fate of the defaulting debtor was slavery. The creditor had the right to seize him and sell him into slavery. It was at this unlimited power of the creditor, which tended to reduce large numbers of free-born people into slavery, that...laws...of the Hammurabi Code were aimed. These laws demand that the defaulting debtor or his free-born pledge shall be released after three years of compulsory service. The right of seizure of the defaulting debtor by his creditor was in like manner exercised in Palestine.

---

[5]Period of the eleventh dynasty (626–539 B.C.), when Babylonia achieved its greatest power.

In II Kings 4:1–2 the creditor seized the children of a deceased debtor and the widow appealed to Elisha for help: "The creditor has come to take unto him my children as slaves." This practice of seizure and the subsequent sale into slavery of the unsolvent debtor is reflected in the prophetic literature: "Because they have sold the righteous for a pair of sandals" (Amos 2:6), and "Which of my creditors is it to whom I have sold you?" (Isaiah 50:1). Nehemiah 5:1 ff. shows that creditors foreclosed the land of their defaulting debtors and reduced pledged children to slavery. Like the Hammurabi Code, the Old Testament codes (Ex. 21:2–3 and Dt. 15:12–18) sought to arrest the power of the creditor by demanding that the Hebrew defaulting debtor should be released after six years of compulsory labor.

Legally the slave was considered a chattel. He was a commodity that could be sold, bought, leased, or exchanged. In sharp contrast to the free man, his father's name was almost never mentioned; he had no genealogy, being a man without a name.... Family ties were disregarded in the disposal of slaves. Husbands were separated from their wives, wives were sold without their husbands, and even young children were not spared. The only exception made was in the case of infants "at the breast" who were sold with their mothers.

Babylonia had a class legislation but it was not a caste state. The inequality and discrimination before the law, displayed in the Hammurabi Code in regard to the three main classes which constituted Babylonian society, were based not on race or birth but primarily on wealth. To be sold or to sell oneself into slavery, because of poverty or indebtedness, was a misfortune that could befall any man. This new status, however, was not irrevocable. The fact that the slave could, theoretically at least, be freed, made him a member of a low, dependent class, but not a member of a caste. However, as long as he remained a slave, he was subject to the wearing of a visible property mark.... It may have been an incised mark upon the forehead, a tattooed sign upon some visible part of the body, or a small tablet of clay or metal hung on a chain around the neck, wrist, or ankle. In the Neo-Babylonian period the prevailing custom of marking slaves was to tattoo the name of the owner (and in case of a temple slave the symbol of the god) on the wrist of the slave. There is no evidence that the Assyrian slave was marked....

The Biblical law prescribes that he who voluntarily submits to perpetual slavery shall have his ear pierced with an awl (Ex. 21:6; Dt. 15:17).... We may, therefore, conclude that just as in Babylonia, the Palestinian slaves were marked with a property sign either in the form of a suspended tag attached to the ear, or with a tattoo mark bearing the owner's name on the wrist.

While, legally, the slave was a mere chattel, classed with movable property, both law and society were forced to take into consideration the constantly self-asserting humanity of the slave. We thus have the highly contradictory situation in which on the one hand, the slave was considered as possessing the qualities of a human being while on the other hand, he was recognized as being void of the same and regarded as a mere "thing." The slave's status as a chattel, deprived of any human rights, was clearly and unmistakably emphasized in his relation to a third party. If injured, maimed, or killed by a third party, his owner was compensated for the loss, not the slave. The Biblical legislation mentions only the case of a slave who was killed by a goring ox and provides that the owner shall be compensated for his loss (Ex. 21:32).

... The slave's fate was in fact in his master's hand. Beatings and mal-treatment of slaves seem to have been ... common. ... The Biblical legislation does not prohibit the maltreatment of a Hebrew slave by his master "for he is his money." It is only when the slave dies immediately (within three days) as a result of the beating that the master becomes liable to punishment (Ex. 21:20–21). In Ancient Babylonia a runaway slave was put in chains and had the words "A runaway, seize!" incised upon his face. The Hammurabi Code decrees the death penalty for those who entice a slave to flee from his master and also for those who harbor a fugitive slave. Furthermore, a reward of two shekels is promised to anyone who captures a fugitive slave and brings him back to his master.

The Old Testament slave legislations (Ex. 21, Dt. 15, Lev. 25) do not mention the case of the fugitive slave although the tendency to run away was prevalent in Palestine as it was in the adjacent countries. ... Fugitive slaves were extradited when they fled into foreign countries (I Kings 2:39 ff.). In view of these facts how should the Deuteronomic ordinance (chap. 23:16) "You shall not deliver a slave unto his master who escapes to you from his master" be interpreted? It is a most extraordinary law for its application in life would have spelled the end of slavery in Palestine. Perhaps this ordinance should be explained from a national-economic point of view. It was most probably drawn up in favor of Hebrew slaves who had fled from foreign countries. If this interpretation be correct, then the Deuteronomic law would have its parallel in ... the Hammurabi Code according to which a native Babylonian slave who had been sold into a foreign country and fled from there was set free by the state ....

The slave enjoyed certain privileges which neither law nor society could deny him. According to the Hammurabi Code a slave could marry a free-born woman and a female slave could become her master's concubine. In both cases the children born of such unions were free. The slave could amass a peculium[6] and enjoy it during his life-time, though legally it belonged to his master. And finally the slave could be manumitted. The Hammurabi Code recognizes four legal ways by which a slave received his freedom ipso facto: (1) wives and children sold, or handed over as pledges, are to be freed after three years of service ...; (2) a slave concubine and her children become free after the death of the master ...; (3) children

[6]Small savings.

born of a marriage between a slave and a free woman are free...; and (4) a native Babylonian slave bought in a foreign country and brought back to Babylonia is unconditionally freed.... In addition to these laws which applied only to certain classes and to specific cases of slaves, there were two other ways of manumission: release by adoption and by purchase. Release by adoption was, like that by purchase, a business transaction.... The manumitted slave entered into a sonship (or daughtership) relation to his former master and took upon himself the obligation to support him as long as he lived. After the death of the manumitter, the fictitious relationship and the very real material support were terminated and the "son" became completely free. If the adopted slave failed to live up to his promise of support, that is, repudiated his "parents" by saying "you are not my father" or/and "you are not my mother," the adoption was annulled and the "son" reverted to his former slave status. The difference between release by adoption with the condition to support the manumitter (or release with the condition of support without adoption) and that of release by purchase is that in the former case the released slave still remains in a state of dependency to his former master and becomes completely free only after the death of his former master, while in the second case, the slave severs all connections with his master and becomes immediately and irrevocably free.

According to the Biblical law there were five ways by which a Hebrew slave obtained his freedom. These were: (1) a debtor-slave is freed after six years of service (Ex. 21:2, Dt. 15:12); (2) he who sold himself into slavery is to be freed in the year of the jubilee (Lev. 25); (3) a free-born girl who was sold by her father with the condition that her master or his son marry her, is to be freed if the master refuses to abide by the conditions of the sale (Ex. 21:7–11); (4) by injury (Ex. 21:26–27); and (5) by purchase (Lev. 25:47 ff.). The six-years service limit of the defaulting debtor has its parallel in the Hammurabi Code ... which demands the release of a debtor-slave in the fourth year. We have no evidence to prove that the Hammurabi law was ever enforced in Ancient Babylonia. We have hundreds of documents showing that this law was not enforced in Neo-Babylonia. Debtors were foreclosed and sold into slavery if the loans were not paid on the date of maturity. In view of the fact that we have no private documents from the Biblical period we cannot say whether the law of release of the debtor-slave was enforced in Palestine.... The law of the release of the Hebrew slave in the year of the jubilee is part of a great land reform utopia according to which all land, whether sold or given as security, must revert to its original owners in the year of the jubilee.... Was the law of the jubilee ever enforced in life? The sages of the Talmud[7] were very much in doubt about it. The law of release by injury presents considerable difficulties. The meaning of the law is, of course, quite clear. The loss of limb, as a result of beatings administered by the master, is considered sufficient ground for meriting release.... It seems ... that the only plausible

[7]The books of Jewish law.

interpretation... would be to assume that the law ... applies to the Hebrew defaulting debtor. From the point of view of the law, the Hebrew defaulting debtor is not a slave at all but merely a debtor temporarily in the service of his creditor. When such a debtor is permanently injured by his creditor, the loss of limb is considered to be the equivalent of the amount of the debt and hence he is to be released.

There were three main classes of slaves in the Ancient Near East, viz., state slaves, temple slaves, and privately owned slaves. Of these, the first group, recruited from war prisoners, was economically the most important. In Babylonia and Assyria the state slaves, with the assistance of corvee[8] gangs and hired laborers, constructed roads, dug canals, erected fortresses, built temples, tilled the crown lands, and worked in the royal factories connected with the palace. The small city-states of Syria and Palestine also had their state slaves. In the El-Amarna period (c. 1400 B.C.) Syrian and Palestinian "kings" sent large numbers of slaves and war captives... as gifts to their Egyptian overlords.... That this institution existed in Palestine from the days of David down to the period of Nehemiah and Ezra is attested by the numerous references to the state slaves in the Old Testament. Since this class of slaves (recruited from war captives and from the tribute paying Canaanites) was officially created by Solomon, they were appropriately called *abde Shelomo* ("Solomon's slaves"). Once formed, this class of state slaves remained in existence until the end of the Judaean kingdom.[9] ... The end of independent statehood marked also the end of the institution of slavery.

Already at the dawn of history the Babylonian temple with its vast wealth constituted the richest agricultural, industrial, and commercial single unit within the community. It was a well organized and efficiently run corporation controlling extensive tracts of land, enormous quantities of raw material, large flocks of cattle and sheep, sizeable amounts of precious metal, and a large number of slaves. This was also true, though to a lesser degree, of the Assyrian, Syrian, and Palestinian temples....

Temple slaves were recruited from two sources: prisoners of war who were presented to the temples by victorious kings, and dedications of slaves by private individuals. The sanctuaries in Palestine recruited their slaves from the same sources. After the successful campaign against the Midianites,[10] Moses is reported to have taken one of every five hundred, or one of every fifty, prisoners, and presented them as a gift to Yahweh (Num. 31:25 ff.). Joshua made the Gibeonites[11] "hewers of wood and drawers of water in the sanctuary" (chap. 9:21 ff.).... We have no evidence to prove that privately owned slaves were dedicated to temples in Palestine. The case of

[8]Forced labor.

[9]586 B.C.

[10]Semitic people who invaded southern Palestine after 1200 B.C.

[11]Palestinian people who derived their name from the city Gibeon.

young Samuel who was dedicated to the sanctuary of Shiloh, however, shows that this practice was known in Palestine. While the number of state and temple slaves was very large, their economic role must not be overestimated. The state ... employed them in non-competitive enterprises and the temple used them primarily for menial work. In its two main branches of activity, agriculture and industry, the temple employed mostly free-born people and not slaves. The land was cultivated by free-born tenant-farmers, and free-born artisans worked in the shops.

Unlike Egypt, where the land belonged to the crown, private ownership of land was the rule in the Sumero-Semitic countries. The case of the Israelite farmer Naboth who chose death in preference to selling his ancestral plot to king Ahab was characteristic of the attitude of all peasantry in the Ancient Near East. With the exception of the large holdings of the crown and the temples, the land was owned by two classes of people: small farmers and large landowners. Since the land property of the average farmer was small and his family large there was no great need for outside help either in the form of hired laborers or of slaves. The labor situation was, of course, different in the second group. These large estates had to be worked with hired help. This help, however, was only to a very small degree drawn from the ranks of hired laborers and slaves. It was drawn primarily and overwhelmingly from the ranks of the dispossessed peasantry croppers. ... Instead of buying, maintaining, and guarding considerable numbers of unwilling slaves, the large landowners (and to a degree even the kings and the temples) preferred to lease parcels of their land to free-born tenant-farmers. ... Like the upper class in the cities, well-to-do farmers owned slaves and employed them on the land, but slave labor was not a decisive factor in the agricultural life of the Ancient Near East.

The counterpart of the free-born tenant-farmer in agriculture was the free-born "hired laborer" in industry. There was, of course, great competition between free laborers and slaves in the field of unskilled labor, but the skilled fields were dominated by the free artisans. The reasons for this phenomenon, that is, the small number of slave artisans in the Ancient Near East, were: (1) the apprenticeship period lasted from two to six years, a period during which the slave not only did not bring in any profit, but the owner had to spend money for his upkeep; (2) the number of slaves in well-to-do families averaged from one to three and therefore only a few of them could be spared to be used as an investment with a view to future returns; and finally (3) the general unwillingness of the employer to hire slaves because they could not be trusted to operate with expensive tools even when they possessed the skill to handle them. We thus come to the conclusion that the role played by slaves in the skilled industries was very insignificant indeed. Ancient Near Eastern craftsmanship was the product of free labor.

We have seen that economically the Ancient Near Eastern civilization was not based on slave labor. We have also seen that society was unable to maintain consistently the legal fiction that the slave was a mere chattel, and hence some freedom was accorded to him. There remains one more aspect to be considered and that is the attitude of religion toward slavery, the ownership of man by man. Nowhere in the vast religious literature of the Sumero-Accadian world is a protest raised against the institution of slavery, nor is there anywhere an expression of sympathy for the victims of this system. The Old Testament justifies perpetual slavery of the Canaanites, but demands the release of the Hebrew defaulting debtor in the seventh year and of those who sold themselves in the year of the jubilee. The first case—the release of the debtor-slave after a limited term of service—has a parallel in the earlier Hammurabi Code which also demands the release of the defaulting debtor. But in the second case where the release is demanded of even those who had sold themselves voluntarily into slavery, we have for the first time an open denial of the right of man to own man in perpetuity. This denial of the right of possession of man by man is as yet restricted to Hebrews only (cf. Nehemiah 5:8), but it is a step which no other religion had taken before. The first man in the Ancient Near East who raised his voice in a sweeping condemnation of slavery as a cruel and inhuman institution, irrespective of nationality and race, was the philosopher Job. His was a condemnation based on the moral concept of the inherent brotherhood of man, for

> "Did not He that made me in the womb make him (the slave) also? And did not One fashion us in the womb?" (31:15)

Afterlife: Ancient Israel's Changing Vision of the World Beyond

BERNHARD LANG

Ancient Semites (Israelites and their Mesopotamian and Syro-Palestinian neighbors) viewed the world as containing the heavens, the earth, and the netherworld (Sheol). How did humans communicate with the gods of heaven and those of the underworld? What type of worship was familial and which rituals were community functions?

How did the ancient Semites bury their dead? Unlike the Egyptians, for example, the Semites did not express great interest in life after death, even though they evidently believed in some sort of afterlife. Why did they believe it necessary to venerate and placate dead ancestors? How did the living make contact with the dead? What was life in the netherworld like?

Religion is a cultural creation and changes over time. In what ways did Israel's vision of the world beyond develop? For instance, attitudes toward ancestor worship and toward the existence of other gods and goddesses underwent transformation. What was the "Yahweh-alone movement" and how did it bear on Israel's conceptions of the world beyond? How did it alter religious ritual? What effect did the destruction of the northern kingdom of Israel in 722 B.C. have on Hebraic religion? How did this religion now view the dead and their significance? In this regard, what was the import of the Book of Job? What did Sheol become in the minds of the Hebrews?

The ancient Hebrews, through their dietary laws, keeping of the Sabbath, and circumcision, cut themselves off from their neighbors. By eventually creating a this-worldly religion, Hebrew theology distanced itself from some of the other ancient Near Eastern religions. The Egyptians, for example, spent much religious energy on preparing for and worrying about a life after death. Hebraic religion concentrated on life above ground.

But Judaism continued to evolve. How did the Babylonian conquest of the southern kingdom of Judah in 586 B.C. lead the Hebrews to rethink their beliefs about the dead? How did the new Persian religion, Zoroastrianism, influence Judaism? By what means did Ezekiel link the new belief in individual bodily resurrection with national aspirations?

From an early date, the Hebrews were concerned with elaborating a theodicy, an attempt to explain the presence of evil in this world. Pain inflicted on sentient beings brought into question their god's attributes of omnipotence and perfect goodness, so Judaism rationally tried to explain how God would permit suffering to exist. How did the belief in resurrection provide a new answer to the problem of evil for some Jews?

Bernhard Lang argues that the Jews became seriously divided on their views of a life after death. What were the beliefs of those who accepted a philosophical and individualistic response to an afterlife? What new role did heaven play? How was heaven pictured? As a result of Greek influence, what ideas emerged about the immortality of the soul?

By the first century A.D., there were three distinct Jewish views of the afterlife. What were these interpretations?

Lang emphasizes the diversity and evolution of Jewish attitudes in the ancient world. The precise extent to which the populace, as opposed to simply a religious elite, held these views is impossible to determine, but, in light of the support that Jews gave to their religion, it is safe to assume that common Jews shared the various attitudes toward life after death and toward Sheol that Lang describes. The changing visions of the world beyond joined together Jewish religious thinkers and the population in an attempt to fathom the unfathomable.

The earliest Hebrew understanding of the cosmos grew out of prevailing Mesopotamian and Canaanite mythology. Even before the time of the Hebrews, ancient Semites pictured the world as a three-tiered structure: an upper realm of the gods (heaven), a middle world given by the gods to humans (earth) and a lower domain consisting of a great cave far below the surface of the earth (the netherworld or Sheol). While the gods inhabited heaven, and humans during life inhabited earth, Sheol housed both the dead and the infernal gods.

Although the ancients envisioned Sheol as a dark and silent place, we should not think of it as hell. A deity called Mot, "Death," reigned there and ruled over both the dead and the infernal gods.

Human beings living on earth, between heaven and Sheol, were affected and influenced by both the upper and lower worlds. Human communication with the deities of the upper world, as well as with the gods of the lower world, was of paramount importance. All the inhabitants of the earth—whether wealthy landlords, merchants, proud warriors, aristocrats, princes or fashionable ladies—had to regard themselves as essentially weak and dependent on the gods. Only by establishing temples, sponsoring priests and temple choirs, offering lavish sacrifices, chanting elaborate prayers, and heeding sorcerers and prophets could human beings be assured of divine benevolence. Fertile flocks, abundant harvests, victories in battle and success, prosperity and peace depended on the graciousness of the gods residing in either heaven or Sheol.

Ancient Near Eastern ritual was varied and complicated. Only priests, thoroughly trained in public and private ritual and lore, knew the intricacies of communication with the upper and lower worlds. Their ritual appealed either to the powers of heaven or to the gods of the netherworld and the dead who shared that habitation and who might influence the infernal gods with whom they lived. To appeal to the dead meant basically to call upon expired ancestors, residing in Sheol, to aid the living.

Ancestor worship—on behalf of genealogically related individuals—venerated forefathers and, perhaps, foremothers, from whom the living expected personal protection and, more important, numerous offspring. Gradually, formalized rituals developed to express the veneration of ancestors. In one such ritual, the living drank huge quantities of wine and also poured out wine for the dead, who were the objects of appeal; in this ritual everyone, including the dead, supposedly got drunk. Another, less elaborate, ritual consisted simply of placing offerings of water and food at the family tomb.

Ancestor worship did not involve the community at large; we may therefore refer to it as a private ritual. Small groups of family members would venerate their ancestors in private worship without the participation of any larger political or ethnic grouping.

However, when the gods of heaven, rather than the dead, were invoked, the entire community was involved. Priests in state temples offered regular sacrifices to the gods of heaven on behalf of the king, and, through him, on behalf of the whole society. These were public rituals that extended far beyond the confines of an individual family or family lineage. The more important public rituals celebrated the cycle of the agricultural year: the sowing and reaping of grain, or the eating of the first fruits of the season. These public rituals connected the people not with their dead relatives, but with the gods of the sky who were responsible for rain. Without this communion with the sky gods, they believed, no vegetation could grow in the arid zones of the ancient Near East.

Both kinds of ritual—the public one addressed to the celestial gods and the private one directed to the ancestors in the netherworld—coexisted. Indeed, they were practiced by the same people. The types of rituals depended not on what the supplicant hoped to gain, but for whom the gain was intended. If a family member would benefit, then a private ritual was performed. If the community as a whole benefited, a public ritual was conducted.

In this cosmic conception, to die meant to change one's place in the ritual universe. But transfer to the netherworld required some earthly actions. The family was required to bury the body, thereby removing it from the sight of the celestial gods and bringing it into contact with the dead person's new realm of being. Burial usually occurred in an underground vault or was carried out simply by covering the body with earth. Although the flesh decayed and the bones dried out, a shadowy replica of the deceased became manifest and descended into the vast underground mausoleum where it would continue its existence.

What was life like there? The ancient Semites, unfortunately for 20th-century students of the past, have left us no speculations about life in Sheol. The ancients were apparently uninterested in this question. Their concern was with establishing ritual contact with the world of the dead. Hence, we do not know what they believed existence was like in Sheol. We know only of their belief that in the netherworld the dead would meet their own ancestors, a belief that may have prompted the biblical expression that a person who dies "goes to his fathers [ancestors]" (see Genesis 15:15) or is "gathered to his people [kin]" (Genesis 25:8).

The shadowy life of the dead was permanent and did not fade away. There were, however, different degrees of life in the netherworld, depending on one's past earthly existence and on the regularity with which one's descendants engaged in certain rituals. Someone who died in ripe old age and who received regular offerings of food and water (placed near the tomb) achieved the best fate. Residing in the upper, and perhaps somewhat lighter part of Sheol, such an ancestor could assist his or her descendants by bestowing powerful blessings. But ancestors could also become angry and withhold blessings and cause harm. The ancestors thus became like "gods" who could affect the lives of the living in dramatic ways (see 1 Samuel 28:13).

If earthly relatives neglected their ancestor offerings, the fate of the dead worsened. Rather than residing in the lighter parts of Sheol, they would descend to the lower and more unpleasant parts of the netherworld. People who died the death of criminals or on the battlefield without having their bodies properly buried populated the lowest regions.

Isaiah provides us with a vivid picture of the lower parts of Sheol in a prophecy against Babylon. The king of Babylon will be brought down by Yahweh, the prophet tells us, and Israel will sing a song of scorn to taunt her former oppressor (Isaiah 14:3). The song, a mock dirge, describes how the king of Babylon will die:

How you are fallen from heaven,
  O Day Star, son of Dawn!
How you are cut down to the ground,

you who laid the nations low!
You said in your heart,
* 'I will ascend to heaven;*
above the stars of God
* I will set my throne on high;*
I will sit on the mount of assembly
* in the far north;*
I will ascend above the heights of the clouds,
* I will make myself like the Most High.'*
But you are brought down to Sheol,
* to the depths of the pit.*

Isaiah 14:12–15

On his arrival in Sheol, the king of Babylon is met by the kings who preceded him. They are mere shades, leading shadowy lives of their own, with dreamy pomp and ceremony. The king of Babylon is to lie in mud and filth, covered with worms.

Sheol beneath is stirred up
* to meet you when you come,*
it rouses the shades to greet you,
* all who were leaders of the earth;*
it raises from their thrones
* all who were kings of the nations.*
All of them will speak
* and say to you:*
'You too have become as weak as we!
* You have become like us!'*
Your pomp is brought down to Sheol,
* the sound of your harps;*
maggots are the bed beneath you,
* and worms your covering.*

Isaiah 14:9–11

The king of Babylon will live in Sheol like one who has been unburied:

Those who see you will stare at you,
* and ponder over you:*
'Is this the man who made the earth tremble,
* who shook kingdoms,*
who made the world like a desert
* and overthrew its cities,*
* who did not let his prisoners go home?'*
All the kings of the nations lie in glory,
* each in his own tomb;*
but you are cast out, away from your sepulchre,
* like a loathed untimely birth,*

> *clothed with the slain, those pierced by the sword,*
> *who go down to the stones of the Pit,*
> *like a dead body trod under foot*
> *You will not be joined with them in burial,*
> *because you have destroyed your land,*
> *you have slain your people.*
>
> Isaiah 14:16–20

The living contacted the dead in Sheol not only through ancestor worship, but also through mediums, sorcerers, witches and necromancers who had special access to the netherworld. In one episode described in the Bible, King Saul, nearly deranged, seeks to learn the outcome of an imminent battle with the Philistines by consulting the witch of En-dor. After his normal channels of communication with the divine realm—dreams, priestly manipulation of lots, the advice of prophets—fail, Saul, desperate and disguised, pays a nocturnal visit to a necromancer. The witch of En-dor digs a hole in the crust of the earth so that the world of the living may be joined to the realm of the dead. At Saul's request, the witch raises the Prophet Samuel, once Saul's supporter—who anointed him king and who is now his sworn detractor. The scene is one of high drama and emotion:

> Then Samuel said to Saul, 'Why have you disturbed me by bringing me up?' Saul answered, 'I am in great distress; for the Philistines are warring against me, and God has turned away from me and answers me no more, either by prophets or by dreams; therefore I have summoned you to tell me what I shall do.'
> And Samuel said, 'Why then do you ask me, since the Lord has turned from you and become your enemy?'
> 'The Lord has done to you as he spoke by me; for the Lord has torn the kingdom out of your hand, and given it to your neighbor, David. Because you did not obey the voice of the Lord, and did not carry out his fierce wrath against the Amalek,[1] therefore the Lord has done this thing to you this day. Moreover the Lord will give Israel also with you into the hand of the Philistines; and tomorrow you and your sons shall be with me; the Lord will give the army of Israel into the hand of the Philistines.'
> Then Saul fell at once full length upon the ground, filled with fear because of the words of Samuel (1 Samuel 28:15–20).

Although this communication occurred between Saul and Samuel, only the medium could see the dead Samuel. Saul had to ask the medium, "What do you see? . . . What is his appearance?" (1 Samuel 28:13,14). She describes "an old man wrapped in a robe."

After the conversation with Saul, the fading spirit returns to the darkness and silence of Sheol. Saul, of course, dies as foretold during the consultation.

---

[1]In Exodus 17:8–16, the Amalekites attacked the Israelites shortly after they crossed the Red Sea. For that reason, God cursed the Amalekites and commanded their annihilation.

The episode gives us a glimpse of an afterlife in which the dead, although apparently deprived of material substance, retain such personality characteristics as form, memory, consciousness and even knowledge of what happens on the other side. While life in the netherworld is less than appealing, the dead have the power to aid or to harm the living. Such powers permit the dead to function as gods. Private rituals, conducted by kin, emphasize the bonds between the residents of earth and the residents of the netherworld. These private rituals contrast with public rituals that focus on the concerns of the larger community.

Although our knowledge of this early stratum of Semitic thought is sketchy, we can discern a belief in a shadowy afterlife in which the status of the dead depends on the veneration of the living; conversely, the state of the living may be influenced by the gods of the netherworld.

Later biblical writers condemned ancestor worship and necromancy as an inherently pagan practice that cannot be a legitimate part of the religion of Israel. Note that the author of 1 Samuel 28 has Saul outlawing resort to such necromancers, although Saul is recklessly violating his own prohibition.

Ancestor worship was outlawed in the eighth century B.C. as a part of a new prophetic movement. At that time, the powerful Assyrian empire was exerting increasingly intolerable pressure on the small vassal kingdoms of Israel and Judah. In this situation of almost permanent crisis, a prophetic movement formed that advocated the exclusive worship of one God, Yahweh. The worship of all other gods and goddesses was to be abandoned.

According to this prophetic movement, Israel's God Yahweh, the only one with real power, would eventually intervene and alter the political scene in favor of his people. This new religious movement has been called by scholars the "Yahweh-alone movement." It not only banned the worship of the sky gods but also outlawed the cult of the dead.

The Yahweh-alone-ists outlawed ancestor worship because they perceived it as a magical deviation from true worship.... [M]agic "is not part of an organized [communal] worship, but private, secret, mysterious" and is therefore often prohibited by the controlling group. The Yahweh-alone-ists believed that ancestor worship, which gave preference to kin, slighted national concerns. For them, national and public matters assumed clear priority over private and family affairs.

Ironically enough, after the Assyrians conquered and destroyed the northern kingdom of Israel in 722 B.C., the Yahweh-alone-ists became even more convinced of their cause. They attributed the military disaster at the hands of the Assyrians to the neglect of the one God whose exclusive worship they advocated. In the now truncated Israel—the small southern kingdom of Judah alone survived—the Judahite king Hezekiah (716–687 B.C.) attempted a cultic and legal reform, emphasizing the exclusivity of Yahweh worship.

King Hezekiah's reform either failed or remained partially unimplemented. In any event, almost a century passed before the Yahweh-alone-ist movement became the decisive factor in official Judahite policy. In 623 B.C., the Judahite king Josiah proclaimed that Yahweh was the only god to be worshipped, apparently accomplishing the aim of the earlier reform. The biblical report of Josiah's reform tells us that "Josiah got rid of all the mediums and necromancers [literally, those who called up the ghosts and spirits of the dead], of all household gods and idols, and all the abominations" (2 Kings 23:24).

By taking this decisive step toward monotheism, Josiah drastically reduced private worship, and especially ritual activities relating to the dead. The placing of food near or in the tomb as a funerary offering—a ritual that formerly was a real sacrifice to the gods of the underworld—was reduced to a simple gesture of convention or tradition. The ritual was stripped of its cosmological significance. The dead could be fed and thereby kept vital, but any other contact was forbidden by the reformers. Denied their exercise of influence over the living, the ancestors faded into the distance, into the eternal darkness of Sheol.

While King Josiah's reform outlawed certain traditional practices concerning the dead, it did not create new beliefs to replace earlier traditions regarding life after death. A more philosophical examination of the meaning of death and the afterlife appears, however, in the Book of Job, which dates from the fifth century B.C. Continuing the trend begun in the eighth century with King Hezekiah, the Book of Job devalues the role of the dead. It recognizes that, when one's earthly life ceases, one is cut off permanently from life on earth, without communication either way, and, perhaps worse, one is cut off from God himself. Job, in his suffering, longs to go to Sheol until the time when God will remember him, but he knows that will not be; there is no hope of this. The Book of Job proclaims that the dead have no knowledge of the living; they cannot influence those on earth. Although a dead man's descendants may honor him, he knows nothing of it (Job 14:21). The communication between ancestor and offspring, so vital in polytheistic thought and ritual, disappears. The living and the dead are eternally separated:

> For there is hope for a tree,
>   if it be cut down, that it will sprout again,
>   and that its shoots will not cease.
> Though its root grow old in the earth,
>   and its stump die in the ground,
> yet at the scent of water it will bud
>   and put forth branches like a young plant.
> But man dies, and is laid low;
>   man breathes his last, and where is he?
> As waters fail from a lake,
>   and a river wastes away and dries up,
> So man lies down and rises not again;
>   till the heavens are no more he will not awake,
>   or be roused out of his sleep.
> Oh that thou wouldest hide me in Sheol,

that thou wouldest conceal me until thy wrath be past,
that thou wouldest appoint me a set time, and remember me!
If a man die, shall he live again?
All the days of my service I would wait,
till my release should come.
Thou wouldest call, and I would answer thee;
thou wouldest long for the work of thy hands.
For then thou wouldest number my steps,
thou wouldest not keep watch over my sin;
my transgression would be sealed up in a bag,
and thou wouldest cover over my iniquity.
But the mountain falls and crumbles away,
and the rock is removed from its place;
the waters wear away the stones;
the torrents wash away the soil of the earth;
so thou destroyest the hope of man.
Thou prevailest for ever against him, and he passes;
thou changest his countenance, and sendest him away.
His sons come to honor, and he does not know it;
they are brought low, and he perceives it not.

Job 14:7–21

Job and his contemporaries agreed with older, pessimistic traditions of the Semitic world that the fate of the dead was a deplorable one. Who wants to exist in "a land of gloom and chaos, where light is as darkness" (Job 10:22; 3:17–19)? We are reminded of the Old-Babylonian epic of Gilgamesh, which portrays the netherworld as "the house wherein the dwellers are bereft of light, where dust is their fare and clay their food." Despite this gloomy view of the land of the dead, at least death ends our earthly misery, as Job points out in a skillful eulogy (Job 3:17–19). Death also resolves the problem of social inequality by releasing us from servitude. Since the dead cannot help the living, the dead are released from the burden of being involved in human troubles. Sheol, if not a place of happiness, is at least free from the trials of earth.

But for the devout worshipper of Yahweh, Sheol held another deprivation. Even Yahweh is not worshipped there.

"Who will praise the Most High in Sheol?" asks Ecclesiasticus,[2] written in the second century B.C. "When a man is dead and ceases to be, his gratitude dies with him" (Ecclesiasticus 17:27,28). There can thus be no relationship between Yahweh and the dead.

The two taboos—prohibiting relating to any deity but Yahweh and prohibiting a relationship between the dead and Yahweh—condemned the dead

---

[2]Ecclesiasticus, or the Book of Sirach, is part of the Catholic canon and is contained in the Septuagint, the first translation of the Bible from Hebrew to Greek—made for the Jews of Alexandria in about the third century B.C. Ecclesiasticus is in the apocrypha of Jews and Protestants. (Author's note.)

to a meaningless existence. They could not even ask for consolation from the living. Since the realms of the living and the dead were completely separated, no communication could take place between them. The residual veneration in the form of funerary offerings notwithstanding, the dead expected nothing from their descendants. And those on earth no longer waited for their ancestors' help. Priests especially avoided any ritual connection with the dead; they were not even allowed to attend the funerals of their own parents (Leviticus 21:11).

In contrast to the earlier Semitic ritual universe, the ritual universe created by King Josiah's seventh-century B.C. reform ultimately sealed off the netherworld. Israelite rituals simply excluded the dead from ritual consideration. Instead of being powerful and influential ancestors, the deceased became weak shadows of negligible vitality. Not being able to praise the only God, they were doomed to a meaningless existence in the eternal silence of Sheol. Israelite theology focused on the practices of a this-worldly religion rather than on the futile speculations of the life of the dead. The pious who meet with unfortunate circumstances on earth had to be promised rewards in this life. Job, faced with a miserable earthly existence, is not promised rewards after death. Whatever other messages his story presents, the implications of its last page are clear: God rewards Job for his patience and devotion with health, family and wealth. Job receives his blessing—"twice as much as he had before"—*on earth and not in the afterlife* (Job 42:10). The Judaism of King Josiah's reform held no promise for the dead.

The Babylonian destruction of Jerusalem in 586 B.C. brought the kingdom of Judah to an abrupt end. Israel no longer existed on the political map of the Near East. In the centuries that followed, many Jews of course continued to dream of an independent Israel restored by divine intervention. Especially in times of political upheavals and turmoil, the fire of independence flared; whenever one superpower vanished, giving way to new rulers—the Babylonians to the Persians, the Persians to the Greeks, and, eventually, the Greeks to the Romans—the hope of a national restoration swelled.

The most extreme version of this hope assumed that Yahweh not only intended to restore Israel as a state but would also permit the dead to live in the new Jewish commonwealth. The belief in a "bodily resurrection" held that the dead must not be deprived of the blessings of the new age that was to come. Restored fully to bodily life, they would live for many years in the new world, enjoying a renewed life.

The concept of a bodily resurrection and life in a restored world had nothing in common with the views of the afterlife reflected in King Josiah's reform. Indeed, the concept of bodily resurrection was borrowed from the ancient Iranians. It first appears in the teachings of the Iranian prophet Zoroaster (about 1500 B.C.). According to Zoroaster, the soul's fate after death depended on the character of its life on earth; after death, the soul would be judged, and either rewarded in heaven or punished in a less pleasant place, hell. Complete happiness, however, required more than this:

Some day the souls of the just would be reunited with their bodies, not in a heavenly paradise, but on earth. Zoroaster anticipated a general resurrection of the dead, following a universal divine judgment and an eventual cleansing of the earth. Restored to its original perfection and beauty, the world would then serve as the eternal kingdom of Ahura Mazda, the creator. In this new world, men and women would live forever.

Jews living in Babylonia, later Persia, and other areas within the orbit of Iranian influence in the sixth century B.C., absorbed Zoroastrian beliefs and adapted them to their own aspirations. Iranian religion helped Jewish theologians shape their own tradition.

The idea of a bodily resurrection in Israel first appears in the prophecies of Ezekiel (c. 585–568 B.C.). Ezekiel delivered a series of oracles of hope that included visions of a gloriously rebuilt Jerusalem with a magnificent temple. In one of his visions, Ezekiel saw a vast plain covered with dry human bones, bleached by the sun (Ezekiel 37:1–15). A plain with dried bones is reminiscent of a Zoroastrian funeral ground where the bodies of the dead remained unburied. Worshippers of Ahura Mazda allowed the bodies to lie in the sun for a year until the rains turned the flesh into carrion and the birds devoured it, leaving only the bones. According to Zoroastrian doctrine, at a later resurrection the creator would reassemble the scattered parts of the body. Similarly in Ezekiel, after the prophet is shown the plain covered with human bones, he is commanded to prophesy to the bones and announce their resurrection; immediately the skeletons reassemble themselves and form bodies. God then tells Ezekiel to order the winds to breathe into the bodies—and the bodies come back to life. The resurrected people return to their homeland in Israel from their exile in Babylonia.

Zoroastrian resurrection was of course adapted to the religious and political outlook of Jews at the time. Ezekiel linked the idea of resurrection to national concerns, rather than to universal, cosmological expectations. The original Iranian doctrine implied the end of human history, as well as the end of death; Ezekiel, however, related resurrection to a miracle that would inaugurate a new era in Israel's national life. Ezekiel expected not a new universe, but a renewed Jewish commonwealth free from foreign oppression.

In later centuries, in times of persecution or when the spirit of national pride was rekindled, religious leaders and political rebels alike would envision a national revival accompanied by a bodily resurrection.

The Book of Daniel, written in the second century B.C. during a time of Greek persecution, anticipated a national revival when "many of those who sleep in the dust of the earth will awake" (Daniel 12:2).

While the kingdom God would create would be never-ending and eternal, the life span of the resurrected would be limited. According to the Book of Enoch,[3] for instance, the resurrected would live "five hundred years" or as "long life on earth as [their] fathers lived." Their "fathers" were not

---

[3] A non-biblical book that originated in third-century B.C. Judaism. (Author's note.)

their immediate ancestors, but rather the biblical patriarchs who, according to Genesis, lived to ripe old ages like 895, 987, etc. After a long and peaceful second life on earth, which would more than make up for the difficulties encountered in their first life, the resurrected would eventually die.

The expectation of resurrection, with its accompanying establishment of the divine kingdom, provided an answer to the question of why God did not intervene on behalf of his suffering people. Far from being indifferent to Israel's political fate, God was simply waiting for that special day that he, in his wisdom, had chosen. Then would the faithful be resurrected, fully restored to bodily life, and God's universal kingdom on earth established.

Not all Jews, of course, shared this hope. Many simply made their peace with their various overlords and accepted foreign rule. As long as their overlords allowed them freely to exercise their religion, they saw no reason to be dissatisfied. Many such Jews, especially those with a more philosophical outlook, explored the fate of the dead in a way vastly different from that of the nationalists. For them, the idea of a glorious communal future with a restored Israelite nation faded into the background. They focused instead on the post-mortem future of individuals.

The earliest effort to formulate a more philosophical, individualistic response to life after death may be found in Psalms 73 and 49. The authors of these psalms are troubled by the seeming prosperity of the wicked and the ease of the rich. The poet-author of Psalm 73 laments that the wicked "are always at ease, they increase in riches. All in vain have I kept my heart clean" (Psalm 73:12–13). But then he realizes that eventually the wicked will be "destroyed in a moment, swept away utterly" (Psalm 73:19). The psalmist, on the other hand, having led a righteous life, will be with God (Psalm 73:23): "Afterward [that is, after life on earth] thou will receive me with glory. Whom have I *in heaven,* but thee?" (Psalm 73:24–25).

Psalm 49 is even more explicit. The rich, boastful and arrogant will be unable to bargain with God. They will perish and be sent to Sheol, without their riches and denied any glimpse of light. As for the righteous psalmist, however, God "will take me from the power of Sheol . . . he will receive me" (Psalm 49:15).

Both psalms reveal a strong personal element; they reflect personal concerns; they speak in the first person, "I."

By proclaiming that God will eventually "receive" them after their deaths, these individualistic poets are boldly reusing vocabulary traditionally associated with figures like Enoch (the sixth descendant after Adam) and the prophet Elijah. Enoch and Elijah did not die; God bodily assumed them into heaven (Genesis 5:24 and 2 Kings 2:11). From the viewpoint of the authors of Psalms 73 and 49, what was possible for Enoch and Elijah was possible for others as well. Thus, the concept of heavenly assumption was redefined in less extraordinary terms. God "received" his faithful "after" death, without having to resort to the miraculous procedure of taking them away while still alive. Searching the Scriptures, the psalmists found the ancient myth of heavenly assumption and creatively expanded it. They translated the myth of heaven, once only possible for the special few like Enoch and Elijah, into a hope and expectation for the many.

The psalmists, however, give no description of this heavenly realm, where the righteous would go. The psalmists speak only of a continuing fellowship with God and refer only vaguely to future glory. Their reflections were "but jets of religious feeling, spasmodic upleapings of the flame of love of existence." . . . Convinced of the love of God for the righteous, the psalmists made the bold assertion that God recognizes the goodness of his creatures and has the power to place them in a celestial realm.

The psalmists combined an ethical argument—that righteousness must be rewarded—with a mythical argument—that God confers upon the righteous the privilege of residence in heaven instead of in Sheol. Eventually these two notions were supplemented by a third—the immortality of the soul. Wherever Diaspora Jews met Greek intellectuals, the idea of an immortal soul surfaced. In cities like Alexandria, Jewish philosophers confronted the notion that an immortal and immaterial soul existed quite independently from the body. This soul was not subject to decay and eventual death. Moreover, it was the soul that contained the essence of the individual. Unlike Jewish tradition, in which the person continued after death as a shade—a weak, emaciated replica of the individual, Greek tradition held that the soul, which was immortal, contained the most vital aspects of the person. Once released from the restrictions of the body, the soul became not weaker but stronger and more powerful. It tended to ascend upwards, rather than to sink into the netherworld. Under favorable circumstances, the individual soul not only survived death, it found its ultimate home in the transcendent, celestial realm of Platonic ideas.

The Greek belief in an immortal soul made a lasting impression on Jewish thought, and eventually on Christian beliefs. Both the Book of Wisdom (also called the Wisdom of Solomon) (first century B.C.)[4] and the work of the Jewish philosopher Philo of Alexandria (20 B.C.–45 A.D.) reflect a deep concern with the nature of the soul. The Wisdom of Solomon accepts the soul's immortality as a simple fact. Philo, on the other hand, developed a unique synthesis of Platonic philosophy and biblical traditions. For Philo, death restored the soul to its original, prebirth state. Since the soul belongs to the spiritual world, life in the body was nothing but a brief, often unfortunate, episode. While many human souls lose their way in the labyrinth of the material world, the true philosopher's soul survives bodily death and assumes "a higher existence, immortal and uncreated."

In heaven, Philo tells us, the soul joins the incorporeal inhabitants of the divine world, the angels. In certain cases the soul advances even higher and

---

[4]The Book of Wisdom, or Wisdom of Solomon, is part of the Catholic Bible. It reflects the concerns of Jewish intellectuals living in first-century B.C. Alexandria, Egypt. (Author's note.)

lives in the world of ideas. If it moves still higher, it can live with the deity itself. Enoch, according to Philo, lived among pure ideas; only the soul of Moses, however, entered the very highest realm, to live with God.

But the soul might also descend again into the material world. By adopting the Platonic view that "some, longing for the familiar and accustomed ways of mortal life, again retrace their steps," Philo recognized the possibility of reincarnation.

Hellenistic Jews, like Philo of Alexandria, showed no interest in recreating a Jewish national state. They considered Judaism a philosophy, a system of belief, rather than the ideology of a state. Ideally, the Jew would be a philosopher, who like Philo led the retired life of a thinker, preparing his soul for its celestial ascent. Preparation for death, rather than hope for a resurrected society, served as a basis for mediation with life here on earth.

Philo and his fellow Hellenistic Jews deepened the musings of the poets who composed Psalms 73 and 49, discussed above. These Psalmists sang of the mercy and justice of a God whose powers saved them from a meaningless existence in Sheol. They did not explain, however, how this would be done. Platonic thought provided the system for transforming the weakened shade trapped in Sheol into an immortal soul destined for the highest realms of existence. For some Hellenistic Jews who retreated from the idea of overthrowing the seemingly endless stream of colonial rulers, an individualistic heaven appeared more appealing—and more realistic— than the promise of a renewed kingdom of Israel where people lived to be 900 years old. They rejected both the early Israelite idea of the futility of any afterlife and the nationalistic hope for a restored communal existence. Instead, they answered their questions about life after death by a belief in the immortal individual soul freed from its bodily confines.

By the first century A.D., in the period before the Roman destruction of the Temple in 70 A.D., three Jewish responses to the question of afterlife competed with one another in the major Jewish sects or religious divisions. The ancient sources are sketchy in their details, but the broad outlines are clear.

The first group originated with the Josianic reform movement of the seventh century B.C., whose heirs were the Sadducees.[5] According to the Jewish historian Josephus (37–100 A.D.), the Sadducees held "that the soul perishes with the body." Because all ancient sources concerning the Sadducees are unsympathetic to them and do not attempt to understand their perspective on death, we can offer only a tentative and somewhat speculative evaluation of why they held this belief. Tradition attributes to the Sadducees a this-worldly attitude, reporting that they "use vessels of silver and gold all their lives" and do not "afflict themselves in this world" as did ascetic-minded Jews.

---

[5]A Jewish sect that represented the priesthood and the wealthy and that stood for a strict interpretation of Mosaic law.

Paul viewed the necessary conclusion of a disbelief in the soul as "Let us eat and drink, for tomorrow we die" (1 Corinthians 15:32).

While the Sadducees expressed their skepticism on the soul's fate after death, the Jewish sect of Pharisees probably shared the view of some of the prophets who predicted a glorious reestablishment of a renewed state of Israel and the destruction of her enemies. This popular movement sought to reconstruct Judaism as a culture whose identity was shaped by meticulous observance of religious law, especially regulations concerning purity.

We can only speculate about how the Pharisees viewed the possibility of life after death. The sources give only fleeting indications of their beliefs concerning the afterlife. From Acts, we learn that the Pharisees accepted the resurrection of the dead. Paul, who admitted to being a Pharisee "born and bred," must already have developed a perspective on the resurrection before becoming a Christian (Acts 23:6ff.). According to Josephus, the Pharisees maintained that every soul was imperishable, "but the soul of the good alone passes into another body." Did the doctrine of the resurrection supplement the Pharisees' expectation of a restored Jewish nation? Our sources do not provide a clear answer.

A third Jewish movement adopted a more individualistic perspective on the afterlife. The philosophic view that at death the immortal soul ascended to heaven, appealed not only to cosmopolitan Hellenistic Jews. Some evidence indicates that the Essenes too hoped for freedom from bodily constraints and eventual rest in a heavenly kingdom. Unlike Philo, the Essenes seem to have speculated about a new Jewish state under the leadership of a messianic king. Yet, they withdrew from active anticolonial politics and led their lives in such secluded communities as Qumran, an isolated site in the Judean Wilderness near the Dead Sea. The Essenes rejected the skepticism of the Sadducees as well as the crude, materialistic notions implied in the belief in a future resurrection. According to Josephus, the Essenes held that "the body is corruptible," while the soul is "immortal and imperishable." As in Philo's thought, the Essenes believed that, at death, souls are released "from the prison house of the body . . . and are borne aloft." For the virtuous, "there is reserved an abode beyond the ocean, a place which is not oppressed by rain or snow or heat but is refreshed by the ever gentle breath of the west wind coming from the ocean." Like the philosophers, the Essenes looked forward to a calm and comfortable hereafter.

The ancient Jewish attitude toward the afterlife reflects the complicated and developing relationship among individual, family and national concerns and theological concepts. Far from being static, belief in the nature of Sheol, and eventually heaven, changed considerably over the centuries. Religious reform movements found new meanings in the nature of God as they coped with the demise of Israel as a state, and tried to survive under non-Jewish governments. They also formed new ideas on life after death.

Religious and Social Order in Ancient Egypt

JOHN BAINES

Perhaps because of the fame of its archaeological discoveries or because of the grandeur of its monuments, we tend to think of ancient Egypt as a wealthy and prosperous kingdom. The regular flooding of the Nile River, the temperate climate, and the relative geographic isolation that protected the country from frequent invasion likewise incline historians to see Egypt as a self-assured and optimistic civilization. In this selection, John Baines challenges such assessments by emphasizing the great religious and social disparity between the few who made up the elite and everyone else in Egypt.

According to Baines, how did the organization of Egyptian society affect religious beliefs? How did Egyptian religion order the cosmos? How did the view of the cosmos reflect the social order? How did the divine cult function? How did the gods treat society? What was the role of the king (pharaoh) in maintaining religious and social order?

What was the moral tension within the elite's attitudes? Who were the members of the elite? In what ways did the lives of the elite differ from the masses? How did demographic conditions affect the structure of the Egyptian family?

Do you agree with Baines's harsh assessment of life in ancient Egypt?

Egyptian religion consisted of a vast range of beliefs and practices and is difficult to comprehend as a whole. It must be subdivided greatly for study, while on a theoretical level it may be best not to think of religion as a unity. The Egyptians lived with and participated in this diversity. It would hardly have occurred to them to question the basis of religious beliefs and practices or to ask whether all of them belonged together. They had no single term for "religion" that would have facilitated any discussion of such issues. "Religious" beliefs were essential and largely unquestioned presuppositions underlying the conduct of life. These beliefs related additionally to the character and the organization of society. Society interacted with religious beliefs, but these beliefs cannot be interpreted in exclusively social terms. The connection between the two was, however, closer in Egypt than it usually is in lands where world religions hold sway, because Egyptian religion belonged to a single society.

There are various possible approaches to the study of religious practice. One is to examine beliefs about creation and about the nature of the gods, and to move from there to relations between the gods and humanity. Another is to start from society, and to see religious practice from that perspective.... I attempt the second. The basic difficulty in the study of social life lies in the nature of the ancient evidence. Most of what is known about ancient

Egypt relates to the small elite; there is little direct evidence for the lives and attitudes of the rest of the people. The beliefs of the elite existed in relation to the wider society, even though they often ignored that society. Where the elite did present the wider society, it would be unwise to take their picture at face value.

Connections between central beliefs, society, and the wider natural world are not straightforward, but there was a continuity between the elite's presentations of the created order of the cosmos and its social hierarchies and the role humanity played in that cosmos. In the cosmogony, the world, including the gods, the king, and humanity, was created at a definite but remote past time, and would ultimately come to an end. In the present, the king took on for humanity the task of dealing both with the gods and with the negative forces that surrounded the ordered world. Disorder lurked at the edges of Egypt—in the desert and in the underworld—and the ordered cosmos was shot through with "uncreated" elements that threatened to engulf it and had to be countered. Whereas order was determinate, disorder was indeterminate and could never be vanquished completely. Constant vigilance was needed. In contrast with largely negative "uncreated" disorder, the god Seth[1] embodied the positive aspects of the brute force and destructiveness that exist within creation. The Egyptians came to reject Seth and persecute him as an enemy only in the first millennium B.C.E.[2]

Ordered creation had constantly to be affirmed against the forces of disorder. Not only the king and humanity but also the gods were involved in this enterprise. All beings, except perhaps the creator, were mortal. Among the gods, Osiris, who once lived and ruled on earth, was distinctive for being dead and ruling in the underworld.

This problematic and ultimately pessimistic view of order and disorder is the opposite of what a monument like the Great Pyramid may symbolize. The pyramid affirms overpowering human, or rather royal, achievement. As a medieval Arabic poem proclaims, it is "feared by time, yet everything else in our present world fears time." Documents of that period, which show that people had a conception of a perfect "antiquity," may confirm that it was built in the hope of instilling such fear, but in the awareness that the triumph over time which it promised could not ultimately be achieved.

In evaluating this instability of the Egyptian cosmos, one should recall that many societies consider the present world to be short-lived. Many Christians have thought that the Second Coming of Christ and the end of the world could occur at any time. Contemporary society could be consumed in a nuclear holocaust. In comparison, the Egyptians had a very long perspective both on the beginning of time and on its end, but they conceived of order

[1]Evil god, murderer of Osiris (judge and ruling god of the underworld).

[2]Before the Common Era. B.C.E. and C.E. are equivalent to B.C. and A.D. but avoid Christian nomenclature.

as being insecurely founded. One could see their view as a cosmic analogy for the fragility of any social order, or as tempering the apparently unchanging character of Egyptian order. Whichever of these perspectives may be nearer the truth, the Egyptians' local and cosmic visions were connected. The insecurity of the foundations of order did not need to be a constant concern in everyday life. Nonetheless, the problems of order in society and of how and why events affect the individual could gain urgency from their cosmic background. Yet that background could be a source of reassurance, because it showed that all, from the highest to the lowest, might be affected by the untoward, which could be seen as a manifestation of chaos or disorder. Everyone, including the gods, was in it together.

Thus the Egyptians' general conceptions of order were relevant to mundane events throughout society. On public monuments of the state and of the elite, these conceptions are embodied in a system of decorum which presents a restricted view of society within the context of celebrating the gods and the king. Temples and other major structures on which this system was displayed related chiefly to the official cults. In discussing religious practice, I am not primarily concerned with those cults, whose relevance for most people was rather limited. Instead, I focus on religious actions of any kind that responded to the problems of people's lives, particularly problems that threatened ordinary existence or social relations, or that threatened continued life. If Egyptian beliefs and practices are to be comprehended, it is necessary to review a vast range of phenomena, to study how they relate to one another, and to view them without prejudice. Distinctions between religion and magic or superstition do not help understanding. It is difficult to define what counts as religion, and it may not be relevant to try to do so.

It may seem one-sided to concentrate on misfortune in relation to religion, because Egyptian rituals focused on celebrating the gods and what the gods continually did for the world, and on the positive aspects of the cosmos. But most of these rituals formed part of the official temple cults, from which people were largely excluded. The king and his priestly deputies were the main beneficiaries of the sweetness and light they presented as pervading the cosmos. In practice, the elite as a whole received these benefits through their privileged position and, for many of them, through their participation in the cults. King and elite presented the cosmos in positive terms because rules and conventions required it to be so, and because the function of the divine cult was to honor the deity and induce in him or her the good disposition that would continue to confer benefits on the king and humanity. Cult consisted of regular daily service for the deity, which was performed on a cult statue. In daily rites the deity was purified, fed, clothed, and praised. Periodic festivals took the deity out of the temple in procession, sometimes to visit other deities in other temples. These festivals were the occasions when the majority who were not involved in the cult came closest to the gods, but even then the cult image was shut inside a shrine and invisible. The outward form of rituals thus appears to be more material than spiritual. The cost of maintaining these cults was borne by endowments, but estates of the gods did not become economically significant until the New Kingdom.[3]

Since in theory the gods provided for all of humanity, and humanity responded with gratitude and praise, the cult could be seen as having universal implications. In practice, however, the gods' benefits were unequally divided. The privileged received the rewards of divine beneficence and returned gratitude, while the rest suffered misfortune in greater measure and had no official channel for interacting with deities. In this inequality Egypt was not and is not unique.

The condition of ordinary Egyptians was probably comparable with, or only a little worse than, that of most people in premodern societies. The small elite were the exceptions. The elite's presentation of their ideology on public monuments is so persuasive, however, that scholars often neglect or fail to comment on its omission of most of humanity and their conditions of life. Other Egyptians may not have found the elite's presentation so convincing, and they must surely have been aware that they were omitted. Here gaps in the evidence, of which very little shows participation by ordinary people in official religious practice, are almost as significant as the evidence itself.

The beneficence of the gods could not be taken for granted. They might not be so well disposed as they were said to be. They could be capricious, or vent their fury on humanity, as the creator had once done near the beginning of time. If neglected, they might abandon humanity—as they did in the time of Akhenaten (1353–1336 B.C.E.), according to his successor Tutankhamun (1332–1322 B.C.E.). But gods and people were still ultimately thrown on one another for support.

The official division of the cosmos is presented in a brief text, probably of the Middle Kingdom,[4] which describes the king's role in the cult of the sun god. The text is worth quoting because of the place it assigns to moral concerns and to humanity. Kingship was both the central institution and the main focus of power in Egyptian society, and the text correspondingly incorporates generalized ideas of social order. Kingship also provided a metaphor for the way others were to conduct their lives, so some aspects of the king's morality were to be emulated by the elite. The text says that the king (in a sense the kingship) is on earth "for ever and ever, judging humanity and propitiating the gods, and setting order in place of disorder. He gives offerings to the gods and mortuary offerings to the spirits (the blessed dead)." (Here "order" is the fundamental religious, social, and abstract concept of *ma'at*, and "disorder" is *izfet*, the opposite of *ma'at*, associated with the world outside creation.)

In this statement the role of the king is more critical for the maintenance of order than that of any single deity. He performs the cult of the gods, an

---

[3]1539–c.1075.
[4]c.1970–1540.

assertion that refers primarily to his provision for them from the abundance of the land and its imports of exotic products. The king is said to "propitiate" the gods rather than to "worship" them; he "judges" humanity, setting them in order but also providing justly for them; and he makes mortuary offerings. The spirits to whom he offers could be either his own ancestors or the blessed dead in general. In the former case, the king may acknowledge the importance of lineage to his position, perhaps placating his ancestors as a normal mortal would. Ancestor cults were not widespread or long-lasting among the nonroyal in Egypt, but the recently dead were important to the living in various ways. There is much evidence from the New Kingdom in particular for the significance of earlier kings in ideology and religion, but this does not constitute a formal royal "ancestor cult." In the case of the spirits in general, the king may take on a burden of care that is vital for the cohesion of society and is common to, or aspired to, by all. The cult of the gods, which is always presented as being performed by the king, was in fact carried out by relatively small numbers of priests. The rest of humanity had far better contact with the dead than with the gods.

The text presents society as consisting of four parts: the gods, the king, the blessed dead, and humanity. They are bound together by moral obligations. Evil people who are found wanting in an ethical judgment after their death are cast out of creation. The four parts of society act together to create and maintain order, while the condemned remain to be tortured eternally in the disordered realms outside the cosmos. Nonhuman, nondivine living beings are absent from this model. Their omission probably relates to the text's brevity, but it also fits with a particular style of presenting the moral universe.

A more expansive style, in which all living beings owe their productive existence to the creator's benevolence, is exhibited in reliefs from an Old Kingdom[5] solar temple and in a list incorporated into a Middle Kingdom mortuary text. This style was the forerunner of important developments. Hymns from a cycle to be pronounced hourly in the cult of the sun god give an opposite picture. In these hymns the sun god's passage is threatened by hostile forces, and the officiant cajoles and commands the continuance of the "natural" order. Such texts were rarely written down in contexts that have been preserved, perhaps partly because of their central significance for the cult and partly because of the problematic nature of what they said. Their assumption that order was threatened was part of the Egyptians' basic world view, but decorum seldom allowed it to be openly presented in a this-worldly context.

The Egyptians made a clear division between normal, ostensibly optimistic religious action, which took place in the restricted context of the cult, and reactions to misfortune. This division makes it possible to concentrate on the less well-known aspect of misfortune, which is universally one of

[5]c.2600–2150.

the foci of religious action. Misfortune threatens the individual's and the group's sense of life's meaning. In Egyptian terms, it may also be part of still broader threats to order that concern all of society. In other words, human misfortune may acquire more general significance as an analogy for the threatened cosmos. Misfortune poses crucial and continuing tests of a society's viability and solidarity. In earlier periods, Egyptians seem to have reacted to it on a local basis and in small groups, in keeping with a social structure that was not fully centralized. This social structure contrasted with the highly centralized political organization of the country. In some later periods, Egypt had a more integrated, urban society, which appears to have responded to adversity in rather different ways.

A discussion of the way in which people confronted the untoward requires presentation of the social context, so far as there is evidence for it. Where evidence is lacking, a hypothetical context must be supplied. Practical religious action needs to be related to conceptions of ethics and morality. These two terms do not refer to two different things so much as to two aspects of the same thing. Society is a "moral system" that is held together by moderated self-interest (and altruism) but is also threatened with dissolution by tensions between self-interest and the interests of wider groups. Morality is integral to the normal interchanges of social life. People reflect on and systematize the problematic of social tensions and of tensions between the individual and the group. In the process they create ethics, which is a second, more abstract level of engagement with moral issues. Official pronouncements and works of literature are often oriented toward ethics, while more indirect sources reveal a little of the workings of morality.

Hardly any Egyptian texts are so abstract as Western works on ethics. Their presentation is rooted in examples, not in general principles, but it can nonetheless be comprehensive and can approach abstraction indirectly, as in the complex ethical discourses of the story of the Eloquent Peasant.[6] In the name of ethics, the most immoral things have been done in many places and periods. Morality, which is more local and less grandiose, may bear less blame here. The contrast between the two is important, because ideology and ethics rationalize the basis for social inequality, which Egypt had in great measure, yet the king and the elite who benefit from the ideological underpinning of their position cannot ignore morality. This moral tension within the position and attitudes of the elite is a complex analogy for the general tension between interests in society.

The sources for investigating practical religion and morality are sparse and indirect. Widespread participation in religious practices that leave archaeological traces is attested from the New Kingdom, from about 1500 B.C.E., and on a much larger scale in the Late Period[7] (from about 700 B.C.E.).

---

[6] A popular tale during the Middle Kingdom intended for educated Egyptians.
[7] c.718–332.

In studying earlier periods, it is necessary to use analogies from these better-documented times. It is difficult, however, to say how far such analogies from later periods can be taken. If similar practices cannot be posited for earlier times, were early society and religion very different from their descendants? If they can be posited, why did the practices leave little trace? These little-studied questions are important for a rounded picture of any period. A small number of sites have yielded a wide range of evidence relating to social life during a few short, well-documented periods in dynastic history, but for most such questions only Ptolemaic and Roman times[8] are well documented. I focus on the third and second millennia B.C.E., for which it is necessary to reconstruct social conditions by indirect methods.

Although ancient Egypt had the largest and most stable state of its time, its world was small and uncertain—the antithesis of the size, confidence, and self-proclaimed certainty of the Great Pyramid. Despite their mass, monuments such as the pyramid leave no record, except the stones themselves, of the people who built them (as opposed to those who commissioned them). Their essential meaning and symbolism even for those who were buried in them is not understood with any assurance. But something can usefully be said about the group of elite people who were involved in planning the pyramids, which, apart from their own tombs, were surely the central undertakings of their lifetimes. This is not my main concern here. Instead, I present, more hypothetically, important conditions of life among the rest of the society. Much of what follows would apply in greater or lesser measure to almost any premodern complex society.

In most periods, the elite who ran affairs of state were a close-knit group of a few hundred. They were all men, and they were the fathers of the next generation of the elite. Although no rule required that positions be inherited, elite children stood an altogether better chance of reaching high office than others. The core elite with their families numbered two or three thousand people. There were perhaps five thousand more literate people, who with their families would have brought the total ruling and administrative class to fewer than 50,000, of whom perhaps one in eight were literate officeholders. They might have formed 3 to 5 percent of the population, which, in the Old Kingdom, was perhaps one to one and a half million.

The rest of society lived in relative poverty and simplicity. Their material culture was little different from that of neolithic times, and may not have been so prosperous. Elite and nonelite had many children. They needed to if they were to increase or even reproduce themselves, because only a minority of children survived to become adults. Adults could not look forward with confidence to long careers. Evidence from Roman Egypt suggests a life expectancy at age 14 of 29.1. At birth, average life expectancy must have been

---

[8]The Ptolemaic dynasty governed from 305–30 B.C.; Rome ruled Egypt between 30 B.C. and A.D. 395.

much less than 20. These figures may seem startling, but their plausibility for all but the elite is corroborated from a number of sources.

Thus most of the elite could only hope for, rather than expect, a long career. This lack of an assured future is exemplified by statistical work on the elite of imperial Rome, whose basic conditions of health and life were probably better than but not essentially different from those of Egypt. The rest of society, in their harsher circumstances of life, will have had fewer expectations. Many people throughout society will have died unexpectedly or developed sudden severe illnesses. Egyptian medicine was the best of its time, but it could do little against disease and could achieve only limited success with accidents and injuries. As in most societies, the full range of medical treatment was probably available only to the elite.

Such frequent, almost routine experience of loss is something modern Westerners find hard to comprehend, and it has led to theories about periods as recent as early modern times, when it has been suggested that parents avoided emotional attachment to their children because of the exposure to grief it would bring. People in many societies, including the Egyptians, dramatize their loss and involve the community, making loss bearable by making it public. Loss creates loose ends: widows of greatly varying ages, orphans, widowers who wish to marry again, aging grandparents with no source of support, and so forth. Many people suffer mutilation through disease and through accidents, which renders them unable to perform useful work because most labor is heavy and physical. These people must then depend on others for support. A notable proportion become mentally unable to sustain their roles in society. In the contemporary world, such people are said to be suffering from stress or to be mentally ill; in most premodern and many modern societies, diagnoses of this common phenomenon and methods of coping with it have been different. Thus, even in periods of peace and stability, the amount and range of untoward occurrences affecting most people was much greater than is the case in modern Western society.

The central context for all these occurrences, for guarding against them and providing for their consequences, was the family. As a unit, the family reaped the benefits of success, but had to care for children, for misfits, for the incapacitated, and for those who had the good fortune to become old. The basic family unit was probably large, consisting of parents, children (including married ones, often with their own children), unattached and widowed relatives, perhaps grandparents, and, among the relatively well-to-do, servants or slaves. Housing was scarce, and people lived at close quarters, accommodating remarkable numbers. Visitors and unrelated people might also be present in the household, because they could not easily find somewhere to stay by themselves.

In contrast with this diverse reality, the ideal of the elite would be relatively familiar today, except that its context was in state service: one grew up, trained for a career, got married, and set up house with one's wife and children. In the grandest of circumstances, one lived on a vast, seemingly rural estate with hundreds of subordinate officials, workmen, peasants, and others. Such a career, with its focus on the nuclear family, might have been possible for few, and it provided a suitably rootless ideal for those who were in theory dedicated to royal service. Their estates and positions depended on the patronage of the king to whom they owed their allegiance, and their wider kinship ties were not displayed on their monuments. They appeared to owe nothing to anyone but the king. This image is the essential one projected by the great Old Kingdom tombs. In Theban New Kingdom tombs it is modified into a part-urban, part-rural presentation. For neither period should this presentation be taken at face value, because it masks realities of competition and independent ambition, but the fact that social forms were presented in these terms remains important.

The experience of most people was very different from the ideal of the elite. Most were tied to the land, which they worked for the state or for a high official. The unfortunate might be taken from their homes to work on major state works in the Nile Valley or, worse, in the desert, becoming little more than expendable units of labor. On an expedition to quarry stone in the Wadi Hammamat during the reign of Ramesses IV (c. 1155 B.C.E.), more than 10 percent of the people who set out did not return. This was not the harshest or most distant place from which minerals were extracted, and the fact that these figures were publicly recorded shows that they were not considered discreditable. Some kings of the later New Kingdom made capital of their efforts to mitigate these somber conditions, setting up inscriptions vaunting their concern and provision for their workers. But even in these cases, the groups addressed were professional workmen rather than the conscripted unskilled laborers who made up the majority on most expeditions. The laborers must have been taken temporarily from their normal environment and made completely dependent on state provision. As the Wadi Hammamat inscription makes clear, they had no special reason to trust the quality of the state's provision.

Such cases highlight one concomitant of life's uncertainty: life was cheap, especially that of the poor and of those who did not conform. Most ancient complex societies were brutal. Egypt's bland public image should not mislead people into thinking that Egyptian society was very different in this respect. A second corollary of life's uncertainty, one that is not quite so apparent, was the importance of age. The material from Roman Egypt used for assessing life expectancy did not include any individual who was with certainty more than sixty-four years old, but some, such as King Ramesses II, who reigned sixty-six years (1279–1213 B.C.E.), lived much longer. Even if most people died young, many still survived to an advanced age, and those who did survive were resilient. Because they were few, they selected themselves as leaders, frequently forming the power behind much younger kings. In the wider society, too, some men pursued active lives to remarkable ages. High mortality and gerontocracy go together. This authority of the aged may also have related to that of their elders, the dead.

Thus the king and the elite appropriated a high proportion of the resources of Egyptian society and rendered society very unequal. Inequality lessened people's capacity to be self-sufficient in facing life's problems. The means of provision for calamity were largely removed from ordinary people, most of whom either lived on the land or lived in towns but derived their livelihood from the land. They paid their rent, taxes, or dues and retained little more of what they produced than they needed for subsistence. In a disastrous flood or a year when the inundation of the Nile was inadequate for a harvest, the state, or in decentralized periods the local grandee, had either to supply people's needs for subsistence or to face the threat of social dislocation. Late Old Kingdom and First Intermediate Period[9] inscriptions contain numerous references to famine and to how their dedicatees averted or mitigated its effects for their people or for a region. Social dislocation, when it came, did not lead to a new order with greater equality or individual self-reliance. Instead, another grandee took over. Although one extant text states that all were created equal, people had no conception of a social order of a different type from the one they had long known.

[9]c.2150–1970.

II

CLASSICAL GREECE
AND ROME

In the eighteenth century, Voltaire, the French intellectual, wrote that true glory belonged only to "four happy ages" in the history of the world. The first was ancient Greece, specifically the fifth and fourth centuries B.C., and the second the Rome of Julius Caesar and Augustus, the first emperor. (The other two were Renaissance Italy and Louis XIV's France.) Voltaire praised classical Greece and Rome because he believed them civilized, holding the arts, literature, and refined living in high regard. The social historian, aware of the underside of classical civilization, cannot share Voltaire's optimism.

There is much to admire in Greek civilization. The political competition of its many independent city-states promoted some freedom of experimentation, evidenced in art, in literature, and in the diversities of philosophical schools. Greek social life too was more heterogeneous than that of other cultures, such as Egypt. Yet Greek civilization was rooted in slavery and oppression; life was difficult for most Greeks, and warfare among the city-states was constant. The Olympics and other games show that the Greeks admired brawn as well as brains. In Athens, the cradle of democracy and the center of classical Greek civilization, well-to-do males virtually locked up for life their wives and daughters. The family in Athens is as distinguishable historically as its philosophy and art are distinguished. Greek sexuality is also rather notorious and the subject of much speculation, if not myths.

Law, engineering, architecture, and literature bear witness to the glories of Rome; gladiatorial combats, mass murders in the Colosseum, and the persecution of Christians remind us of the streak of cruelty that was as Roman as an aqueduct. The Roman historian Tacitus remarked about imperial conquest: "Where they make a desert, they call it peace." Slavery, infanticide, and other brutalities were basic features of life in Roman civilization, as they had been in Greece and in the Near East. Women in Rome, however, seem to have fared better than their counterparts in Athens.

Certainly much has been written about the legacy of Greece and Rome to Western civilization. One of the great developments in classical Rome was the rise of Christianity, which has had a tremendous impact on Europe until the present day. Historians have documented the classical heritage in the Middle Ages, in seventeenth-century France, eighteenth-century Germany, Victorian Britain, and in American universities. When the term renaissance *is applied to a culture such as twelfth-century France or fifteenth-century Italy, it refers to a rebirth of classical art, literature, style. But social structures, people's attitudes, and lifestyles are as significant and as rich as the cultural developments more commonly studied.*

Organized Greek Games

WILLIAM J. BAKER

The history of sports, like women's history and the history of children, is a relatively new area of interest for scholars. A culture's games and its perception of sports and athletes tell us much about that society's priorities, values, and beliefs. No longer do historians view sports and leisure activities as unimportant.

Virtually everyone knows that the modern Olympics are patterned on the Olympic Games of ancient Greece, yet few people have more than a hazy understanding of the original Olympics. This selection describes the Greek games and points out their differences from the modern games (which date only from 1896).

One should bear in mind that, while the ancient Olympics were the most famous athletic contests in Greece, there were other games, including some limited to women. Baker is careful to use Greek athletics as a means to raise larger questions about Greek culture. Why were women excluded from the Olympic Games? What was the relationship between religion and athletics in Greece? How did Greek philosophers perceive the role of athletics? Answers to such questions lead one to conclude that sports were not a mere sideshow but a basic component of Greek civilization.

If that is so, then the Greeks were violent, for wrestling, boxing, and the pancration were more brutal than any modern Olympic contest (of course, such current professional sports as boxing, ice hockey, and rugby are violent). On the other hand, some events, such as footraces, appear almost identical to those staged today. The professionalism of the athletes and the honor they derived from their victories resemble the culture of sports in our society. On balance, were the ancient games vastly different from our Olympics? What does the role of games in ancient civilization suggest about the significance of sports in any society?

The story of organized athletics in the ancient world is primarily the story of Greece. A land of sunshine, mild climate, and rugged mountains rimmed by sparkling seas, Greece spawned philosophers and civic leaders who placed equal value on physical activity and mental cultivation. A vast array of gymnasiums and palaestras (wrestling schools) served as training centers for athletes to prepare themselves to compete in stadiums situated in every major city-state.

For more than a thousand years athletic festivals were an important part of Greek life. Originally mixtures of religious ceremony and athletic competition, hundreds of local festivals were held each year throughout the country and in Greek colonies in Egypt, Sicily, and on the banks of the Bosporus. By the fifth century B.C. four major festivals dominated the scene, forming a kind of circuit for ambitious athletes. The Pythian Games, held every fourth year at the sacred site of Apollo in Delphi, crowned victory with a laurel wreath. The Isthmian Games at Corinth in honor of Poseidon, the god of the sea, were conducted every other year, providing a victor's wreath of pine from a nearby sacred grove. The Nemean Games at Nemea, honoring Zeus every second year, awarded a sacred wreath of celery. The oldest and most prestigious of all the festivals, the Olympic Games, bestowed the olive wreath every four years in honor of Zeus.

The Olympics were the Super Bowl, the World Cup, the Heavyweight Championship of Greek athletics. By Olympic standards were the other festivals judged; at Olympia the sweet "nectar of victory" filled athletes with self-esteem and accorded them public acclaim....

The Olympic Games originated in a most unlikely place. Far removed from Athens, Corinth, and Sparta, the teeming centers of Greek culture and power, Olympia was a little wooded valley in the remote district of Elis on the northwestern tip of Peloponnesus (the peninsula that makes up the southern half of Greece)....Mount Olympus, a site readily associated with the gods, lay far to the northeast. Yet according to ancient lore, little Olympia was the place where gods and heroes mingled to accomplish feats worthy of immortal praise.

The origins of the Olympic Games are shrouded in mystery and legend. According to one yarn, Hercules founded the games in celebration of his matchless feats. Some Greeks insisted that their two mightiest gods, Zeus and Cronus, contested for dominance on the hills above Olympia, and that the games and religious ceremonies held later in the valley were begun in commemoration of Zeus's victory. Others clung to the legend of Pelops, who won his bride in a daring chariot escape. The girl's father was an expert with the spear, and according to tradition, thirteen suitors had met death while attempting to steal the daughter away. But Pelops was shrewd. He loosened the axle of his adversary's chariot, took off with his prize, and breathed a sigh of relief when his lover's father broke his neck in the ensuing crash....[S]upposedly on that hallowed ground Pelops instituted the games and religious sacrifices in celebration of his god-given victory.

Significantly, all these tales involve competition, physical aggressiveness, and triumph....[L]ike most sporting activities in the ancient world, the competitive games associated with Olympia grew out of religious ceremonies and cultic practices. With all their emphasis on man and his achievements, the Greeks were extremely religious. Polytheists, they looked to particular gods for assistance and blessing in every sphere of life....Most of all they feared the wrath and sought the favor of Zeus, the mightiest of the gods.

In prayers, processions, and sacrifices, the ancient Greeks sought diligently to appease their gods. Religious festivals, accompanied by feasts, music, dancing, and athletic contests, were scattered throughout the Greek world. About 1000 B.C. Olympia became a shrine to Zeus. In addition to their religious ceremonies, young Greeks competed athletically in honor of Zeus, himself reckoned to be a vigorous warrior god who cast his javelinlike thunderbolts from on high. Competitors at Olympia swore by Zeus that they would play fair and obey all the rules. When they broke their oaths, they were required to pay fines, which in turn were spent to erect statues to Zeus.

The actual date of the first competitive games at Olympia is unknown. But the year 776 B.C. stands as a milestone, for in that year the Greeks first recorded the name of the victor in a simple footrace. For a time the footrace—a sprint of about 200 meters—was the only event associated with the religious festival at Olympia. In 724 B.C., however, a "double race" (400 meters) was added, and in 720 B.C. a long-distance race of 4,800 meters became a fixture. Within the next hundred years other events were established: wrestling and the pentathlon in 708 B.C., boxing in 688 B.C., chariot races in 680 B.C., and boys' footraces, wrestling, and boxing between 632 and 616 B.C. Finally in 520 B.C. the Olympic program was completed with the introduction of a footrace in armor. For almost a thousand years the list of events remained essentially intact. Every four years, strong, young Greeks gathered to compete, to strive for the victory wreath of olive branches.

In the beginning, however, Olympia was a simple site unadorned with buildings. A few scattered stone altars to Zeus stood in the *altis*, the sacred grove.... Competitive events were held in randomly selected open spaces, as near to the *altis* as possible. Not until about 550 B.C. were buildings constructed.... Finally a hippodrome and stadium were constructed, the latter ... providing space for about 40,000 spectators. A gymnasium and palaestra completed the athletic complex.

In the spring of every fourth year three heralds departed from Olympia to traverse the Greek world, announcing the forthcoming games and declaring a "sacred truce." By the authority of Zeus, competitors and spectators making their way to Olympia were allowed to pass safely through the countryside, even in times of war. The athletes and their trainers arrived in Olympia a month before the games. First they had to prove their eligibility—that they were Greek, freeborn (not slaves), and without criminal records. Then they had to swear by Zeus that they had been in training for the previous ten months. Participation in the Olympic Games was no lighthearted matter. Strict judges supervised a grueling month-long training program in order to ensure the fitness of prospective competitors, and they arranged elimination heats for those events that had attracted an unusually large number of athletes....

While the athletes sweated and grunted through their preparatory exercises, little Olympia and the surrounding countryside took on a carnival atmosphere. Spectators came from all directions, and official delegations from Greek city-states arrived with gifts for Zeus. Food and drink vendors did a brisk business, as did hawkers of souvenirs and pimps with their prostitutes. Jugglers, musicians, dancers, and magicians displayed their talents, and soothsayers dispensed their wisdom. Deafening noise and stifling dust added to the midsummer heat, making attendance at the Olympic Games something of an ordeal.

Until late in the history of the games, tiny Olympia was ill-prepared to cope with the crowds. A few springs and the nearby rivers provided water for drinking and bathing, but sanitation and planned water facilities were not available until the second century A.D. Flies were everywhere. As one first-century visitor complained, life at the Olympics would have been unbearably crude and unpleasant were it not for the excitement of the games themselves: "Do you not swelter? Are you not cramped and crowded? Do you not bathe badly? Are you not drenched whenever it rains? Do you not have your fill of tumult and shouting and other annoyances? But I fancy that you bear and endure it all by balancing it off against the memorable character of the spectacle."

The athletes fared little better. Although they ate well during their month's training, they, too, received scant provision for physical comfort. Housing, or the lack of it, was a main problem. Servants of wealthy spectators and official delegations pitched richly embroidered tents on the hillsides, but most athletes simply wrapped themselves in blankets, slept under the stars, and hoped it would not rain. Not until about 350 B.C. was housing provided for the athletes, and even then it was too spartan for comfort. Certainly nothing approximating a modern Olympic village was ever constructed....

For three centuries after the first recorded Olympic victor in 776 B.C., the sequence and duration of the games fluctuated from Olympiad to Olympiad according to the whims of the judges. In 472 B.C., however, the games were reorganized and fixed into a pattern that remained virtually unchanged for the next eight hundred years. The duration of the entire festival was set at five days, with only two and a half days devoted to the games themselves. The first day was given to religious ceremony: oaths, prayers, sacrifices, and the singing of hymns. Some athletes presented gifts and offered prayers to the statues of past victors who had been deified, at the shrines of various patron gods, and especially to the several statues of Zeus.

On the second day the sports competition began. Spectators gathered at the hippodrome, a level, narrow field about 500 meters long, to witness the chariot race. Amid great fanfare, splendid two-wheeled chariots pulled by four horses lined up in staggered starting places. Here was the most costly and colorful of all the Olympic events, a signal to the world that the owners were men of great wealth. Their drivers, decked out in finely embroidered tunics, tensely awaited the start. They could scarcely afford to relax. Their course was not a rounded oval but rather around posts set at each end of the hippodrome about 400 meters apart, requiring 180-degree turns for twelve laps. Rules forbade swerving in front of an opponent, but bumps and crashes and even head-on collisions around the posts were inevitable. In one race only one of forty chariots finished intact.

As soon as the dust settled and battered chariots were removed from the hippodrome, single horses and their jockeys moved into starting positions. Riding without saddles or stirrups, the jockeys were nude. Even more than the charioteers, jockeys got little credit if they won. They were the hirelings of wealthy owners, whose names were recorded as the winners of the race. Even the olive crown was placed on the owner's head, not the jockey's.

The morning having been given to these equestrian events, the afternoon was devoted to an altogether different contest, the pentathlon. Spectators crowded onto the grassy slopes of the stadium. Except for a few marble slabs provided for the Olympic officials, no seats were ever built. Through a narrow passageway at one end of the stadium the competitors entered. Naked and bronzed by the sun, they more than any of the other contestants at Olympia represented the Greek ideal of physical beauty. Pentathletes had to be fast as well as strong, with muscles well-proportioned and supple but not overdeveloped....

Like the modern decathlon, the pentathlon rewarded the versatile athlete. First he had to throw the discus, a round, flat object originally made of stone and later of bronze. Five throws were allowed, and only the longest counted. Next came the javelin throw. About six feet long, the javelin had a small leather loop attached near the center of gravity. The athlete inserted one or two fingers in the loop, wound the thong around the javelin, and thus obtained leverage to make the javelin spin in flight. In the third event, the standing broad jump, the athlete carried weights in his hands, swung them forward to shoulder height, and then down as he leaped. Made of stone or metal in the shape of small dumbbells, the weights both increased the distance and helped the jumper to keep his balance when landing. A 200-meter sprint and a wrestling contest were the last two events in the pentathlon, but they were often not held: The athlete who first won three of the five events was declared the victor without further contest.

As the sun set on that second day of the Olympic festival, attention turned from athletic competition to religious ceremony. In honor of the hero-god Pelops, a black ram was slain and offered as a burnt sacrifice—always as the midsummer full moon appeared above the *altis*. On the following morning were religious rites, followed by a magnificent procession of priests, Olympic judges, representatives from the Greek city-states, the athletes and their kinsmen, and trainers. All finally arrived at the altar of Zeus, where one hundred oxen were slain and their legs burned in homage to Zeus. The carcasses were cooked and eaten at the concluding banquet on the final day of the festival.

On the afternoon of the third day, the footraces were held: 200-meter sprints the length of the stadium, 400-meter dashes around a post and back, and long-distance runs of 4,800 meters (twelve laps). Marble slabs provided leverage for quick starts, and a trumpet blast served as the starting signal....

The fourth day of the festival brought on the "heavy" events: wrestling, boxing, the pancration, and armored footraces. The first three were especially violent, brutal contests of strength and will. There were few rules, no time limit, and no ring. More important, there were no weight limits, thus restricting top-level competitors to the largest, best-muscled, and toughest men to be found throughout Greece. In the wrestling contests biting and gouging were prohibited, but not much else. A wrestler won when he scored three falls, making his opponent touch the ground with his knees. Wrestlers therefore concentrated on holds on the upper part of the body and tripped their opponents when possible....

Yet wrestling was mild exercise compared to boxing. Boxers wound heavy strips of leather around their hands and wrists, leaving the fingers free. They aimed primarily for the opponent's head or neck, rather than the body. Slapping with the open hand was permissible, and it was often done to divert the attention, cut the face, or close the eyes of the opposition. The fight went on without a break until one of the competitors was either exhausted or knocked out, or until one raised his right hand as a sign of defeat. Blood flowed freely. Scarcely an Olympic boxer finished his career without broken teeth, cauliflower ears, a scarred face, and a smashed nose. He was lucky if he did not have more serious eye, ear, and skull injuries.

As if boxing and wrestling were not brutal enough, the Greeks threw them together, added some judo, and came up with the contest most favored by spectators at Olympia—the pancration. Pancratiasts wore no leather thongs on the fists, but they could use their heads, elbows, and knees in addition to hands and feet. They could trip, hack, break fingers, pull noses and ears, and even apply a stranglehold until tapped on the back, the sign that the opponent had given up. In 564 B.C. a pancratiast who had won in two previous Olympics found himself in both a leg scissors grip and a stranglehold. Literally in the process of being choked to death, he frantically reached for one of his opponent's toes and broke it. As he gasped his final breath, his opponent, suffering excruciating pain, gave the signal of capitulation. So the strangled pancratiast was posthumously awarded the crown of victory, and in the central square of his native village a statue was erected in his honor.

After the deadly serious business of wrestling, boxing, and the pancration, the final Olympic contest added a farcical touch to the festival. The 400-meter footrace in armor pitted naked men clad only in helmets, shin guards, and shields, a fitting though ludicrous reminder of the military origins of most of the games. Although the armored footrace remained on the Olympic program from its introduction in 520 B.C. until the end, it was never a prestigious event. Apparently it provided comic relief at the end of a gory day.

The fifth and final day of the festival was devoted to a prize-giving ceremony, a service of thanksgiving to Zeus, and a sumptuous banquet at which the sacrificial animals were consumed....

...[S]ome of the limited features of the Olympic Games should be noted. In the first place, the athletic program was narrowly confined to two equestrian contests, six track-and-field events, three physical-contact sports, and the armored footrace. From a modern point of view, conspicuously absent were relay races, hurdles, pole vaults, high jumps, running broad jumps, weight lifting, and shot puts. Nothing approximating a modern marathon ever appeared on the ancient Olympic program....

Given the fact that Greece is a peninsula and half of it virtually an island, it is surprising to find no water sports such as swimming, diving, sailing, or rowing in the ancient Olympic program.... Less apparent was the reason for the lack of competitive ball games. In fact, the Greeks played a number of individual and team games of ball. At Sparta "ball player" and "youth" were synonymous.... Without doubt the Greeks played a kind of field hockey game.... Most common of all competitive ball play in Greece, however, was the game of *episkyros*, a team sport in which opposing sides threw a ball back and forth "until one side drives the other back over their goal line."

Why, then, were no ball games ever played in the ancient Olympics? When the Olympics began in the eighth century B.C., most ball play was still mere exercise, keep-away games at most.... [T]hey were played by women, children, and old men, but not by serious athletes. Not yet rough mock forms of combat, ball games were considered child's play compared to the warrior sports of chariot racing, javelin throwing, wrestling, and the like. By the time competitive ball play became respectable for adult males, the Olympic program was already set on its traditional course....

Another limitation of the Olympics that more tellingly reflected the mentality of ancient Greek society was the exclusion of women from the games. In that patriarchal world, matters of business, government, and warfare were reserved for men. A woman might attend the theater if accompanied by a man, but even in the home she lived in separate quarters. Except for the honorary presence of the priestess of Demeter, women were altogether excluded from the Olympic Games, as spectators as well as competitors. Apparently only one woman ever broke the taboo, and her ploy provoked a rule change. In 404 B.C. a mother who wanted to see her son box slipped into the stadium disguised as a trainer. But when the boy won his match, she leaped over the barrier to congratulate him and in so doing gave herself away. Horrified Olympic officials immediately laid down a new rule: trainers henceforward must appear in the stadium stark naked, like the athletes.

Barred from the Olympic Games, women held their own competitive contests at Olympia in honor of Hera, the sister-wife of Zeus. Their competition was largely in the form of footraces, wrestling, and chariot races. Apparently these Heraean Games even predated the Olympic Games as fertility rites representing an early matriarchal society. During the history of the Olympic Games, however, Olympic officials proved to be a highly conservative group of men committed primarily to maintaining a successful formula, thus inadvertently protecting traditional male interests. Their conservatism is best seen by comparison with the other major Panhellenic games. As Greek women increasingly became emancipated (primarily in the cities) toward the end of the pre-Christian era, short-distance races for girls were introduced as an integral part of the program in the Pythian, Isthmian, and Nemean Games.

Olympia's relation to the other festivals on the athletic "circuit" calls to mind another myth long entertained about athletes in the ancient world: Olympic victors received no cash prizes or other material rewards with their olive crowns; thus it would appear that they were purely amateur, competing for the honor of victory. The appearance was a mere shadow of reality. Throughout the history of the Olympics, only aristocrats could afford the horses and chariots for the equestrian events. For the first 300 years or so, the games were dominated by athletes from wealthy families who could afford trainers and coaches, a proper diet (plenty of meat), full-time training, and travel. Around 450 B.C., however, lower-class athletes began participating in the track-and-field and physical-contact sports. Financed by local patrons and public funds drawn from taxes on wealthy citizens, they ran and fought to bring honor to their city-states as well as to themselves. Their city-states, in turn, rewarded them with cash prizes, free food, and lodging. Therefore, although the Olympic Games paid no direct material rewards, they existed in a maze of commercial enterprise. A victory at Olympia dramatically raised an athlete's value as he went off to sell his talents and brawn for further competition at the Pythian, Isthmian, and Nemean Games. Whether or not he received money for his Olympic exploits is beside the point. Well paid for his full-time efforts, he was a professional athlete.

A sure sign of this professionalism was the emergence of athletic guilds in the second century B.C. Like today's unions or players' associations, the guilds originated on the principle of collective bargaining. And bargain they did: for the athletes' rights to have a say in the scheduling of games, travel arrangements, personal amenities, pensions, and old-age security in the form of serving as trainers and managers.

When Greek poets, philosophers, and playwrights turned a critical eye on the athletes of their day, they seldom attacked professionalism.... Yet athletics were scarcely beyond criticism. For well-born, highly cultured Greeks, athletics appeared to be a lamentably easy way for lower-class citizens to rise quickly to affluence, then to fall back into poverty once the strength of youth waned....

Worse still, the successful athlete had to specialize to such an extent that he made a poor soldier....

Yet of all the barbs directed against Greek athletics, the most common had to do with the glorification of physical strength to the detriment of mental and spiritual values. To the philosopher and satirist Xenophanes, it was "not right to honor strength above excellent wisdom." ... Milo of Croton was the butt of numerous jokes and slurs on the mindlessness of the muscle-bound athlete. "What surpassing witlessness," declared a moralist when he heard that Milo carried the entire carcass of a bull around the stadium at Olympia before cutting it up and devouring it. Before it was slaughtered, the bull carried its own body with much less exertion than did Milo. "Yet the bull's mind was not worth anything—just about like Milo's." The image of the "dumb jock" is as old as athletics.

... "How very unlike an athlete you are in frame," Socrates once chided a young Athenian weakling. "But I am not an athlete," retorted the literal-minded youth. "You are not less of an athlete," shot back the wise Socrates, "than those who are going to contend at the Olympic Games. Does the struggle for life with the enemy, which the Athenians will demand of you when circumstances require, seem to you to be a trifling contest?" For Socrates, the key words were *contend, struggle,* and *contest.* Moreover, for Socrates the athlete provided the model for the principle that "the body must bear its part in whatever men do; and in all the services required from the body, it is of the utmost importance to have it in the best possible condition."

Socrates' prize pupil, Plato, agreed fully with his master. Plato, in fact, trained under the best wrestling teacher in Athens and reportedly competed in the Isthmian games. Originally his name was Aristocles, but his wrestling teacher changed it to Plato, meaning "broad shouldered." In *The Republic,* Plato set up a dialogue with Socrates to argue logically that gymnastic exercise was the "twin sister" of the arts for the "improvement of the soul." His ideal was the body and mind "duly harmonized."

This sense of balance between the physical and the mental prompted the third of the great Greek philosophers, Aristotle, to devote several sections of his *Politics* to the training of children to be good Greek citizens. "What is wanted," he insisted, "is not the bodily condition of an athlete nor on the other hand a weak and invalid condition, but one that lies between the two." Coming to manhood a hundred years or so after Socrates, Aristotle was more critical of "the brutal element" involved in organized athletics. Yet he, too, held the Olympic victors in awe....

Critical as they were of overspecialized athletes, the great philosophers still did not reject athletics. For them, the association of body and mind was literally intimate: gymnasiums were places where men not only exercised, but gathered to hear the lectures of philosophers and itinerant orators. Plato's Academy and Aristotle's Lyceum in Athens were, in fact, gymnasiums, centers of training "for the body and the soul." Ironically, the terms "academy" and "lyceum" have come to refer solely to intellectual pursuits, wholly divorced from physical training....

Marriage and the Family in Athens

W. K. LACEY

In the last two decades, historians of the family have demolished any lingering notion that families have not changed appreciably over time. Recent studies demonstrate that husbands, wives, and children, and their relationships with one another and with society at large, possess a complex past. In the long history of the family, that of classical Athens stands out because of its rigidity and connection to the politics of the city.

For example, one would be hard-pressed to think of another society that kept women of wealthy families hidden. Athenian men felt their betrothed had to be virgins and their wives chaste. Why were Athenian males so uncompromising in these matters? How did the laws of the state serve to maintain the virtue of citizens' wives? Citizenship was the key, and the concept of citizenship affected marriage and children. Attitudes toward adultery also related to worries about citizenship.

Athens may have been the "cradle of democracy," but it was a very limited democracy. In what ways did Athenian legislation concerning the family discriminate against those groups, such as foreigners or slaves, excluded from the democratic system? What kind of "democratic" values could be nurtured in such families?

Finally, how did Athenian males treat their wives, children, and parents? What explains their behavior and attitudes toward those groups? Is there evidence of love in these relations?

... In 451 Pericles[1] persuaded the assembly[2] to modify the rules for entitlement to citizenship by a law which decreed that a man's parents must both be citizens for him to be a citizen.... The motives for Pericles' law have been much discussed; selfishness—*i.e.* not wanting to share the profits of empire; race-consciousness—*i.e.* fear of diluting the Athenian autochthonous stock;... but, from the point of view of the family, much the most convincing reason was the desire of Athenian fathers to secure husbands for their daughters....

Prior to the law Athenians had always been able to contract legal marriages with non-Athenian women....

That is not to say that there were no such people as illegitimate children before Pericles' day; bastards are known in the Homeric poems, mostly the children of slave girls or concubines begotten by the great heroes...; but their status and rights depended upon the decision of their father about them while he lived, or of their kinsmen when he had died. When a man had no son by his recognized wife he might adopt a bastard as his heir....

Slave girls' children, and the children of common prostitutes, must always have been classed as bastards, and so, presumably, were the offspring of parents who did not live together, such as the children of the victims of rape or seduction....

Pericles' law, however, added a new class of persons to the illegitimate, by declaring the offspring of unions with non-citizen mothers non-citizens... however formal the marriage agreement had been, and thus the procreation of legitimate children became impossible except from the legitimate daughter of an Athenian....

[1]Dominant Athenian statesman, 495–429 B.C.

[2]Popular assembly made up of all male citizens eighteen and older; only legislative body in Athens.

The law required that an Athenian's marriage should be preceded by either a betrothal agreement...or a court judgment.... This latter was the legal process whereby a man's claim to be the legitimate husband of an *epikleros*[3] was established. Otherwise the normal process...was for a girl's *kyrios*[4] to pledge her to a prospective bridegroom. The pledge was a formal one, and witnesses were present on both sides; it also stated what her dowry was to be as one of its conditions. It is uncertain at what age this agreement was normally made for girls.... But it is quite certain that betrothal, though obligatory, did not itself make a marriage.... This was because, if a child's mother was not properly married, the child was a bastard, and suffered severe disabilities in respect of the capacity to succeed to property, and exclusion from civic privileges as a citizen.

Marriages within the *anchisteia* or wider family were extremely common; they were prescribed by the law for *epikleroi*,[5] we hear of half-brothers marrying their half-sisters, and uncles often married their nieces; ...

The normal age for men to marry seems to have been about thirty, an age approved by the philosophers as suitable, but there were sound family reasons as well as those of imaginary eugenics. These lay in the Athenian custom of old men retiring from the headship of (or at least from economic responsibility for) their families in favour of their sons, and the son's marriage was an appropriate moment for this to occur.... A man who married at about thirty would be about sixty when his son reached thirty; fifty-nine was the age at which a man's military service ended and he was therefore considered an old man.

Girls were married much younger; philosophers and other writers recommended about eighteen or nineteen as suitable.... In Athens, girls were presented to the *phratry*[6] on...the third day of the Apatouria,[7] when a sacrifice was made by their (new) husband; this is associated with the boys' sacrifice on the same day, made on the occasion of their cutting their hair as indicating the end of their childhood. Therefore it will have been not later than about sixteen, and the Greeks' fanatical emphasis on premarital virginity will have made it tend to be earlier than this rather than later.

A few instances are known in which a woman is said to have chosen her own husband, but in every case it is clear that it was most unusual.... It is important to stress that all these women belonged to the highest social class, in which the women have always had markedly more independence than among the bulk of the population.

Society demanded that a man procure marriages for his daughters, and, if necessary, sisters; it was regarded as a slight on his excellence if he did

---

[3] A woman to whom property was attached. She was thus an attractive bride.

[4] The male guardian of a woman. An Athenian woman was an eternal minor; she always had a guardian.

[5] Plural of *epikleros*.

[6] Tribe or clan.

[7] An annual festival.

not do so. Nature, however, ordained ... that more girl-babies than boys should survive infancy, and battle casualties were at least as numerous as deaths in childbirth; the excess of brides seeking husbands therefore created a competitive situation for the fathers of girls, which ensured that a dowry was an invariable accompaniment (though by no means a legal requirement) of a marriage. Girls who had no dowry could not get married, and therefore to marry a girl without a dowry, or with only a very small one, was to do her a very great honour, and was a matter for self-congratulation by orators, especially when the girl was an *epikleros*. Unmarried girls had either to remain at home, or enter the world of the demimondaines[8] if they were destitute orphans. After marriage, however, a girl seems to have had more ability to determine her lot. ... [For] most married couples divorce was easy, and widows were often remarried.

In the choice of their second husband widows were certainly sometimes able to exercise some element of choice. ... There can be little doubt, however, that young widows, even if they had children, were expected to remarry.

Moreover, Athenian women had as much right to divorce their husbands as their husbands had to divorce them, and we even hear of a father taking his daughter away when he quarrelled with his son-in-law; divorce by consent was also possible, especially in connection with a suit for an *epikleros*. In all cases, however, the woman's dowry had to be repaid to her *kyrios,* and a large dowry is said to be something which protects a woman and prevents her being divorced. It is therefore alleged that a woman whose citizenship was doubtful would necessarily have a large dowry so that her husband would not easily get rid of her.

The dowry was a field in which it is accepted that a man would express his self-esteem. ... Nobody failed to give a dowry if he could help it; an uncle, it is said, guardian to four nieces and one nephew, would be sure to see that the girls were given dowries; friends gave dowries to the daughters of the poor; the daughters of *thetes,* the lowest financial class, who lacked brothers had by law to be given dowries by their relatives in accordance with their means; even the state stepped in very occasionally (in return for outstanding public services) to dower a man's daughters. ... Dowries consisted of cash, or real-estate valued in cash. ... Widows on their remarriage received dowries in exactly the same way as unmarried girls, and this is only natural since a woman's dowry was deemed to be her share of her paternal estate, a share set apart for her maintenance, and it is an unfailing principle of Athenian law that the head of the family who had a woman's dowry in his possession had to maintain her. ...

... [A] dowry was intended primarily for a woman's maintenance. It remained in her husband's control while he lived; if he predeceased her and there were no children, it returned with her to her own family; if there were children, it was part of the children's inheritance provided that they supported their mother if adult, or their guardian did if they were infants. ...

[8]Women who lost social standing owing to their sexual promiscuity.

After the betrothal...came the wedding..., at which the bride was brought to the bridegroom's house and the marriage really began..., so that the various songs of the wedding were then appropriate. It was living together which made a marriage a marriage; its existence was therefore essentially a question of fact. Living together...is the Greek for being married, and the procreation of children was its explicit object. Xenophon's[9] Socrates says: 'Surely you do not suppose that it is for sexual satisfaction that men and women breed children, since the streets are full of people who will satisfy that appetite, as are the brothels? No, it is clear that we enquire into which women we may beget the best children from, and we come together with them and breed children'....[9]

The Athenians were even a bit sentimental about children, if about anything; weeping children were a stock-in-trade of the defendant at a trial....

Formal marriage and the birth of children from it also had a public side; this was due to the importance of asserting the child's legitimacy. With this in view a marriage was registered with the *phrateres*,[10] the husband's *phrateres* in most cases, but also, when the girl was an *epikleros*, with her family's. Similarly, when a child was born, it was exhibited at least to relatives on the tenth day festival, at what seems to have been a big celebration; and on this occasion the father named him.... [T]he father swore 'that he knew that the child had citizen-status, being born to him from a citizen mother, properly (*i.e.* formally) married'.

Children who could not substantiate their claim to legitimacy were bastards; they not only lacked rights of succession after 403...they were also excluded from the family religious observances, and they did not enjoy citizen-rights. This did not mean that they had no rights.... Bastards resembled outsiders...in that they lacked the right to claim citizens' estates, but they must have had rights at law....

...Apollodorus[11] cites a law forbidding a foreigner to live with a citizen woman as his wife...and a foreign woman to live with a citizen, on pain of enslavement or a heavy fine; clearly this did not mean a prohibition of sexual intercourse across these boundaries, nor a prohibition on keeping a concubine, or, in the case of a woman, a lover, but it prohibited such people from pretending that they were formally married, and from claiming to breed citizen children....

During the Peloponnesian War, after the Sicilian disaster in 413, we are told that the Athenians temporarily abandoned their rules about requiring a child's father and mother to be formally married because of the shortage of men, and citizens were allowed to marry one wife, and breed children (that

---

[9]A student of Socrates who, like Plato, wrote an *Apology* (a work purporting to be what Socrates said on his own behalf at his trial).

[10]Tribe or clan (phratry).

[11]Important only because of his involvement with a famous legal case.

is, legitimate children) from another. This has shocked commentators, . . . but it accords fully with the Athenian view of marriage—as an arrangement for maintaining the *oikoi*,[12] and (in the case of the city) for replenishing the supply of citizen-soldiers. . . .

The importance of being able to prove legitimacy had two principal results; it made adultery a public as well as a private offense, and it made the Athenians excessively preoccupied with the chastity of their womenfolk, with the result that they were guarded in a manner nowadays thought to be intolerable.

Adultery in Athens (it is sometimes said) meant 'the sins of a wife'. The evidence is not quite so unequivocal; in the first place, the punishment of death is prescribed for the adulterer and not the adulteress—she was punished, naturally, but it is odd that, if the offense was only hers, her lover should be put to death, not she.

Secondly, . . . it is stated that a man may with impunity kill an adulterer caught in the act with any of the women in his *kyrieia*[13]—his mother, sister and daughter are mentioned as well as his wife. . . .

. . . Plato's laws on sexual matters are revealing. They were intended to be as severe for men as for women, but, as he admitted, he had to compromise; though he wished to brand all sexual intercourse with anyone other than a wife as adultery, and claimed that the law of nature was to preserve virginity until the age of procreation, then to remain faithful to one's mate, he admitted that most men, both Greeks and non-Greeks, did not do this; he therefore fell back on 'the possible', which was to prohibit all sexual intercourse with freeborn or citizen women other than a man's wedded wife, to forbid sodomy, and impose secrecy on intercourse with any other (*i.e.* non-free) woman on pain of disfranchisement. Obviously Plato was reacting against contemporary attitudes, which did allow men extra-marital sexual relations provided that they were not with women in the *kyrieia* of other citizens. This is to say that adultery was not *solely* an offense by a female; a man was punishable as an adulterer if he seduced a woman he was forbidden to seduce, and his punishment was apt to be more severe, as his liberty of action was greater.

Athenian women had no sexual liberty, but the explanation of the Athenians' attitude was primarily civic, not moral. Euphiletus[14] says that 'the lawgiver prescribed death for adultery' (though not for rape) '. . . because he who achieves his ends by persuasion thereby corrupts the mind as well as the body of the woman . . . gains access to all a man's possessions, and casts doubt on his children's parentage'. This was the point; if an Athenian had an affair with a citizen-woman not his wife, a baby would not have any claim on his property or family or religious associations, nor

[12]Households or families.

[13]Headship of a family.

[14]An aggrieved husband in a famous Athenian law case dealing with adultery.

impose on them a bogus claim for citizenship; but the woman would be compelled to claim that her husband was the father, and his kinship-group and its cult was therefore deeply implicated, since it would be having a non-member foisted upon it, and if she were detected, all her husband's children would have difficulty in proving their rights to citizenship if they were challenged. An unmarried Athenian girl who had been seduced could be sold into slavery according to Solon's laws; Hypereides[15] implies that it was more usual 250 years later merely to keep her at home unmarried—when he hints that neither she nor a widow who had been seduced would be able to get a husband.

Death for an adulterer, even if caught in the act, was quite certainly not always demanded; comedy speaks of payment, depilation and other humiliating, vulgar but comical indignities being inflicted on an adulterer, which would prevent him appearing in public, certainly from appearing in the wrestling-school, for some time. Divorce for a woman taken in adultery was compulsory, but we may be pretty certain that the demand was not always complied with; a woman with a large dowry would have to have it repaid, and this might be impossible for her husband, or be something he was unwilling to do....

Non-citizens could contract legally valid marriages and dower their daughters to non-citizens, and the Athenian law upheld their contracts; what the Athenian law was concerned to prevent was non-citizens claiming to be citizens, and making claims on the property of citizens....

The attitude of the Athenians to old age was somewhat unusual. On the one hand they hated old age with its loss of the youthful beauty which they so much admired, and they dreaded the time when they would no longer have the strength to earn their daily bread. Senility moreover was one of the causes which made an Athenian's acts invalid at law in that it was deemed that he was out if his mind if senile.... On the other hand the city laid it on children as a legal obligation, not merely a moral duty, to ensure that their parents were looked after when they were old. Maltreatment of parents ranks with maltreatment of orphans and *epikleroi* as a prosecution in which a prosecutor ran no risk of punishment.... [E]xpectations did not stop at refraining from maltreatment; positive services were required, especially the provision of food-supplies.... Hence getting children in order to have someone to tend their old age is a frequently mentioned motive for parenthood, and equally for adoption.

The state also made provision for looking after old women; here the law was explicit; the person who had charge of her dowry had the obligation to maintain her.... The class of people most obviously concerned are widows, whose situation at the death of their husbands was possibly that they could remain in their husband's *oikos* and be maintained by its new *kyrios*, who was sometimes a son, sometimes the guardian of an infant, or (if she were

---

[15]Mid-fourth-century speechwriter and orator.

childless) a relative; alternatively the widow could return to her own family, if she had no children, and get her dowry back, or interest on it at a prescribed rate, or, if she were young enough, she could be remarried with an appropriate dowry..., or she could be adjudicated as *epikleros* if her situation warranted it. But whatever happened, the person who was *kyrios* of her dowry had to support her.

On the other hand, one effect of the law about senility was that fathers of adult sons often handed over the management of their *oikos* to their sons, and virtually stepped down from the management of the house....

Throughout his life an Athenian was essentially a part of his *oikos;* as a baby his birth had to be accepted by the *kyrios* of his *oikos* (his father) and registered by the *phrateres* of the phratry to which his *oikos* belonged—the city was not interested in him directly until he was ready to be trained to serve it in war; as a man he married usually at an age at which his father was ready to retire from economic responsibility for the *oikos,* and his *phrateres* took note of his marriage, so that his son in turn would readily be accepted as a member of the *oikos;* when he retired in his turn, his *oikos* continued to support him under its new *kyrios,* his son. An Athenian woman was equally a part of her *oikos* until she married, at which time she removed into her husband's *oikos* taking with her a portion out of the possessions of her own *oikos;* this was designated for her support until her dying day whether she was wife or mother or widow or even divorcée. All the Athenian law was framed with this membership of the *oikos* in view; a man's *oikos* provided both his place in the citizen body and what measure of social security there was, and this helps to account for that passionate determination to defend the *oikoi* alike against foreigners and against grasping individual Athenians which is characteristic of the democratic period.

Classical Greek Attitudes to Sexual Behavior

K. J. DOVER

In this article, K. J. Dover analyzes Greek standards of sexual morality. Male citizens had numerous opportunities for sexual activity, yet there were restrictions. Why? How were Greek adolescents supposed to behave sexually? How did the city and family influence the adolescents' sexual activity? At an early age, males learned responsibility and moral values. What were those values? How did the Greeks view love and lovemaking?

Homosexuality (more properly, bisexuality) is a frequently noted feature of ancient Greece. Dover offers a nuanced interpretation of the sexual relationship

between men, or between men and boys. How do you account for the Greeks'
tolerance of homosexuality? Why were men so attracted to other men? What
qualities did the Greeks praise in men?

What did Greek males think of women as sexual beings? Did they believe
that women had different sexual appetites? Dover discusses the sexual roles that
daughters, wives, slaves, and prostitutes played in ancient Greece. Why was there a
double standard?

Dover's sources for this essay include public speeches, the theater, art, and the
works of philosophers. Do these sources present different views of Greek attitudes
toward sex? Dover notes that the reality of sexual activity may have been different
from attitudes expressed in speech and in writing.

The Greeks regarded sexual enjoyment as the area of life in which the
goddess Aphrodite[1] was interested, as Ares was interested in war and other
deities in other activities. Sexual intercourse was *aphrodisia,* 'the things of
Aphrodite.' Sexual desire could be denoted by general words for 'desire,'
but the obsessive desire for a particular person was *eros,* 'love' in the sense
which it has in our expressions 'be in love with...'...and 'fall in love
with....'...Eros, like all powerful emotional forces, but more consistently
than most, was personified and deified....

Eros generates *philia,* 'love'; the same word can denote milder degrees
of affection, just as 'my *philoi*' can mean my friends or my innermost family
circle, according to context. For the important question 'Do you love me?'
the verb used is *philein,* whether the question is put by a youth to a girl as
their kissing becomes more passionate or by a father to his son as an anxious
preliminary to a test of filial obedience.

Our own culture has its myths about the remote past, and one myth
that dies hard is that the 'invention' of sexual guilt, shame and fear by the
Christians destroyed a golden age of free, fearless, pagan sexuality. That most
pagans were in many ways less inhibited than most Christians is undeniable.
Not only had they a goddess specially concerned with sexual pleasure; their
other deities were portrayed in legend as enjoying fornication, adultery and
sodomy. A pillar surmounted by the head of Hermes[2] and adorned with an
erect penis stood at every Athenian front-door; great models of the erect penis
were borne in procession at festivals of Dionysus,[3] and it too was personified
as the tirelessly lascivious Phales.[4] The vase-painters often depicted sexual
intercourse, sometimes masturbation (male or female) and fellatio, and in
respect of any kind of sexual behaviour Aristophanic[5] comedy appears to
have had total license of word and act....

[1]Goddess of love and beauty.

[2]Messenger of the gods.

[3]God of wine and fertility.

[4]Personification of the phallus, often said to accompany Dionysus.

[5]Aristophanes (c.448–c.380 B.C.) was an Athenian writer of comedy.

There is, however, another side of the coin. Sexual intercourse was not permitted in the temples or sanctuaries of deities (not even of deities whose sexual enthusiasm was conspicuous in mythology), and regulations prescribing chastity or formal purification after intercourse played a part in many Greek cults. Homeric epic, for all its unquestioning acceptance of fornication as one of the good things of life, is circumspect in vocabulary, and more than once denotes the male genitals by *aidos*, 'shame,' 'disgrace.' ...Poets (notably Homer) sometimes describe interesting and agreeable activities—cooking, mixing wine, stabbing an enemy through a chink in his armour—in meticulous detail, but nowhere is there a comparable description of the mechanisms of sexual activity. Prose literature, even on medical subjects, is euphemistic ('be with...' is a common way of saying 'have sexual intercourse with...')....

Linguistic inhibition, then, was observably strengthened in the course of the classical period; and at least in some art-forms, inhibition extended also to content. These are data which do not fit the popular concept of a guilt-free or shame-free sexual morality, and require explanation. Why so many human cultures use derogatory words as synonyms of 'sexual' and reproach sexual prowess while praising prowess in (e.g.) swimming and riding, is a question which would take us to a remote level of speculation. Why the Greeks did so is a question which can at least be related intelligibly to the structure of Greek society and to Greek moral schemata which have no special bearing on sex.

As far as was practicable..., Greek girls were segregated from boys and brought up at home in ignorance of the world outside the home; one speaker in court seeks to impress the jury with the respectability of his family by saying that his sister and nieces are 'so well brought up that they are embarrassed in the presence even of a man who is a member of the family.' Married young, perhaps at fourteen (and perhaps to a man twenty-years or more her senior), a girl exchanged confinement in her father's house for confinement in her husband's. When he was invited out, his children might be invited with him, but not his wife; and when he had friends in, she did not join the company. Shopping seems to have been a man's job, to judge from references in comedy, and slaves could be sent on other errands outside the house. Upholders of the proprieties pronounced the front door to be the boundaries of a good woman's territory.

Consider now the situation of an adolescent boy growing up in such a society. Every obstacle is put in the way of his speaking to the girl next door; it may not be easy for him even to get a glimpse of her. Festivals, sacrifices and funerals, for which women and girls did come out in public, provided the occasion for seeing and being seen. They could hardly afford more than that, for there were too many people about, but from such an occasion (both in real life and in fiction) an intrigue could be set on foot, with a female slave of respectable age as the indispensable go-between.

In a society which practices segregation of the sexes, it is likely that boys and girls should devote a good deal of time and ingenuity to defeating society, and many slaves may have co-operated with enthusiasm. But Greek laws were not lenient towards adultery, and *moikheia,* for which we have no suitable translation except 'adultery,' denoted not only the seduction of another man's wife, but also the seduction of his widowed mother, unmarried daughter, sister, niece, or any other woman whose legal guardian he was. The adulterer could be prosecuted by the offended father, husband or guardian; alternatively, if caught in the act, he could be killed, maltreated, or imprisoned by force until he purchased his freedom by paying heavy compensation. A certain tendency to regard women as irresponsible and ever ready to yield to sexual temptation... relieved a cuckolded husband of a sense of shame or inadequacy and made him willing to seek the co-operation of his friends in apprehending an adulterer, just as he would seek their co-operation to defend himself against fraud, encroachment, breach of contract, or any other threat to his property. The adulterer was open to reproach in the same way, and to the same extent, as any other violator of the laws protecting the individual citizen against arbitrary treatment by other citizens. To seduce a woman of citizen status was more culpable than to rape her, not only because rape was presumed to be unpremeditated but because seduction involved the capture of her affection and loyalty; it was the degree of offense against the man to whom she belonged, not her own feelings, which mattered.

It naturally follows from the state of the law and from the attitudes and values implied by segregation that an adolescent boy who showed an exceptional enthusiasm for the opposite sex could be regarded as a potential adulterer and his propensity discouraged just as one would discourage theft, lies and trickery, while an adolescent boy who blushed at the mere idea of proximity to a woman was praised as *sophron,* 'right-minded,' i.e. unlikely to do anything without reflecting first whether it might incur punishment, disapproval, dishonour or other undesirable consequences.

Greek society was a slave-owning society, and a female slave was not in a position to refuse the sexual demands of her owner or of anyone else to whom he granted the temporary use of her. Large cities, notably Athens, also had a big population of resident aliens, and these included women who made a living as prostitutes, on short-term relations with a succession of clients, or as *hetairai,* who endeavoured to establish long-term relations with wealthy and agreeable men. Both aliens and citizens could own brothels and stock them with slave-prostitutes. Slave-girls and alien girls who took part in men's parties as dancers or musicians could also be mauled and importuned in a manner which might cost a man his life if he attempted it with a woman of citizen status....

It was therefore easy enough to purchase sexual satisfaction, and the richer a man was the better provision he could make for himself. But money spent on sex was money not spent on other things, and there seems to have been substantial agreement on what were proper or improper items of expenditure. Throughout the work of the Attic orators,[6] who offer us by far the best evidence on the moral standards which it was prudent to uphold in addressing large juries composed of ordinary citizens, it is regarded as virtuous to impoverish oneself by gifts and loans to friends in misfortune (for their daughters' dowries, their fathers' funerals, and the like), by ransoming Athenian citizens taken prisoner in war, and by paying out more than the required minimum in the performance of public duties (the upkeep of a warship, for example, or the dressing and training of a chorus at a festival). This kind of expenditure was boasted about and treated as a claim on the gratitude of the community. On the other hand, to 'devour an inheritance' by expenditure on one's own consumption was treated as disgraceful. Hence gluttony, drunkenness and purchased sexual relations were classified together as 'shameful pleasures.'...When a young man fell in love, he might well fall in love with a hetaira or a slave, since his chances of falling in love with a girl of citizen status were so restricted, and to secure the object of his love he would need to purchase or ransom her. A close association between eros and extravagance therefore tends to be assumed, especially in comedy; a character in Menander[7] says, 'No one is so parsimonious as not to make some sacrifice of his property to Eros.' More than three centuries earlier, Archilochus[8] put the matter in characteristically violent form when he spoke of wealth accumulated by long labour 'pouring down into a whore's guts.' A fourth-century litigant venomously asserts that his adversary, whose tastes were predominantly homosexual, has 'buggered away all his estate.'

We have here another reason for the discouragement and disapproval of sexual enthusiasm in the adolescent; it was seen as presenting a threat that the family's wealth would be dissipated in ways other than those which earned honour and respect from the community. The idea that one has a right to spend one's own money as one wishes (or a right to do anything which detracts from one's health and physical fitness) is not Greek, and would have seemed absurd to a Greek. He had only the rights which the law of his city explicitly gave him; no right was inalienable, and no claim superior to the city's.

Living in a fragmented and predatory world, the inhabitants of a Greek city-state, who could never afford to take the survival of their community completely for granted, attached a great importance to the qualities required of a soldier: not only to strength and speed, in which men are normally superior to women, but also to the endurance of hunger, thirst, pain, fatigue, discomfort and disagreeably hot or cold weather. The ability to resist and master the body's demands for nourishment and rest was normally regarded

---

[6] Athenians who wrote or gave speeches in law courts or in the assembly.

[7] Greek writer of comedy, 342?–291? B.C.

[8] Greek poet of the mid-seventh century B.C.

as belonging to the same moral category as the ability to resist sexual desire. Xenophon[9] describes the chastity of King Agesilaus[10] together with his physical toughness, and elsewhere summarises 'lack of self-control' as the inability to hold out against 'hunger, thirst, sexual desire and long hours without sleep.'

The reasons for this association are manifold: the treatment of sex—a treatment virtually inevitable in a slave-owning society—as a commodity, and therefore as something which the toughest and most frugal men will be able to cut down to a minimum; the need for a soldier to resist the blandishments of comfort (for if he does not resist, the enemy who does will win), to sacrifice himself as an individual entirely, to accept pain and death as the price to be paid for the attainment of a goal which is not easily quantified, the honour of victory; and the inveterate Greek tendency to conceive of strong desires and emotional states as forces which assail the soul from the outside. To resist is manly and 'free'; to be distracted by immediate pleasure from the pursuit of honour through toil and suffering is to be a 'slave' to the forces which 'defeat' and 'worst' one's own personality.

Here is a third reason for praise of chastity in the young, the encouragement of the capacity to resist, to go without, to become the sort of man on whom the community depends for its defence. If the segregation and legal and administrative subordination of women received their original impetus from the fragmentation of the early Greek world into small, continuously warring states, they also gave an impetus to the formation of certain beliefs about women which served as a rationalization of segregation and no doubt affected behavior to the extent that people tend to behave in the ways expected of them. Just as it was thought masculine to resist and endure, it was thought feminine to yield to fear, desire and impulse. 'Now you must be a *man;*' says Demeas[11] to himself as he tries to make up his mind to get rid of his concubine, 'Forget your desire, fall out of love.' Women in comedy are notoriously unable to keep off the bottle, and in tragedy women are regarded as naturally more prone than men to panic, uncont. ollable grief, jealousy and spite. It seems to have been believed not only that women enjoyed sexual intercourse more intensely than men, but also that experience of intercourse put the woman more under the man's power than it put him under hers, and that if not segregated and guarded women would be insatiably promiscuous.

It was taken for granted in the Classical period that a man was sexually attracted by a good-looking younger male, and no Greek who said that he was 'in love' would have taken it amiss if his hearers assumed without further enquiry that he was in love with a boy and that he desired more than anything to ejaculate in or on the boy's body. I put the matter in these coarse and clinical terms to preclude any misapprehension arising from modern

---

[9]Greek general and historian, 430?–355? B.C.

[10]Spartan king (444–360 B.C.) who begin his reign in 399.

[11]Character in a play by Menander.

application of the expression 'Platonic love' or from Greek euphemism (see below).... Aphrodite, despite her femininity, is not hostile to homosexual desire, and homosexual intercourse is denoted by the same term, *aphrodisia*, as heterosexual intercourse. Vase-painting was noticeably affected by the homosexual ethos; painters sometimes depicted a naked woman with a male waist and hips, as if a woman's body was nothing but a young man's body plus breasts and minus external genitals, and in many of their pictures of heterosexual intercourse from the rear position the penis appears (whatever the painter's intention) to be penetrating the anus, not the vagina.

Why homosexuality—or, to speak more precisely, 'pseudo-homosexuality,' since the Greeks saw nothing surprising in the coexistence of desire for boys and desire for girls in the same person—obtained so firm and widespread a hold on Greek society, is a difficult and speculative question. Segregation alone cannot be the answer, for comparable segregation has failed to engender a comparable degree of homosexuality in other cultures. Why the Greeks of the Classical period accepted homosexual desire as natural and normal is a much easier question: they did so because previous generations had accepted it, and segregation of the sexes in adolescence fortified and sustained the acceptance and the practice.

Money may have enabled the adolescent boy to have plenty of sexual intercourse with girls of alien or servile status, but it could not give him the satisfaction which can be pursued by his counterpart in a society which does not own slaves: the satisfaction of being welcomed *for his own sake* by a sexual partner of equal status. This is what the Greek boy was offered by homosexual relations. He was probably accustomed (as often happens with boys who do not have the company of girls) to a good deal of homosexual play at the time of puberty, and he never heard from his elders the suggestion that one was destined to become *either* 'a homosexual' *or* 'a heterosexual.' As he grew older, he could seek among his juniors a partner of citizen status, who could certainly not be forced and who might be totally resistant to even the most disguised kind of purchase. If he was to succeed in seducing this boy (or if later, as a mature man, he was to seduce a youth), he could do so only by *earning* hero-worship.

This is why, when Greek writers 'idealize' eros and treat the physical act as the 'lowest' ingredient in a rich and complex relationship which comprises mutual devotion, reciprocal sacrifice, emulation, and the awakening of sensibility, imagination and intellect, they look not to what most of us understand by sexual love but to the desire of an older for a younger male and the admiration felt by the younger for the older. It is noticeable also that in art and literature inhibitions operate in much the same way as in the romantic treatment of heterosexual love in our own tradition. When physical gratification is directly referred to, the younger partner is said to 'grant favours' or 'render services'; but a great deal is written about homosexual eros from which the innocent reader would not easily gather that any physical contact at all was involved. Aeschines,[12] who follows Aeschylus[13] and Classical sentiment generally in treating the relation between Achilles and Patroclus in the *Iliad*[14] as homoerotic, commends Homer for leaving it to 'the educated among his hearers' to perceive the nature of the relation from the extravagant grief expressed by Achilles at the death of Patroclus. The vase-painters very frequently depict the giving of presents by men to boys and the 'courting' of boys (a mild term for an approach which includes putting a hand on the boy's genitals), but their pursuit of the subject to the stage of erection, let alone penetration, is very rare, whereas depiction of heterosexual intercourse, in a variety of positions, is commonplace.

We also observe in the field of homosexual relations the operation of the 'dual standard of morality' which so often characterizes societies in which segregation of the sexes is minimal. If a Greek admitted that he was in love with a boy, he could expect sympathy and encouragement from his friends, and if it was known that he had attained his goal, envy and admiration. The boy, on the other hand, was praised if he retained his chastity, and he could expect strong disapproval if he was thought in any way to have taken the initiative in attracting a lover. The probable implication is that neither partner would actually say anything about the physical aspect of their relationship to anyone else, nor would they expect any question about it to be put to them or any allusion to it made in their presence.

Once we have accepted the universality of homosexual relations in Greek society as a fact, it surprises us to learn that if a man had at any time in his life prostituted himself to another man for money he was debarred from exercising his political rights. If he was an alien, he had no political rights to exercise, and was in no way penalized for living as a male prostitute, so long as he paid the prostitution tax levied upon males and females alike. It was therefore not the physical act *per se* which incurred penalty, but the incorporation of the act in a certain deliberately chosen role which could only be fully defined with reference to the nationality and status of the participants.

This datum illustrates an attitude which was fundamental to Greek society. They tended to believe that one's moral character is formed in the main by the circumstances in which one lives: the wealthy man is tempted to arrogance and oppression, the poor man to robbery and fraud, the slave to cowardice and petty greed. A citizen compelled by great and sudden economic misfortune to do work of a kind normally done by slaves was shamed because his assumption of a role which so closely resembled a slave's role altered his relationship to his fellow-citizens. Since prostitutes were usually slaves or aliens, to play the role of a prostitute was, as it were,

[12] Athenian orator 397?–322? B.C.

[13] Athenian tragic poet, 525–456 B.C.

[14] Achilles was the great hero and Patroclus his friend in the *Illiad*, Homer's epic poem.

to remove oneself from the citizen-body, and the formal exclusion of a male prostitute from the rights of a citizen was a penalty for disloyalty to the community in his choice of role.

Prostitution is not easily defined—submission in gratitude for gifts, services or help is not so different in kind from submission in return for an agreed fee—nor was it easily proved in a Greek city, unless people were willing (as they were not) to come forward and testify that they had helped to cause a citizen's son to incur the penalty of disenfranchisement. A boy involved in a homosexual relationship absolutely untainted by mercenary considerations could still be called a prostitute by his family's enemies, just as the term can be recklessly applied today by unfriendly neighbours or indignant parents to a girl who sleeps with a lover. He could also be called effeminate; not always rightly, since athletic success seems to have been a powerful stimulus to his potential lovers, but it is possible (and the visual arts do not help us much here) that positively feminine characteristics in the appearance, movements and manner of boys and youths played a larger part in the ordinary run of homosexual activity than the idealization and romanticisation of the subject in literature indicate. There were certainly circumstances in which homosexuality could be treated as a substitute for heterosexuality; a comic poet says of the Greeks who besieged Troy for ten years, 'they never saw a hetaira . . . and ended up with arseholes wider than the gates of Troy.' . . . A sixth-century vase in which all of a group of men except one are penetrating women shows the odd man out grasping his erect penis and approaching, with a gesture of entreaty, a youth—who starts to run away. In so far as the 'passive partner' in a homosexual act takes on himself the role of a woman, he was open to the suspicion, like the male prostitute, that he abjured his prescribed role as a future soldier and defender of the community.

The comic poets, like the orators, ridicule individuals for effeminacy, for participation in homosexual activity, or for both together; at the same time, the sturdy, wilful, roguish characters whom we meet in Aristophanes are not averse to handling and penetrating good-looking boys when the opportunity presents itself, as a supplement to their busy and enjoyable heterosexual programmes. . . . [T]here is one obvious factor which we should expect to determine different sexual attitudes in different classes. The thorough-going segregation of women of citizen status was possible only in households which owned enough slaves and could afford to confine its womenfolk to a leisure enlivened only by the exercise of domestic crafts such as weaving and spinning. This degree of segregation was simply not possible in poorer families; the women who sold bread and vegetables in the market—Athenian women, not resident aliens—were not segregated, and there must have been plenty of women . . . who took a hand in work on the land and drove animals to market. No doubt convention required that they should protect each other's virtue by staying in pairs or groups as much as they could, but clearly . . . the obstacles to love-affairs between citizens' sons and citizens' daughters lose their validity as one goes down the social scale. Where there are love-affairs, both boys and girls can have decided views...on whom they wish to marry. The girl in Aristophanes' *Ecclesiazusae*[15] who waits impatiently for her young man's arrival while her mother is out may be much nearer the norm of Athenian life than those cloistered ladies who were 'embarrassed by the presence even of a male relative.' It would not be discordant with modern experience to believe that speakers in an Athenian law-court professed, and were careful to attribute to the jury, standards of propriety higher than the average member of the jury actually set himself.

Much Classical Greek philosophy is characterized by contempt for sexual intercourse.... Xenophon's Socrates, although disposed to think it a gift of beneficent providence that humans, unlike other mammals, can enjoy sex all the year round, is wary of troubling the soul over what he regards as the minimum needs of the body.... One logical outcome of this attitude to sex is exemplified by Diogenes the Cynic, who was alleged to have masturbated in public when his penis erected itself, as if he were scratching a mosquito-bite. Another outcome was the doctrine (influential in Christianity, but not of Christian origin) that a wise and virtuous man will not have intercourse except for the purpose of procreating legitimate offspring, a doctrine which necessarily proscribes much heterosexual and all homosexual activity.

Although philosophical preoccupation with the contrast between 'body' and 'soul' had much to do with these developments, we can discern, as the ground from which these philosophical plants sprouted, Greek admiration for invulnerability, hostility towards the diversion of resources to the pursuit of pleasure, and disbelief in the possibility that dissimilar ways of feeling and behaving can be synthesised in the same person without detracting from his attainment of the virtues expected of a selfless defender of his city. It is also clear that the refusal of Greek law and society to treat a woman as a responsible person, while on the one hand it encouraged a complacent acceptance of prostitution and concubinage, on the other hand led to the classification of sexual activity as a male indulgence which could be reduced to a minimum by those who were not self-indulgent....

The Roman Mob

P. A. BRUNT

The police force is a modern invention, existing in its current form for only a few centuries. Earlier, to preserve order, governments relied on consensus or on the use of examples, such as grisly executions or the massacre of the inhabitants of a

---

[15]The play *The Assembly of Women*.

rebellious town, to frighten the populace. Rome developed its notorious policy of "bread and circuses," a dole of foodstuffs and a dose of grand entertainments in order to keep the urban masses somewhat content.

As P. A. Brunt indicates, such tactics did not always work, and the mob became a potent force in the last century of the Republic. What powers did the Roman people actually exercise in government? How did the aristocracy view the populace? What political measures concerning the masses did the aristocracy oppose? What did the aristocracy see as the proper duty of government?

What do you see as the weaknesses in the governmental system of the Roman Republic? What factors favored the growth of violence? Did living conditions in Rome incline the population toward violence? Why was it difficult for the government to maintain order in Rome? On the other hand, what limited the mob's ability to influence events?

Do Roman attitudes toward poverty and the poor help to explain the political activities of the masses? What circumstances surrounded the first act of illegal political violence in Rome? Who—commoners or nobles—were responsible for initiating violence? Why did people and groups resort to illegal violence? What political gains did the mob hope to achieve?

Does Brunt believe mob violence contributed greatly to the fall of the Roman Republic? Does he think the urban masses were better off under the Republic or under the monarchy that followed?

In February 56 B.C., Publius Clodius, the patrician leader of the urban proletariat at Rome, had indicted his enemy, Titus Annius Milo, on a charge of seditious violence before the popular assembly. (Milo had successfully disputed Clodius' control of the streets by hiring gladiators and other bravados.) Pompey[1] had undertaken to appear for Milo at a preliminary hearing.

> Pompey spoke [wrote Cicero][2] or intended to; in fact, as soon as he rose, the Clodian gang raised a clamour, and throughout his speech he was interrupted not only by shouting but by loud abuse and insults. When he had finished—in this he certainly showed courage; he was not frightened away, said his piece to the end, and now and again secured silence by his authority—up got Clodius. Our people made such a clamour—we had decided to show him the same courtesy—that he could not control his mind, tongue or expression. Pompey had barely finished at noon; this went on till two o'clock; every kind of insult and the most bawdy verses were shouted at Clodius and his sister. Livid with fury, Clodius asked his followers who was starving the people to death. The gang replied: "Pompey". Who wanted to go to Alexandria? "Pompey". Whom did they want to go? "Crassus".[3] ... At about three o'clock, as if at a signal, Clodius' people began to spit in unison at ours. A crescendo of anger. They began to shove our people out. We charged; the gangsters fled; Clodius was thrown off the platform, and I too took to flight; there might have been an accident.

[1] Pompey the Great, 106–48 B.C., Roman general who conquered additional territory, cleansed the Mediterranean Sea of pirates, and lost the civil war against Julius Caesar.

[2] Orator and politician, 106–43 B.C.

[3] Marcus Licinius Crassus (c.115–53 B.C.), perhaps the wealthiest Roman, shared power with Pompey and Julius Caesar in the First Triumvirate (60 B.C.).

This was a relatively peaceful scene in the 50s. In 58, when Clodius was driving Cicero into temporary exile, a senator was killed in street fighting. The day after Cicero left Rome, before he had been condemned in law, his house on the Palatine was sacked and burned, and the mob marched out to treat his Tusculan villa in the same way. Later that year, Pompey kept to his house in fear for his life. In 57 the efforts of Milo and Sestius as tribunes to restore Cicero were met by violence; Sestius was left for dead in the street; Clodius brought gladiators into the senate-house. Milo and Sestius repelled force with force, until at last the gentry and bourgeoisie of all Italy came in to vote for Cicero's return. In November, an armed band drove off the workmen who were rebuilding his house, demolished a neighbouring portico and set fire to the mansion of his brother "with the city looking on". A week later, Cicero was going down the Sacra Via, the principal street in the city centre which ran from where the Colosseum now stands to the foot of the Capitol and was lined with great houses and luxury shops, when Clodius' gang attacked: "there were shouts, stones, clubs, swords, all without a moment's notice". Cicero was saved by his escort. Next day Clodius tried to storm Milo's house in a fashionable residential quarter. "Quite openly in the middle of the morning, he brought up men with shields and drawn swords and others with lighted torches". A successful counterattack was made and Clodius fled for his life.

Such violence reached a climax in early 52 when Milo at last succeeded in murdering Clodius outside Rome and a frenzied mob brought the body into the senate-house, tore down tribunal and benches, seized the clerk's papers and burned everything up, the senate-house itself and the adjacent Porcian basilica, in a great funeral pyre. A rather similar scene recurred in 44 when Caesar's[4] body was burned, and the mob tore to pieces the poet, Helvius Cinna, under the misapprehension that he was a praetor[5] who had publicly sympathized with Caesar's assassins. But, though the proportions of violence were unprecedented, violence itself was not something novel in Rome; for almost a century it had been growing more frequent.

I propose here to examine the conditions which favoured or caused it, to sketch its progress, and to consider the composition of the mobs and their aims; I shall conclude by assessing what the mob achieved.

The true governing organ of the Roman Republic was the senate which acted through annual magistrates elected by the people but drawn from its own ranks. The senate itself was dominated by a few noble families whose power reposed on their wealth and on the number of their dependents, and on the prestige they derived from their past services to the state. Candidates for office seldom stood on programmes, and organized parties did not exist. Men were returned to office occasionally for personal merits (talent could carry outsiders like Cicero to the highest place), more often by reason of

---

[4] Julius Caesar (c.102–44 B.C.), Roman general, conqueror of Gaul, eventually dictator of Rome.

[5] A Roman magistrate who administered justice.

their munificence and lavish bribes, in general because of their family and connections. Birth and wealth usually went together. Cicero describes Lucius Domitius Ahenobarbus as a man destined for the consulship since he was born; in 49 he could offer farms of thirty acres apiece to some thousands of soldiers. Such nobles had numerous dependents or clients who were morally expected and often economically compelled to support them. They used their power to grow richer from the profits of war and empire, and to oppose every measure to relieve the poor, the provision of cheap grain, the distribution of land or the remission of debt. Here they had the backing of the upper class in general, whose spokesman, Cicero, declared that the prime duty of government was to ensure "that every man kept his own". And public largesses, which did not infringe property rights, could be rejected on the ground that they were more than the treasury could bear, the treasury from which senators drew handsome allowances for themselves.

In theory the people at Rome possessed great power. They elected the magistrates, declared war and ratified treaties, passed laws, and until the creation of standing courts in the late second century decided the most important criminal cases; to the end of the Republic some political charges came before them. From the late second century they voted by ballot; this naturally diminished aristocratic control.

There was more than one popular assembly. Of these the *comitia centuriata*[6] was timocratically organized.[7] Decisions were taken by a majority not of heads, but of voting units called centuries; the well-to-do, if they were of one mind, could decide the issues; the citizens with no property at all, and who are said to have outnumbered all the rest put together by the time of Augustus,[8] formed only a single century, which might never even be called. The rural poor therefore had little influence in this body the importance of which was great, for it elected the chief magistrates; and it was men who had held the highest offices who dominated the senate itself.

This assembly was also competent to legislate, but laws were more generally passed by a less cumbrous body, in which the voting units were thirty-five tribes. The tribes were local divisions of the people; thirty-one were rural and four urban, though all freedmen (except such as were substantial landowners) were registered, wherever domiciled, in the urban tribes. In the tribes, rich and poor had equal votes.

At all times by far the greater number of citizens lived in the country, and it might seem that the organization of the tribal assembly ensured that the wishes of the rural majority would prevail, perhaps even to an undue extent; thirty-one to four was not the true proportion between town and country dwellers. However,... the system of primary democracy, in which the citizen can exercise his voting rights only by attending the sovereign assembly in

---

[6]Centuriate assembly.

[7]That is, there were property qualifications for membership in the assembly.

[8]First Roman emperor, 27 B.C.–A.D. 14.

person, can only work democratically if voters have not to spend more than two nights away from home. Even in the third century many citizens were a hundred miles distant from Rome, and after 80 they comprised the free population of Italy south of the Po. It was only on rare occasions that the peasants came in to vote. If the censors [9] who held office every five years were careful to register every citizen who moved from the country into the city in an urban tribe instead of a rural, the votes of the rural tribes must have been exercised by the minority of their members who had the leisure and means to visit Rome for the purpose, the very same class of wealthy landowners who controlled the centuriate assembly.

It seems, however, that the censors did not do their work thoroughly. Dionysius of Halicarnassus[10] sharply contrasts the centuriate assembly controlled by the respectable classes and the tribal, composed of artisans with no hearths of their own. He purports to be describing the early Republic, but the picture is imaginary and drawn from the conditions known to the annalists of the first century. In the Principate urban dwellers are attested in rural tribes. One piece of evidence suggests that this was possible as early as 133. Tiberius Gracchus,[11] who had hitherto relied on the rural voters (one of the few known instances in which they swarmed in to vote), began to court the urban plebs, as his followers were occupied with the harvest. His action would have had little purpose, if the urban plebs had been confined to the four urban tribes. It may be indeed that even a few immigrants who had moved into Rome since the last census and had not yet been reregistered might have balanced or outvoted the wealthier members of their tribes, and that it was to such a handful of citizens that he appealed. Even so, urban dwellers were evidently influential in the rural tribes. And between 70 and 28 it is not clear that any census was completed. It seems probable then that normally the urban plebs had a majority in the tribal assembly.

However, the assemblies could do nothing except with the collaboration of a magistrate. They could meet only on his summons, and only vote "Yea" or "Nay" on his proposals; a private citizen could not even speak except on his invitation. The plebs could not obtain redress of its grievances, unless a magistrate drawn from the upper classes was prepared to take the initiative. Genuine social concern or personal ambition led nobles like the Gracchi, Caesar and Clodius to come forward as "popular" leaders from time to time, but there was no consistent and continuous opposition, no organized and enduring popular party.

Even if a magistrate submitted a popular proposal, it did not follow that it would go through. It could be obstructed on religious pretexts, or vetoed. A single tribune[12] could veto what all his nine colleagues proposed.

[9]Two censors oversaw the census of Roman citizens and property.

[10]Greek historian of Rome, first century B.C.

[11]Tiberius Sempronius Gracchus (163–133 B.C.), statesman and reformer.

[12]Government office designed to protect the rights of the plebeians (plebes or plebs).

The tribunate had arisen in the class struggles of the early Republic for the protection of popular interests, and in the second century Polybius[13] could still say that it was the tribune's duty to do always what the people approved. To the end most of the champions of the commons acted as tribunes. None the less, Polybius' statement did not correspond to the constitutional practice that had evolved by his time. The senate could almost always find at least one tribune to act on its behalf and ... to use the tribunician veto to dissolve the tribunician power. Tribunes were often nobles themselves, or in Livy's[14] words "chattels of the nobility". . . .

According to Burke[15] "a state without the means of some change is without the means of its conservation". At Rome there were too many checks and balances in the constitution, which operated in practice only in the interest of the ruling class. Reformers had to use force, or at least to create conditions in which the senate had reason to fear its use. . . . This was the first factor which favoured the growth of violence at Rome.

In the second place, Rome was even by modern standards a populous city, in which there was no garrison and no police to control the multitude.

To the total size of the population there is no direct testimony. But the number of recipients of free grain had risen to 320,000 in the 40s. Only adult males were normally eligible, and we therefore have to estimate the number of women and children in this class. The grain recipients were partly freeborn, partly freedmen. Appian[16] implies that in 133 the poor were unable to raise children. Abortion and infanticide were not forbidden by the law, and many parents must have exposed their babies, some of whom might then be brought up as slaves by the finders. The infanticide of female infants must have been common even in the senatorial class, among whom in Augustus' reign men outnumbered women; if we make the reasonable assumption that it was still more prevalent with the poor, the birth-rate would also have been depressed by a scarcity of reproductive women. There is some ground, however, for thinking that the urban plebs consisted preponderantly of freedmen ... and particularly after Clodius made grain distributions free in 58 masters were very ready to manumit slaves, who could still be required to work for them, while obtaining rations from the state. Now it seems to me unlikely that there were so many female slaves or freedwomen as male slaves or freedmen. In this period slave-women were not needed to keep up the stock of slaves, most of whom were "made" by capture in war or kidnapping. And they were employable only for household duties and to some extent in spinning, weaving and making clothes, occupations perhaps more common on country estates than in town-houses. Slaves might enter

[13]Greek historian, c.203–120 B.C., who described the rise of Rome.

[14]Titus Livy, Roman historian, 59 B.C.–A.D. 17.

[15]Edmund Burke (1729–1797), English statesman and political writer, best known for *Reflections on the Revolution in France* (1790).

[16]Greek historian of Rome, second century A.D.

into a quasi-marriage, but both spouses were not necessarily freed together, and any children born in slavery, who were slaves themselves, might be manumitted only at a later date. In many thousand sepulchral inscriptions of freedmen at Rome (mainly imperial) under thirty percent record offspring, and still fewer marriage. For these reasons I doubt if we need more than double the figure of 320,000 to include both women and children of corn[17]-recipients.

Well-to-do residents were presumably not numerically significant. There remain the slaves. A rich man required a large staff of domestic servants, secretaries, etc.; and his standing might be measured by the number of his attendants and flunkeys. There might also be women engaged in textile work. Under Nero[18] an eminent senator had four hundred slaves in his town-house. However, in the 50s the scale of manumissions should have diminished the slave population. I guess that 100,000 would be a liberal estimate. The city population might then have been more or less than 750,000. Clodius' bill probably accelerated the drift from the country, but it had been going on before, and the number of slaves and freedmen had been progressively increasing. However, no numerical estimate can be ventured for any earlier date.

In the early Principate the government had at least 12,000 soldiers in Rome, not to speak of seven cohorts, which ultimately and perhaps from the first comprised 7,000 men, raised to deal with fires; they were military units and could also be used as police. Even so, it was hard to keep order. In 39 B.C., though there were troops at hand which saved him in the end, Octavian[19] was almost lynched in a riot, and Claudius[20] later was only rescued by soldiers from a famished mob. The narrow, winding streets and high buildings . . . did not help in suppressing riots. In A.D. 238 the populace, armed by the senate, besieged the depleted praetorian guard[21] in its camp; when the soldiers sallied out and pursued them into the streets,

> the people climbed up into the houses and harassed the soldiers by throwing down on them tiles, stones and pots of all kinds; the soldiers dared not go up after them, not knowing their way about the houses; but as the houses and workshops had their doors barred, they set fire to the many wooden balconies; the tenements were set close together, and large parts of the buildings were wooden; so the flames soon devastated a very great part of the city, one section after another.

Something of the same kind nearly occurred in 88, when Sulla[22] marched into the city. No doubt it was such dangers that made the emperors ready to

---

[17]Grain.

[18]Emperor, 54–68.

[19]Augustus's name before he achieved control of the Roman world.

[20]Emperor, 41–54.

[21]The emperor's guard.

[22]Lucius Cornelius Sulla (138–78 B.C.), general, leader of the supporters of the Roman Senate, and temporary dictator.

spend large sums on "bread and circuses". In other towns they had no such motive to care for the poor and did not do so.

The aristocratic government of the Republic had no police available; the magistrates had but a few attendants. Nor were troops normally found in the city, though in 121 the consul[23] happened to have at his disposal Cretan archers whom he used in suppressing the Gracchans.[24] How could the nobility ever hold the mob in check, when it was inflamed against the government?

The mob was generally unarmed and relied on sticks and stones. To carry arms was a capital offence, and in any event the poor would possess none, except knives. Moreover, as legions were recruited in the country, not the city, the urban poor were not trained in the use of arms. The well-to-do would have their own equipment, including body-armour, and had mostly seen military service; and the senate could authorize the arming of their followers. On occasions popular leaders distributed arms illegally to the mob, but even then, man for man, their followers were probably unequal to their opponents. Though armed, the partisans of Gaius Gracchus in 121 put up but a feeble resistance. The numerous clients of the great houses in the city itself often enabled the governing class to make a stand against the mob, reciprocating or even initiating violence....

Given time, the senate or magistrates or individual nobles could call up clients with military experience from the country. In 100, men from Picenum took part in the suppression of Saturninus.[25] The armed followers with whom Cicero surrounded himself during the Catilinarian conspiracy[26] of 63 included chosen young men from Reate. In 59 he was hoping to resist Clodius by force; his friends and their clients, freedmen and slaves would band together in his defence. A great concourse of substantial citizens from all over Italy ensured that he was recalled from exile in 57, although his enemy, Clodius, remained dominant over the city proletariate. In 56 Pompey summoned followers from Picenum and the Po valley for his protection. To end the uproar ensuing on Clodius' murder in 52, the senate authorized a levy all over Italy, and soldiers restored order in the city. But between 59 and 52 the senate was generally impotent, because Pompey with his veterans and Caesar with his great army in the north could marshal forces stronger than the senate could command.

The third factor in the turbulence of the city population may be found in the misery and squalor in which they lived, which naturally made them responsive to politicians who promised to improve their conditions and

[23]One of the two chief executives of the Roman state.

[24]Followers of Gaius Sempronius Gracchus (153–121 b.c.), statesman, reformer, and brother of Tiberius Sempronius Gracchus.

[25]Lucius Appuleius Saturninus, tribune who attempted to push extreme bills through the Senate in 100 and who staged a revolt in 88.

[26]Lucius Sergius Catilina (Catiline), c.108–62 b.c., politician who led a conspiracy against the Republic in 63. Cicero thwarted the plot.

engendered hostility (if only intermittent) to the upper classes who showed little care for their interests.

For lack of modern means of transport, the people were crammed into a small built-up area, not much larger than that of modern Oxford, with a density seven or eight times as great. The streets were winding and narrow, even main thorough-fares under twenty feet wide. While the rich had their luxurious mansions on the Palatine or spacious gardens in the suburbs, most inhabitants were penned into tiny flats in tenements, which had to be built high; Augustus imposed a limit of seventy feet (which suggests that this had been exceeded), and Trajan[27] pronounced that dangerous, reducing it to sixty. Cicero contrasts a newly planned city with Rome "situated on hills and in valleys, lifted up and suspended in the air, with no fine streets to boast of but only narrow paths".

The lower parts of the city were subject to periodic floods, and the collapse and conflagration of buildings were common occurrences. In the Principate it is said that not a day passed without a serious fire, yet then there were 7,000 *vigiles*[28] to put them out, in the Republic only a small force of publicly owned slaves. Crassus had a gang of five hundred builders, and bought up houses that were afire or adjacent to a blaze at knock-down prices with a view to rebuilding on the sites. These dangers were aggravated by bad methods of construction. Owners would not or could not afford to employ skilled architects or suitable materials. The local travertine cracked in fires, but it was too costly to bring better stone even fifty miles by land. A thin facing of stone might conceal a filling of soft rubble. To conserve space, party walls had to be not more than a foot and a half thick; given this limit, only baked brick was strong enough for high buildings, yet sun-dried brick was often used. Walls were sometimes of wattlework, the more dangerous as it was too expensive to bring larchwood, relatively impervious to fire, all the way from the Adriatic. In 44 Cicero reported to Atticus[29] that two of his tenements had fallen down, and that cracks were showing in others; the tenants—and the mice—had all fled.

The houses of the poor must also have been ill-lit, ill-ventilated and unwarmed; facilities for cooking were inadequate; water had to be fetched from the public fountains, and the supply cannot have been abundant until the old conduits were repaired and new aqueducts built under Augustus; further, the tenements were not connected with the public sewers. We may fairly suppose that most of the inhabitants of Rome lived in appalling slums. They offered shelter, but little more. As for furniture, Cicero speaks of the poor man as having no more than a stool and a bed where he lived, worked and slept.

[27]Emperor, 98–117.

[28]Literally "guards," but meaning professional firemen here.

[29]Titus Pomponius Atticus (109–32 B.C.), a wealthy Roman businessman living in Athens who corresponded regularly with Cicero.

From such tenements men like Cicero drew as landlords a good income. Cicero's property on the Aventine and in the Argiletum, probably two lower class districts, was in 44 bringing him in 80,000 HSS,[30] enough to have paid 160 legionaries for a year under the rates that had obtained until recently; he appropriated it to the allowance for his undergraduate son at Athens, and was anxious to have tenants who would pay on the nail. Perhaps that was not so easy to ensure. Then, as later, it is probable that the return on investment in house-property was high precisely because the risk was great.

In the 40s there was a prolonged agitation about urban rents. In 48 the praetor, Marcus Caelius, who proposed a year's remission, was driven out of the city by the consul, but only after bloodshed. Caesar, however, granted the remission in the same year, and perhaps extended it in 47, after further tumults, when barricades were raised, soldiers called in and eight hundred rioters killed. It applied to rents up to 2,000 sesterces in Rome, and 500 elsewhere, an indication that the cost of living in Rome was exceptionally high. (A generation earlier, Cicero gave the daily wage for an unskilled labourer as three sesterces; obviously he could not have afforded 2,000 for a year's rent. We cannot say whether wages had risen in the interim, or whether the remission was intended to benefit people at a rather higher level, such as shopkeepers.) Cicero's comment is characteristic. "There is no equity in abolishing or suspending rents. Am I to buy and build and repair and spend, and you to have the benefit against my will? Is this not to take away the property of some and give to others what does not belong to them?"

How did the people of Rome live? Rome was never a great industrial city; indeed there never was any large-scale industry in the ancient world of the kind familiar since the industrial revolution: the high cost of transport alone forbade the production of factory goods for a world-wide market. Adjacent to Rome there were no abundant supplies of fuel or raw materials. The Tiber is not well suited to navigation, and the port of Ostia had not yet been developed; the larger ships had to discharge in an open roadstead into lighters. None the less far more use was made of the river and its affluents (for downstream traffic as well as for transport from the mouth) than we should expect from present conditions; the growth of the urban population left no alternative. The supply of this population created a great demand for wholesale and retail traders, dock labour, carters and so on. So too large numbers must have been employed in the building trade: more fine public edifices were now being put up; the rich were continually erecting more luxurious town-houses and villas in the vicinity of Rome, and the increase of the population in itself required more tenements and shops, a demand augmented by the frequency of fires and collapses. Evidence from pre-industrial cities in other times may help to supply the lack of ancient statistics. In 1586 up to 6,000 workmen were engaged on public buildings at Rome, of whom 800 with 150 horses were needed to move the obelisk into the

---

[30]Sesterces, silver coins introduced in the third century B.C.

Piazza of St. Peter's; at the time the total population seems to have been under 100,000. In 1791 a third of all Paris wage-earners were occupied in the building trade. In addition, there were artisans and shopkeepers of all kinds, many of whom must have sold goods they made themselves, perhaps to the order of clients. Beggars, curiously, are hardly ever mentioned, perhaps because the Romans (unlike the Jews, and the Christians after them) recognized no special obligation to relieve the poor as such; it was another matter if the great houses supported idle dependents, whose votes and strong arms they could employ; on them they conferred benefits in accordance with the usual principle of Roman morality: "do ut des".[31]

According to tradition king Numa[32] had organized craftsmen into *Collegia* or corporations of flautists, goldsmiths, carpenters—the word *fabri* came to mean builders in all sorts of material—dyers, shoemakers, coppersmiths and potters. If only these particular corporations were in fact ancient, they go back to a very remote time, when for instance the use of iron was still unknown; in the historic period there must have been many ironworkers, especially to make arms for the legions which were regularly enrolled and equipped just outside the city. The list also does not include bakers; according to Pliny[33] there were none down to the middle of the second century; the women used to grind and bake at home; presumably they ceased to do so, when so many of the poor were lodged in houses without suitable ovens. In the course of time many more corporations came into existence. The fishermen who fished in the Tiber had an old festival. Fulling ceased to be a domestic craft. Plautus[34] casually mentions a score of other trades. Cato[35] in the second century recommended buying at Rome tunics, togas, cloaks, patchwork cloth and wooden shoes (though some of these things were also made on his estates), and in addition jars, bowls, ploughs, yokes, locks and keys and the finest baskets.

As in medieval towns men of one craft tended to congregate. There was a pottery district, and streets were named after the silversmiths, grain merchants, sandal-makers, timber merchants, log-sellers, perfumers and scythemakers, probably many more. *Collegia* of artisans would thus be composed of neighbours.

Many traders and artisans were not of free birth. Slaves were employed in every trade, craft and profession. Freedom was a necessary incentive to good work and seems often to have been granted fairly soon, or bought by the slave from the wage or share of the profits he was allowed. The freedman

---

[31] "I give in order that you give" (that is, scratch my back and I'll scratch yours).

[32] Successor to Romulus, Numa Pompilius was the semi-mythical second king of Rome, thought to have established the Roman calendar and religion.

[33] Pliny the Younger, statesman and civil servant, 61/62–113.

[34] Roman playwright, c.254–184 B.C.

[35] Marcus Porcius Cato ("the Elder"), 234–149 B.C., statesman famous for his opposition to Greek refinement and his recommendation of the simple, rustic life.

naturally worked at his old trade and was probably often still financed by his old master. . . . [I]n the urban population as a whole, as well as in the crafts and trades, men of servile origin preponderated. . . .

Many freedmen (perhaps most in Rome) came from the east and probably brought with them new skills; with the capital their patrons provided, they thus had an advantage over native workmen. Freeborn Italians, some of whom were displaced peasants, would then have had no means of employment except casual, unskilled labour. They could go out into the country for the harvest, vintage and olive-picking. . . . The Roman landowner preferred to rely on a permanent labour-force of slaves, but as Cato makes clear, he did not wish to feed idle mouths. For seasonal operations, therefore, he required supplementary labour provided by free hired men. On the same principle we must suppose that most dock labour and the ancillary carting of supplies was free; there was little sailing for half the year, and work must have bunched in a few months or weeks. And it required no special skill. Similarly building contractors, whose business is likely to have fluctuated, would not have found it profitable to keep enough slaves throughout the year for *all* their work. The builders on Cicero's Tusculan villa went back to Rome to collect their free grain rations as citizens. It has been plausibly conjectured that the distress Tiberius Gracchus sought to alleviate had been newly aggravated by unemployment resulting from the completion of the Marcian aqueduct. The emperor Vespasian[36] was to refuse to adopt a labour-saving device; if he did so, he asked, how could he feed his poor commons?

Sallust[37] and others tell of the drift of countryfolk into Rome; Sallust speaks of young men who had barely made a livelihood with labour in the fields and were attracted by the private and public largesses in the city, and Cicero could urge the urban plebs with some success in 63 not to forsake the advantages of life there, their votes (which could of course be sold), games, festivals and so on, for land allotments in barren or malarial places. What Sallust says of the private largesses is probably important; the great houses could afford to maintain clients, and they might even be given rent-free lodgings. Sometimes magistrates, to enhance their popularity, distributed grain or oil at low prices, bearing the cost themselves. Above all there were the cheap or free public corn-doles instituted generally by popular leaders, partly perhaps to reduce the dependence of the plebs on noble patrons. However, the distributions were not free until 58, the liberality of the cheap distributions provided under Gaius Gracchus' law in 123 was soon reduced and not restored till 100, and distributions were in abeyance from 80 to 73 and restricted to only some 40,000 recipients from 73 to 62. Moreover men could not live on bread and shows alone; there was other food, and clothes to be paid for, and rent. Augustus was to introduce a quicker method of

[36]Emperor, 69–79.

[37]Roman historian, 86–c.34 B.C., known for his *War of Catiline*, an account of the conspiracy of Catiline.

distributing free grain which did not take the recipients away from their work so long as in the past. The people of Rome had to earn much of their living, and for many of them casual employment was the only means. Gaius Gracchus must have won much support by his programme for building roads and granaries.

The feeding of the city population was also a grave problem. There were large imports from Sicily, Sardinia and Africa, but the supply was precarious, liable to be interrupted by piracy and wars. Much grain must still have come from Italy, or else the population could not have survived the years 43–36, for most of which it was cut off from oversea supplies. The public rations did not suffice for a family, and some, if only a minority, of the recipients must have had wives and children. Some grain had to be bought on the market, even in the years when there were public distributions to most of the free population. In 57–6 it seems likely that there was not enough in the public granaries to honour the state's obligation; the market price was a matter of general concern and might soar to famine rates.... And market prices fluctuated sharply, soaring when the harvests were poor and when hoarding by growers and merchants aggravated the shortage. It is an illusion that in the late Republic the urban plebs was usually well and cheaply fed by the state. As for modern scholars who repeat ancient gibes that the doles corrupted the urban population, one must wonder if they would also condemn all modern measures of social welfare; in Rome there were no charitable foundations for the poor, and no unemployment benefits.

The progress of violence may now be sketched. In 133 Tiberius Gracchus proposed to redistribute among the poor public lands which the rich had occupied. His colleague, Octavius, interposed a veto; Gracchus had him deposed by vote of the assembly, an unprecedented act which set aside the most important of the constitutional checks. His bill was then carried. Actual violence was not used, but the menacing attitude of the peasantry who had flocked in to back Gracchus may explain why Octavius did not dare to veto the motion for his own deposition. Later in the year the senators charged Gracchus with aspiring to tyranny and lynched him in public. The first open act of illegal political violence came from the nobility.

In 123–2 Gaius Gracchus as tribune carried many anti-senatorial measures. (In 123 no other tribune had the will or courage to oppose him; he had the backing of both urban and rural plebs and of the *equites*, rich men outside the senate, on whom he conferred important benefits; he did not need to use force.) But eventually he lost popular favour and office, and as a private person in 121 armed his followers to obstruct the repeal of one of his laws; he and they were massacred by senatorial forces quite legally.

In 103 and 100 the tribune, Saturninus, who also proposed land-distribution and revived the grain dole on the Gracchan scale, did not scruple to murder opponents and rivals; he too was suppressed by the senate. In 88 the tribune Sulpicius, promoting the interests of the newly enfranchised Italians, and also of the freedmen whom he proposed to redistribute among all the tribes, drove his opponents from the forum by force; the consul, Sulla, appealed to his army (where his ability and generosity assured him of support), marched on Rome and proscribed Sulpicius and his friends. This was the first occasion on which the army was employed to overturn decisions made at Rome; once again, it was a noble and conservative who took the fatal step. Sulla's successor, Cinna, revived Sulpicius' proposals; the streets ran with blood in conflict between him and his colleague, Octavius. Defeated in the city, Cinna imitated Sulla in appealing to the army and with like success. Only a great civil war concluded this phase of the revolution and enabled Sulla to restore and consolidate the senate's control of the state.

So far it is not clear that the urban proletariate, even though it owed cheap grain to popular leaders, took a strong part against the senate, which in 100 and 87 is said to have had the support of the townsmen. The Gracchi and Saturninus relied chiefly on the rural poor, Cinna and perhaps Sulpicius on the new Italian citizens. Sulla, however, severely limited the powers of tribunes and put an end to corn doles. The latter measure directly injured the urban poor, and the former denied them hope of redress for their grievances.

In the 70s the prevalence of piracy began to affect the corn-supply. In 75 the price of grain was cruel, and a mob attacked the consuls proceeding along the Sacra Via[38] and put them to flight; this riot does not seem to have been "incited by demagogues". The senate itself re-instituted corn doles in 73, but on a miserably limited scale. Pompey in 70 forced through the restoration of the tribunes' powers; he probably envisaged that tribunician legislation could be advantageous to him (as it proved); and his wishes could not be denied, as he had a large and loyal army outside the city. Three years later, the tribune Gabinius had a great command conferred on Pompey to put down the pirates. Almost all the senators opposed the bill; the mob stormed the senate-house and put them to flight. Tribunes who tried to interpose their veto were overawed by a threat of deposition. The people would not tolerate any opposition to a measure that might end the scarcity. Pompey's mere appointment resulted in fact in an immediate and abrupt fall in the price of grain, and within a few weeks he cleared the seas of pirates. His prestige was such that he could not be debarred from another great command in the east. It could be foreseen that on his return with a large army he would be potentially master of the state. This was why the senate had resisted the proposal in 67 to grant him extraordinary powers.

The years from 67 to 62 (when Pompey came back) were full of violence and threats of violence. In 63 Catiline rose in arms against the government with a band of discontented peasants. The urban plebs had at first favoured him, perhaps because his proposal to cancel debts would have relieved them of some payments of rent-arrears. Cicero won them over to the government by alleging that Catiline's friends in the city intended to burn it down and deprive them of their miserable shelter and few personal belongings.

---

[38]Sacred way, the road that wound through the forum.

But his execution without trial of Catiline's accomplices violated the principle on which the humblest Roman relied for the protection of his own person. Cicero incurred the lasting hatred of the masses. When Clodius had him banished in 58, he erected a shrine to Liberty on the site of Cicero's town house; he had vindicated the freedom of citizens against arbitrary ill-treatment by magistrates.

Early in 62 Marcus Cato[39] greatly extended the scale of distribution of cheap grain. He was the staunchest champion of the senate's power. It seems paradoxical that he should be the author of this measure. But the urban masses were volatile, and it was necessary to assuage their discontents, when Catiline was still in arms and there was a proposal to bring Pompey back to deal with the crisis.

The fears entertained of Pompey proved unjustified. On his return he disbanded his army. But he needed to reward his veterans with land-allotments. Senatorial obstruction threw him into alliance with Caesar, who had consistently identified himself with popular aims, and as consul in 59 Caesar carried agrarian laws by the help of the strong arms of Pompey's veterans. In return, he received the great command in Gaul. To check senatorial reaction, once Caesar had left for his province, Pompey and Caesar promoted the election to the tribunate of Publius Clodius, and it was Clodius who finally made the grain distributions free. This was the prime source of the enormous popularity he enjoyed with the plebs so long as he lived. Another measure, to be considered presently, ensured that he, unlike previous demagogues, remained powerful in the city even when out of office.

This sketch will have shown that violence at Rome did not proceed from any single section of the people. Before Sulla "popular" leaders drew support mainly from citizens who came in from the country to vote and fight in the streets; in 70 it was Pompey's army (recruited in the country) that made the restoration of tribunician power irresistible; in 59 it was again his veterans who forced through Caesar's bills. On the other hand, in 67 it was the *urban* plebs which broke the opposition to Gabinius' law, and in most of the post-Sullan period it is their riots that we hear of. But the senate also, or some of its members, initiated illegal violence from time to time, or at least met force with force. They could mobilize their clients not only from other parts of Italy . . . but within the city itself. The urban plebs was not an united body, and sometimes we are not told what section of it took this or that action.

In annalistic accounts of the class-struggles in the early Republic, which are coloured in detail by the experience of the second and first centuries, we hear much of the dependents (clients) of the nobility supporting them against plebeian leaders. In 133 the assailants of Tiberius Gracchus included, besides members of the upper classes, "the plebs uncontaminated by pernicious

[39]Marcus Porcius Cato ("the Younger"), 95–46 B.C., statesman and opponent of Caesar, Pompey, and Crassus.

schemes". The nobility drew support within the city against Saturninus in 100 and Cinna in 87; and it may be that we should think of this coming rather from their own clients than from the urban masses in general (though Saturninus' followers were countrymen, and Cinna's new citizens from Italy, and neither is known to have had much urban backing). Cicero's claims that his return in 57 was popular, if true at all, may be so only in the sense that the dependents of the nobility demonstrated in his favour. Tacitus'[40] distinction for A.D. 69 between "the sound section of the populace, attached to the great houses" and the "sordid plebs, habitués of the circus and theatres" may be relevant. But perhaps some republican acclamations of "anti-popular" figures in the theatres might be explained by the hypothesis that they were crowded with clients, for whom their patrons had procured places.

Sallust asserts that in 63 the whole plebs was at first on Catiline's side against the government, which he explains by saying that invariably men who have nothing are envious of the "good"—the term is in practice indistinguishable from "rich"; "they hate the old order and yearn for a new; in detestation of their own lot they work for total change; to them turmoil and riots are a source not of anxiety, but of nourishment; for the destitute cannot easily suffer any loss". Cicero too more than once says that the property and fortunes of the rich were endangered by Clodius' gangs; and the existence of class-hatred in Rome can hardly be doubted; it is significant that in 52 the mob killed anyone they met wearing gold rings or fine clothes. But it was not felt or evinced by *all* the poor there; a large number depended on the upper classes.

Sallust thought that the plebs was at a disadvantage against the nobility in that it was less organized. It could do nothing except with leadership from inside the ruling class. It was also notoriously volatile, and could be persuaded to desert its leaders by the plausible demagogy of senatorial spokesmen, as in 122 and 33. And no popular leader before Clodius sought to organize his supporters in such a way that they would effectively support him beyond the brief period for which he held office.

The Twelve Tables, the ancient code of Roman law, apparently allowed freedom of association, if there was no conflict with public law. Many *collegia* of artisans as such or of persons living in the same district (*vicus*) thus arose, some at a very early date. Evidently some of them were implicated in riots in the 60s, and in 64 the senate dissolved all "except a few named corporations required by the public interest". At the time Catiline was standing for the consulship, and it was probably feared that they would exert themselves on his behalf. In 58 a law of Clodius restored the right of association, and he himself organized *collegia,* old and new, on a local basis in para-military units and provided a supply of arms. The proximity of Caesar's army and the backing the consuls who also had some soldiers gave Clodius, made it impossible for the senate to resist; and henceforth Clodius was an

[40]Roman historian, c.55–c.117.

independent power in Rome, even when a private individual, thanks to his control of the *collegia*.

Only from Cicero do we know anything of the composition of Clodius' bands. He speaks of slaves, including runaways and thugs whom Clodius had bought himself for the purpose of terrorism, criminals—"assassins freed from the jail", which Clodius "emptied into the forum"—foreigners; at best they were hirelings.... Clodius was a rich man, and according to Cicero he acquired illicit funds to distribute; no doubt he could afford to buy or hire armed escorts. Freedmen and indeed slaves were admitted to *collegia* in large numbers (as inscriptions show), and such people, foreigners by extraction, naturally formed a substantial element in his gangs. Wherever slavery is found, there are always runaways, and in the unpoliced purlieus of Rome they could easily lurk. Rome must also have provided armed robbers with ample opportunities, though it may be noted that in Roman law imprisonment was not a penalty, and if Clodius freed prisoners, they may have been not only persons merely awaiting trial but also men seized for debt. Cicero's descriptions are, however, suspect; he admits himself that it was a common rhetorical device to vilify all who attended political meetings as "exiles, slaves, madmen", and we know of at least one occasion when he chose to speak of freedmen as slaves. In his view Clodius was Catiline's heir and enjoyed the support of survivors from his movement; we may recall that Catiline had originally had the favour of the whole urban population.

Cicero writes of Clodius' followers much as contemporaries of the better classes wrote of the mobs which rioted in Paris in 1789–95 or 1848, or in English towns of the eighteenth and early nineteenth centuries; they were, it was said, banditti, desperadoes, ragamuffins, convicts and the like.... [W]herever records exist to check these descriptions they prove to be largely false. Men with criminal convictions were never more than a minority among the rioters; mostly they were men of "fixed abode and settled occupation".... In Rome the Catilinarians tried to raise "the *artisans* and slaves", and Cicero lets out that Clodius' following included shopkeepers; when he wished to gather a mob, he had the shops closed, a practice common with seditious tribunes. We should not assume on his biased testimony that artisans and shopkeepers needed to be incited or hired on every occasion to give up their day's earnings and risk their lives and limbs in a demonstration, without real grievances to demonstrate about. In 41, when famine was raging, "the people closed their shops and drove the magistrates from their places, thinking that they had no need of magistrates or crafts in a city suffering from want and robbery [by soldiers]". Then at least they acted without any demagogue to instigate and pay them. I suspect that when Shakespeare makes a carpenter and a cobbler typical members of the Roman mob, he was, by intuition, right, and that Clodius would have had little power over such people but that they had complaints and looked on him as their champion. But even if most of them (freedmen included) were artisans and shopkeepers, that would not have endeared them to Cicero; he had once spoken of "artisans, shopkeepers and all the scum in cities whom it is so easy to excite". He characterizes the Clodians as "destitute" (*egentes*); but their plight did not evoke his compassion; the word is almost a synonym with the epithet which often accompanies it—"scoundrels" (*perditi*). He recognized that the plebs was "wretched and half-starved", but added at once that it was "the bloodsucker of the treasury". It was such attitudes on the part of the governing class which gave Clodius his opportunity.

Violence was actuated by many different aims. The clients of the great houses used it simply in their patrons' interest, the followers of popular leaders sometimes merely from loyalty to their leaders. But they were attached to the "demagogues" because the demagogues were active for their welfare. Country people, including the veterans, usually sought land distributions. The burden of rent, indignation at arbitrary punishments, proposals to redistribute freedmen among all the tribes could sometimes raise an urban mob. But in 75, 67, in the heyday of Clodius' ascendancy and again in 41 and 39 hunger seems to have been the chief motive force.

When Cicero was banished, there was a scarcity; his sarcasm that the bands who pulled down his house were not going to satisfy their appetite on tiles and cement implies that they were hungry. Clodius' grain law may have increased the effective demand, which certainly outran the supply. In July 57 there was a food riot. A few days later, when the senate voted for Cicero's restoration, the price of grain providentially sank. It was but a temporary improvement. For days together the senate debated the corn supply. Cicero gave three possible explanations for the shortage: exporting provinces had no surplus, or they sent it elsewhere to get higher prices, or the suppliers held grain in store in the expectation of famine rates. On the 5th September he boasted that plenty had returned with him. This was an illusion. Prices continued to oscillate (a familiar phenomenon in many ages). On the next two days they went sky-high, and the mob rose; Cicero acknowledged that there was suffering and hunger. He and others did not venture to the senate-house. But a day or two later he risked attendance; the streets were evidently quiet again. If the rioters had been merely Clodius' hirelings, out for Cicero's blood, this would be strange; if they were exasperated artisans and shopkeepers, with work to do, they could not be kept in the streets continuously. On Cicero's motion Pompey was now invested with the procurement of grain and given wide powers, probably enabling him to requisition grain from recalcitrant suppliers. Plutarch[41] thought he secured abundance as by magic, but soon all was not well again, and now the blame could be laid on Pompey. Hence, in the scene with which I opened, the mob shouted that Pompey was starving them. In April 56 there were renewed debates on the high price of grain, and Pompey was voted more money. In August Cicero deplored high costs, the infertility of the fields, the poor harvest. Persistent scarcity was the background to continual violence....

[41]Greek moralist and biographer, c. 46–120.

If we look beyond the ambitions and machinations of the great figures of the late Republic, the main cause of its fall must in my view be found in agrarian discontents; it was the soldiers, who were of peasant origin, whose disloyalty to the Republic was fatal. The rôle of the *urban* mob was more restricted. Still, it was their clamour that gave Pompey his extraordinary command in 67 and set in motion the events that led to his alliance with Caesar in 59. And the violence in the city from 58 to 52, which was itself one result of that alliance, produced such chaos that it finally brought Pompey and the senatorial leaders together again, and helped to sever his connection with Caesar; hence the civil wars in which the Republic foundered.

Popular leaders sometimes proclaimed the sovereignty of the people. But the people who could actually attend meetings at Rome were not truly representative and were incapable of governing an empire. The only workable alternative to the government of the few was the government of one man. The interventions of the people in affairs led on to monarchy.

To the urban proletariate this was no disadvantage. It was the aristocracy who suffered from loss of liberty. Tacitus says that Augustus won over the people with bread, and this was the greatest need. They also benefited from improvements in the supply of water, from better fire-protection, better preservation of water, more splendid shows, more expenditure on buildings which gave employment. The emperors for their own security had to keep them content, and their misery was somewhat reduced. This was all they could expect in a world whose material resources remained small.

Roman Marriage

SUZANNE DIXON

There is great disagreement among historians about the nature of Roman marriage, the status of women in marriage, and whether or not spouses cared for one another. Suzanne Dixon discusses the many aspects of matrimony and firmly presents her view that Roman marriage could be harmonious, companionate, and virtuous as opposed to being an aspect of supposed Roman moral decay.

Why did Romans marry? How was a match made? Did other family members have a role in the marriage plans? What constituted a valid marriage? Was there a ceremony?

The dowry, the property a wife brought to the marriage, was an important institution. How did the dowry operate to provide protection to the wife?

What was the relationship of husband to wife? Did they often—ever—love one another? Did society expect them to be in love? Rome was a slave society in which female slaves had to submit to their owners' sexual demands. Prostitution was common. But, given these readily available sexual outlets for males, did Romans derive sexual pleasure from marriage? Did society view adultery differently for husband and for wife? Was divorce an option for both?

Dixon has the arduous task of dealing with many centuries of Roman history, and marriage certainly evolved over time. She states that the most significant change in marriage was its evolution from a merged to a separate regime. What does she mean by that? Do you see other developments in Roman marriage? Did Christianity influence marriage?

Dixon sometimes compares Roman marriage to marriage in the West today. What do you see as major similarities?

If two Roman citizens with the legal capacity to marry one another each had the consent of the *paterfamilias*[1] and lived together with the intention of being married, that was recognized as a valid marriage (*iustum conubium* or *iustae nuptiae*), and children born of the union were Roman citizens in the power of their father. This gives us a basic definition of marriage and a notion of its purpose in Roman society....

[T]he state and the community at large tended to agree that marriage was above all an institution for the production of legitimate children, and Roman legal discussions of marriage commonly focus on this question of the status of children. Illegitimate children could still be Roman citizens and suffered few legal disadvantages, but marriage remained the chief means of determining status from one generation to the next.

Marriage performed a number of roles, many of them common to marriage in most societies. It linked different families both immediately on the marriage and in subsequent generations if children resulted from the union. Dowry and inheritance, the two major forms of property transmission in the ancient world, were both tied to marriage. It should be pointed out, however, that inheritance between husband and wife, though common, was not seen as an obvious or obligatory form of inheritance (as it was between parents and children). Within the political elite, marriage was an important means of forging alliances, and thus mentions of Roman marriages crept into the works of historians, who normally disdained domestic or economic detail. Senatorial men married earlier than men lower down the social scale precisely because they needed the support of two family networks to assist them in gaining political office. Pliny[2] commends a candidate for marriage to his friend's niece by pointing out that the potential groom has already achieved office, so that his in-laws would not be put to the usual expense and trouble expected of the bride's family as part of an electoral campaign. ...Marriage extended the network of support available for routine family needs and for emergencies.

Roman marriage was clearly perceived as a family affair, not an individual decision based on personal attraction. The marriage of Cicero's[3] brother

---

[1]Father of the family; head of the household.
[2]Pliny the Younger, statesman and civil servant, A.D. 61/62–113.
[3]Roman orator and politician, 106–43 B.C.

Quintus to Pomponia, sister of Cicero's great friend Atticus, was intended to cement the ties between the two friends. Delighted to be asked to suggest a husband for his friend's young niece, Pliny enthuses: "You could not entrust me with anything which I value or welcome so much, nor could there be any more befitting duty for me than to select a young man worthy to be the father of Arulenus Rusticus's grandchildren."...He is aware of the young woman's interests and for her benefit mentions the potential groom's good looks, but the matter is clearly seen as one for family discussion, since it will have an impact on the family for generations to come. Apart from the stress on generations past and future, the letter reads rather like a standard *commendatio*[4] for a political candidate or a young man suitable for attachment to a governor's retinue. Romans saw it as quite reasonable that friends of the family would offer up such suggestions, arguing the credentials of the candidate, to be considered by the members of the other family.

This public and rather communal approach to the arrangement of marriage contrasts greatly with the modern Western norm, which is pervaded by the ideology of young romantic love, in which two people after courtship decide to marry and announce their decision to their families. It is usually at this stage that families become involved and, if the marriage transgresses the understood marriage groups (class, age, ethnic, or religious), it is borne upon the couple that the decision does have ramifications for families. If it is acceptable, the match is welcomed (though often with a certain ritual grumbling or conflict symbolically played out over wedding arrangements, timing, or gifts from the parents) and the families of the engaged couple accept that they are now linked in some way.

Roman matches were clearly arranged by the older generation. The partners probably had some say in them, depending on their own age and status within family and society. A young upper-class girl, married in her early or mid-teens, might barely be consulted, and someone like young Quintus, Cicero's nephew, would be pressured by his parents and the older generation generally to accept their choice. Widows and widowers and the divorced tended to be involved actively in the process, but it was still a communal one, a matter of discussing candidates with their supporters. One of Cato the elder's[5] lower-class *clientes* assured him that he would not dream of arranging his daughter's marriage without consulting Cato, and Cicero lists finding a husband for a daughter as one of the problems on which an orator's advice might be sought.

Legally, the *paterfamilias* arranged a match. His consent was essential for its validity. So, in theory, was the consent of the bride and groom, but jurists' quibbles make it clear that this was assumed, and even express refusal could be discounted, particularly in the case of the bride....[T]he mother of the bride (or groom) assumed the right to be actively involved in the process,

---

[4]Recommendation.
[5]Cato the Elder (234–149 B.C.), a statesman of the Roman Republic.

although she had no legal basis for this social assumption. The decision was usually celebrated by an engagement party, at which agreements ... and gifts were exchanged. Unfortunately, we do not know whether the couple then courted in the style familiar in modern societies practicing arranged matches, in which the groom conventionally woos the bride in a romantic way. It is logical to assume that matches lower down the social scale were more amenable to individual decision making, but this is not certain.

We know a little more about the marriage ceremony and the dowry arrangements, although neither dowry nor a ceremony was a legal requisite of a valid marriage. Parties and general hilarity attended the wedding rites, which probably began in the home of the bride, who then processed, attended by torchbearers, to the home of the groom. Small boys would dance around the procession making ribald jokes and grabbing at nuts thrown in their midst. The groom probably awaited the bride in his home, and on her arrival they joined in a religious rite to mark her entry into her new home. A small image representing her *Genius*[6] would be placed on the symbolic conjugal couch in the *atrium.*[7] ... Some aspects of the ceremony would vary according to personal preference, wealth, and the age of the partners. Probably the first marriage of a young girl was more elaborate than that of a mature widow or divorcée. Many funeral sculptures show bride and groom at the wedding grasping right hands symbolically, with figures in the background bearing torches. It is indeed interesting that Roman men whose sarcophagi were decorated with scenes of their military and public achievements should also have chosen their wedding and in many cases the common domestic scene of husband and wife reclining to eat dinner as images to be passed on to posterity....

...Rules gradually arose about the timing and mode of payment and return of dowry. It seems to have been generally assumed that after an initial transfer of real property—a piece of land or a house, for example—the cash component would be paid over in annual installments and that this basic arrangement would be followed by the husband in repaying the dowry at the end of the marriage.

Such rules constituted a kind of safety net for people who had not made specific arrangements or could not agree on the terms. It seems to have been usual to draw up contracts ... stating the rules for payment and return....

In the event of the husband's death, the dowry was normally returned to the widow fairly speedily. If the wife died, in the absence of special conditions the dowry was returnable only if it had been given by her father. If the marriage ended in divorce, the wife and her father had a right to sue jointly for its return, but they probably did not do this unless the usual mechanisms broke down. We have some information about the repayment of dowry on the divorce of Cicero from Terentia and on the divorce (and

[6]Guardian spirit.
[7]The entrance room.

subsequent death) of his daughter Tullia. This information suggests that negotiations about the dowry were conducted through intermediaries and that there was some flexibility in adapting the original agreement. The legal sources, for example, imply that a wife who initiated a divorce without cause might forfeit the right to the return of dowry and that the husband's right to retain part of the dowry for the maintenance of children was dependent on the wife's misconduct. In practice, however, the notion of fault seems to have been of little significance in late republican divorce. The arrangements were determined by the social assumption that children were entitled to part of the mother's dowry for their maintenance (or a daughter's dowry, which perhaps amounted to the same thing) and that a divorced mother (like a widow) needed a dowry to remarry. The provision of dowry (and, by implication, marriage) is explicitly seen as a matter of public interest:

> It is a matter of state concern that women should have secure dowries which enable them to marry. (*Dig.*[8] . . .)
> A case involving dowry takes priority at any time and in any place for it is actually in the public interest that dowries be preserved for women, since it is of the utmost necessity that women are dowered for the purpose of bringing forth progeny and replenishing the state with [citizen] children. . . . (*Dig.* . . .)

The tablets or papyrus scroll in which the dotal agreement was recorded did not constitute a marriage contract or a wedding certificate in the modern sense, but it could be used to demonstrate that a marriage had taken place, and it would be invoked in the reassignment of property and money on the dissolution of the match. This forethought again conflicts somewhat with modern romantic notions of marriage. It is not clear whether the Romans were more materialistic than moderns or simply more realistic and efficient about their materialism. The common law tradition encouraged the presumption that the property of husband and wife was held in common. Perhaps as a result of this tradition (or because the law reflected an entrenched social assumption), Anglophone married couples today, regardless of their legal claims, still tend to treat their property as joint for the duration of the marriage. Divorce or death then forces a decision on them at a time when they are least likely to be capable of rational decision making. The trauma of divorce is exacerbated by the modern perception that it constitutes a personal failure to measure up to society's ideal of a lifelong partnership. The Romans also had an ideal of marriage as a lifelong union, while in fact they practiced remarriage (on the death or divorce of spouses), very much as modern Western cultures do. They seem to have been more pragmatic about their solutions, and the custom of bargaining through intermediaries (a general feature of Roman social relations) apparently worked fairly well. In

[8]The Digest, statements of renown jurisprudents, contained in the *Corpus iuris civilis,* the "body of civil law," a collection of Roman laws, decrees, and imperial orders drawn up during the reign of the Emperor Justinian (527–565).

the modern world, negotiation tends to be carried out directly by the parties or through lawyers. Prenuptial agreements and that most recent innovation, mediation, are closer to the Roman system, except that Romans began the process of mediation before marriage, then renewed it at its end.

I stated at the outset that the purpose of Roman marriage was the production of legitimate citizen children. It is from this that so many other consequences flow for subsequent generations. The production of legitimate citizen children is perennially the basis of any state's concern with marriage. When the Roman census was held, it was traditional for the censors [9] to put to men of the equestrian[10] and senatorial orders the question, "Have you married for the purpose of creating children?" ... [A]necdotes and comments imply that the public and private ideology of Roman marriage was continually associated with the desire for progeny but that the concept of marriage included other elements, such as compatibility, partnership, and love. This is more obviously the case from the first century B.C. on, though perhaps it is merely a reflection of the greater quantity and variety of sources available to the historian from that period. It is, however, plausible that there was a change in sentiment, just as there was in marriage preference. For example, anecdotal stories about the earlier period tend to focus on the "external" aspects of married life—the wife's fertility, industry, and chastity—rather than the feelings husband and wife held for each other. It becomes clear that marriage, while still firmly associated with the hope of children, was also expected to produce other satisfactions.

It is interesting that the apparent change coincides with the greater incidence of divorce, which is no longer associated with the adultery of the wife. In his *Life* of the general Aemilius Paullus, Plutarch[11] mentions Paullus's divorce of his first wife Papiria, which seemed inexplicable to his contemporaries. Plutarch then cites a general anecdote about "a Roman" who divorced his wife in spite of his friend's remonstrances that she was fertile, discreet, and altogether a good wife. The man picked up his sandal and said that it looked sound to the onlooker, but only the wearer could tell where it hurt. Plutarch agrees that it is the little everyday irritations that make some marriages unbearable. The old idea that divorce was rare and shameful seems to have passed away by the second century B.C. Probably the husband had to initiate divorce if the wife were in his *manus*,[12] but an agreement could probably be reached in many cases, and gradually the separate marital regime, in which women could also initiate divorce, became dominant. In a society where so much was public, divorce now became

[9]Two censors oversaw the census of Roman citizens and their property.

[10]Economic rank below senator. In the late Republic, a member of the equestrian order was usually a businessman.

[11]Greek moralist and biographer, c. 46–120.

[12]Legal control.

a matter for speculation, because the reason for divorces was not known. Aemilius Paullus's divorce was the precursor of the new style.

Partnership becomes an automatic inclusion in discussions of marriage. Livy,[13] writing in the Augustan period[14] about early Rome, creates a portrait of a virtuous soldier symbolic of the simplicity of the past who enjoys a partnership with his wife in his fortunes, his estate, and his children. Such references—usually expressed from the husband's perspective—proliferate. The notion that a wife was a welcome partner in prosperity and adversity was invoked, for example, by the emperor Augustus in Dio's[15] representation of his attempt to persuade the men of the upper classes to marry and by senators arguing that provincial governors should be permitted to take their wives with them on tours of duty rather than be deprived of their companionship. The notion of marriage as partnership and companionship was so established, then, as to be part of the civic rhetoric and the public sphere. The many literary and epigraphic references to companionship, mutual loyalty and support, and the ideal of a happy and harmonious marriage show that this was part of a popular ideal as well as public and imperial ideology.

The notion of *concordia,* or harmony, in marriage was frequently mentioned in literature and in epitaphs boasting that marriages, especially long marriages, had been without discord.... Ovid[16] has the aged bucolic couple Baucis and Philemon speak of their harmony throughout their long marriage leading to their wish to die together. The elder Arria[17] defends her decision to commit suicide on her husband's condemnation by arguing that she and he had such a long and harmonious marriage. When this ideal was attached to the imperial family, it carried the implication that harmony ensured stable rule and succession....

... [T]he point to note is that the *ideal* of harmony was almost as strongly embedded in the Roman notion of marriage as was its reproductive purpose. Like the association of marriage and children, it is reflected in public and private discourse. Marriage was viewed, therefore, as the proper vehicle for continuing the citizenship and serving the state into the next generation, for maintaining an individual family or a particular order. It was also viewed, both privately and officially, as a partnership in which each side supported the other and which was ideally harmonious and long-lasting.

At Rome, marriage was essentially a private arrangement, but it had legal implications, and the state occasionally intervened to remedy what

---

[13]Titus Livy, Roman historian, 59 B.C.–A.D. 17.

[14]During the reign of Emperor Augustus, 27 B.C.–A.D. 14.

[15]Dio Cassius, statesman and historian, late second to early third century A.D.

[16]Poet (43 B.C.–A.D. 18), known for his love poems, especially *The Art of Love,* and for his mythological work, *The Metamorphoses.*

[17]Arria the elder was the model of a dutiful wife because she accompanied her husband into exile and because she courageously committed suicide in order to show him that it was not difficult.

were perceived as injustices or anomalies. . . . Legal aspects of marriage—the capacity to marry, the payment of dowry, its return on the dissolution of the marriage—are set in the context of marriage as a social phenomenon, an important element of Roman family relations embedded in Roman notions of status, sentiment, and economic exchange. It is important to test any legal principles against practice as far as it can be ascertained not only from individual decisions recorded in the *Codices*[18] but from literary evidence (particularly the law court speeches of Cicero and the letters of Cicero and Pliny) and from inscriptions and papyri. . . . Some scholars now are more inclined to speak of strategies than of legal rules and make a persistent attempt to plot change over time, relating developments in marriage to other trends in Roman society. This presents a contrast with the earlier tendency to theorize from the *Digest* as if it were timeless and perfectly reflected Roman society.

We have seen that the partners in a Roman marriage were Roman citizens or, more rarely, people with the *ius conubii*, the right to contract a valid Roman marriage with Roman citizens, and that they had to have the *affectio maritalis*, the intention of being married. The contract itself was legally drawn up between two families through the heads of the families. If neither bride nor groom had a living father, the groom would be a *paterfamilias*, and the bride would be a full party to her own contract, with her *tutor*[19] giving his assent to the dotal arrangements and, if applicable, to her transfer to the husband's power or *manus*. Marriage for the most part was governed by customary rules rather than formal law. The legal history of marriage at Rome could be seen as a slow tendency for the state to regulate aspects of an essentially private arrangement.

It is particularly difficult to determine the nature of marriage in early Rome. Later sources are understandably vague or confidently oblivious of the distinction between law and custom, and the picture is blurred by the tendency to mythologize the past. Indeed, reference to marriage in early Rome is almost always part of a moral argument deploring contemporary practice. The traditional extent of the husband's power is a popular theme. Dionysius of Halicarnassus,[20] writing in the time of Augustus, comments approvingly on regal Rome of the eighth century B.C.:

> By passing a single law, Romulus[21] reduced women to modesty. The law was as follows: that a proper wife, who had passed into the *manus* of her husband by a sacral marriage (by *confarreatio*), should have a partnership with him in all his goods and rites. . . . Four relatives would decide the following issues in conjunction with the husband: these included adultery and whether the wife

---

[18]Late imperial (third through early sixth centuries) orders.

[19]Guardian.

[20]Greek historian of Rome, first century B.C.

[21]One of the mythical founders of Rome.

proved to have drunk wine, for Romulus allowed that either of these offences could be punished by death.

This "law" is, then, an affirmation of the power of the family to hold a *consilium*[22] to determine vital issues, including the discipline of family members, and represents a limitation on the husband's power in that capital punishment had to be a group decision. In Livy's account of the traditional story of Lucretia, set at the close of the regal period (late sixth-century B.C.), Lucretia[23] summons a meeting of her husband, her father, and two of their friends to announce that she has been raped, intends to commit suicide, and expects them to avenge her. The presumption here is that the families of husband and wife would be represented at a *consilium*. Perhaps the most frequently quoted passage on the subject is the statement by Cato the elder in the second century B.C. that a husband had the right to sit in judgment on his wife, even for offenses such as drunkenness, but that she had no such right to judge him, even if she caught him in the act of adultery. Dionysius of Halicarnassus reinforces this picture with the statement that Romulus gave the Roman *paterfamilias* full powers over wife and child, and Plutarch, writing in the second century A.D. in Greece, continued the tradition with the comment that Romulus's laws one thousand years earlier had allowed the husband the right to divorce his wife but she had no such right.

It is very likely that the husband's powers were restricted by custom and the relative interest and power of the wife's relations. It is, however, plausible that divorce, insofar as it occurred in early Rome, was initiated only by the husband and implied a severe marital fault—almost necessarily adultery—on the part of the woman. It is also generally agreed that although there were in archaic Rome two distinct types of marriage, one marking the woman's full legal entry into the family of her husband and the other allowing her to retain her legal status as a member of the family of her birth, most marriages in the early period did involve the transfer of the woman to the husband's family and to his power.... This legal transfer could occur by *confarreatio, coemptio*,[24] or *usus*.[25] *Confarreatio* was an elaborate ceremony open only to patricians and included a joint sacral meal of prescribed foods. Divorce was not possible from this form of marriage, which became very rare.

The "imaginary sale" of *coemptio* remained a common way in which a woman passed into the husband's *manus*. The "sale" resembled other legal ceremonies, such as the emancipation of a child from *patria potestas*,[26] the manumission of a slave, or a Roman will. A woman could also come into

---

[22]Council, usually of family and friends. (Author's note.)

[23]Legendary model of the perfect Roman wife, chaste and hard-working.

[24]A formal "sale" involving change of legal status, for example, by a woman before making a will. (Author's note.)

[25]Use.

[26]The father's power.

her husband's *manus* if she spent a full year under his roof (*usus*) but this consequence of marriage could be avoided if she spent three nights away from the conjugal home. This practice seems to have become obsolete or unusual by the late Republic and certainly by the early Empire. In fact, by the middle of the first century B.C. there seems to have been a general preference for the form of marriage in which the woman retained her natal status and separate property.

... A woman who had entered her husband's *manus* on marriage became one of his *sui heredes,* or direct heirs, and inherited equally with their children on his death. Any property she owned at the time of marriage or acquired afterwards became part of the joint family holding owned by the husband as *paterfamilias.* In practice, such property seems to have been treated as dowry, which she could recover separately on the husband's death by the second century B.C. ...

... Cicero tells us that all property of a wife *in manu mariti*[27] was legally classified as dowry by the middle of the first century B.C. This must have been a response to the popularity of the "separate regime" form of marriage, because it virtually restored the widow who had been *in manu mariti* to full ownership of "her" property, which as dowry was now recoverable in its own right rather than being merged with the conjugal holding so that the whole could be evenly divided between herself and her children.

The most significant historical development in Roman marriage is surely this shift from a merged to a separate regime, that is, from the earlier form in which the woman normally entered the husband's *manus* to the later form in which the wife retained her status as *filiafamilias*[28] or, if her father were dead, *sui iuris.*[29] It is frustrating that nobody has been able fully to explain the shift or to plot it precisely. Authors have sometimes called the separate-regime style of marriage "free marriage" and have interpreted the shift as one to greater individual female power. ...

Certainly, the wife was not in the husband's formal control and had greater freedom to manage her own property and to initiate divorce. The problem is in determining how the *ancients* viewed the different marriage styles and, therefore, what moved them to alter their preference over time. It was probably a corporate decision based on corporate interest. At first glance it seems to be in the interest of the bride's family to defer the final division of the patrimony in any generation until the father's death. The dowry seems to have represented a smaller share of the family holding than a daughter's intestate (or testamentary) portion. This must be offset against the likelihood that so many women would be *sui iuris* at the time of marriage or within a few years of it because of the death of the father. The shift might have

---

[27]In the legal control of the husband.

[28]Daughter of the family.

[29]Independent of the father's or the husband's power.

conferred on the woman's brothers greater control of her fortune, but...the tendency was to view a woman's property as destined eventually for her children, and even brothers who were *tutores* must have given permission for their sisters to make wills in favor of the brothers' nephews and nieces. In time, the *tutela*[30] of male relations over women was abolished, surely because the men of the family had no particular interest in it and did not see it as a means of keeping property in the family or under their control.

The Roman sources do not discuss the shift explicitly. The change could well be linked with economic transformations in Roman society, for the attitude towards wealth, particularly landed wealth, altered significantly from the third century B.C. Without reverting to Roman myth about the simplicity of the past, we can still acknowledge that after the second Punic War[31] and the subsequent expansion into the eastern Mediterranean, Romans of the elite class became more involved in conspicuous consumption, such as the building of elaborate private homes and gardens and public buildings such as temples, and less tied to the concept of maintaining landed holdings within the same family. The preferred early system of marriage, like the ideal system of inheritance enshrined in the rules on intestate succession, seems to have been posited on a more static society in which a woman moved physically from the holding of her father to that of her husband and remained there for life, sinking her own property into her husband's and identifying with his family and therefore with the children of the marriage (who necessarily belonged to his family).

From the second century B.C., this scenario was no longer followed by an aristocracy that treated land as a commodity to be exploited in any way offered. In spite of legislation directed against the concentration of wealth in female hands, we hear increasingly of wealthy women such as Aemilia and her daughter Cornelia (mother of the Gracchi)[32] in the second century B.C. In the first century B.C. women such as Caecilia Metella, Servilia, Clodia, and Fulvia seem to be characteristic of the political elite, prominent for their wealth, their patronage, and, to an extent, their public activity and image. The establishment of an *actio rei uxoriae*[33] for the return of dowry to a woman after divorce or widowhood slightly precedes these other developments and suggests that divorce and the departure of the widow from her marital home had already become more common than in early Rome. Even allowing for the recurrent historical problem of the greater abundance and reliability of sources for the later Republic, it is difficult to avoid the conclusion that the changing character of upper-class wealth and spending, the greater public

---

[30] A form of guardianship imposed on women and young children *sui iuris*. (Author's note.)

[31] 218–201 B.C.

[32] Tiberius Sempronius Gracchus (163–133 B.C.) and Gaius Sempronius Gracchus (153–121 B.C.), brothers who were Roman statesmen and reformers.

[33] A legal action for the recovery of dowry on the dissolution of marriage. (Author's note.)

profile of upper-class women, and the change in marriage preference and frequency of divorce are all somehow linked.

The affiliation of married women seems also to have changed from the early stress on the *univira*, the woman with one husband who came to him as a young *filiafamilias* and died as his *materfamilias*.[34] The term was extended to the widow who declined remarriage out of loyalty to her husband's memory. From the time of the late Republic at least, widows were likely to remarry, and divorce became quite common and casual. The relative instability of marriage might have been tied to the volatility of elite political alliances in that period, but the tendency continued in times of political calm. Perhaps the earlier ideal, elaborated in ritual and sentimental ideology, was actually grounded in the assumption of a static property system in which women moved only once in a lifetime, taking with them their intestate portion, which remained with their conjugal family whether they died in the marriage or not. The presumption of the late Republic is that women will move into other marriages, taking their property with them but on the understanding that their children will eventually share it. Politically, married women of the elite promoted the interests of their brothers and sons rather than those of their husbands. Economically, they favored their children. Emotionally, they showed great affection and loyalty towards their husbands. All of these characteristics are not only displayed by the actions of the elite women best documented by the sources but lauded as the proper behavior of an ideal wife, mother, or sister.

In a general way, the history of marriage and the family seems to be characterized by a very slow erosion of the powers of the *paterfamilias*, both as father and as husband. . . . [S]tories about early Rome are typically examples of extreme husbandly harshness, but even they reveal the importance of the *consilium* as a possible check on his arbitrary exercise of power. . . . Even the shocking story of the husband who successfully defended his fatal assault on his wife with the excuse that she was a drunkard reveals that he was tried for the murder, however unsatisfactory we might find the outcome. By the early Empire, the *consilium* as a medium for passing judgment on wives seems to have become obsolete, presumably because wives were no longer seen as being in their husband's power and because divorce was a remedy readily available to both parties. . . .

. . . The Augustan legislation[35] on adultery transferred much of the power of adultery trials to the public sphere, and such powers as remained tended to lie with the father of the errant woman rather than with the husband, although he had a right to punish summarily a male adulterer caught in the act in his own home.

---

[34]Mother of the family.

[35]Worried about the family life of the Roman elite, Emperor Augustus established laws that, in addition to making the state responsible for the punishment of female adultery, concerned marriage and divorce procedures and rewarded couples that had more than three children.

Approximately one century after the Augustan legislation on marriage and the family, Tacitus[36] wrote that in characterizing the act of adultery as a breach of the religious and legal code Augustus exceeded the more lenient attitude of the ancestors and even went further than his own laws. It is not quite clear what he meant by this, but the gist of his statement is that marriage and offenses against marriage had belonged traditionally to the private realm. Any problems that arose, including adultery committed by the wife, were dealt with by the families involved. The legislation sponsored or actually inspired by Augustus represents a strong and significant incursion by the state into this private sphere.

This statement needs some qualification. We have already seen that the censors regularly put to men the question whether they had married for the purpose of producing children. . . . There were also times when the aediles[37] had, as public officials, judged cases of adultery and other female sexual transgressions. There had, moreover, been rules limiting intermarriage even between citizens. Until the *Lex Canuleia*,[38] of ca. 445 B.C., marriage between patricians and plebeians could not produce legitimate issue and was in effect invalid. Yet at this time Latins and many Italians had *conubium* with Roman citizens; that is, they had the capacity to contract proper legal marriages with Romans which could produce legitimate Roman citizen children. There is some suggestion that marriage between freed and free-born Roman citizens was either illegal or subject to strong social sanctions, including condemnation by the censor. Such unions were not prevented or punished by the law in the modern sense, but the effect of the law was to invalidate the union, that is, to determine that any children of the union were not legitimate Roman citizens. . . .

In sum, the law had always had some relevance to issues of marriage and related questions, such as betrothal, dowry, divorce, and the status of children. Notwithstanding, the Augustan legislation passed in at least two blocks, in 18 B.C. as the *Lex Papia Poppaea*[39] and in A.D. 9 as the *Lex Iulia*,[40] did represent a new development. Augustus saw himself as a moral crusader, one who was bound to restore the pristine virtue of the Roman state. He perceived a failure, particularly in the upper class, to marry and have children, and his legislation was designed to provide incentives in the form of more rapid promotion through the political and administrative ranks and advantages in inheritance for those who married and produced children, with penalties for those who failed to conform to his requirements. In addition, his legislation

[36]Roman historian, c.55–c.117.

[37]Elected officials who supervised the grain trade, public buildings, archives, public games, and the physical fabric of the city.

[38]Canulean Law, which allowed marriage between patricians and plebeians.

[39]The Papia-Poppaean Law attempted to have Romans marry others in the same social class.

[40]With the intent of increasing the population, the Julian Law established marriage as a duty for Roman patricians.

attempted to formalize divorce by requiring a formal letter of divorce and witnesses and by compelling husbands to divorce adulterous wives. Men were also to be punished as criminals for committing adultery with married women or fornication . . . with single women.

The laws were not markedly successful in suppressing adultery or propagating the Roman population. Marriage was probably already popular with those who could afford it and had marriageable partners available; indeed, some made a career of marriage, like their modern equivalents. It is therefore not clear whether there genuinely was a serious demographic and moral problem in Augustus's day. Nor is it entirely clear whether he hoped that his legislation would affect all echelons of society, since the rewards and penalties were largely directed towards the upper class, with significant property to bequeath and with political ambitions to satisfy. The legislation aroused strong protests from men of the upper classes, and Augustus chose to respond to these in a variety of ways. He himself mounted a demonstration of sorts by appearing in public with his grandchildren, in effect presenting a counter-example to errant citizens. He also harangued recalcitrant upper-class bachelors and praised married men in speeches. . . .

The legislation itself has not been well preserved, so we must rely heavily on ancient summaries of the laws. The provisions on adultery were retained in the sixth century A.D. *Digest*, but Justinian finally eradicated many references to rewards for marriage and parenthood because of the new Christian regard for celibacy and theoretical dislike of the remarriage of widows. From what can be pieced together we get a sense of Augustus's moral purpose. He seems, in part, to have aimed at providing a eugenically sound ruling class for the empire, furnishing Italian soldiers for the imperial army and ensuring the survival of the great estates of the aristocracy. His methods were not successful; overall, their greatest significance is for the violence and extent of his intrusion into the private sphere. Henceforth, adultery was a criminal offense which could, moreover, be prosecuted by anyone moved by moral outrage, malice, or the hope of gaining a percentage of the confiscated wealth of convicted miscreants. This ensured the persistence of accusations and trials, and the legislation, slightly modified from time to time, was maintained by subsequent emperors. . . .

Just as marriage continued to consist of two Romans with the capacity and desire to marry cohabiting, so divorce continued to be a matter of mutual agreement or unilateral repudiation, instantaneous in its effect in either case and requiring no recourse to state authorities unless the parties failed to agree on the restitution of dowry. In many respects, then, Roman marriage was more "private" than many of its modern equivalents. The theory and practice of marriage was monogamous, but there was no equivalent to the penalties of some modern states for bigamy as a crime.

It was to be expected that Christianity would have some impact on Roman marriage, but in fact the legal and social impact was less immediate and less strong than one might have imagined, given the early theological decision that marriage was a sacrament. Divorce by mutual consent remained straightforward even under Justinian's legislation, but it became more difficult for one partner—especially the wife—to institute divorce even in the face of clear hardship. Among themselves, Christians imposed social penalties on those who remarried or who married out of the proper groups, and in time they formulated many complicated prohibitions on marriage between quite distant relations or between people related only by marriage or betrothals (or even by relations of godparenthood).

In earlier Roman law, marriages between close kin had been subject to sanctions, but it is not clear that it was ever illegal in the sense that it was a crime. There was a tradition that cousin marriage had been illegal or discountenanced in archaic Rome, but it seems to have been acceptable from an early period. . . . Authors of the late Republic and early Empire certainly seem to find nothing worthy of comment in the marriage of cousins. Cousin marriage has some obvious advantages for the preservation of estates in families and is in many societies a favored mode (given the usual prohibition on marriage between siblings). . . .

New prohibitions were introduced from time to time in the imperial era. The prohibition against a provincial governor marrying somebody within his province, against a *tutor* or his son marrying a *pupilla* (ward), against senators marrying freedwomen or actresses, and so on, all show a certain tendency to intervene in the private sphere of marriage, which by modern standards is surprising only in the emphasis on status. In general, then, it can be said that marriage remained as essentially private affair on which the state intermittently intruded, particularly where there was some economic advantage to be gained from the imposition of penalties. In other cases, the state tended to impose as rules accepted community norms. It is, for example, improbable that a great number of senators were ever given to marriage with freed slaves, and such rules (like the earlier prohibition on marriage between patricians and plebeians in an era when the distinction was meaningful) reflected the actual marriage groups. Subsequent legislation prohibiting marriage between Jews and Christians reflected the ideology of the official religion. It is not clear how strictly such rules were applied at any stage. They could have been enforced by recourse to the Julian laws on adultery, since people living in such relationships were actually committing adultery or fornication in legal terms, but . . . there was considerable acceptance of certain types of *de facto* marriage, e.g., soldier marriage or unions between slave and free partners.

The ground was certainly laid in the classical period for the harder line eventually followed by Christian rulers, who saw marriage as a matter for public regulation. The earlier trend away from husbands' absolute rights was also undermined in late antiquity, and women, subject to public penalties for adultery, gradually lost their relative equality with the increasing Christian stress on wifely endurance and one-sided virtue in marriage and on the impropriety of widow remarriage.

No Roman thinks it shameful to take his wife to a dinner party. At home the wife, as mistress of the household, takes first place in it and is the center of its entertaining. Things are very different in Greece, where the wife is never present at dinner, except for a family party, and spends all her time in the Women's Quarter, separated from the rest of the house—an area broached only by close male relatives.

—*Cornelius Nepos*[41]

...We have seen that partnership and harmony were Roman marital ideals. The relative social visibility of Roman women and the fact that men such as Cicero and Pliny had women friends, their references to the literary interests of such women (e.g., Juvenal's[42] savage attacks in the Sixth Satire on women who talk incessantly about politics, literature, or philology) all suggest a society in which a married couple might have interests and activities in common that give some meaning to the ideal of partnership beyond a community of interest in their children and the family generally.

There are serious problems in attempting to analyze relationships and feelings even in a contemporary society, where taped interviews and questionnaires give a more solid base to speculation. The evidence of attitudes within Roman marriages is difficult to interpret....

...We know that matches were commonly arranged by the older generation with an eye to material and political advantage, that divorce was easy and common, that many marriages ended fairly soon with the death of one partner and subsequent remarriage. Scholars have argued that Roman marriage, especially within the political elite, therefore engaged little of the partners' emotions and that there was scant likelihood that affectionate feelings would develop in such a milieu. Yet the four surviving letters from Cicero to his wife during his exile 58–57 B.C. reveal his dependence on her emotional and practical support. Consider, for example:

If these misfortunes are permanent, I truly desire to see you, light of my life...as soon as possible and for you to remain in my embrace, since neither the gods whom you have cultivated so virtuously nor the men whom I assiduously served have rendered us our proper return.

He ends his letter with the following:

Take good care of yourself, as far as you are able, and believe me when I say that I am more desperately perturbed by your wretched position than by my own. My Terentia, most faithful and best of wives, and my most beloved little daughter and our one remaining hope, Cicero—farewell.

Letters to Terentia are replete with expressions of longing for her and terms of endearment: "most faithful and best of wives," "light of my life, my longing," "my own life," "dearer to me than anything ever." Ovid,

[41] Roman biographer, c.99–24 B.C.
[42] Roman satirist, c.55–c.140.

exiled to the Levant a generation later, uses the same or similar expressions to his wife: "dearest," "light of my life," "best of wives." ...

... Arria the elder was famous for following her dissident Stoic husband into exile and taking the lead in showing him how to commit suicide heroically. Pliny noted that she had also committed other brave acts which were less well known. She had, at one stage, attended her husband and son, who were both critically ill. The boy died, but she kept the sad news from her husband until he recovered. Pliny preserved her deeds for posterity:

> Indeed, that was a glorious act of hers, to draw the blade, to plunge it into her breast and to pull out the dagger and offer it to her husband, to utter besides the immortal, almost divine words, "It does not hurt, Paetus." But fame and posterity were before her eyes when she did those deeds and said those words. How much more glorious it was for her, without the incentive of immortality and fame, to hold back her tears, to suppress her grief, to go on acting the part of a mother, when she had lost her son.

There was a *genre* of such inspirational tales. ...

We have already seen the great popularity of the tombstone formulae celebrating marriages without discord. There was another, somewhat less common formula, used more by wives and typically following a statement of the length of the marriage, that the only unhappy day in that time was the day of the husband's death. Sometimes these briefer epitaphs also give sufficient detail to make it clear that the sentiments are no empty convention. Such is [the inscription] where the bereaved husband follows his recital of his wife's virtues with the statement that he has added these details so that people reading the epitaph would understand how much they loved each other. Consider, too, the woman whose husband had befriended her as a young slave girl, bought her out of slavery, and married her. This suggests that even the most conventional formulae, far from being "essentially loveless," might represent a shorthand for much stronger emotions which could not be spelled out for reasons of custom and economy.

It has also been claimed that Roman men did not expect to gain sexual satisfaction from their wives but sought this with mistresses. Certainly the tradition of passionate attachment is associated with mistresses of a lower social group, but the literary conventions are adopted by authors speaking of married love. This is the case with Sulpicia's[43] love poetry to her husband, with Ovid's yearning for his absent wife, with Statius's[44] claim that he had been struck as by a thunderbolt with love for his wife, and with Pliny's letter to his young wife lamenting her absence and stressing his longing for her:

> I am seized by unbelievable longing for you. The reason is above all my love, but secondarily the fact that we are not used to being apart. This is why I spend the

[43]Roman poetess, late first century B.C.

[44]Poet, c. 45–96.

greater part of the night haunted by your image; this is why from time to time my feet lead me (the right expression!) of their own accord to your room at the times I was accustomed to frequent you; this is why, in short, I retreat, morbid and disconsolate, like an excluded lover from an unwelcoming doorway. The only time free of these torments is time spent in the forum and in friends' law cases. Just imagine what my life is like—I, for whom you are the respite from toil, the solace of my wretchedness and anxieties. Farewell.

There are probably elements of literary conceit in all of these, but all see it as appropriate to adopt the language and imagery of passionate, romantic love when speaking of married love.

Cato the elder's famous punishment of the senator who embraced his wife passionately before their young daughter, Seneca's[45] insistence that men should not make love too ardently to their wives, Lucretius's[46] contrast between the modest immobility of a wife and the unseemly coital gyrations of a prostitute, and Plutarch's caution against the use by wives of aphrodisiacs on their husbands all imply a dominant ideology of moderation and decorum in married relations, particularly as displayed in public behavior. Yet the very fact that these warnings are seen as necessary is an indication that married couples did show the symptoms of sexual infatuation celebrated by the lyric poets. Plutarch's contrast between the heady, obsessive attachment of newlyweds and the stabler and more profound love between long-married partners is a modern commonplace. The references in Catullus[47] . . . to burning passion and jealousy between the bridal pair imply that such references are stock elements of wedding songs and other ritual. Tacitus's account of the murder of a woman by her husband after a stormy night of alternating reconciliation and quarreling and the references to the well-known passion of the Stoic Seneca himself for his young wife remind us that this decorous ideal was not always realized (and that we should not take philosophical generalization too seriously?). Consider Seneca's own words:

> This is what I said to my Paulina, who tells me to watch out for my health. Because I know that her life is inextricably bound with my own, I begin to be considerate of myself as a way of considering her. And although old age has made me brave in many respects, I am losing this advantage of my state of life . . . . Sometimes, however pressing the reasons are for ending it, life must be maintained for the sake of our loved ones even at the cost of extreme pain. . . . He who does not think enough of his wife or friend to hang on longer to life but is obstinate in choosing death, is effete.

In the end Nero[48] gave him no choice about the suicide.

---

[45] Roman statesman and philosopher, 3 B.C.–A.D. 65.

[46] Roman poet, c.99–55 B.C.

[47] Roman lyric poet, c.84–c.54 B.C.

[48] Emperor, A.D. 54–68.

There is no doubt that men did have extramarital sexual relationships with women of their own class—Augustus's laws against adultery did not, after all, stop the practice!—and with others who were not seen as marriageable. Such phenomena are hardly unknown in the modern world, where sexual satisfaction is a highly publicized expectation of the partners. A dual sexual standard certainly prevailed—again, this is hardly unique to Roman society, upper-class or otherwise. In the ancient world, sex outside marriage might even have been seen as a means of limiting the legitimate family, and gratification of male sexual whims was easy in a society with an abundance of slaves of both sexes lacking any rights. Many men probably did find casual and adulterous sex an exciting variation from sex with a respected and even beloved wife of many years' standing. I have no difficulty in believing that wives might have felt the same. Yet this scarcely justifies a firm statement that Romans saw sexual satisfaction as entirely distinct from marriage. There is enough contrary evidence to give us pause in making absolute pronouncements on the subject.

It will be apparent by now that most of the examples of legendary married love and heroic conjugal *fides*[49] concern women. It is also true that wives are overrepresented in epitaphs. This reflects the generally masculine orientation of the sources and probably the notion that men should be identified primarily by their jobs or public offices, and women by their position in the family. There are, to be sure, husbands known for their extraordinary love, such as Tiberius Sempronius Gracchus, who virtually chose to predecease his young wife Cornelia when faced with an omen in the form of two snakes, one male and one female, and husbands who killed themselves on the death of a wife. The usual trend, however, is to laud the courage and loyalty of wives. Given the historical tendency for women to retain their status after marriage as members of their own natal families and the acknowledged identification of elite women with their brothers' interests rather than their husbands', the ideal and reality of wifely loyalty in an age of frequent divorce is quite striking.

Another curiosity already noted above is the persistence of the ideal of the *univira,* the woman with only one husband. This soubriquet was applied originally to the woman who had come to her husband as a young virgin in her father's power, transferred to the husband's *manus,* and died before him. By the late Republic it came to be applied approvingly to widows who chose to remain single out of loyalty to their husband's memory and their children's interest. The ideal is celebrated in tombstones and literature against a background of frequent remarriage occasioned by divorce and spousal death. The law ... acknowledged the right of widows and divorcées to the full or partial return of dowry so that they could marry but increasingly applied safeguards for the children of the earlier marriage against the designs of a stepfather. How did the ideal manage to persist, then? Because, like many

---

[49]Faith, reliance, promise.

ideals, it was sometimes met, and because people accepted it as part of their culture. This paradox (if it is a paradox) is perfectly paralleled in modern states, where people promise to marry until parted by death and plan their happy life together as if unaware of the statistics that give them such a high chance of divorce and widowhood. The ideal of romantic love—once only and for life—is active today, promoted by literature, the visual media, and pop songs, all produced by industries not distinguished by great individual adherence to the ideal. But hope springs eternal. Perhaps it is not so ironic that Augustus, himself scarcely chaste, should have promoted moral legislation and the ideals of marriage and family, for he and Livia[50] were known for their devotion to each other and, once they had contracted the "right" marriage, stuck with it.

It is worth repeating that feelings are very difficult to reconstruct historically. It is possible to argue both ways about Roman marriage. Evidence of cold-blooded political marriage and divorce abound, and it could be maintained that tombstones and tales of model marriages are empty conventions against a background of arranged matches and frequent remarriage. This is the sort of evidence that influences scholars . . . to characterize Roman marriage, especially within the elite, as emotionally unrewarding. Yet the references to the ideal of happiness or harmony, the relative trouble taken to comment on marriages and the dead spouse in tombstones, and the popularity of stories of overriding conjugal love all suggest that these matches, arranged by the older generation for reasons of material and political advantage, were expected to yield affectionate, companionable relationships and that this happened in numerous cases.

. . . Roman marriages, undertaken for the purpose of producing legitimate citizen children, performed legal and emotional functions. The legal aspects involved the status of the partners and the children of the union and, to an extent, their economic rights and obligations. Such considerations would have loomed large in people's lives, but marriage was also viewed ideally as a source of comfort and happiness. Scholars have questioned whether these ideals could have been achieved against a background of arranged matches and casual divorce, but there is sufficient evidence to suggest not only that the political elite often formed loving and loyal conjugal partnerships but that slaves and soldiers, their lives subject to so much external disruption and control, also sought and sometimes fulfilled these ideals even when denied the full legal benefits of marriage.

Those studies of marriage (or concubinage) which were not entirely concerned with legal detail have often been dominated by the view that Roman marriage showed all the symptoms of the Roman moral decline so beloved of popular films and novels. This picture of decline probably owes much to the legislation of Augustus and the writings of the early church fathers and it has been fleshed out by the satirists' racy accounts of adultery

---

[50](58 B.C.–A.D. 29), wife to Augustus, the first Roman emperor.

and grossness. Augustus's assumption of resistance to marriage is difficult now to assess, and Christian distaste for concubinage and divorce have given an impression that is difficult to sustain in face of the evidence that Romans generally wished to marry and that they hoped for and often found harmony and comfort in marriage. Some also committed adultery, some divorced, and many remarried repeatedly on the death or divorce of spouses. The overall picture does not seem to be one of depravity or disregard for marriage. On the contrary, epitaphs proclaim the virtues of spouses (and, by implication, of the married state), and dramatic stories circulated of model spouses, especially wives, whose love and loyalty gave inspiration and sentimental gratification to a wide audience.

It is frustrating that we cannot adequately explain the changes which did take place in Roman marriage. These changes rest in the alteration of preference whereby women (or their fathers or families for them) chose to retain their status as a member of their own natal families after marriage. These women fully acknowledged their obligations to the children of the marriage and were encouraged to do so by the community, including their own relations, so it is not entirely explicable in terms of retention of family holdings. Husband and wife seem to have looked to each other more for emotional than for financial support; this is reflected in the inheritance laws giving low priority to succession between them and the custom limiting their gifts to one another. Yet there are so many exceptions to this tendency that it is difficult to make too much of it beyond the statement that a married woman owed great loyalty to her husband but that that relationship, which could be severed, was probably not perceived, if it came to the crunch, as being on quite the same level as duty to children and close natal kin.

... The close analysis of ideals and of texts and inscriptions describing actual marriages continues to yield important material which is changing our conception of Roman marriage and might eventually enable us to make sound statements about class and regional differences. In the meantime, it is clear that marriage, beset by the mortality patterns of the preindustrial world and the oppression of economic demands and a hierarchical social structure, yet provided comfort and some measure of material and emotional security for many and remained a desirable ideal for those whose circumstances excluded them from it.

The Motivations for
St. Perpetua's Martyrdom

MARY R. LEFKOWITZ

Why did many Christian women become martyrs? Christians might like to believe that the martyrs' steadfast faith led them to suffer atrocious treatment and terrible death at the hands of the Romans. While not discounting the martyrs' commitment to Christianity, Mary R. Lefkowitz offers additional perspectives and great insight into the motives for religious suicide. Her method is the case study, an examination of the martyrdom of St. Perpetua, which allows Lefkowitz to draw conclusions applicable to other female martyrs and to relations between the sexes during the period of Christianity's formation.

The question of motives is intriguing, for many Christians, such as the Gnostics, denied that God wanted what they considered to be human sacrifice. But the debate over martyrdom lies beyond Lefkowitz's article. She stresses the role of family and especially St. Perpetua's relationship with her father. Where did the idea of family intersect with the decision to accept martyrdom? Lefkowitz uses St. Perpetua's autobiographical account to explore her problems with her father and with men. Were her problems strictly personal or did they address the common relationship between men and women in that society? Did St. Perpetua revolt against her father or against a patriarchal social order, or against both? Her motivations, after all, must have been deeply felt, for she readily gave up her infant son as well as her life.

Lefkowitz concludes with a tragic irony. If indeed St. Perpetua chose Christianity over family and death over life because she desired release from a male-dominated society, and her martyrdom thus constituted a political rebellion against the social hierarchy, then her death was ultimately futile. The church she died for would soon become as patriarchal as the world she rejected. For women, martyrdom did not prove to be the path toward social change.

In case there is someone here who does not know by heart the story of St. Perpetua's martyrdom, let me summarize briefly how and what we know about it. A narrator tells us about a group of Christians who were executed in Carthage in 203, including Vibia Perpetua, "a newly married woman of good family and upbringing . . . about twenty-two years old . . . with an infant son at the breast"; with her is her brother, also a Christian convert. The narrator then quotes directly from Perpetua's own memoirs, which consist of her account of her imprisonment and of the dreams she had in prison; she tells how her father, who has remained a pagan, pleads with her to abandon her religion and tries to get the authorities to let her out; detailed, explicit visions tell her meanwhile that she must die. The narrator then tells the story of her fellow martyrs and their joint execution: they were exposed to wild beasts in the arena; Perpetua herself was attacked but not seriously wounded by a wild cow, and finally killed by a gladiator, whose sword she willingly guided to her neck.

...[T]here is ample subject matter here for many sermons.... The *Acts of SS. Perpetua and Felicity* is, of course, a document that is meant to convert and persuade.... But the story even so can tell us much about the working beliefs of the early church and in particular about the experience of a female martyr. In this paper I would like to suggest, on the basis of her autobiographical account, that part of the appeal of the new religion lay in its encouragement to the convert to break traditional family patterns, and in its promise of enabling the convert to share in a new existence in a more egalitarian community.

In her dreams and in her life, Perpetua gives up her old family for a new one of brothers and sisters in Christ: she refuses to give in to her father, who visits her twice in prison, and finally throws himself at her feet in despair; she never mentions her brother or her mother after she sees in her dream that she must die, and she allows her father to take her nursing baby from her. We can recognize in Perpetua's resistance to her father and gradual withdrawal from her family the standard behavior pattern of conversion; a wish to break with the past, a need to substitute strong new ties that can replace the old. The martyrs Agape, Irene, and Chione[1] of Salonica (we are told) "abandoned their native city, their family, their property, and possessions because of love of God, and their expectation of heavenly things," and to avoid their persecutors went for two consecutive years (303 and 304) to live with each other on a mountain. One thinks of Lucius in Apuleius[2] *Metamorphoses,* who after his dream of Isis and transformation back into human shape, does not go home again, but joins a priesthood that serves and respects the feminine power he once tried to control and to exploit. Jerome[3] advises Heliodorus, who wants to become a monk, to trample his father underfoot if his father lies down on the doorstep to block his passage.... So Perpetua's father throws himself at her feet, and she dreams of treading on a snake to climb a ladder to heaven, and of stepping on the head of an Egyptian who opposes her in single combat. The metaphor in Jerome's advice and in Perpetua's dreams is the same, but it is noteworthy that in Perpetua's case the aggressive child is a woman.

There is a distinctive emphasis in stories of Christian women's martyrdom on separation from the family and on death as a means to life. Pagan women martyrs were celebrated by their contemporaries for their defiance of tyranny and loyalty to their husbands, and courage in the face of death. One thinks especially of Arria[4] thrusting the sword into her breast, and saying to

---

[1] Three sisters martyred in the early fourth century.

[2] Latin writer, second century A.D., author of *The Golden Ass* or *Metamorphoses.*

[3] Saint Jerome, Christian theologian and translator of the Bible, c.347–420.

[4] When her husband was condemned in A.D. 42 for his part in a conspiracy, Arria stabbed herself first.

her husband in encouragement, "Paetus, it doesn't hurt". Arria's immortality . . . consists only of being assured of continued fame, through celebration of her achievement in literature. . . . The Christians Perpetua, Agape, Irene, and Chione die courageously but in noticeable isolation from their families, in defiance of, rather than in loyalty to, their husbands or fathers. We find in the stories of the Christian women martyrs a surprising eagerness to abandon young infants: Perpetua, who at first is concerned for her nursing baby and is relieved to get permission to keep him, after her dream about the snake and the ladder and a confrontation with her father, is miraculously relieved of her responsibility, "and as God willed, the baby wanted no more of the breast, nor did they (her breasts) give me fever, so that I was not tormented by care for the baby or the pain in my breasts". Felicity, the slave girl who is imprisoned along with her, prays that she may be delivered of her child in time to be executed along with the others, and rejoices when she does in fact give birth to a little girl prematurely. Similarly, Eutychia, one of the women tried in Salonica along with Irene, though seven months pregnant, insists, in spite of danger of imprisonment and death, to keep the faith. To celibate male scholars this behavior may appear less remarkable (or perhaps more commendable) than it does to us. It might more accurately be viewed as an abnormal, extreme form of social protest: we can compare the accounts in Greek myth of groups of Theban women who fled to the mountains to worship a new god, abandoning their homes and children, and in some cases even murdering their sons. Euripides[5] in the *Bacchae* portrays Agave's condition as a kind of temporary insanity; modern anthropologists would compare it to the sudden ecstatic experiences that bring oppressed groups a sense (albeit transient) of political power. Were the Christian women who fled their families by rushing to the wilderness, or to prison, abandoning their babies, also seeking a new freedom from the traditional patterns of their lives?

That the nature of these women's conduct was regarded as something more than simple impiety is indicated by the nature of their punishment: Irene, because she had concealed forbidden written material before she "ran away" into the wilderness, is sentenced to be placed naked in the brothel, on a subsistence diet. The judge Aquila in Alexandria (ca. 210) threatens to let his gladiators rape the Christian Potamiaena, but then has her executed by having boiling pitch poured drop by drop over different parts of her body. As in the case of the woman who murdered her husband, child, and husband's sister in Apuleius and is condemned to be mounted by the jackass in the arena, male superiority must be publicly reasserted in case of female attack on familial or governmental norms. . . . In Perpetua's case, where the principal antagonist is not a Roman governor, but rather her own father, there are also sexual overtones. Her dreams reveal a concern with destroying threatening male figures: she treads upon a snake and in her final vision becomes a man

---

[5]Greek tragic poet, 480?–406 B.C.

in order to step on the head of an Egyptian. The explanation of the repeated metaphor of trampling becomes apparent when we remember that her father, in their last interview, threw himself at her feet. In her dreams there is a curiously consistent association of feet with power: she describes how the Egyptian "tried to get hold of my feet, but I kept striking him on the face with the heels of my feet". In her descriptions of the kind deacon who leads her to victory, and of the trainer who presides over her successful contest, she calls attention to their sandals, "elaborate" and "complex, made from gold and silver". Her desire to compete in these dream-contests successfully against her father indicates that, in her perception at least, more than theological issues are involved in her martyrdom. . . . Perpetua's death is in part a result of an adolescent rejection necessary for personal individuation.[6] But the consistent emphasis in the narrative on sexual definition suggests a more specific motivation, what psychotherapists call "unconscious incest," a close emotional pairing of father and daughter, which results from a desperate attempt to keep a disintegrating family together. You will recall that while the narrator of Perpetua's story says that she was honorably married, her husband is never mentioned by name, and appears nowhere in the narrative. Because she appears to be in her father's custody, we might assume that she is widowed or divorced. More noteworthy than the absence of her husband is the shadowy role played by her mother in the story (she seems to be imprisoned with Perpetua at the beginning, and Perpetua turns the child over to her care; the father begs Perpetua to think of her mother; thereafter the mother disappears from the narrative). Perpetua's main concern throughout is with her father ("for a few days I gave thanks to the Lord that I was separated from my father, and was comforted by his absence"); she feels pity for him, she tries to console him. She records first his rage ("he moved toward me as though he would pluck my eyes out"), then his sorrow ("pity me . . . if I am worthy to be called your father, if I have favored you above all your brothers," "with tears in his eyes he no longer addressed me as daughter, but as woman". But her reply to his plea is remote, "it will all happen . . . as God wills," and she accepts death eagerly, as the narrator observes, "she screamed as she was struck on the bone, then she took the trembling hand of the young gladiator and guided it to her throat. It was as though so great a woman, feared as she was by the unclean spirit could not be dispatched unless she herself were willing". Similar patterns of actions and reactions are found in unconscious (and conscious) incestuous father-daughter relationships: the absent husband and the absent mother, and to replace her, the close emotional pairing of the daughter with the father, and the daughter's eventual withdrawal and self-destructive behavior. . . . St. Dymphna,[7] according to the legend, after her father lost his wife and decided to take his daughter as her successor, fled from Ireland to Belgium, where

[6] That is, development of her personal identity.

[7] Irish martyr, sixth or seventh century.

she founded (not inappropriately) a mental hospital; in the French tale of the Donkey-skin[8] again it is the daughter who must find an escape, and atone for her predicament by disfiguring herself. In patriarchal society, ancient and modern, the guilt for an incestuous relationship is (remarkably) felt only by the younger, passive partner: self-destruction or self-negation in some form results, suicidal depression, inability to have a mature sexual relationship with another man.

It is not without significance that the religion which Perpetua adopts appears to encourage more a-sexual, fraternal relationships between men and women, and that the men with whom she dies and whom she sees in her visions are benign, supportive, and beautiful, as opposed to the hostile (her father wants to tear out her eyes) and mutilated (her father tears out his beard, she sees in a dream her young brother who had died of skin ulcers). Her willingness to die is not only an act of faith and maturity, but in existential terms, a political act against her environment. In seeking martyrdom she was as much concerned with solving problems in this life as with attaining perfection in the next. The Church Fathers . . . would praise Perpetua and Felicity for acting uncharacteristically for women, in overcoming the inherent weakness and sinfulness of their flesh. We may regret that these men did not also wish to realize how Christianity in its earlier stages also met a social need of releasing women from the hierarchical structure imposed by patriarchal society, which the church in its own organization would increasingly incorporate and emulate. The persistent emphasis on breaking with family, and on sexually defined conflict with authority in the *Acts* of Perpetua, Irene, and Potamiaena express a perceived concern of women in the early centuries of the Christian era.

[8] A fairy tale in verse by Charles Perrault (1628–1703).

III

THE MIDDLE AGES

Covering the years roughly from 500 to 1500, the Middle Ages included a number of cultures and territories. Western civilization during this epoch was increasingly confined to western Europe, leaving the eastern Mediterranean to the expanding Islamic world. Opening with Germanic invasions of the western Roman Empire, the Middle Ages concluded with European invasions of exotic and distant lands as men crossed the oceans in the guise of explorers, soldiers, and missionaries in the fifteenth and sixteenth centuries to discover, fight, and convert the indigenous peoples.

Some historians further subdivide the medieval epoch into the early (500–1000), high (1000–1300), and late (1300–1500) Middle Ages. The early Middle Ages, often misnamed the Dark Ages, witnessed Germanic invasions, political fragmentation, a rural economy, small population, little international trade, and a decline in education, urbanization, and commercialization. Christianity spread throughout western Europe so completely that the entire Middle Ages is sometimes branded the Age of Faith or the Christian centuries. Following Charlemagne's reign (768–814), which saw administrative innovations and a small cultural flowering, invasions by the Vikings, Hungarians, and Saracens plunged Europe back into the chaotic conditions that recalled the collapse of Roman rule in the fifth and sixth centuries. But the ninth and tenth centuries also provided the final elements that defined rural life and the method of governance, feudalism.

The high Middle Ages was an era of relative prosperity that saw medieval civilization approach its zenith, marked perhaps by the prodigiously tall cathedrals built according to a new architectural and artistic style, the Gothic. The population expanded as a result of the surplus provided by improved agricultural techniques; towns and commerce grew; education (though highly limited in social scope) blossomed, first in cathedral schools and later in universities; and the slow accumulation of power in fewer hands offered a greater measure of political stability. Religion infused the economy, social order, politics, art, and mentality of the Middle Ages. The crusades exemplified the brash exuberance and confidence of this period. It took the unprecedented disasters of the fourteenth and fifteenth centuries to end this vibrant civilization, though there was certainly much continuity with succeeding centuries. A worsening climate, famines, economic depression, international warfare, peasant revolts, and the worst scourge in history—the Plague—made the later Middle Ages a bleak era in many ways. But this was also, in Italy, the age of the Renaissance, a cultural flowering that coincided with economic depression and severe population loss. Humanism (the major intellectual movement of the Renaissance), artistic innovation, and political experimentation made Italy arguably the most dynamic area in Europe at the end of the Middle Ages.

The selections that follow describe basic subjects in the social history of the Middle Ages: the nobility, the family, marriage, children, peasants, pollution, religion, social behavior, women, and crime. They show medieval societies to have been violent, intense, severe, patriarchal, and devoted to professed values and traditional modes of conduct from which nonetheless they often enthusiastically broke away. This was an energetic culture, difficult to categorize because of the substantial gap between people's ideals and the harsh reality of their daily life and behavior.

Rural Economy and Country Life in the Medieval West

GEORGES DUBY

Europe of the ninth and tenth centuries was a rural civilization, in which seasonal rhythms and patterns of cultivation determined the lifestyles of all, even the few who lived in small towns. In contrast, today less than twenty percent of the population in the Western world live in rural areas, large-scale mechanized agriculture is the norm, and farmers are linked to the outside world by television, automobiles, and the computer.

Georges Duby begins his study of medieval agricultural communities by describing peasant settlements. What did a village comprise? Beyond the living area and the fields were forests. How did medieval people use the forests? What type of food did peasants consume? How effectively did the agricultural technology of the time exploit the land? Put another way, what factors limited the production of more food?

For most of history, people have stood rather helpless before the inadequacies of their land, the unpredictability of the weather, and their own inability to influence their environment in a stable, effective way. Medieval peasants proved no exception. Their constant battle against the soil and climate, not to mention the parasitic aristocracy and clergy, gave them little food and much insecurity. In theory at least, the lords and clergy provided certain forms of security, but the reality was that the peasantry faced an epic struggle, with few material rewards.

One fact is outstanding: in the civilization of the ninth and tenth centuries the rural way of life was universal. Entire countries, like England and almost all the Germanic lands, were absolutely without towns. Elsewhere some towns existed: such as the few ancient Roman cities in the south which had not suffered complete dilapidation, or the new townships on trade routes which were making their appearance along the rivers leading to the northern seas. But except for some in Lombardy, these 'towns' appear as minute centres of population, each numbering at most a few hundred permanent inhabitants and deeply immersed in the life of the surrounding countryside. Indeed they could hardly be distinguished from it. Vineyards encircled them; fields penetrated their walls; they were full of cattle, barns and farm labourers. All their inhabitants from the very richest, bishops and even the king himself, to the few specialists, Jewish or Christian, who conducted long-distance trade, remained first and foremost countrymen whose whole life was dominated by the rhythm of the agricultural seasons, who depended for their existence on the produce of the soil, and who drew directly from it their entire worldly wealth. . . .

Another thing is also certain. It was a countryside created by man around a few fixed points of settlement. Western Europe was peopled by a stable peasantry rooted in its environment. Not that we should picture it as totally immobile. There was still room in rural life for nomadic movements. In high summer cartage and pastoral activities took many peasants to distant places, while others were occupied in gathering the wild products of the woodland, in hunting, in raiding their neighbours, and in some other activities that were necessary to acquire vital food supplies for survival. Other members of the rural population regularly participated in warlike adventures. However, most of these were only seasonal or part-time nomads. They spent most of their days on land which housed their families and formed part of organized village territories. They give the impression of belonging to villages.

Indeed the countryman's life was very rarely conducted in solitude. Dwelling houses appear to have been close together and very seldom isolated. Clusters of houses were usual.... [T]he village, whatever its size or shape, provided the normal background of human existence. In Saxon England, for instance, the village served as the basis for the levying and collection of taxes. Around these fixed points was laid out the pattern of the cultivated land, and particularly the network of trackways and paths, which appear in the landscape of today as the most tenacious relic of our ancient heritage, the reality which provides the starting point for archeological study of the village territory.

In western Europe, pioneer excavations are under way which will one day help us to know better what medieval rural dwellings were like. Already evidence exists which leads us to believe that, except in the Mediterranean coastal lands where building was in stone, men's habitations in the early, and even the not-so-early, Middle Ages were huts of wattle and daub, short-lived and destructible; even at the beginning of the thirteenth century an English peasant was found guilty of having destroyed the house of his neighbour by merely sawing through the central beam.

... [T]he land on which the village stood was subject to a particular legal status, different from that of the surrounding land, and enjoying customary privileges which made its boundaries unalterable. Legal historians have shown that the village was made up of contiguous parcels of land which most Carolingian documents describe by the word *mansus,* and which the peasant dialects of the earliest Middle Age called variously *meix, Hof, masure, toft....* We understand by this an enclosure, solidly rooted to its site by a permanent barrier such as a palisade or a living hedge, carefully maintained, a protected asylum to which the entry was forbidden and the violation of which was punished by severe penalties: an island of refuge where the occupant was assumed to be the master and at whose threshold communal servitude and the demands of chiefs and lords stopped short. These enclosures provided a haven for possessions, cattle, stocks of food, and sleeping men, protected them against natural and supernatural dangers, and taken together, constituted the kernel of the village, and expressed in terms of land and territory the essence of a society of which the family was the nucleus. Furthermore, it is probable that occupation of such a *manse* carried with it a place in the village community with collective rights over the surrounding fields. By the same token newcomers remained dwellers in a secondary zone of habitations outside the enclosures. . . .

. . . The soil which lay nearest to the house and to the stable was especially rich and fertile. By proximity alone the site of peasant settlement fertilized itself: household waste and the domestic animals were sufficient to establish around the dwelling, precisely because it was immovable, a permanent condition of fertility. Moreover, this land, because it was so conveniently placed, could be repeatedly dug over. In no other spot could the natural state of the earth be so profoundly modified to meet the needs of man; the constant manuring and digging created there an artificial soil and raised on it a specialized and particular plant life. Thus each domestic fence enclosed and protected a vegetable garden, . . . in other words a continually cultivated plot, where the ground was never left to rest, and where in carefully protected conditions grew tender plants, the herbs and roots of the daily diet, hemp and the vine. These plots were undoubtedly most productive and the atmosphere of garden care which they cast over their surroundings did much to anchor the village to its site.

Beyond the encircling hedges, nature was also subject to a certain, even if a not very rigorous, discipline. Without the need to tame her, men could win from nature a large part of their subsistence. River, marsh, forest and thicket offered to whoever could take advantage of them, fish, game, honey and many other edible substances in generous measure. . . . We are encouraged to believe that [the countryman] was as skilled in the use of the hunting spear, the net and the warrener's stick as he was with the plough. In 1180 when Alexander Neckham, an English teacher in the schools of Paris, wrote his treatise *Du Nom des Outils*,[1] he listed nets, lines, and snares for trapping hares and deer amongst the ordinary tools of the peasant household. It is certain that the thinly growing forest of the early Middle Ages, with its numerous clearings, and its varied vegetation ranging from thick woodland to grassy glades, formed an essential background to the domestic economy. Apart from the livelihood that it bestowed generously on foodgatherer and hunter, it furnished the larger domestic animals with their chief sources of nourishment. Sheep and cows grazed there and war- and farm-horses were let loose in it. But above all else the woods were the domain of pigs. . . . Indeed over vast stretches of northern Europe in the ninth century bacon was an essential ingredient in the household economy. Herds of swine yielding both meat and lard formed everywhere the mainstay of every farming system, large and small. . . . In fact agrarian archeology leads us to suppose that many villages and especially those in the north-west and north-east, in England, Frisia and Saxony, possessed no cultivated lands, apart from the 'tofts'. And in the eleventh century we know of communities in the English fenlands, on the Wash and in the flooded valley of the Saône which lived solely by fishing.

[1] *The Names of Tools.*

However, because of man's customary eating habits the cultivation of the small plots around the dwelling houses and the quest for the gifts of nature were nearly everywhere allied to the efforts to farm more extensively. We know very little about the food of early medieval man in western Europe outside the monastic communities. . . . It is clear that at this period not only were men unable to feed themselves on what they found by chance, but they were driven to grow what custom decreed they should consume. . . . [T]he expansion of winegrowing in Gaul was a direct consequence of the social habits of the nobles, with whom it was a point of honour to drink and to offer their guests none but the best wine. But on a much humbler level also the whole system of agricultural production was organized to fulfil the social requirements which determined eating habits.

References in documents . . . reveal the universal acceptance of bread as a basic foodstuff, even in the least civilized regions of the Christian world. . . . Indeed, all the documents indicate that peas, vetches, beans—the leguminous plants—together with 'herbs' and 'roots', the ancestors of our garden vegetables (the hermits were praised for restricting their diet to these) and of course meat, a most desirable item of consumption from which the clergy ostentatiously abstained, comprised only the *companaticum*, the accompaniment to bread. It was the latter that was the mainstay of existence.

It is reasonably clear that bread was not baked solely from wheat, rye or spelt, but also from other, lesser, cereals, such as barley and even oats, which [were] eaten as much by humans as by animals. What is less easy to distinguish is in what measure these food grains were consumed in the form of porridge . . . or brewed into ale, the commonest beverage throughout north-western Europe. Ale had often the consistency of thick soup and so could be counted perhaps more as a food than a drink. Eleventh-century peasants had to grow cereals even when climatic conditions were not favourable. As arable fields had to be laid out around the villages, the least exposed and most easily worked sites had to be cleared for the purpose, in close proximity to habitations and in the midst of woods and pastures.

Here and there, in places where the climate allowed grapes to ripen, a few vines were planted for the masters on the most suitable and permanently enclosed plots. Meadows were confined to damper ground, and the hay, together with the grass and rushes which could be gathered in the marshes, provided winter fodder for the cattle. Nevertheless neither vines nor meadows covered more than a very limited part of the cultivated area since the cereal crop was the really important one, and almost the whole of the area given over to agricultural activity was reserved for its culture. These fields had also to be protected against the depredations of animals, both domestic and wild. They can thus be visualized as separated from the uncultivated lands, which were open to pasture, by enclosures which in the country of the Franks seemed generally to have been temporary. In spring as soon as the new grass began to push up and the corn to sprout these mobile barriers made of wooden stakes . . . were erected and signs were put up forbidding shepherds to let their animals stray there. For a season therefore these strips seemed, like the cultivated 'tofts' of the village, to be the territory of individual owners. But after the harvest, signs and fences were removed, and the strips returned for a time to pastoral use, and were reincorporated into the larger areas where access to animals was free. To a greater or lesser extent then, according to the quantity of bread men were used to eating, the arable appeared as a limited and temporary extension of the cultivated 'toft' area and thus private property, at the expense of the wild area which was left to collective use.

Can we ever hope, even in the best documented regions, to plot the portion of village lands occupied by the arable fields? . . . What we know now suggests that this area was small everywhere and that a large space was being left to natural vegetation, the forest and pasture, whose presence 'had helped to form this combination of agriculture and animal husbandry which was the principal feature' of rural economy in the west. . . . This union indeed appears constant and fundamental throughout the Middle Ages. What we might describe as three concentric zones formed the picture . . . —the village enclosures, the *coûtures,* that is the arable, and finally surrounding all, a broad uncultivated belt. These were the three zones in which the effects of man's labour became less and less visible as the distance from the inhabited centre grew greater, but which were of equal importance to him as a means of subsistence.

Village communities thus found themselves hemmed in with no way of absorbing the increase in their birth rate. Periodic waves of mortality, such as those caused by military activity and, increasingly in the second half of the ninth and in the tenth centuries, raids of invaders, rather than any systematic clearing of the wastes and the resulting hiving off of colonists, relieved demographic pressure at intervals. Such a situation suggests a peasantry poorly equipped with efficient tools and incapable for this reason of taming the encircling wilderness.

Was the undoubted technical progress to which the diffusion of the water mill bears witness accompanied in Europe of the ninth and tenth centuries by the spread of ploughs with wheeled foreparts, by improvements in harness, and by the adoption of a more efficient ploughshare? This important problem of technique cannot be resolved, but it is reasonable to assume that even in the most favoured sectors of rural life, those of the great farming complexes described by inventories, men used feeble wooden implements. They found themselves ill-equipped to come to grips with nature and worked with their bare hands for a great part of the time. The primitive technical equipment obviously restricted narrowly the individual's productive capacity. And this observation agrees completely with the impression gained from land settlement. Villages teemed with people whose efforts were needed to work the soil on the home fields, but they were situated in clearings separated by stretches of wild country because agricultural tools were not robust enough to overcome the obstacles of heavy, wet and thickly wooded land. Areas of natural vegetation adjoining the villages were of course actually necessary because the cultivation of cereals was so demanding of manpower that each rural community had to supplement its means of livelihood by making the most of the products of the wastelands—animal husbandry, hunting and foodgathering.

These limited portions of the village lands suitable for grain growing and therefore providing the village's main food supply . . . , or 'furlongs' to use the English term, were not given over wholly to food production every year. Unlike the cultivated 'tofts' whose soil, manured by the household waste and stable dung, could be cultivated without interruption, the fields demanded a periodic rest if fertility was not to be lost. Every spring a section of the arable was not sown; it remained open, unenclosed, available for pasture, in the same way as the wild area of wastes and commons. For an understanding of the productivity of the land and the manner in which it was able to support human life, we need to know the rhythm of the resting periods. What was the place of the fallow and what the place of spring-sown corn, oats and leguminous crops? How much land was devoted to autumn-sown corn, that is the bread grains—wheat, rye and spelt (the most widely grown grain in the Rhineland and north-west France), and lastly barley, which was in those days often a winter-sown crop? . . .

1. The description of harvest and sowing and, more often, that of dues in the form of grain exacted from peasant tenants proved that the fields of peasants as well as lords very frequently produced spring as well as winter corn and especially oats.

2. The arrangement of the ploughing services exacted from manorial dependants in the agricultural calendar shows that the cycle of ploughing was often divided into two sowing 'seasons', one in the winter . . . , and the other in the summer or the spring. . . .

3. Ploughing units on the great properties appear often in groups of three. . . . This arrangement leads us to think that cultivation was organized on a ternary rhythm. . . . By this arrangement, a third portion was prepared in May by a preliminary ploughing, and was turned over again by the plough in November before sowing; the following year after harvest the same fields were left throughout autumn and winter for the animals to graze on, and were then ploughed in Lent and sown with spring grain, after which they rested for a year. Thus at least a third of the agricultural area produced nothing, while another third produced bread grains and the last third the ingredients of porridge and soup.

I do not consider, however, that these indications are sufficient for us to conclude without further consideration that a regular three-year rotation was general, or even widespread. What argues against any such conclusion is that none of our examples is in southern Europe where climatic conditions, and above all early spring droughts, made March sowings somewhat hazardous, and also that our documents describe none but the great monastic or royal farms which were run in an unusually rational and even scientific manner. . . .

... It is therefore safest to conjecture that there was considerable variation in the crop rotation in use. Man was forced to bow to the natural capacity of the soil because he was poorly prepared to alter it. We can imagine an infinite variety of systems in use ranging all the way from the strict three-course rotation to temporary cultivation based on burning where bits and pieces of land on the outer fringes of the village enclave would be tilled after the undergrowth had been burned, and continued to be cropped for years until fertility was exhausted. It is also probable that oats and other spring grains were often a supplementary crop taken from the fallow, and that such a system, even when the regular ploughings in winter and early spring... were adhered to, frequently lasted more than one year on the largest part of the available arable. It must be added that seed corn was sown very thinly.... The agricultural practice of those early days demanded not only plentiful manpower, but wide open spaces.

The insistent demands for long fallow periods, and the need to scatter the seed thinly arose at least partly because of mediocre ploughing implements which could not turn the ground over properly, but they were also due to the virtual absence of manure. It is true that animal husbandry was always complementary to agriculture and the draught oxen whose task was to plough the fields could also fertilize them with their dung. In reality the combination of arable with pasture was not close enough to enable animal manure to make much impression. Men who were so inadequately equipped with tools were forced to devote all their energies to producing their own food, and cattle had to take second place. A little fodder was harvested, but barely enough to keep those few beasts which had not been slaughtered in the autumn alive during the lean winter months when nature's offerings failed. But for the rest of the year the herds grazed alone in the open air on the land which was not enclosed. They must also have ranged over the fallow fields and in doing so deposited their manure on them; but the deposit was quite insufficient to maintain fertility. Scarce fodder meant restricted periods of stall-feeding, and the limited quantities of stable manure thus available were almost wholly devoured by the cultivated 'tofts' in the inner fertile belt of the village territory. No wonder areas of fallow had to be huge. And we can appreciate afresh the need of each family to dispose of as large a space for subsistence as possible which had to cover, besides pasture, an arable area much more extensive than the portion actually in use each year. Even so, despite the long resting periods, output remained extremely low.

... These elusive details allow at any rate one firm conclusion. Carried out with rudimentary equipment and in a generally unfavourable climate, the cultivation of cereal crops was at the mercy of the caprices of the weather. Even on the best equipped farms an excessively wet spring or summer could render the heavy toil in the fields totally unproductive. Despite an enormous expenditure of manpower and the disproportionate size of the village lands country folk could be racked with hunger. Obviously their main preoccupation was to survive through spring and early summer, that period of backbreaking toil. When the scraps of food remaining to them after the demands of their masters had been exhausted, the yearly nightmare of hand-to-mouth existence began, and the pangs of hunger had to be stilled by devouring garden herbs and forest berries and by begging bread at the gates of the rich. At such moments the threat of starvation overshadowed the whole village world.

Medieval Children

DAVID HERLIHY

In this survey of children in the Middle Ages, David Herlihy emphasizes the complexity of the subject. There is first the problem of documentation. Children did not write about themselves and adults usually did not specifically detail their attitudes and behavior toward children. Herlihy thus has had recourse to many different types of source materials. What sources does he rely on in his discussion of children in classical society, among the barbarians, and, finally, in the Middle Ages? Second, Herlihy notes that the information available about medieval children can lead the historian to quite opposite conclusions, that the Middle Ages either maltreated offspring or took pleasure in their spirituality and goodness. Which conclusion does Herlihy adopt? Does the evidence support his interpretation?

What explains the different treatment of children in classical, barbarian, and medieval cultures? Instead of looking within the family for the causes of these changes, Herlihy usually points to outside influences, such as Christianity, and socioeconomic developments. Christian theologians disagreed on the basic nature of children, stressing their ties to original sin or their holy innocence. According to Herlihy, changing attitudes toward the baby Jesus reflected the way in which society viewed all children. Of course, the impact of theology and Christian art on the family is impossible to measure exactly—one wonders, for example, about peasant children, a subject Herlihy neglects in favor of urban social groups. Increasing commercialization and urbanization in the eleventh and twelfth centuries led to a new concern for children, one that was both practical and psychological. The establishment of schools and orphanages suggests that children received more attention and care. Pedagogues, both religious and lay, worried about children's education, health, and spiritual well-being. The result, says Herlihy, was an idealization of childhood in the Middle Ages, long before many historians place that development. Herlihy thus refutes those historians who argue that a concept of and an appreciation for childhood did not emerge until the sixteenth and seventeenth centuries.

. . . Many, perhaps most, children in most traditional societies did no more than come and go. And most never acquired, or were given, a voice which might have recorded and preserved their impressions concerning them-selves, their parents, and the world they had recently discovered. Of all social groups which formed the societies of the past, children, seldom seen and rarely heard in the documents, remain for historians the most elusive, the most obscure.

The difficulties of interviewing the mute have doubtlessly obstructed and delayed a systematic investigation of the history of childhood. But today, at least, historians are aware of the commonplace assumption of psychologists, that childhood plays a critical role in the formation of the adult personality. Perhaps they are awakening to an even older wisdom, the recognition that society, in the way it rears its children, shapes itself. . . .

Today, the literature devoted to the history of children in various places and epochs may be described, rather like children themselves, as small but growing daily. It remains, however, difficult to discern within that literature a clear consensus, an acceptable hypothesis, concerning the broad trends of children's history, even within Western societies. To be sure, there is frequent allusion within these recent publications to a particular interpretation which, for want of a better name, we shall call the "theory of discovered childhood." The principal formulator of this interpretation, at least in its most recent form, has been the French social historian Philippe Ariès. In a book published in 1960, called in its English translation *Centuries of Childhood*, Ariès entitled the second chapter "the discovery of childhood." In it he affirmed that the Middle Ages of Western history did not recognize childhood as a distinct phase in life. Medieval people allegedly viewed and treated their children as imperfectly formed adults. Once the infant was weaned, medieval parents supposedly made no concessions to its special and changing psychological needs and took little satisfaction in the distinctive traits of the young personality. The corollary to this assumption is that, at some point in the development of Western society and civilization, the young years of life were at last discovered: childhood needed a Columbus.

Proclamations of the alleged discovery of childhood have become com-monplace in the growing literature, but wide differences in interpretation still separate the authors. When, for example, was childhood first recognized? On this important question, Ariès himself is indefinite, even evasive, and seems to place the discovery over three or four hundred years, from the fifteenth to the eighteenth centuries. . . .

If historians of the modern world do not agree concerning the date of childhood's discovery, their colleagues, working in more remote periods, show signs of restiveness with Ariès' postulate, that medieval people did not distinguish children from adults. A number of scholars . . . have noted among the pedagogues, humanists, and even artists of fifteenth-century Italy a new orientation toward children, a new awareness of their problems, and an appreciation of their qualities. The fat and frolicksome babies, the *putti*, who cavort through many solemn paintings of the Italian Renaissance, leave little doubt that the artists of the epoch knew how to depict, and they or their patrons liked to contemplate, children. A still more radical departure from Ariès' views was proposed, in 1968, by the French medievalist Pierre Riché. Riché accepted Ariès' phrase, the "discovery of childhood," but radically changed his chronology. The initial explorers of childhood were, for Riché, the monastic pedagogues active in Western Europe between the sixth and eighth centuries. Their sensitivity toward the psychology of children allegedly transformed the harsh educational methods of classical antiquity and developed a new pedagogy which was finely attuned to the personality of the child-monk. Thus, over an extended period of time, from the early Middle Ages until the present, one or another author would have us believe that a consciousness of childhood was at last emerging.

The lessons that I would draw from this confusion of learned opinions are the following. Historians would be well advised to avoid such categoric and dubious claims, that people in certain periods failed to distinguish children from adults, that childhood really did lie beyond the pale of collective consciousness. Attitudes toward children have certainly shifted, as has the willingness on the part of society to invest substantially in their welfare or education. But to describe these changes, we need terms more refined than metaphors of ignorance and discovery. I would propose that we seek to evaluate, and on occasion even to measure, the psychological and economic investment which families and societies in the past were willing to make in their children. However, we ought also to recognize that alternative and even competitive sets of child-related values can coexist in the same society, perhaps even in the same household. Different social groups and classes expect different things from their children; so do different epochs, in accordance with prevailing economic, social, and demographic conditions. In examining the ways in which children were regarded and reared in the past, we should not expect either rigorous consistency across society or lineal progress over time.

In the current, lively efforts to reconstruct the history of children in Western civilization, the long period of the Middle Ages has a special importance. The medieval child represents a kind of primordial form, an "eo-pais," a "dawn child" as it were, against whom Western children of subsequent epochs must be measured if we are to appreciate the changes they have experienced. To be sure, the difficulties of observing medieval children cannot be discounted. Medieval documentation is usually sparse, often inconsistent, and always difficult.... We can hope to catch only fleeting glimpses of medieval children in their rush through, or out of, life. On the other hand, even glimpses may be enough to dispel some large misconceptions concerning medieval children and to aid us toward a sound reconstruction of the history of children in the Western world.

In surveying medieval children, it is first necessary to consider the two prior traditions which largely shaped the medieval appraisal of the very young—the classical and the barbarian. It is important also to reflect upon the influence exerted upon child rearing by a special component of the ancient Mediterranean heritage: the Christian church.

Classical society, or at least the elites within it, cultivated an impressive array of intellectual traditions, which were founded upon literacy and preserved over time through intensive, and expensive, educational methods. Classical civilization would be inconceivable in the absence of professional teachers, formal instruction, and numerous schools and academies. But as social historians of antiquity now emphasize, the resources that supported ancient society were in truth scant. "The classical Mediterranean has always been a world on the edge of starvation," one historian has recently written, with much justice if perhaps some exaggeration. Scarce resources and the high costs of rearing children helped form certain distinctive policies regarding the young. The nations which comprised the Roman Empire, with the exception only of the Jews, refused to support deformed, unpromising, or supernumerary babies. In Roman practice, for example, the newborn baby was at once laid before the feet of him who held the *patria potestas*[1] over it, usually the natural father. Through a ritual gesture called *susceptio,* the holder of paternal authority might raise up the infant and receive it into his family and household. But he could also reject the baby and order its exposure. Infanticide, or the exposure of infants, was a common and accepted social practice in classical society, shocking perhaps to modern sensibilities but rational for these ancient peoples who were seeking to achieve goals with limited means.

Here however is a paradox. Widespread infanticide in ancient society does not imply disinterest in or neglect of those children elected for survival. On the contrary, to assure a good return on the precious means invested in them, they were subject to close and often cruel attention and to frequent beatings. St. Augustine[2] in his *Confessions* tells how his father, Patricius, and even his pious mother, Monica, urged him to high performance at school, "that I might get on in the world and excel in the handling of words, to gain honor among men and deceitful riches." "If I proved idle in learning," he says of his teachers, "I was soundly beaten. For this procedure seemed wise to our ancestors; and many, passing the same way in the days past, had built a sorrowful road, by which we too must go, with multiplication of grief and toil upon the sons of Adam." The memories which the men of antiquity preserved of their childhood were understandably bleak. "Who would not shudder," Augustine exclaims in the *City of God*, "if he were given the choice of eternal death or life again as a child? Who would not choose to die?"

The barbarian child grew up under quite different circumstances. Moreover, barbarian practices of child rearing seem to have been particularly influential in the society of early medieval Europe, between the fifth and

[1] Paternal authority.

[2] Christian theologian, 354–430, and Bishop of Hippo in North Africa.

eleventh centuries. This is not surprising. Early in the Middle Ages, the cities which had dominated society and culture in antiquity lost importance, the literate social elites of classical society all but disappeared, and their educational institutions and ideals went down amid the debacle of the Western empire. On the other hand, barbarian practices were easily preserved within, and congenial to, the semibarbarized society of the early medieval West.

In a tract called *Germania*, written in A.D. 98, the Roman historian Tacitus has described for us the customs of the barbarian Germans, including their treatment of children. Tacitus, to be sure, likes to contrast barbarian virtues with Roman vices and doubtlessly exaggerates in his depictions of both, but his words are nonetheless worth our attention. The Germans, he claims, did not, like the Romans, kill their supernumerary children. Rather, the barbarians rejoiced in a numerous progeny. Moreover, the barbarian mother, unlike her Roman counterpart, nursed her own baby and did not hand it over for feeding to servants or a hired nurse. On the other hand, Tacitus notes, the barbarian parents paid little attention to their growing children. "In every household," he writes, "the children grow up naked and unkempt...." "The lord and slave," he continues, "are in no way to be distinguished by the delicacy of their bringing up. They live among the same flocks, they lie on the same ground...." Barbarian culture did not depend for its survival on the costly instruction of the young in complex skills and learned traditions; barbarian parents had no need to invest heavily in their children, either psychologically or materially. The cheap costs of child rearing precluded the adoption of infanticide as standard social policy but also reduced the attention which the growing child received from its parents. Only on the threshold of adulthood did the free German male re-establish close contacts with adult society. He typically joined the following of a mature warrior, accompanied him into battle, observed him, and gained some instruction in the arts of war, which, like the arts of rhetoric in the classical world, were the key to his social advance.

A casual attitude toward children seems embodied in the laws of the barbarian peoples—Franks, Lombards, Visigoths, Anglo-Saxons, and others—which were redacted into Latin largely between the sixth and the ninth centuries. The barbarian laws typically assigned to each member of society a sum of money—a fine, or wergeld—which would have to be paid to the relatives if he or she was injured or killed. The size of the wergeld thus provides a crude measure of social status or importance. One of the barbarian codes, the Visigothic, dating from the middle seventh century, gives a particularly detailed and instructive table of values which shows how the worth of a person varied according to age, sex, and status. A free male baby, in the first year of life, was assigned a wergeld of 60 solidi. Between age 1 and age 9, his social worth increased at an average rate of only 3.75 solidi per year, thus attaining the value of 90 solidi in the tenth year of life. Between ages 10 and 15, the rate of increase accelerated to 10 solidi per year; and between ages

15 and 20 it grew still more, to 30 solidi per year. In other words, the social worth of the free Visigothic male increased very slowly in the early years of childhood, accelerated in early adolescence, and grew most substantially in the years preceding full maturity. Considered mature at age 20, he enjoyed a wergeld of 300 solidi—five times the worth of the newborn male infant—and this he retained until age 50. In old age, his social worth declined, to 200 solidi between ages 50 and 65 and to 100 solidi from age 65 to death. The old man, beyond age 65, was worth the same as a child of ten years.

The contrast between the worth of the child and the worth of the adult is particularly striking in regard to women. Among the Visigoths, a female under age 15 was assigned only one-half the wergeld enjoyed by males—only 30 solidi during her first year of life. Her social worth, however, increased enormously when she entered the years of childbearing, between ages 15 and 40 in the Visigothic codes. Her wergeld then leaped to 250 solidi, nearly equal to the 300 solidi assigned to the male and eight times the value of the newborn baby girl. The sterile years of old age brought a reduction of the fine, first to 200 solidi, which she retained to age 60, and then to 100 solidi. In old age, she was assigned the same worth as the male. . . .

The low values assigned to children in these barbarian codes is puzzling. Did the lawgivers not realize that the supply of adults, including the especially valued childbearing women, was critically dependent on the protection of children? This obvious truth seemingly escaped the notice of the barbarian lawgivers; children, and their relation to society, did not loom large in their consciousness.

Apart from laws, one other source offers some insight into the treatment of children in the early Middle Ages: surveys of the population settled on particular estates and manors. These sporadic surveys have survived from the Carolingian period of medieval history, the late eighth and ninth centuries. The largest of them, redacted in the first quarter of the ninth century, lists nearly 2,000 families settled on the lands of the abbey of Saint-Germain-des-Prés near Paris. The survey gives no exact ages, but of 8,457 persons included in it, 3,327 are explicitly identified as *infantes*, or children. . . .

The proportion of known children within the population is very low—only 85 children for every 100 adults. Even if all those of uncertain age are considered *infantes*, the ratio then becomes 116 children for every 100 adults. This peasant population was either singularly barren or it was not bothering to report all its children. Moreover, the sexual composition of the population across these age categories is perplexing. Among the known adults, men and women appear in nearly equal numbers. But among the known children, there are 143 boys for every 100 girls—a male-to-female ratio of nearly three to two. Among those of uncertain age, the sex ratio is even higher. The high sex ratio among the known children may indicate widespread female infanticide, but if this were so, we should expect to find a similarly skewed ratio among the known adults. The death of numerous baby girls inevitably would affect over time the proportions of adult women in this presumably closed population. But the proportions of males and females among the known adults are reasonably balanced. The more likely explanation is that the monastic surveyors, or the peasants who reported to them, were negligent in counting children and were particularly deficient in reporting the presence of little girls in the households. As the barbarian legal codes suggest, children, and especially girls, became of substantial interest to society, and presumably to their families, only as they aged.

The low monetary worth assigned to the very young, and the shadowy presence of children in the statistical documents of the early Middle Ages, should not, however, imply that parents did not love their children. Tacitus notes that the barbarian mother usually nursed her own babies. Kinship ties were strongly emphasized in barbarian society, and these were surely cemented by affection. The German epic fragment the *Song of Hildebrand* takes as its principal theme the love which should unite father and son. The warrior Hildebrand flees into exile to live among the Huns, leaving "a babe at the breast in the bower of the bride." Then, after sixty years of wandering, he confronts his son as his enemy on the field of battle. He recognizes his offspring and tries to avoid combat; he offers the young warrior gold and, as the poet tells us, his love besides. . . . If classical methods of child rearing can be called cruel but closely attentive, the barbarian child grew up within an atmosphere of affectionate neglect.

The Christian church also powerfully influenced the treatment of children in many complex ways. Christianity, like Judaism before it, unequivocally condemned infanticide or the exposure of infants. To be sure, infanticide and exposure remained common social practices in Western Europe across the entire length of the Middle Ages. Church councils, penitentials, sermons, and secular legal codes yield abundant and repeated references to those crimes. As late as the fifteenth century, if we are to believe the great popular preachers of the period, the streams and cesspools of Europe echoed with the cries of abandoned babies. But medieval infanticide still shows one great difference from the comparable practice in the ancient world. Our sources consistently attribute the practice to two motivations: the shame of seduced and abandoned women, who wished to conceal illegitimate births, and poverty—the inability of the mother, and often of both parents, to support an additional mouth. The killing or abandonment of babies in medieval society was the characteristic resort of the fallen, the poor, the desperate. In the ancient world, infanticide had been accepted practice, even among the social elites.

Christian teachings also informed and softened attitudes toward children. Christian scriptures held out several examples of children who enjoyed or earned God's special favor: in the Old Testament, the young Samuel and the young Daniel; in the New, the Holy Innocents and the Christ child himself. According to the evangelists, Jesus himself welcomed the company of children, and he instructed his disciples in the famous words: "Unless you become as little children, you will never enter the Kingdom of Heaven."

This partiality toward children evoked many echoes among patristic[3] and medieval writers. In a poem attributed to St. Clement of Alexandria,[4] Christ is called the "king of children." Pope Leo the Great[5] writes . . . "Christ loves childhood, for it is the teacher of humility, the rule of innocence, the model of sweetness." . . .

A favorable appraisal of childhood is also apparent in the monastic culture of the early Middle Ages. Western monasteries, from the sixth century, accepted as oblates to the monastic life children who were hardly more than toddlers, and the leaders of the monastic movement gave much attention to the proper methods of rearing and instructing these miniature monks. In his famous rule, St. Benedict of Nursia insisted that the advice of the children be sought in important matters, "for often the Lord reveals to the young what should be done." St. Columban[6] in the seventh century, and the Venerable Bede[7] in the eighth, praised four qualities of the monastic child: he does not persist in anger; he does not bear a grudge; he takes no delight in the beauty of women; and he expresses what he truly believes.

But alongside this positive assessment of the very young, Christian tradition supported a much harsher appraisal of the nature of the child. In Christian belief, the dire results of Adam's fall were visited upon all his descendants. All persons, when they entered the world, bore the stain of original sin and with it concupiscence, an irrepressible appetite for evil. Moreover, if God had predestined some persons to salvation and some to damnation, his judgments touched even the very young, even those who died before they knew their eternal options. The father of the Church who most forcefully and effectively explored the implications of predestination for children was again St. Augustine. Voluminous in his writings, clear in his logic, and ruthless in his conclusions, Augustine finally decided, after some early doubts, that the baby who died without baptism was damned to eternal fires. There were heaven and hell and no place in-between. "If you admit that the little one cannot enter heaven," he argued, "then you concede that he will be in everlasting fire."

This cruel judgment of the great African theologian contrasts with the milder views of the Eastern fathers, who affirmed that unbaptized children suffer only the loss of the vision of God. The behavior of Augustine's God seems to mimic the posture of the Roman paterfamilias, who was similarly arbitrary and ruthless in the judgment of his own babies, who elected some for life and cast out others into the exterior darkness. And no one in his family dared question his decisions. . . .

[3]Referring to the fathers, or theologians, of the early Christian Church.
[4]Greek Christian theologian, c.150–c.215.
[5]440–461.
[6]Irish monk and missionary, c.543–615.
[7]English monk, historian, and saint, c.673–735.

Augustine was, moreover, impressed by the early dominion which evil establishes over the growing child. The suckling infant cries unreasonably for nourishment, wails and throws tantrums, and strikes with feeble but malicious blows those who care for him. "The innocence of children," Augustine concludes, "is in the helplessness of their bodies, rather than any quality of soul." . . .

The suppression of concupiscence thus becomes a central goal of Augustine's educational philosophy and justifies hard and frequent punishments inflicted on the child. While rejecting the values of pagan antiquity, he adheres to the classical methods of education. Augustine prepared the way for retaining under Christian auspices that "sorrowful road" of schooling which he, as a child at school, had so much hated.

Medieval society thus inherited and sustained a mix of sometimes inconsistent attitudes toward children. The social historian, by playing upon one or another of these attitudes, by judiciously screening his sources, could easily color as he pleases the history of medieval children. He could compile a list of the atrocities committed against them, dwell upon their neglect, or celebrate medieval views of the child's innocence and holiness. One must, however, strive to paint a more balanced picture, and for this we obviously need some means of testing the experiences of the medieval child. The tests we shall use here are two: the social investment, the wealth and resources which medieval society was apparently willing to invest in children; and the psychological investment, the attention they claimed and received from their elders. The thesis of this essay, simply stated, is that both the social and psychological investments in children were growing substantially from approximately the eleventh and twelfth centuries, through to the end of the Middle Ages, and doubtlessly beyond.

The basic economic and social changes which affected medieval society during this period seem to have required a heightened investment in children. From about the year 1000, the medieval community was growing in numbers and complexity. Commercial exchange intensified, and a vigorous urban life was reborn in the West. Even the shocking reduction in population size, coming with the plagues, famines, and wars of the fourteenth century, did not undo the importance of the commercial economy or of the towns and the urban classes dependent upon it. Medieval society, once a simple association of warriors, priests, and peasants, came to include such numerous and varied social types as merchants, lawyers, notaries, accountants, clerks, and artisans. A new world was born, based on the cultivation and preservation of specialized, sophisticated skills.

The emergence of specialized roles within society required in turn a social commitment to the training of children in the corresponding skills. Earlier educational reforms—notably those achieved under Charlemagne[8]—had largely affected monks and, in less measure, clerics; they had little

[8]Carolingian emperor, 768–814.

impact on the lay world. One novelty of the new medieval pedagogy, as it is developed from the twelfth century, is the attention now given to the training of laymen. Many writers now comment on the need and value of mastering a trade from early youth. Boys... should be taught a trade "as soon as possible." ... "Men from childhood," Thomas Aquinas[9] observes, "apply themselves to those offices and skills in which they will spend their lives.... This is altogether necessary. To the extent that something is difficult, so much the more must a man grow accustomed to it from childhood."

Later in the thirteenth century, Raymond Lull,[10] one of the most learned men of the epoch, compares society to a wheel upon which men ride ceaselessly, up and down, gaining and losing status; the force which drives the wheel is education, in particular the mastery of a marketable skill. Through the exercise of a trade, a man earns money, gains status, and ultimately enters the ranks of the rich. Frequently, however, he becomes arrogant in his new status, and he neglects to train his children in a trade. His unskilled offspring inevitably ride the wheel on its downward swing. And so the world turns. A marketable skill offers the only certain riches and the only security....

One hundred and fifty years later, the Florentine Dominican Giovanni Dominici voices exactly the same sentiments. Neither wealth nor inherited status offers security. Only a marketable skill can assure that children "will not be forced, as are many, to beg, to steal, to enter household service, or to do demeaning things." ...

Although statistics largely elude us, there can be little doubt that medieval society was making substantial investments in education from the twelfth century.... The chronicler Giovanni Villani[11] gives us some rare figures on the schools functioning at Florence in the 1330s. The children, both boys and girls, who were attending the grammar schools of the city, presumably between 6 and 12 years of age, numbered between eight and ten thousand. From what we know of the population of the city, better than one out of two school-aged children were receiving formal instruction in reading. Florentine girls received no more formal instruction after grammar school, but of the boys, between 1,000 and 1,200 went on to six secondary schools, where they learned how to calculate on the abacus, in evident preparation for a business career. Another 550 to 600 attended four "large schools" where they studied "Latin and logic," the necessary preparation for entry into the universities and, eventually, for a career in law, medicine, or the Church. Florence, it might be argued, was hardly a typical medieval community. Still, the social investment that Florentines were making in the training of their children was substantial.

[9]Saint and theologian, c.1225–1274.

[10]Missionary and philosopher, c.1223–c.1315.

[11]Florentine, d.1348.

Another indicator of social investment in children is the number of orphanages or hospitals devoted to their care, and here the change across the Middle Ages is particularly impressive. The care of the abandoned or orphaned child was a traditional obligation of Christian charity, but it did not lead to the foundation and support of specialized orphanages until late in the Middle Ages. The oldest European orphanage of which we have notice was founded at Milan in 787, but we know nothing at all concerning its subsequent history or that of other orphanages sporadically mentioned in the early sources. The great hospital orders of the medieval Church, which sprang up from the twelfth century, cared for orphans and foundlings, but none initially chose that charity as its special mission.

The history of hospitals in the city of Florence gives striking illustration of a new concern for abandoned babies which emerged in Europe during the last two centuries of the Middle Ages. In his detailed description of his native city, written in the 1330s, Villani boasts that Florence contained thirty hospitals with more than a thousand beds. But the beds were intended for the "poor and infrm," and he mentions no special hospital for foundlings. A century later, probably in the 1420s, another chronicler, Gregorio Dati,[12] ...composed another description of the marvels of Florence. By then the city contained no fewer than three hospitals which received foundlings and supported them until an age when the girls could marry and the boys could be instructed in a trade....

Even a rapid survey of the foundling hospitals of Europe shows a similar pattern. Bologna seems not to have had an orphanage until 1459, and Pavia not until 1449. At Paris, the first specialized hospital for children, Saint-Esprit en Grèves, was founded in 1363, but according to its charter it was supposed to receive only orphans of legitimate birth. Care of foundlings, it was feared, might encourage sexual license among adults. But the hospital in practice seems to have accepted abandoned babies, and several similar institutions were established in French cities in the fifteenth century.

This new concern for the survival of children, even foundlings, seems readily explicable. Amid the ravages of epidemics, the sheer numbers of orphans must have multiplied in society. Moreover, the plagues carried off the very young in disproportionate numbers. Parents feared for the survival of their lineages and their communities.... The frequent creation of foundling hospitals and orphanages indicates that society as a whole shared this concern and was willing to invest in the survival of its young, even orphans and foundlings.

The medieval social investment in children thus seems to have grown from the twelfth century and to have passed through two phases: the first one, beginning from the twelfth century, largely involved a commitment, on the part of the urban communities, to the child's education and training; the

[12]Florentine writer, businessman, and statesman, 1362–1435.

second, from the late fourteenth century, reflected a concern for the child's survival and health under difficult hygienic conditions.

This social investment also presumes an equivalent psychological investment, as well as a heightened attention paid to the child and his development. This is evident, for example, in the rich tradition of pedagogical literature intended for a lay audience, which again dates from the twelfth century. One of the earliest authors to provide a comprehensive regimen of child care was Vincent of Beauvais, who died in 1264.... [H]e gives advice on the delivery of the baby; its care in the first hours, days, and months of life; nursing and weaning; the care of older children; and their formal education. Later in the century, Raymond Lull ... is similarly comprehensive, including passages not only on formal schooling but also on the care and nourishment of the child. "For every man," he explains, "must hold his child dear." ... The learning of the scholars seems to have spread widely, even among the humble social classes.

These medieval pedagogues also developed a rudimentary but real psychology of children. Vincent of Beauvais recommends that the child who does not readily learn must be beaten, but he warns against the psychological damage which excessive severity may cause. "Children's minds," he explains, "break down under excessive severity of correction; they despair, and worry, and finally they hate. And this is the most injurious; where everything is feared, nothing is attempted." A few teachers ... wanted to prohibit all corporal punishment at school. For them physical discipline was "contrary to nature"; it "induced servility and sowed resentment, which in later years might make the student hate the teacher and forget his lesson."

The teacher—and on this all writers agree—should be temperate in the use of force, and he should also observe the child, in order to identify his talents and capacities. For not all children are alike, and natural differences must be recognized and developed. Raymond Lull affirms that nature is more capable of rearing the child than the child's mother. The Florentine Giovanni Dominici stresses the necessity of choosing the proper profession for the child. Society, he notes, requires all sorts of occupations and skills, ranging from farmers to carpenters, to bankers, merchants, priests, and "a thousand others." ...

To read these writers is inevitably to form the impression that medieval people, or some of them at least, were deeply concerned about children. Indeed, Jean Gerson[13] expressly condemns his contemporaries, who, in his opinion, were excessively involved with their children's survival and success. In order to gain for them "the honors and pomp of this world," parents, he alleges, were expending "all their care and attention; they sleep neither day nor night and often become very miserly." In investing in their children, they neglected charitable works and the good of their own souls....

[13]French theologian, 1363–1429.

Medieval society, increasingly dependent upon the cultivation of sophisticated skills, had to invest in a supporting pedagogy; when later threatened
by child-killing plagues, it had to show concern for the survival of the very
young. But the medieval involvement with children cannot be totally described in these functional terms. Even as they were developing an effective
pedagogy, medieval people were re-evaluating the place of childhood among
the periods of life.

One indication of a new sympathy toward childhood is the revision
in theological opinion concerning the salvation of the babies who died
without baptism. Up until the twelfth century, the leading theologians of
the Western church ... reiterated the weighty opinion of St. Augustine, that
such infants were surely damned. In the twelfth century, Peter Abelard and
Peter Lombard, perhaps the two most influential theologians of the epoch,
reversed the condemnation of unbaptized babies to eternal fires. A thorough
examination of the question, however, awaited the work of Thomas Aquinas,
the first to use in a technical theological sense the term *limbus puerorum*, the
"limbo of children." The unbaptized baby, he taught, suffered only the
deprivation of the Beatific Vision.[14] ...

Aquinas' mild judgment on babies dead without baptism became the
accepted teaching of the medieval Church. Only one prominent theologian
in the late Middle Ages, Gregory of Rimini,[15] resisted it, and he came to be
known as the *tortor puerorum*, the "torturer of children."

No less remarkable is the emergence, from the twelfth century, of a
widespread devotion to the Child Jesus. The texts from the early Middle
Ages which treat of the Christ Child ... present Christ as a miniature wonder
worker, who miraculously corrects Joseph's mistakes in carpentry, tames
lions, divides rivers, and even strikes dead a teacher who dared reprimand
him in class. All-knowing and all-powerful, he is the negation of the helpless,
charming child. A new picture of the Child Jesus emerges, initially under
Cistercian auspices, in the twelfth century. For example, between 1153 and
1157 the English Cistercian Aelred of Rievaulx composed a meditation, "Jesus
at the Age of Twelve." Aelred expatiates on the joy which the presence of
the young Christ brought to his elders and companions: "...the grace of
heaven shone from that most beautiful face with such charm as to make
everyone look at it, listen to him, and be moved to affection.... Old men
kiss him, young men embrace him, boys wait upon him.... Each of them, I
think, declares in his inmost heart: 'Let him kiss me with the kiss of his
mouth.'"...

Doubtlessly, the special characteristics of Cistercian monasticism were
influential here. Like other reformed orders of the twelfth century, the
Cistercians no longer admitted oblates, the boys placed in the monastery at

[14]The immediate vision of God in Heaven.

[15]d.1358.

tender ages, who grew up in the cloister with no experience of secular life. The typical Cistercians . . . were raised within a natural family, and many were familiar with the emotions of family life. Grown men when they entered the monastery, they carried with them a distinct mentality—a mentality formed in the secular world and open to secular values. Many doubtlessly had considered and some had pursued other careers before electing the monastic life; they presumably had reflected upon the emotional and spiritual rewards of the married state and the state of parenthood. While fleeing from the world, they still sought in their religious experiences analogues to secular and familial emotions. . . . In celebrating the joys of contemplating a perfect child, they find in their religious experience an analogue to the love and satisfaction which parents feel in observing their growing children. The Cistercian cult of the Child Jesus suggests, in other words, that lay persons, too, were finding the contemplation of children emotionally rewarding.

In the thirteenth century, devotion to the Child Jesus spread well beyond the restricted circle of Cistercian monasticism. St. Francis of Assisi,[16] according to the *Legenda Gregorii*[17] set up for the first time a Christmas crèche, so that the faithful might more easily envision the tenderness and humility of the new-born Jesus. St. Francis, the most popular saint of the late Middle Ages, was thus responsible, at least in legend, for one of the most popular devotional practices still associated with Christmas. . . .

This cult of the Christ Child implies an idealization of childhood itself. "O sweet and sacred childhood," another Cistercian . . . writes of the early years of Christ, "which brought back man's true innocence, by which men of every age can return to blessed childhood and be conformed to you, not in physical weakness but in humility of heart and holiness of life."

How are we to explain this celebration of "sweet and sacred childhood"? It closely resembles other religious movements which acquire extraordinary appeal from the twelfth century—the cults of poverty, of Christian simplicity, and of the apostolic life. These "movements of cultural primitivism" . . . point to a deepening psychological discontent with the demands of the new commercial economy. The inhabitants of towns in particular, living by trade, were forced into careers of getting and spending, in constant pursuit of what Augustine had called "deceitful riches." The psychological tensions inherent in the urban professions and the dubious value of the proferred material rewards seem to have generated a nostalgic longing for alternate systems of existence, for freedom from material concerns, for the simple Christian life as it was supposedly lived in the apostolic age. Another model for an alternate existence, the exact opposite of the tension-ridden urban experience, was the real or imagined life of the child, who was at once humble and content, poor and pure, joyous and giving joy.

[16] Founder of the Franciscans, c.1182–1226.

[17] *Legends by Gregory.*

The simple piety of childhood remained an ideal of religious reformers for the duration of the Middle Ages. At their close, both Girolamo Savonarola[18] in the south of Europe and Desiderius Erasmus[19] in the north urged their readers to look to pious children if they would find true models of the Christian life. . . .

Moreover, the medieval cult of childhood extends beyond religious movements and informs secular attitudes as well. . . . Later in the Middle Ages, a Florentine citizen and merchant . . . , reflecting on his own life, calls childhood "nature's most pleasant age." In his *Praise of Folly*, Erasmus avers that the simplicity and unpretentiousness of childhood make it the happiest time of life. "Who does not know," Folly asks her audience, "that childhood is the happiest age and the most pleasant for all? What is there about children that makes us kiss and hug them and cuddle them as we do, so that even an enemy would help them, unless it is this charm of folly?" Clearly, we have come far from Augustine's opinion, that men would prefer eternal death to life again as a child.

The history of medieval children is as complex as the history of any social group, and even more elusive. This essay has attempted to describe in broad outline the cultural attitudes which influenced the experiences of medieval children, as well as the large social trends which touched their lives. The central movements which, in this reconstruction, affected their fate were the social and economic changes widely evident across Europe from the twelfth century, most especially the rise of a commercialized economy and the proliferation of special skills within society; and the worsening health conditions of the late Middle Ages, from the second half of the fourteenth century. The growth of a commercialized economy made essential an attentive pedagogy which could provide society with adequately trained adults. And the deteriorating conditions of hygiene across the late Middle Ages heightened the concern for, and investment in, the health and survival of the very young. Paradoxically, too, the growing complexities of social life engendered not truly a discovery but an idealization of childhood: the affirmation of the sentimental belief that childhood is, as Erasmus maintains, a blessed time and the happiest moment of human existence. . . .

[18] Dominican reformer who ruled Florence from 1494 to 1498.
[19] Dutch humanist, c.1466–1536.

Vendetta and Civil Disorder in Late Medieval Ghent

DAVID NICHOLAS

Faced with plague, warfare, and economic depression, fourteenth-century cities were hotbeds of social antagonisms and daily violence. Ghent, the greatest city of Flanders, in present-day Belgium, provides a case study for an understanding of late medieval criminality, the underside of urban life.

Unlike most historians who have studied revolts and discontent in medieval cities, David Nicholas eschews class struggle as the source of medieval troubles with law and order and instead focuses on family life. He offers a cogent argument that family relationships explain the proliferation of feuds and thus of beatings, mutilations, and homicides. Moreover, the families involved included not only the nuclear unit of parents and children, but also grandparents, uncles, and cousins— not to mention the dozens of clients, retainers who wore the colors of and bore arms for the wealthy families that plagued Ghent with their violent and bloody ways.

The family was the only unit that could provide adequate protection against personal attack in Ghent. When it came to homicide, the city government sought to arbitrate rather than to punish. We are far from the modern notion that the state bears the primary responsibility for the protection of its citizens. Fourteenth-century Ghent had a relatively weak government but a strong family structure, rather than the opposite situation in existence today.

What exactly did the government of Ghent do to curb violence? How did the principle of collective responsibility serve to restrain family members from committing crimes and to resolve feuds already begun? What notions of honor and morality contributed to the bloodletting that often characterized interfamily relations? How did the blood price function? How does Philip van Artevelde's scheme of revenge illustrate the familial and urban ethos of late medieval Ghent?

Western Europe underwent a social and economic upheaval in the late Middle Ages. In the late thirteenth or early fourteenth century, population virtually everywhere reached levels that could only be supported with difficulty. Death rates were high even before the famines and plagues that visited Europe with numbing regularity began about 1310; beginning with the "Black Death" of 1348–1349, mortality became catastrophic. Faced with shrinking markets, the occupational guilds in the cities began restricting the entry of persons who were not kinspeople of masters [fully trained and enfranchised members of the organization]. The cities were filled with unskilled workers, many of them recent immigrants, who could not join guilds and were unable to find steady work.

The classic situation of the rich getting richer while the poor got poorer is found in virtually all major cities. There was a dramatic increase in the extent

143

of unemployment and poor relief. Most towns began providing assistance to churches, hospitals, orphanages, and parish organizations for poor relief in the fourteenth century. Yet the virtually constant threat of war and the fiscal demands of the territorial princes forced city governments to spend such enormous amounts of money on fortifications and weaponry that their domestic spending was severely limited. Much of what they did spend went into pageantry and building.

It thus comes as no surprise to learn that most late medieval cities were extremely violent and dangerous places. Studies of such diverse places as Siena, Venice, Florence, Oxford, and Paris have shown a desensitizing succession of street wars, gang rapes, individual sexual assaults, and fights that could erupt for anything from a misinterpreted stare to a personal insult. A brawl began at Ghent when one young man, accompanied by a band of his friends, called mockingly to the leader of another group across the square "Tra la la la la, Parijs [the man's family name] has a long cock."

Most historians have interpreted this urban violence as a reflection of class struggle: the unemployed fought the employed, and poorer crafts fought wealthy guilds for political power. But recent studies of family bonds have shown that economic rivalries were supplemented virtually everywhere, and in some places were actually less important as causes of violence than powerful families and their clienteles. An offense to any member of the family, including affines [in-laws] in most cities, could lead to bloodshed and vendettas that could involve non-combatants on both sides and might last for many years. Family alliances created a maze of patronage and influence from which few could escape.

Flanders, the most densely urbanized part of northwestern Europe, offers a particularly instructive example of late medieval urban problems. The Flemish cities based their prosperity on manufacturing luxurious woolen textiles, but they had to import most of their food from France and the finer wools for their cloth from England. In addition, the counts of Flanders were Frenchmen who were often at odds with their subjects, most of whom spoke a dialect of Dutch. As political hostilities deepened in the thirteenth century between Flanders' major suppliers, France and England, the Flemish textile industry began to decline, and parties formed in the major cities.

Ghent, the metropolis of Flanders, was the second largest (after Paris) city of northern Europe in the fourteenth century. Its records provide a superb case study of the vital importance of the vendetta in exacerbating urban violence. It had a population of perhaps 80,000 around 1300 but had declined to 30,000 by 1390 after a century of plagues, foreign and civil wars, and decline of its textile industry. The city was racked by the feuds of powerful extended families that the government had little power to curb. The city was governed by two councils of thirteen members who were chosen after 1360 on the basis of guild affiliation. One council functioned as Justices of the Peace. The Justices held mass trial days several times a year where uncontested cases of slander and petty violence involving minimal bloodshed were judged and punished. The Justices sent the miscreants on pilgrimages and awarded personal damages in most of these cases, usually acting on the basis of the prior rulings of arbitrators who had been agreed upon by the parties. Between 1350 and 1379, the Justices handled an average of 151 cases a year, but the problem of crime was worsening: the average in the 1370s was 185, and by 1370 the population of Ghent was only about three-fifths of its level of 1350. Fewer people were responsible for more violent deeds.

For a population the size of Ghent's, these figures are not large, but the convictions at the trial days of the Justices of the Peace are only a part of the larger pattern of violent behavior. The aldermen, who constituted the higher of the two councils, tried criminal cases in which the facts were disputed, but the records of these actions have not survived. The prince, the count of Flanders, also appointed a bailiff to assist the aldermen in keeping order. He had a miniscule staff, consisting of a deputy bailiff and four sergeants. By the fourteenth century the only arrests that the bailiff could make on his own authority were in cases of thieves caught in the act, homicide, and assault so serious that it might eventually result in a death. For all other crimes, he could make arrests only in the presence of the aldermen. He could put citizens on trial only before the aldermen, who had the right to release any culprit whom he had arrested.

Thus the bailiff of Ghent handled mainly cases involving transients and citizens whom the town fathers did not care to protect. The bailiff had jurisdiction outside the city as well as within the walls, but even there he could not try people of Ghent unless the aldermen agreed. In 1373 the bailiff of Eeklo, a small town northwest of Ghent, reported that "several burghers of Ghent, together with others who were not burghers, came into Eeklo and hit and slashed at Henry de Ketelboetere's house during the day. On this account the bailiff conducted an inquest with the aldermen to have justice for the misdeed." The culprits apparently went unpunished. The next year the victimized men of Eeklo retaliated against them. This attack was handled by arbitration at Ghent, to the considerable advantage of the Ghent citizens.

Although the bailiff and the town government had some quarrels over jurisdiction, relations between them were generally correct. The bailiffs had to render trimesterly accounts to the counts, and these include the emoluments of justice. Between 1373 and 1378, when complete records survive, they handled an average of 158 cases a year that in principle should have been heard by the aldermen, but most of these actions did not come to formal trial. Rather, the bailiffs exacted a fine, called "composition," before they would release suspects whom they thought that the aldermen would not convict, and they were brazen enough to state this as their reason. In 1373 the bailiff of Ghent released a man whose guilt was undeniable because "he thought he would not get anything through the court, so he made peace for lack of a better alternative."

In addition to functioning as judges in formal trials, both the Justices and the aldermen could act as arbitrators whenever the parties to a legal action agreed to it. More often, private citizens, usually members of the families of the two protagonists, served as arbitrators. The aldermen could try homicide cases. The Justices of the Peace could not, but they had the duty of arranging arbitration between sets of kindred who wanted to avoid having one of their number go to trial. The city's constitution of 1191 made homicide a capital offense, but there was no *ex officio* prosecution: someone had to press charges before the aldermen would intervene and hold a formal trial. Thus most homicides in Ghent were settled by private arrangements between extended families, rather than in trials. In modern terms, such cases were torts rather than crimes. Between 1350 and 1380 the deaths of 725 persons were atoned by arbitration, an annual average of twenty-four per year. Most of these were cases in which multiple homicides and other acts of original and retaliatory bloodletting were settled as part of a general peace settlement between "kinsmen and friends."

How did this state of affairs come about? Why did the magistrates not intervene directly more often, despite the limitation of the law of 1191, forcing the parties into trials? How did the extended families gain such power? For what ends did they exercise it? The answers to these questions will reveal the forces of order in Ghent negotiating a delicate course between the Scylla of chaos and the Charybdis of savagery.[1]

First, the rivalry between the English and French parties in Flanders contributed to but did not cause this dangerous situation. Matters reached a crisis in the struggles between the Flemish count Guy of Dampierre (ruled 1278–1305) and his feudal overlord, King Philip IV (1285–1314) of France, who hoped to annex Flanders. Parties called "Claws" (for the lion on the Flemish counts' coat of arms) and "Lilies" for the French fleur-de-lys formed in the Flemish cities. Although most aristocratic families were Lilies, some became Claws, usually because their rivals within the ruling group were not.

A particularly flagrant example of a feud that assumed political overtones after beginning as a family struggle racked Ghent between 1294 and 1306. Two ancient lineages, the Borluuts and the van Sint Baafs, were already enemies when John Borluut the younger answered a verbal slight by striking a kinsman of Matthew van Sint Baafs, the rival patriarch. His act broke the existing truce between their families, and the aldermen exiled him. Before he left, he took a gang at night to the abbey village of Saint Bavo, where his rivals had property and clients, and butchered several people in a fight in which the Borluut forces outnumbered their rivals by at least three to one. While in exile, he remained in touch with his ally, Peter de Visschere, brother of the abbot of St. Peter's, the great rival of Saint Bavo. Alerting each other to movements of enemies, the pair engineered several more homicides and mutilations by stealth. In one of these cases, a servant of the van Sint Baafs

---

[1]In Greek mythology, Scylla was a sea monster and Charybdis a whirlpool. They assumed positions on opposite sides of the straits of Messina, and sailors who tried to avoid the one fell victim to the other. (Author's note.)

had his hands and feet hacked off before expiring from his injuries. Peter de Visschere was finally killed during a brief truce in 1296 by a van Sint Baaf ally, in a brawl that erupted when the men of both sides came to a funeral with knives concealed under their coats. Borluut then returned in disguise and used the shelter of St. Peter's abbey to avenge his friend by murdering two more people, one by a knife thrust in the back.

The personal feud between the van Sint Baafs and Borluuts corresponded to a political stance: the Borluuts were Claws, while the van Sint Baafs, who were more closely associated with the older patrician ruling element of Ghent, were Lilies. When Count Guy in 1297 ordered the Lily patricians arrested, the van Sint Baafs had to flee the city. They returned in 1300, when French troops occupied Flanders and installed Lily governments in the cities. The French were in serious trouble elsewhere in Flanders by the spring of 1302, but they held out at Ghent. When Courtrai, a town south of Ghent, joined the Claws, John Borluut came there from exile and sent word that men of Ghent who wanted to fight against the French invasion could join him. The government of Ghent did not send the city militia to fight at the battle at Courtrai, where a crushing defeat was administered to the French on July 11, 1302, but Borluut's contingent of guildsmen and Claw patricians did so. The Lily regime at Ghent was quickly ended, and Borluut was acclaimed as a hero. He was the first but not the last mass murderer who has become a hero of the Ghent working classes through the sheer accident that his pursuit of family goals forced him to seek allies with the guildsmen who were outside the governing elite.

When the Lilies were again repatriated in 1305, the van Sint Baafs returned to Ghent. The son of the murdered bailiff of 1296, now an adult and taught to seek revenge, stalked John Borluut. He failed in two attempts on his life but finally knifed him as he left a drinking bout at the town hall in December 1305. By this time the families were ready to hold a peace conference. The result of the nine homicides and countless mutilations and injuries was twenty-seven pilgrimages and damage assessments that nearly cancelled out between the sides.

Several protagonists in the Borluut–van Sint Baafs feud served on the town council and used their positions in the government to further their families' interests. Yet there is considerable evidence that however readily the magistrates would rush to the defense of one of their own relatives, most of them saw in principle the need to contain family violence. The endemic disorder in Ghent was not caused by an abdication of responsibility, but rather by legal limitations on the magistrates' power and by an ethic that saw bloodletting to avenge family injuries not as a mere right, but as a moral obligation.

The vendetta was thus as alive in Flanders in 1360 as it had been in 960. Although no formal *wergeld* scales [blood price listed in Germanic law codes to compensate the homicide victim's kindred] survive this late, an enormous sum was paid to the males of the clan for their slaughtered brother. Homicide, as an affair of honor, did not involve women as principals and only rarely as victims. The most important determinant of the blood price was clearly the wealth or social standing of the deceased; there is no evidence that the status of the killer had anything to do with setting the blood price. The penalties for violence perpetrated during truce were more severe than those where no formal peace existed between the families. They might be imposed by the aldermen rather than the antagonists.

But the countless feuds show that atonement for homicide, indeed of any injury in which blood was drawn, was the sacred duty of every kindred, not the town government. The aldermen never accepted a homicide case until the parties had tried private mediation. Litigants had the right to refuse the aldermen's arbitration, and the magistrates only intervened when private arbitrators had failed to reach a verdict. The aldermen would record any agreement acceptable to both feuding parties. So minimal was respect for public authority that when one party took another to court, and the legal action resulted in the latter's execution, the former was obligated to offer his kinsmen a blood price, just as if he had been killed in a street fight. When enough blood had been shed to exhaust their energies, the senior males of the families concerned arranged settlements by which injuries on both sides might be cancelled out, more serious injuries paid for by a fee, and homicides handled by pilgrimages and always a blood price. These reconciliations involved not individuals, but entire families, all of whom were brought into the peace terms and were required to post bond guaranteeing that they would abide by the terms of the settlement.

The blood price was divided among the family members according to a fixed formula, but the mechanics of division caused some brotherly friction. Half of the blood price went to the closest surviving male blood relative of the deceased party, preferably his oldest brother. He in turn had the obligation of avenging his brother's death by, if he wished to satisfy all demands of honor, killing his brother's murderer. Failing that, he should kill one of his relatives, or at the very least demand as high a blood price as the market would bear. After expenses of reaching the settlement were deducted, the rest of the money was divided into shares for the other blood kin. Support of the widow and orphans was in principle the duty of her father or brothers. It was not to come from the blood price, and exceptions to this were entirely at the discretion of the decedent's male relatives.

A few well documented cases illustrate the pride and arrogance of the prominent men of Ghent. In 1358 Soy van der Dorent, who was leasing a farm at Vurste, near Ghent, from John van der Zickelen, one of the richest men of the city, was assaulted by a youth who was acting on orders of van der Zickelen's personal enemies. John van der Zickelen, not the injured farmer who was part of his clientele, took matters into his own hands. After waiting in vain for several months for an atonement to be offered, he sent formal notice to the culprit and his patron, Cornelius van Prendale. The next Sunday Cornelius' brother was given lethal wounds from the van der

Zickelens. To prevent further violence, the parish priest of Vurste arranged an arbitrated settlement in which John van der Zickelen not only forced the van Prendales to pay for Soy van der Dorent's injuries, but also obliged Cornelius van Prendale himself to atone John's own killing of Cornelius' brother. That noble spirit in turn gave it to the parish priest of Vurste to support the dead man's orphan. The Justices of the Peace at Ghent recorded this settlement on the same day when it was reached.

No moral or legal stigma was attached to any deed that was paid for. Few would ally with a family enemy; yet Philip van Artevelde, who as we shall see had a maniacally strong consciousness of family responsibility, served in the government of Ghent in 1382 alongside John van Merlaer, who had killed Philip's brother James in 1370. Since van Merlaer had paid the blood price rather than paying with his own life, he had satisfied his debt to the van Arteveldes.

The principle of compensating all injuries regardless of fault or motive was followed to the letter. When the victim of an assault injured his assailant by defending himself, he had to pay for the person's damages. In 1355 a butcher's son admitted that he had entered a house "saying that he had been fighting and drinking all week and had paid for all that, and he was now ready for more and would pay for that too." They did indeed pay enormous sums that would have ruined persons who lacked their wealth. This fray, in which he was joined by three other youths of prominent families, cost one innocent man his life and left the homeowner with life threatening wounds and his wife and son with less serious injuries. Despite the clear culpability of the invaders, the homeowner had to pay one of them 9 lb. parisis, which was roughly what a continuously employed master carpenter would earn in a month and a half, to compensate him for the injuries that he sustained during the assault. There was thus open season on human flesh. Indeed, there is surprisingly little evidence of persons defaulting blood prices for homicide or damage assessments. Most of the bloodletting was done by persons of property who saw nothing wrong with what they were doing but rather considered it a mark of honor.

Wives and widows and their blood kin were expected to pay half the blood prices, while the perpetrator and his relatives paid the other half, and this in turn simply multiplied exponentially the number of persons involved in family-related violence. When an individual was unable to pay the blood price, his relatives were expected as a matter of honor to help him. Although this obligation was usually not legally enforceable, very few family members legally excused themselves from liability in homicide atonements. Since relatives could be injured or killed by the enemies of any of their kinspeople, even if they had no knowledge of what was going on, it was very risky to remove oneself from the warmth of the family circle. The attitude that the kindred should help was sanctioned by the aldermen. In a case of 1370, they noted that the killer "can hardly do this [pay the blood price] without the help and grace of his kinsmen and friends." The magistrates thus suggested pointedly that they help him "insofar as kin or friends help their kinsman and should do it out of grace, to the extent that you would want help or assistance from your kinsman, which we promise you in equal or even greater measure."

Although the Justices normally would not force innocent relatives to help with blood prices, arbitrators frequently did, and the Justices recorded their verdicts and enforced them. This was true even when the other relatives had urged the malefactor to modify his behavior. In 1369, one Henry van Heedevelde had collected a 10 lb. groot [the pound groot was worth twelve times the pound parisis] damage settlement from Arnold van der Borch. Then, contrary to his two brothers' advice, he resumed hostilities, and eventually he and his family became liable for 25 lb. 10s. groot [roughly what a continuously employed master carpenter would earn in four years] for another death and injury. Henry's personal liability, however, was only for the 10 lb. that he had collected for his own injuries. He successfully sued his brothers to pay everything over this from their own property. Henry had no obligation to repay them; they probably lost more money from his bad behavior than he did.

No tactic was too odious to use on one's enemies. Numerous homicides involved large groups ambushing an isolated person or two. Tempers were hot, and while some insults were visited with immediate retribution in the view of a crowd, others were the result of premeditation and stealth: the back stab, the tracking of an antagonist until he got into a place where his own clan could not protect him or where the city government could not enforce its regulations. Children and non-combatants were fair game. Persons with the same family name as an enemy were forced to swear in the presence of the magistrates that there was no blood relationship or face immediate extinction. Gangs that might include scores of persons roamed the streets. Some families had their own uniforms or colors by which their retainers could be recognized. Several cases in the Borluut–van Sint Baafs feud show that servants were particularly vulnerable; they were considered part of the clan and thus were subject to retribution that really was aimed at the patriarch. Servants were often ordered into enemy territory in the city or the surrounding abbey villages where the family leaders had sense enough not to go. Of course, since they were part of the household, their own masters would avenge their injuries.

Ghent was an armed camp. The rural areas near the city were not exempt from its violence. In 1373 a brewer of Ghent was seriously injured by other men of Ghent in a tavern in a nearby town, despite the fact that he had taken the precaution of wearing an iron helmet while he dined. Although statutes forbade the inhabitants to carry deadly weapons, and the bailiff regularly fined a few people for infractions, several cases show that it was expected that everyone would have weapons on his person. In 1365, one fistfight led to retaliation with a knife; the fray escalated to a battleaxe, whose victim then chased his victim with an iron morning star [a heavy iron ball studded with spikes and attached to a chain, from which it could be flailed]. The aldermen simply set personal damages for the knife and battleaxe injuries, but drew the line at the morning star, which "is not an honorable man's weapon, but rather it is forbidden among all decent people," and set its user on a pilgrimage. Most cases even of assault in which no deadly weapon is involved specify a beating "with the fist and its contents."

To combat this chaos, the city government of Ghent had an official personnel of only about 150 persons in the fourteenth century, although the extensive use of arbitrators, and the fact that many cases were handled in guild courts that have left no records, make the picture somewhat less bleak. All persons in an official capacity, from the aldermen to the city messengers, could make arrests. Yet, except when there was open revolt in the city, the government maintained only seventeen full-time police officers during the 1360s and 1370s. Their task was complicated by the total absence of a notion that violence was anything other than completely ethical. Cases survive showing that contracts to commit premeditated murder were enforceable in the very courts that were supposed to be trying to quell the violence. Even more cases show that while named individuals are legally responsible for deeds of violence, the damages that are owed to their victims would be paid openly for them by their patron, most often a prominent man of the city.

The problem of peacekeeping was exacerbated by the persistence of enclaves outside the jurisdiction of the city government, notably the two great abbey villages of Saints Peter and Bavo, where malefactors such as John Borluut's ally Peter de Visschere could take refuge. Even within the city fugitives and exiles could take shelter in the churches and adjacent cemeteries, for the city government generally respected the right of asylum that prohibited secular powers from functioning on ecclesiastical immunities.

Even when cases reached the magistrates, they often imposed punishments that were more symbolic than deterrent. Imprisonment was rarely used as a punishment for crime. As was generally true in medieval Europe, the town prison of Ghent was used mainly for debtors and for persons who were being detained awaiting trial. Only the bailiff could impose blood justice, which involved penalties of death or loss of a limb, ear, or the nose; when the aldermen convicted someone of a capital crime, they had to have the bailiff execute him. Perhaps for this reason and also because arbitration was possible for any misdeed except treason, few mutilations are mentioned, and the bailiff rarely executed as many as ten persons per year, and many of these were for heresy or witchcraft. At the mass trial days, the Justices usually sent the person considered primarily responsible for a fight on a pilgrimage, usually to a nearby shrine, but would order his victim to compensate the assailant for his injuries. This meant that the victim often suffered greater financial loss than the instigator.

Pilgrimages to more distant places, of course, amounted to a temporary exile. The problem with exile was that while the city government could banish a convicted felon from Flanders, it had no means of enforcing this judgement outside the town. Thus even the suburbs of the city were havens for persons banished by the aldermen. As exiles, however, they could be summarily dispatched by anyone catching them; in practice, this meant that their personal enemies, whose grievances had led to the banishment in the first place, had open season on them. The exiles were accordingly desperate enough to do anything. Some of them lived openly on their rural estates, and some homicide atonements specifically forbid a guilty man's wife to send him provisions during his exile. The smaller towns around Ghent resented the power of the metropolis, which was often used to their political or economic disadvantage, and many of them gave haven to exiles from Ghent. The municipal accounts of Ghent record numerous armed expeditions to dislodge exiles from Ghent from the small towns.

Evidence is ambiguous about the extent of family solidarity during the numerous political upheavals of the later fourteenth century in Ghent, but there can be no doubt that political and personal rivalries fed each other. The careers of James and Philip van Artevelde, the legendary father and son who became captains of Ghent and to this day are considered heroes of both nationalist and socialist movements in Flanders, afford a chilling example of the political impact of the vendetta. James van Artevelde became chief captain of Ghent in 1338 in the emergency caused by Flanders being caught in the middle between France and England in the opening stages of the Hundred Years War. He maintained his position virtually unchallenged until early 1343, when he survived a coup attempt led by people who felt that the English alliance into which he had led the city was catastrophic. The new government of Ghent that took office on August 15, 1344 contained several men who had no objection to the English alliance—indeed, they adhered to it after van Artevelde's death—but were van Artevelde's personal enemies who disliked him for playing the prince as ruler of Ghent and in fact the rest of Flanders. Van Artevelde was deposed from his captaincy in late March 1345, but he continued to perform diplomatic missions for the city government. In the last week of his life, he was negotiating with the English when he was summoned home into a trap by the captain John de Scouteete. When van Artevelde returned to Ghent on the evening of July 17, 1345, he was ambushed and killed at his home. One source says that he was given the death stroke by an anonymous "maker [restorer] of old shoes," evidently a disgruntled neighbor, in the alley behind his house as he tried to escape the mob. James van Artevelde was killed by personal enemies, not as an act of policy.

When peace was restored in 1349, van Artevelde's sons were exiled. They evidently knew that John de Scouteete had been involved in enticing their father back to Ghent. In 1361, just after they were repatriated, the oldest, John, killed John de Scouteete; although de Scouteete had living relatives, they demanded no blood price, evidently feeling that the homicide had been a consequence of John de Scouteete's official duties and that their kinsman had compromised himself with the van Arteveldes.

The van Arteveldes of the second generation thus seem at first to have thought that their father's death had been avenged. This did not stop them from getting into other feuds. James van Artevelde the younger was killed in 1370 by his family's neighbors at the polder village of Weert, a village along the Scheldt where James the elder had owned land. The killers in turn were bound in a tangled kinship net with the van Arteveldes' political opponents in Ghent. The leaders of the killers were the de Mey and van Merlaer families, who were related to one another and to other van Artevelde enemies in Ghent. The principal assassin was Walter de Mey, but John, son of Walter van Merlaer, was also responsible. His mother was Catherine Parijs, a kinswoman of uncertain degree of Simon Parijs, a dyer who had been dean of the "small guilds" [the fifty-nine locally based trades that had individual guild organizations but a common overdean] of Ghent in 1345 and had been implicated with John de Scouteete in James van Artevelde the elder's death. Before her marriage, Catherine had had a liaison with another prominent Ghent burgess, Gilbert son of Baldwin de Grutere.

John van Artevelde died in 1365. James the younger then assumed control of his father's economic interests in rural Flanders and eventually was killed by persons who had family ties to his father's enemies in the city. After James' death in 1370, only one van Artevelde son was left: Philip, who was much younger than his brothers. But Philip was now the oldest son, and the duty of avenging any wrongs done to the family thus descended on him. But as far as any of the van Arteveldes then knew, the scores had been settled: the death of John de Scouteete had avenged James the elder, and payment of the blood price by the de Meys and van Merlaers avenged James the younger.

On December 27, 1381, when Ghent was in a civil war against most of the rest of Flanders, Philip van Artevelde, who had never held public office before, was suddenly made commissioner in charge of handling property confiscated from fugitives. Contemporary chroniclers tell us that the recollection of his father's heroic role in Ghent's earlier struggle led to his elevation. On January 24, 1382, he was made chief of five captains, as his father had been. His first week in office was memorable. On January 26, he participated in a mob scene in which Simon Bette, the first alderman, the equivalent of the mayor of Ghent, was killed. Bette's family had not been implicated in the killing of James van Artevelde the elder, but they had been his political opponents. In 1379, when the war broke out, Bette had been First Justice of the Peace. He and Gilbert son of Gilbert de Grutere, who was first alderman at that time, banished two men who seem to have been van Artevelde partisans, on the spurious grounds that they had led an unauthorized attack on the city of Oudenaarde, south of Ghent.

On January 30 Philip van Artevelde enticed this Gilbert de Grutere, by then dean of the "small guilds," into an assembly, read a list of particulars accusing him of treason, and stabbed him on the spot. Some de Gruteres had been openly hostile to Philip's father's regime in the 1340s, but the family was bitterly split on personal grounds even then between the sons of

Baldwin and those of Gilbert de Grutere. Philip van Artevelde had reason to dislike both branches: for Baldwin de Grutere fathered an illegitimate child by Catherine Parijs, who later gave birth to John van Merlaer, the killer of James van Artevelde the younger; while Gilbert was a political ally of the shippers, who by 1382 wanted peace with the count, while van Artevelde and the weavers who supported him wanted to continue the war.

During his same first week in power, Philip van Artevelde ordered three other men decapitated. Two of them were enemies of John van Merlaer, killer of James van Artevelde but now Philip's ally. On February 21, he murdered James Soyssone, the dean of the butchers' guild. Like the de Gruteres, the Soyssone family was bitterly split. James' branch was hostile to the van Arteveldes, although the other was not. Political affiliation in Ghent in early 1382 thus was a confused maelstrom. Disagreements within families caused different branches to choose opposite sides.

Philip van Artevelde's fury was directed both at persons who opposed his assumption of power in Ghent in early 1382 and against those with whom his family had grievances and specifically those whose ancestors had been implicated in his father's death. Which motive was uppermost in his mind in given cases is sometimes hard to determine. It seems likely, however, that the killings that we have mentioned to this point were not connected to the death of James the elder. Philip knew the Bettes, de Gruteres, and Soyssones personally. None of his documented actions before he became captain suggests that he thought that anyone other than John de Scouteete had been implicated in his father's assassination. He may have heard rumors; but as a youngest son—he was only five when his father died—he could have known little. If he had, he could have taken action on that knowledge; for as we have seen, eldest sons, and Philip van Artevelde had been that since 1370, had a solemn obligation to avenge killings with killings. But when Philip entered the city government in late 1381, he suddenly gained access not only to the records that we now use, but to much more detailed material that is now lost.

Contemporary writers make statements about his homicides in the month after Gilbert de Grutere's death that are sometimes dismissed as wild exaggerations. Philip van Artevelde was certainly in a position to use the forces of the city to accomplish private vengeance. The official accounts of the city mention payment of 2 francs "to Pete, Philip van Artevelde's executioner, for a sword" and of 12 pence "when he cut off ears." The historian Sir John Froissart (c. 1337–1410), who was usually well informed about affairs in Flanders, claimed that Philip had twelve persons beheaded in his presence because "some said" that they had been involved in his father's death.

But the death of James van Artevelde the elder was now thirty-seven years in the past. No one who was directly involved in his death in 1345 was still alive in 1382. The obvious answer to this riddle is that Philip van Artevelde considered the oldest sons of the men involved to bear the taint of their fathers' blood. We have seen that a restorer of old shoes had allegedly given the death stroke to James the elder. Professions often became family names at this time, and the city account mentions that Philip had one "Dennis de Scoemakere," whose name means "shoemaker," brought into his presence, although we are not told directly that the man was executed. Some families whose members felt themselves compromised evidently foresaw the van Artevelde restoration before it occurred and took the precaution of leaving the city. Clearly they suspected the action that he might take if he ever came to power, and with reason; others, who did not move fast enough, did not escape him. The elder son of the alderman of 1345, Francis Sloeve, was evidently killed; his younger brother had left Ghent earlier. The son of the town receiver of 1345, Peter Stocman, was murdered. Nicholas uten Dale, the son of the first Justice of the Peace of 1345, was killed. The clearest case is Lievin van Waes, an alderman of 1345. His older son and namesake, Lievin, left Ghent soon after March 24, 1382. On April 16, his younger brother Peter, who clearly was not considered liable for his father's deeds, bought Lievin's confiscated property from the city. Lievin van Waes was back in Ghent by August 1383, after van Artevelde's death but two years before the war against the count ended. He did not leave because he was opposed to the rebellion against the Flemish count, but because he feared the van Artevelde restoration. We have no way of estimating the number of other persons who left the city from fear of van Artevelde; the cases that we can document are chillingly revealing.

James and Philip van Artevelde have been acclaimed by posterity as democrats, men who had the welfare of the common people at heart, were popular figures, and who brought the guildsmen into power. Contemporary sources, however, inform us that although Philip van Artevelde's rebellion terrified the nobles and helped provoke revolts in some cities of northern France, half the population of Ghent opposed him. Although the city was in a civil war, had little food, no significant allies in Flanders—in contrast to the situation of the 1340s, Bruges and Ypres opposed Ghent now—and was being blockaded by the count's troops, Philip van Artevelde undertook no economic or diplomatic initiatives to relieve this situation until late March 1382 and no military initiatives until May. He had been too busy paying off his family's scores. The last of his homicides and most of the property seizures had been accomplished by February 21. Only when this man of honor had laid to rest the shade of his unavenged and thus dishonored father could he be bothered with the affairs of his afflicted city.

Family antagonisms were not the only causes of civil discord in late medieval Ghent, but they were involved as at least an aggravating element in virtually all breakdowns of public order. Political allegiances, personal enmities and amities, neighborhood solidarities, and occupational guilds were all important social and economic bonds, but they were relative and as transitory as human life itself. Reasonable men might differ about political or ideological issues, but the family was an absolute. To spill kinsmen's blood was to tarnish the family's honor, a sacrilege and shame requiring divine retribution consummated by the shedding of expiatory gore on the altar of vengeance. The males of medieval Ghent cared nothing for the rule of human law; their values were fixed on the holy, transcendent imperative of redemptive bloodshed.

BIBLIOGRAPHY

This essay is derived from information in Andrée Holsters, "Moord en politiek tijdens de Gentse opstand 1379–1385," *Handelingen der Maatschappij voor Geschiedenis en Oudheidkunde te Gent*, n.s. 37 (1983): 89–111; David Nicholas, "Crime and Punishment in Fourteenth-Century Ghent," *Revue Belge de Philologie et d'Histoire*, 48 (1970): 289–334, 1141–76; Nicholas, *The Domestic Life of a Medieval City: Women, Children, and the Family in Fourteenth-Century Ghent*. Lincoln: University of Nebraska Press, 1985; Nicholas, *The Metamorphosis of a Medieval City: Ghent in the Age of the Arteveldes, 1302–1390*. Lincoln: University of Nebraska Press; Leiden: E. J. Brill, 1987; Nicholas, "The Marriage and the Meat Hall: Ghent/Eeklo, 1373–75," *Medieval Prosopography* 10 (1989): 22–52; Nicholas, "The Governance of Fourteenth-Century Ghent." In *Law, Custom, and the Social Fabric in Medieval Europe: Essays in Honor of Bryce Lyon*. Edited, with an Appreciation, by Bernard S. Bachrach and David Nicholas. Kalamazoo, Michigan: Medieval Institute Publications, 1991: 235–260. The section on the Borluut-van Sint Baafs feud is based on Wim Blockman, *Een middeleeuwse vendetta. Gent 1300*. Houten: De Han, 1987. That on the van Artevelde family is based on David Nicholas, *The van Arteveldes of Ghent: The Varieties of Vendetta and the Hero in History*. Ithaca and London: Cornell University Press; Leiden: E. J. Brill, 1988.

"Bastard Feudalism" and the Kiss: Changing Social Mores in Late Medieval and Early Modern France

J. RUSSELL MAJOR

The fourteenth and fifteenth centuries witnessed the development of what historians have stigmatized as "bastard" feudalism. Leading aristocrats in France and England raised their own armies of soldiers loyal to their commander rather than to the king. Vassals previously had held land from their lords, or in some cases received an annual sum of money (the money fief, or fief rente); now the lord's man received wages, wore the lord's livery (uniform), and did not do homage.

In this provocative essay, J. Russell Major focuses on the ceremony of homage, which experienced considerable evolution in late medieval Europe. How does Major relate the appearance of bastard feudalism, as well as transformation of homage, to changing social mores? How did changing attitudes toward kissing alter the political and social relationship between lord and vassal?

The Christian custom of kissing for nonerotic reasons, either between men and women or between members of the same sex, has a long history. What functions did such kissing serve? What dangers did some early Christians believe kissing posed? How did medieval literature and song treat the kiss? What was the link between amatory homage in courtly love and feudal homage? How was the kiss in homage rendered in France during the high Middle Ages? What did the kiss symbolize? How did homage and the kiss accommodate women and ecclesiastics who were vassals?

A less tolerant view toward kissing emerged during the thirteenth century that paralleled the heightened intolerance of medieval society and the Church. Homosexuals, Jews, religious heretics, and social dissidents bore the brunt of the increased persecution. While political and religious authorities during the early Middle Ages, for a variety of reasons, had ignored social and religious nonconformists or treated them with benign forbearance, the late Middle Ages experienced a turn toward increased tension and bitter repression. How did these attitudinal changes, particularly with regard to homosexuality, affect the practice of kissing? What developments then occurred in feudal relationships and in the ceremony of homage?

In sixteenth-century France, jurists began an attack on homage that resulted in new social mores. How exactly did the French alter the practice of doing homage? Why was the ceremony of homage retained there but not in England?

During the late Middle Ages a new relationship between the greater and lesser members of Western European aristocracies emerged in which indentures were made to bind lord and client together but no fiefs[1] were given or homage performed.... The purpose of this essay is, first, to suggest that the failure to require homage in the new aristocratic relationship in France was caused by a change in the attitudes toward kissing; and then to address the question of whether this new relationship that has been given the derogatory name of "bastard feudalism" necessarily involved a decline in the loyalty that a man owed his lord....

...At the base of the traditional feudal system lay the concept of vassalage as cemented in homage and fealty. The ceremony of homage varied, but, in its most common form, the vassal, without sword, belt, or spurs, knelt bareheaded, placed his joined hands between those of his lord, and declared that he was the lord's man in return for a specified fief. The lord then kissed the vassal on the mouth and said that he took him as his man. Fealty consisted of the vassal taking an oath of fidelity, most frequently upon the Gospels. As a result of this double ceremony, a contract came into

---

[1]A fief was a piece of land that one nobleman (a vassal) held as hereditary tenure from another (the lord) in exchange for service.

being in which the vassal became obligated to give military and material aid and counsel to his lord. The lord in return was expected to provide his vassal with protection and maintenance that usually took the form of a fief.

When the ceremony of homage evolved, kissing between unrelated members of the same sex and between the two sexes for non-erotic reasons was widely practiced. The early Christians were especially noted for their custom of kissing. Jesus reproached Simon the Pharisee for not kissing him when he entered his house (Luke 7:45). Paul often urged Christians to "Greet one another with a holy kiss" (Romans 16:16; I Corinthians 16:20; II Corinthians 13:12; I Thessalonians 5:26), and Peter enjoined them to "Greet one another with the kiss of love" (I Peter 5:14). Indeed, the kiss between men was so commonplace that Judas believed that he could use it to identify his Master without arousing suspicion.

The kiss of peace soon became part of the Christian liturgy. At first men and women kissed each other and Tertullian[2], one of the earliest Church fathers, expressed concern that pagan husbands would object to their Christian wives behaving in this fashion. What heathen, he queried, would suffer his wife "to slip into prison to kiss the fetters of a martyr? Or, for that matter, to salute any one of the brethren with a kiss?" Nor was the possibility that the kiss would arouse carnal desires lost on the early Christians. Clement of Alexandria[3] complained:

> There are those that do nothing but make the churches resound with a kiss, not having love itself within. For this very thing, the shameless use of a kiss, which ought to be mystic, occasions foul suspicious and evil reports. The apostle calls the kiss holy. When the kingdom is worthily tested, we dispense the affection of the soul by a chaste and closed mouth, by which chiefly gentle manners are expressed. But there is another, unholy, kiss, full of poison, counterfeiting sanctity. Do you not know that spiders, merely by touching the mouth, afflict men with pain? And often kisses inject the poison of licentiousness.

Nevertheless, Paul's repeated injunctions were so clear that the kiss of peace, of salutation, and of friendship was preserved, but the danger of the liturgical kiss between men and women was diminished when the custom developed of having the two sexes sit on opposite sides of the church.

Little is known concerning the kissing practices of the Germanic invaders, but . . . "Gregory of Tours[4] relates how the Frankish king Gunthramn sealed a pact with his nephew by kissing him, and how King Chilperich kissed his son Merovech and the latter's fiancée Brunichilde in swearing an oath that he would not try to prevent them from marrying." The only kiss in Beowulf, one of the oldest surviving works in a Germanic language, was between men. . . . Examples from German literature between 1160 and 1220 are

[2]Christian theologian, c.160–230.

[3]Greek theologian, c.150–c.215.

[4]Frankish historian and saint, c.538–594.

plentiful enough to provide some certainty as to current practices.... [K]isses between members of the same sex and between different sexes were largely restricted "to the conventional occasions of welcomes, farewells, reconciliations, and treaties." Erotic kisses were infrequent.... [W]hen Isolde decided to forgive Tristan[5] for killing her uncle, she kissed him as a sign of reconciliation and her father did the same.

In many of the medieval love lyrics and in the songs of the troubadours, the kiss was treated as the ultimate reward that a lady could be expected to give to her lover. The first kiss that Queen Guinevere gave to Sir Lancelot[6] has been likened to homage in that "the lady held the position to the lover that in fuedal homage the lord held to the vassal... the act of amatory homage was modeled on the ceremony of the feudal contract of vassalage." ... [W]hen the Provençal[7] poets invented courtly love, the devotion of the vassal to his lord was the model on which they based their conception of the fealty of the perfect lover." ...

... [I]n courtly love, the man is the woman's vassal and ... an essential part of its symbolic system is the kiss." ...

The bishop-elect of Carpentras placed the hands of an infant boy and his female guardian between his own when the former rendered homage in 1322, but he kissed only the infant. The text says that the bishop excluded the guardian from the kiss as a matter of decency.... The dame d'Oisy anticipated the opportunity to kiss the handsome bishop of Cambrai when she did homage, but the latter, on hearing this, designated his bailiff to serve as his proxy, again in the name of propriety. The disappointed lady refused to accept this substitution and transferred her allegiance to the count of Artois. In both these instances it was presumed that the kiss would take place, but the lord, who had taken vows of celibacy, refused in the name of decency. When the woman was doing homage in her own name, a lay proxy was provided to receive the kiss. When she was merely a guardian, only the infant was kissed.... Indeed, some ecclesiastics were less squeamish: the bishop of Langres kissed two female vassals when they did homage in 1328.

During the high Middle Ages the ritual of homage doubtless varied as to time, place, and the individuals concerned, as it certainly did during the centuries that followed when the documentation is much richer. The preponderance of evidence, however, indicates that in France the usual procedure was for the lord and vassal, regardless of sex, to kiss on the mouth. Commoners did not participate in this part of the ritual.

The kiss in homage was given as "a sign of mutual fidelity," as a means "to confirm the promise of fidelity between two parties." The kiss was also used in the high Middle Ages to confirm other types of agreements, such

---

[5]There were many medieval poems about the tragic lovers Tristan and Isolde.

[6]Queen Guinevere and Sir Lancelot were major figures in the legends surrounding King Arthur of Britain.

[7]From Provence, a region in southern France.

as the gift of a piece of property, the renunciation of a disputed claim, and the making of a marriage alliance. Once again, if a monk and a woman were involved, the kiss on the mouth was omitted. Thus, when a married couple and their son made a donation to Saint-Aubin d'Angers, the monk who accepted the gift was kissed by the father and the son, but he refused to be kissed by the wife because "it was uncommon for a monk to be kissed by a woman," and he directed the lady to give the kiss to a lay proxy. In 1143, the viscountess of Turenne kissed only the hands of the prior of Obazine when she made a gift.

The kiss may not have been part of the ceremony of homage in its earliest stage, although too few descriptions of the ritual survive to enable one to speak with assurance. It was first recorded when the abbot-elect of St. Gall did homage to Otto I[8] in 971 and it was firmly incorporated in the ceremony in France by the close of the tenth century. By then kisses had been exchanged for non-erotic reasons for centuries and it was but natural to include the practice in a ritual that was so important in binding society together.

... In the late thirteenth century there was a change in the attitude toward kissing. The danger of kisses being exchanged by members of the opposite sex had been noted by the earliest church fathers. The stories of Lancelot and Guinevere and other romances of chivalry demonstrated clearly that the kiss could lead to unforeseen and disastrous consequences. More striking was a new attitude about the exchange of kisses between members of the same sex. During the ancient period homosexuality had been widely accepted. Even the early church fathers[9] were more tolerant of it than might be expected. There was some tightening of the sexual code in the fourth, fifth, and sixth centuries, which may be attributed in part to a growing asceticism. The emperor Justinian[10] outlawed homosexual practices, but neither the late empire nor the early medieval states were in a position to enforce such legislation, and the church was seemingly unconcerned. Indeed, there was a substantial increase in the amount of homosexual literature during the eleventh and twelfth centuries and prominent prelates were implicated. Not until the late twelfth century was there a concerted effort to stamp out homosexual practices and many years elapsed before it had a telling effect. ... [T]his change in attitude was "probably closely related to the general increase in intolerance of minority groups apparent in ecclesiastical and secular institutions throughout the thirteenth and fourteenth centuries." ... [W]hatever the cause, by 1300 homosexual practices were generally condemned by church and state alike, and kissing between members of the same sex that had once served as a sign of peace, reconciliation, and agreement now became associated with homosexuality.

[8]Otto the Great, King of Germany (936–973) and Holy Roman Emperor (962–973).

[9]Authoritative theologians of the early Christian church who formulated doctrines.

[10]Byzantine Emperor, 527–565.

This change in attitude toward kissing may explain why the English began to abandon the kiss of peace around the middle of the thirteenth century. It had long been customary for men to kiss men and women to kiss women as a sign of reconciliation just before communion, but this practice was now replaced by kissing a plaque on which was implanted a picture of Jesus or some saint. This practice gradually spread to the continent and the kiss of peace between Christians, that had been so meaningful as a token of reconciliation, ceased to exist in the liturgy of the Roman Catholic Church except in the form of a light embrace among the clergy. At about the same time, the kiss to seal the various types of contracts, which once had been very common, ceased to be performed.

That a new attitude toward kissing had developed by the beginning of the fourteenth century is further suggested by the trial of the Templars.[11] Philip the Fair[12] and his advisers were anxious to discredit the Templars by every means at their disposal. They could hardly attack the order because a kiss on the mouth was included in the initiation, since it was also a part of the vassalage ceremony, but they were quick to couple mouth kissing with homosexual practices whenever the opportunity occurred. Thus, when Hugues de Pairaud was interrogated in 1307, he said that he had been kissed on the mouth when he had been inducted, but admitted that he had then been taken to a secret place where he had been kissed on "the lower part of his spine, on his navel, and on his *mouth*" (italics mine).

Kneeling also came under attack. When the ceremony of homage began to evolve, vassals had usually been ordinary freemen or even serfs. They did not object to kneeling humbly before their lord. The Carolingian monarchs[13] had some noble vassals, but they so far surpassed their subjects that they could impose such a ritual. By the close of the thirteenth century, however, a virtual revolution had occurred. Nearly all vassals had achieved noble status and these nobles had become conscious of their dignity, worth, and unity as an order. A pauper might kneel when he was about to receive alms, but for one noble to kneel before another noble was, as an eighteenth century jurist put it, "ridiculous." This opposition to kneeling before a noble was not extended to include kneeling before a king because, by 1300, the growing concept of royal sovereignty had exalted the king above the magnates. Kneeling before the king provoked opposition only from such independent or semi-independent dignitaries as the kings of England and the dukes of Brittany. The situation was therefore ripe for an attack on these two elements of the ritual of homage as the Middle Ages began to draw to a close.

... Feudal relationships had already proved vulnerable to social changes, but the earlier adjustments had been made before the kiss had become

---

[11] The Knights Templar, a military religious order founded in 1128.

[12] King of France, 1285–1314. He attacked the Knights Templar because of its wealth and succeeded in having the order abolished in 1312.

[13] Ruled 751–987.

suspect, and the ceremony of homage had gone unchallenged. When fiefs became hereditary soon after the inception of the feudal system, it became necessary to define the status of clergymen, widows, daughters, and minors who were unable to perform the services required of vassals. A man who held fiefs from more than one lord was faced with the problem of whom he should serve in case of simultaneous or conflicting demands. As a result, when oaths of fealty were taken, it became customary for the vassal to name one or more persons against whom he would not serve. By the late eleventh century, the economy was sufficiently developed for some lords to offer annual payments in money to those who would render them faith and homage. Thus the *fief rente* was established. The *fief rente* added to the flexibility of the feudal system because it enabled a great lord not only to expand his military force but also to extend his vassalage system into areas in which he owned no land.

At first, witnesses were present to testify that faith and homage were performed, but, by the thirteenth century, literacy had developed to the point that lords began to give their vassals letters describing the procedure that had been followed during the ceremony so that their right to the designated fiefs would less likely be challenged. Vassals, in return, repeated the ritual of faith and homage in writing in a document call an *avou*.[14] Within forty days they were also expected to submit a detailed description of their fiefs called *dénombrements*.[15] Finally, although the essence of faith and homage was an agreement between lord vassal taken in person, long absence, sickness, old age, minorities, and other problems often made it necessary for one or the other of the two parties to be represented by proxy. As time progressed, personal convenience and, by the late Middle Ages, dislike of the ceremony itself replaced necessity. The kings delegated the authority to receive homage to their chancellors, bailiffs, seneschals, and other officials, and, during the reign of Charles VII,[16] this delegation became the normal procedure for less important fiefs. Nobles also sometimes abandoned their insistence that homage and fealty be rendered in person.

Since the vassal was expected to perform military service, there was from the start a problem of what to do with women and the clergy.... Around 1475, Sir Thomas Littleton[17] took offense at a woman who did homage having to say "I become your woman; for it is not fitting that a woman should say, that she will become a woman to any man, but to her husband, when she is married. But she shall say, I do to you homage, and to you shall be faithful and true, and faith to you shall bear for the tenements I hold of you, saving the faith I owe to our soveraigne lord the king." ... Abbots, priors, and other heads of religious communities, Littleton thought, who had

[14] Avowal or acknowledgment.

[15] Enumerations.

[16] King of France, 1422–1461.

[17] English legal scholar and judge, c.1407–1481.

given themselves entirely to God, should also be excused from saying "I become your man."

The above changes demonstrated to everyone that aspects of the lord-vassal relationship could be altered and made it all but certain that, when kissing and kneeling fell into disrepute, there would be demands to change the ceremony of homage itself. The most outspoken and most quoted leader of the assault on homage was Du Moulin,[18] who published an influential treatise in 1539. Simple homage, he insisted, implied no personal dependence. To kneel before a noble was ridiculous. One only knelt before a prince. The kiss was "indecent nay reprehensible," and not imposed by custom. The expression *la bouche et les mains*[19] that was used to describe the ceremony of homage in many customs only meant that the mouth was used to promise loyalty, which was done with the hands joined. Furthermore, there was no precise form for the oath of fidelity.

Splendid opportunities to study the efforts to alter the ceremony of homage so as to conform to the new social mores are provided by the redaction and reformation of the customs of the various parts of France and the commentaries of the jurists designed to interpret them. During the Middle Ages a few customs had been redacted—that is, transferred from the oral tradition to a written form—but the task did not begin in earnest until the early sixteenth century. In the latter part of the sixteenth century many of the customs were reformed. The redaction and the reformation of the customs was accomplished by holding large assemblies in which the three estates[20] declared what the law was. There was popular pressure for change but, at the same time, it was difficult to depart much from the oral tradition during the redaction and still more difficult to make significant changes once the custom was in a written form. Nevertheless, because of omissions, vagueness, additions, and occasionally outright corrections, the customs were altered to meet the growing dislike of aspects of the ceremony of homage. . . .

Most troublesome of all was the question of whether a woman had to participate in the kiss in doing homage. . . . [Some] followed Du Moulin in excusing women from the kiss on the grounds that it was not an essential part of homage, but more traditional jurists pointed out that women . . . could no more dispense with this mark of obedience and fidelity than anyone else. . . .

In spite of a tendency on the part of a few to preserve some of the traditional aspects of the ceremony, the trend was clearly in the other direction. . . .

From the sixteenth century, some customs permitted a vassal to present himself before his lord's domicile in his principal fief and announce in a

---

[18]Charles Du Moulin, French legal scholar, 1500–1566.

[19]The mouth and hands.

[20]The first estate was the clergy, the second the nobility, and the third the remainder of the population (although notables represented the third estate in assemblies).

loud voice that he had come to do homage. If neither his lord nor someone authorized to receive homage appeared, the vassal could kneel without hat, sword, or spurs and take the oath before a notary and other witnesses. Then, in some customs, he kissed the bolt of the door. The vassal might feel a little foolish in this procedure, but at least he escaped the humility of doing homage before another man....

The French customs, therefore, provided increasing opportunities to escape the more humiliating aspects of homage, and most of their interpreters did all in their power to further this trend. It is necessary, however, to turn to the documents that actually described individual ceremonies to learn what occurred. In the early fourteenth century the archbishop of Bordeaux required his vassals to kneel and he kissed them on the mouth, but by 1530 a kiss on the cheek had become standard, although one and sometimes both knees were placed upon the ground....

Some noble families appear to have adopted a ceremony or at least a phraseology of their own. By the late sixteenth century the trade mark of the viscounts of Polignac had become the "kiss of peace" which they bestowed upon their vassals "after the fashion of nobles." Once we are told that such a kiss was planted upon the mouth. Always the vassal placed his hands between those of the viscount, but we are not informed if or how he knelt. In 1601 a vassal swore to follow the viscount in all wars and against everyone. Not even the king was specifically excepted. When the parish of Le Brignon did homage to the viscount in 1645, its inhabitants became his "liege men and subjects." In doing so they knelt on both knees, but the "kiss of peace" was not administered to these humble people.

But the Polignac came from one of the most backward parts of France. Elsewhere the ceremony of homage was less impervious to change. Even the duke of Epernon, one of the haughtiest noblemen in France, permitted Pierre de Baritault to escape the kiss when he did homage in 1602. A woman who did homage to him in the name of her children in 1638 swore on the holy Gospels "to be forever a good, loyal and faithful vassal," but she neither knelt before nor was kissed by her now aged lord. Jean d'Anglade knelt bareheaded without belt or arms and placed his hands between the hands of his lord when he did homage in 1658, but although the document that recorded the event was written in Gascon, the ceremony was not so outdated as to include the kiss. Nicolas Fouquet, Louis XIV's celebrated minister, dispensed with the ceremony of homage but preserved his rights by having his vassals sign a statement acknowledging him as their overlord, and perhaps take an oath. Thus, by the early seventeenth century, the kiss was falling before the onslaught of the jurists and public opinion. Homage was becoming an administrative matter.

Homage did not cease altogether, however, because, if a vassal failed to perform this duty, the lord could legally take possession of his fief. Thus, in 1585, we find a woman asking Madame de La Trémoille, the former Jeanne de Montmorency, to delay seizing her lands on the grounds that her husband had twice gone to do her homage, only to find her absent. He was now away in the service of her son, the duke, and was not at the moment free to go a third time.... In 1613, the seigneur and dame of Bosjan tried to regain the lands of Frangi, Villeneuve, and Charni from the seigneur of Sarigny, because he had not done homage in the proper fashion. Among the procedural issues at stake was that Sarigny had failed to place both knees on the ground. In May 1617, the Parlement of Dijon sided in Sarigny's favor on the grounds that the Burgundian custom did not provide a "certain and precise form for doing faith and homage" and that he had met the essential requirements of the ritual. A similar dispute led the Parlement of Bordeaux to spell out in detail how liege homage should be done. In a decree of March 10, 1605, it stipulated that the vassal, bareheaded and without sword, belt, or spurs, should place one knee on the ground and, with his hands between his lord's, promise to be a good and faithful vassal and to assist him against everyone except the king. The lord would then raise the vassal and promise to be a good seigneur. The kiss was conspicuously omitted from the ceremony.

In spite of a tendency on the part of the courts to side with the vassal on questions concerning homage, there were instances in which the lord actually seized fiefs. The dukes of La Meilleraye did so in 1673 and 1692, and there were a number of seizures between 1694 and 1708, when part of the ducal lands reverted to the crown and were administered by royal officials. The dukes themselves were vassals of local lords for some of their lands, but they protected their pride by doing homage through procureurs. Indeed, homage by procuration appears to have become common in Poitou during the seventeenth century. At times both lord and vassal used proctors. Thus, in 1671, the procureur of the dame of Roquefeuil, bareheaded, with both knees on the ground and without belt, sword, or spurs, did homage in her name to Louis XIV,[21] who was represented by his procureur. The oath on the Holy Gospels was administered, but the agents of the dame and the king saw no need to subject themselves to the kiss. The tie between lord and vassal had become totally impersonal. Homage in person, however, did not cease. In an elaborate ceremony in 1699, the duke of Lorraine rendered homage to Louis XIV for the duchy of Bar. Without hat, gloves, or sword, he knelt on a pillow and took the oath, but the kiss was conspicuously omitted. In 1775, the duke La Trémoille did homage to Louis XVI,[22] with the keeper of the seals serving as the royal proxy.... Homage continued to be performed until it was abolished in the Revolution.

The kiss in homage may have come under attack in England also; in the fifteenth century it was part of the ceremony, but by the seventeenth century it was a thing of the past. In 1429, John Nowell did homage to Thomas de Hesketh by kneeling bareheaded, placing his hands between those of the said Thomas, and saying: "Sir, I become your man from this day forward." When

[21] King of France, 1643–1715.
[22] King of France, 1774–1792.

he had finished, Thomas kissed him. John then took an oath upon "a book." In 1439, when "a sekeness called the Pestilence" spread through England, the House of Commons petitioned Henry VI[23] that those "holdyng of yow by Knyghtes service...in the doyng of thair said homage, may omitte the said kissyng of you, and be excused thereof at youre will, the homage beyng of the same force as though they kissed you, and have thair lettres of doyng of thair homage, and kyssyng of you omitted not withstondyng." The king approved this request. Around 1475, Littleton still prescribed kneeling on both knees with head uncovered and terminating the ceremony with a kiss. ...Homage had apparently disappeared altogether in England between the time of Littleton and the age of Coke,[24] except in so far it was preserved in the coronation ceremony....

...The lord-vassal relationship had long been inadequate to meet the military and administrative needs of kings and great nobles, and historians of England have made a great contribution by demonstrating the changes that were introduced to correct the deficiencies. In the reign of Henry I[25] and earlier, the military household of the Norman kings included a number of persons who were neither vassals nor clerics. These men were retained by an annual fee and paid a daily wage when they were called upon to serve. Unlike the vassal, they could be discharged when their term of service expired. For this reason we find them being exhorted on the eve of a battle in 1124 "to fight for their reputation and for their right to continue to draw the king's wages and eat his bread." Since they served for a limited time, it made no sense for each of them to kneel before the king and declare that he had become his man. Homage was reserved for lifetime relationships. Some of these clients were reappointed year after year and, if fortunate, were eventually given fiefs for which they did homage. At this point the relationship became a lifetime one; the patron and client became lord and vassal.

Initially, these non-feudal contracts for service had been verbal, but, by 1270, written contracts called indentures appeared. At first all of these indentures were for limited periods of time, but soon lifetime contracts also began to be made and the so-called "bastard feudalism" was born. The indenture was generally written on parchment, the copy retained by the lord being sealed and signed by the client and the copy retained by the client being sealed and signed by the lord. The new relationship was similar to the earlier one in the military household in that the client received pay for his services and did not do homage; it differed in that it was for a lifetime. The new relationship was similar to the *fief rente* in that it was for life and included financial payments; it differed in that no homage was done....

[23]King of England, 1422–1461.
[24]Sir Edward Coke, English jurist, 1552–1634.
[25]King of England, 1100–1135.

The principal distinction between the lord-vassal relationship and the indenture system was that the vassal in the former rendered both homage and fealty, whereas in the latter the client only swore fealty, which he did by taking an oath on the cross or, more commonly, on the Gospels. . . .

From the latter stages of the Hundred Years' War until the end of the fifteenth century, there was a tendency for indentures in which the high nobility were the senior participants to become shorter, less specific, and more standardized. . . . [P]ayment was rarely specified, although good lordship was certainly anticipated. Thus, in 1429, Gilles de Rais signed a written contract in which he swore to serve his cousin, Georges de La Trémoille, with all his power until death. He stated that he took this step because of the past favors that he had received and the courtesies that he anticipated. Although La Trémoille promised no specific reward in return, within three months he won for his twenty-three-year-old client the post of marshal of France.[26]

In 1451, Gailhard de Durefort promised "to serve, succor, and aid" Charles d'Albret and his children for life against everyone except the king and the dauphin. Homage was not performed and no reward was hinted at, but one was doubtless anticipated. The superstitious and ever-suspicious Louis XI[27] was willing to forego liege homage if the occasion warranted, but fealty remained important to him. He insisted that Jean, count of Armagnac, swear in a document signed in 1465 to be loyal on everything that his fertile imagination could conjure up:

> I swear and promise by the faith and oath of my body, on my honor, by the Baptism through which I have been brought from the depths, on the peril and damnation of my soul, on the holy Gospel of God, and on the holy relics of the Chapel of the Palace at Paris, . . . that I will serve and obey my lord the king always and forever, towards and against everyone, living and dead without any exceptions including my lord Charles his brother or anyone else. I will serve him moreover against mysaid lord Charles as against all others in whatever manner or quarrel that there be and with no exceptions whatsoever . . . I renounce all oaths, promises, seals, or alliances that I have formerly given, made or issued to anyone.

Louis, in return, promised to protect Armagnac from Charles, his brother, and all other persons. That same day, in a separate document, Louis returned to Armagnac the extensive estates that had been taken from his father and grandfather. Thus in France, as in England, homage was dropped from the indenture in spite of its similarity to the *fief rente*.

Can it then be, as has so often been argued, that the failure to include homage in the indenture signaled the fact that a client owed his patron less

[26]The highest military command, after the constable. There were only two marshals of France.

[27]King of France, 1461–1483.

loyalty than a vassal did his lord? Or should we attribute the absence of homage in the new contractual arrangement to a change in social mores? The latter appears more probable. The evidence that the kiss and to a lesser extent the kneeling that was required in the ceremony of homage were unpopular in France by the sixteenth century is overwhelming. Evidence concerning the preceeding centuries is less voluminous, but the abandonment of the kiss to seal many types of contracts, the disappearance of the kiss of peace from the Catholic liturgy, the growing opposition to homosexuality, and the trial of the Templars all point to the fact that aspects of the homage ritual were unpopular when "bastard feudalism" was born in France. For a great noble to have insisted on the ritual of homage would have limited his recruitment efforts under the indenture system. He undoubtedly wanted to receive the same loyalty that he was entitled to under the lord-vassal relationship. The question is whether his wishes coincided with the social mores of the time....

... [F]rom the latter half of the fourteenth century, treatises were written that provide insights into the contemporary mind. They dealt with such problems as "Whether the subjects of a baron are bound to aid their lord against the king," or, "If a baron is vassal to two lords who are at war with each other which should he help?" The authors who treated literally hundreds of such questions, drew no distinction between vassals and indentured knights. Bonet,[28] probably the most widely read of these authors, insisted in *The Tree of Battles* that a knight "should be willing to die to keep the oath of his faith to his lord. I say the same of the knight in receipt of wages from the king or other lord, for since he has pledged to him his faith and oath he must die in defence of him and his honour." Knights "should keep the oath which they have made to their lord to whom they belong, and to whom they have sworn and promised to do all that he shall command for the defence of his land, according to what is laid down by the laws." "If a knight quits his lord in time of peace, whilst in receipt of wages, he should be condemned to go henceforth not mounted, but on foot like a sergeant." In time of war he should be executed.

... Indeed, it was so self-evident to most writers that the hired soldiers owed the same loyalty to their captain as a vassal owed to his lord that they did not bother to discuss the question. Both were subject to the same "law of arms."

The late medieval phase of the patron-client relationship has been given the pejorative name of "bastard feudalism" on the assumption that it was inferior to the traditional feudalism. In actual fact it was the traditional feudalism that was in a state of decay, and the patron-client relationship was invented in part to serve as a new way to tie the greater and lesser nobility together. Indeed, the dukes of Brittany appear to have used indentures to

---

[28]Honoré Bonet, fourteenth-century canonist, whose book, *The Tree of Battles,* described the laws of war.

strengthen their fading ties with their vassals. Homage was not enough to insure loyalty; a written contract was needed. The belief that clientage ties were stronger than vassalage ties was expressed when Mézières,[29] wrote, around 1389, that a king need not worry about his officials doing homage to great nobles for the fiefs that they held from them, but he warned against permitting them to make public or secret alliances with the magnates. Mézières, who was no stranger at the French court, then explained how such alliances lead to the corruption of justice and bad government.

The weakness of feudal ties is also revealed by the efforts of kings and great nobles to tie their vassals more closely to their sides by creating orders of chivalry. In 1351, King John[30] introduced Chivalric orders into France by establishing the Order of the Star, and his unknightly descendant, Louis XI, brought the raft of medieval creations to an end when he founded the Order of St. Michael in 1469. In the intervening period, a number of great nobles created their own orders, the most famous being Philip the Good[31] of Burgundy's[32] Golden Fleece (1431) and René of Anjou's Croissant (1448). These orders undoubtedly were designed to serve a number of purposes, among them: to defend the true religion, to protect noble ladies, and to sponsor tournaments. But, in the minds of most of their creators, one of the greatest purposes was to bind their vassals more closely to them and to seek outside supporters. They put great stress on loyalty to the commander of the order and to one's sovereign lord, who was often one and the same person. Disloyalty and flight from the battlefield after the banners had been unfurled led to disgrace and expulsion from the order. The Burgundian dukes and René of Anjou found their order useful in drawing together the high nobility of their far-flung domains.... So like clientage were these orders that the collar or other insignia of the members was often identical to the livery that clients wore.

Thus, when the ties between lord and vassal weakened, the nobility invented clientage to assume its role in tying together the greater and lesser members of the aristocracy. Homage was not dropped because less loyalty was desired. Indeed, the purpose of clientage was to insure greater loyalty. Homage was dropped because the ritual had become unpopular as a result of the changing social mores in late medieval and early modern France. The problem now left to be resolved is the extent to which clientage was successful in restoring traditional loyalties and the length of time it was able to perform this function.

---

[29]Philip de Mézières, 1327–1405, author of *The Dream of the Old Pilgrim.*

[30]John II, King of France, 1350–1364.

[31]Duke of Burgundy, 1419–1461.

[32]King John II of France gave the duchy of Burgundy to his son Philip the Bold. Under his successors, Burgundy became a wealthy and powerful state. In 1477, the duchy reverted to France.

Concepts of Cleanliness: The Water That Infiltrated

GEORGES VIGARELLO

The West today links cleanliness to bathing (although the frequency varies dramatically among countries) and both to hygiene. The Roman elite had considered bathing and its accompanying rituals to be essential, while medieval castles and towns possessed baths. But the sixteenth and seventeenth centuries shunned baths and saw water as injurious to health.

What developments led to the new belief that bathing was harmful and water dangerous? How did people view the human body? Why was there a fear of social contact? In light of these new attitudes, what sorts of clothes were recommended?

The fear of bathing did not lead to an acceptance of human smells and dirt but to new ways to combat bodily odors and promote cleanliness. How did Europeans now contain smells? Why were only certain parts of the body washed? Without bathing, how did people clean their bodies? For example, how was hair kept clean?

Western civilization has within it both a basic mistrust of the human body and a view of the body as something beautiful and worthy of praise. In the early modern era, the former attitude achieved dominance, with important implications for cleanliness, social interaction, and health. How might these new attitudes have affected relationships between men and women, distinctions among social groups, and the evolution of religious beliefs?

In 1546, Barcelona, in the grip of the plague, was no longer receiving provisions. Neighbouring towns and villages, fearing contagion, refused all contacts and all trade. Worse, the ships dispatched to Majorca in search of supplies by the Council of the Five Hundred[1] were repulsed with cannon fire. Such episodes became common. At the end of the Middle Ages and in the classical period, contact was widely seen as a major risk in times of epidemic. The traditional flight from infected towns became in itself dangerous; it came up against neighbourhoods capable of open violence. Those people who fled from Lyons in 1628 were stoned by the peasantry, and condemned to rove or return to their city. The inhabitants of Digne, compelled in 1629 by a degree of the Parlement[2] of Aix to remain within the town walls, were put under the surveillance of a cordon of armed guards by the neighbouring communities. They threatened to set fire to the town if the cordon was broken. Cities struck by plague became prisons doomed to horror.

Within these communities temporarily shut in on their awful plight, the external constraints accelerated the formulation of internal regulations if only, here too, in the hope of confining the calamity. Mayors, magistrates

---

[1]The expanded city council.

[2]A "sovereign" judicial court.

and provosts of the merchants issued injunctions dealing with social hygiene; social contacts were progressively limited, certain places shut off or condemned. The Salle Légat of the Hôtel-Dieu[3] in Paris, for example, was isolated in 1584 and made ready to receive only victims of the plague. In many towns notaries could not approach stricken houses; wills were dictated at a distance, before witnesses, from upper storeys. The measures also dealt with personal hygiene: to suppress social intercourse was to suppress practices which risked opening up the body to infected air, such as violent labour which heated the limbs, warmth which relaxed the skin, and, above all, bathing. Liquid, by its pressure, or even more by its warmth, could open up the pores and heighten the danger. The fight against plague here reveals ideas which are totally remote from our own; water was capable of penetrating the skin, which had implications for practices of cleanliness.

It was this same fear which led people to cease to frequent schools, churches, steam-baths and bath-houses. Contacts, and thus the possibility of infection, had to be limited. In the case of baths, the dynamic of separation related to the very image of the body and its functioning. Doctors, in times of plague from the fifteenth century on, denounced these establishments, where naked bodies rubbed shoulders. 'People already afflicted with contagious diseases' might be the cause of ill-fated mixing. Disease might spread in consequence. 'Steam-baths and bath-houses, I beg you, flee them or you will die.' These regulations were at first tentative. In the plague of 1450, Des Pars[4] called in vain on the Paris magistrates to prohibit steam-baths, but provoked only the wrath of their owners. Their threats were such that he beat a hasty retreat to Tournai. Regular temporary closure during each epidemic nevertheless gradually established itself within the logic of separations. In the sixteenth century, these closures became official and systematic. An ordinance of the provost of Paris, frequently repeated between the plagues of 1510 and 1561, prohibited anyone 'from going to steam-baths, and steam-bath keepers from heating their baths until after next Christmas, on pain of a summary fine.' A similar resolution was passed in more and more towns. It became general; introduced in Rouen in 1510 and in Besançon in 1540, it had existed in Dijon since the end of the fifteenth century. In most epidemics, it was during hot weather, more favourable to outbreaks of plague, that the prohibition was promulgated.

... Why should historical significance be attributed to these prohibitions? Because behind the fear of social contacts lurked a host of other anxieties, amongst them a fear of the frailty of the bodily shell. The skin was seen as porous, and countless openings seemed to threaten, since the surfaces were weak and the frontiers uncertain. Behind the simple refusal of proximity lay a very specific image of the body: heat and water created openings, the

---

[3]The Salle Légat was the major room in the central Parisian hospital (Hôtel-Dieu).
[4]Jacques Des Pars (1380–1458), physician.

plague had only to slip through. These images were potent and far-reaching, and their consequences for classical hygiene need to be assessed. It is in this context that the prohibitions we have described assume significance. Baths and steam-baths were dangerous because they opened up the body to the atmosphere. They exercised an almost mechanical action on the pores, temporarily exposing the organs to the elements.

It was no longer touch, or a principle of proximity, which was at issue, but a principle of openness. The body had less resistance to poisons after bathing, because it was more open to them. It was as if the body was permeable; infectious air threatened to flood in from all sides. 'Steam-baths and bath-houses should be forbidden because when one emerges, the flesh and the whole disposition of the body are softened and the pores open, and as a result, pestiferous vapour can rapidly enter the body and cause sudden death, as has frequently been observed.' Comparing the body to familiar objects only reinforced this image of penetration. The architectural metaphor played a central role, with the body seen as a house invaded and occupied by the plague. You had to know how to shut the doors. But water and heat undid them at will, opened them up and maintained the breach. The plague had only to move in. 'Bath-houses and steam-baths will from now on be deserted, because, the pores and the little air holes in the skin being, as a result of the heat, more easily opened, pestilential air gets in.'

This fear lasted throughout the seventeenth century. The plague, breaking out in one place or another almost annually throughout the period, engendered the same prohibitions: to heat the body 'would be to open the doors to the poisons in the atmosphere and swallow it in great gulps.' Invariably, such an 'encounter of air and poison' with heated flesh suggested an almost inevitable result. It transformed danger into destiny.

The first concerted actions against the plague, especially from the sixteenth century, thus conjured up a frightening picture of a body with a permeable exterior. Its surface could be penetrated by water and by air, a frontier rendered even more uncertain in the face of an evil whose material basis was invisible. Perhaps the pores were even weak in themselves, independently of being heated. They needed permanent protection from attack. This, for example, rendered the shape and nature of clothing in time of plague all-important: smooth fabrics, dense weave and close fit. Infected air should slide over with no possibility of entry. The ideal of being enclosed varied only in its manifestations. 'One should wear clothes of satin, taffeta, camlet, tabby and the like, with hardly any pile, and which are so smooth and dense that it is difficult for unwholesome air or any sort of infection to enter or take hold, especially if one changes frequently.' Clothing in times of plague confirms this image, dominant throughout the sixteenth and seventeenth centuries, of a body which was completely porous, and which necessitated quite specific strategies: the avoidance of wool or cotton, materials which were too permeable, and of furs, whose deep pile offered a haven to unhealthy air. Men and women alike longed to have smooth and hermetically sealed clothes enclosing their weak bodies. And if taffeta and tabby were too grand, the poor could resort to 'sacking and oil-cloth.'

Practices of hygiene and, in particular, practices of cleanliness could not be considered without reference to these assumptions. If water could penetrate the skin, it needed to be handled with care. It could seep and disturb. In certain cases, as in hydrotherapy, the mechanism might be beneficial. Immersing themselves in the pools of Spa, Pougues or Forges, sixteenth-century bathers confidently expected an amelioration of their diseases. A bath of warm thermal water, like a bath in 'ordinary' water, could, for example, dissolve stone; this was how Montaigne[5] treated his kidney stones. It could also restore some substance to systems which were 'too dry.' It was employed by Rivière[6] for 'emaciated and wasted bodies.' It also acted on the colour of jaundice, and soothed certain congestions. In these cases, liquids mingled. And lastly, the penetration of the water might even correct certain sour or vicious humours. This treatment 'refreshed far more than any medicine.'

But for the most part, baths threatened to disturb an equilibrium. They invaded, damaged, and above all, exposed the body to many more dangers than pestilential air. The very earliest observations on steam-baths and the transmission of plague already referred to more obscure dangers. 'Bath-houses and steam-baths and their aftereffects, which heat the body and the humours, which debilitate the constitution and open the pores, cause death and sickness.' Disease, in the sixteenth and seventeenth centuries, was spreading, even proliferating. People had disquieting visions of contagious communication, as with syphilis, or visions of the most miscellaneous penetrations, such as steam-bath pregnancies resulting from the impregnation of female sexual organs by sperm floating in the tepid water. 'A woman can conceive through using baths in which men have spent some time.' The risks multiplied. Once infiltrated, the skin was not only wide open to pestilence, but also to unwholesome air, to cold, and to nameless ills. The weakness was diffused, and all the more global and imprecise since it was through the pores that humours and thus strength escaped. The openings worked both ways. It was as if internal substances threatened to flee; thus the 'bath debilitated.' It provoked 'feebleness.' It 'diminished hugely strength and vigour.' The risks were no longer confined simply to contagion. And this picture had sufficient success to spread beyond the discourse of doctors. It was absorbed into thinking to the extent of becoming commonplace. It was all-pervasive. It became impossible to contemplate a bath without surrounding it with imperative constraints: rest, staying in bed, protective clothing. The practice could not fail to be a source of anxiety. The accumulated precautions and the impossible protections turned it into something both complicated and rare.

---

[5] French essayist and philosopher, 1533–1592.

[6] L. Rivière, author of a book on the practice of medicine.

When, one May morning in 1610, an emissary from the Louvre[7] found Sully[8] taking a bath in his house at Arsenal,[9] complications ensued; a series of obstacles prevented Sully, for the sake of his body, from attending on the king, who required his presence. The minister's own entourage, even the emissary himself, adjured him not to brave the outside air. 'Having found you in the bath, and observing that you wished to get out to do as the king ordered, he said to you (because we were nearby): Monsieur,[10] do not quit your bath, since I fear that the king cares so much for your health, and so depends on it, that if he had known that you were in such a situation, he would have come here himself.' Henri IV's envoy proposed to return to the Louvre, he would explain to the sovereign and return with his orders. Not one of the witnesses was surprised to see such a situation disrupt relations between the king and his minister. On the contrary, everyone insisted that Sully should not expose himself. And Henri IV's reply justified the precautions taken. 'Monsieur, the king commands you to complete your bath, and forbids you to go out today, since M.[11] Du Laurens[12] has advised him that this would endanger your health.' So there had been a consultation. Advice had been sought and offered. The recourse to Du Laurens, the royal doctor, reveals the nature of the concern. The episode assumed all the aspects of an 'affair.' It immediately involved numerous people, and it was protracted, as the risks lasted several days. 'He orders you to expect him tomorrow in your nightshirt, your leggings, your slippers, and your night-cap, so that you come to no harm as a result of your recent bath.' So it was the liquid experienced in this manner which could be harmful. It was the consequences of the bath as such which were at issue.

This commotion over a bathtub was not mere idle tittle-tattle; it emphasises the strength in the seventeenth century of the association between water and the penetration of the body, and it confirms the dominant image of an exterior which was easily permeable. It emphasises also, paradoxically by its very intensity, the rarity of the practice of bathing.

Half a century later, when Louis XIV's[13] doctors decided to bathe him, it was for explicitly medical reasons. The patient had experienced 'starts, raging fits, convulsive movements... followed by rashes; red and violet spots on his chest.' The bath took place during his convalescence. It was to 'moisten' a body which had been bled eight times within the last few days. Once again there was no shortage of precautions: a purge and an

[7] A royal palace in Paris.

[8] Maximilien de Béthune, duke of Sully (1560–1641), minister-favourite of the French King Henry IV (1589–1610).

[9] Named after the arsenal established there by King Henry IV.

[10] Sir.

[11] Monsieur.

[12] André du Laurens (1558–1606), prolific author and physician to Henry IV.

[13] King of France, 1643–1715.

enema the day before to prevent any possible surfeit which might result from the water infiltrating, rest so as not to exacerbate any over-excitement, and interruption of the treatment at the slightest discomfort to avoid anything untoward. 'I had the bath prepared, the king got in at ten o'clock; for the rest of the day he felt weighed down with a nagging headache such as he had never experienced before, and with the whole demeanour of his body quite changed from what it had been in the preceding days. I did not wish to persist with the bath, having seen enough wrong to have the king get out.' Thus the treatment was quickly interrupted. A year later, Fagon[14] resorted to it again, very cautiously, for a few days. This was the last time. 'The king was never pleased to become accustomed to bathing in his chamber.'

The disquiet was obscure and diffused, as if the mere encounter of water and body was in itself a cause for concern. The penetration might sometimes, by its very force, restore lost equilibrium. But the essential disturbance it involved demanded vigilance. Openings, interchanges and pressure on the humours constituted above all a disorder. Their consequences were ever more various.

> The bath, except for medical reasons when absolutely necessary, is not only superfluous, but very prejudicial to men...The bath destroys the body, and, filling it, renders it susceptible to the effects of the bad properties of the air... slacker bodies are more sickly and have shorter lives than hard ones. Bathing fills the head with vapours. It is the enemy of the nerves and ligaments, which it loosens, in such a way that many a man never suffers from gout except after bathing. It kills the child in the mother's womb, even when it is warm...

The catalogue of ills also included 'weakness of the chest,' dropsy, and various evils humours resulting from the penetrating vapours.

Various attempts were made in the seventeenth century to ward off these dangers, but they served only to render the activity even more complicated. And they confirmed the view of the bodily covering as porous. In 1615 Guyon[15] suggested that the day before bathing the body should be submitted to the heat of a dry steam-bath; the idea was to evacuate the humours so as to render the penetration of the water less pressing. Actions designed to prepare the body for bathing became more numerous and more complex. But whatever was done, penetration and its attendant dangers remained. The most extreme, indeed absurd, suggestion came from Bacon,[16] who in 1623 required the water to have a composition identical to that of the bodily matter. The liquid, after all, had to compensate for the substances which were lost, and do no harm itself by mixing. The constituents of the bath had to be treated till they were similar to those of the body. Interchanges would consequently be less dangerous. 'The first and principal requirement

---

[14]Guy-Cresent Fagon, 1638–1718, Louis XIV's physician.

[15]L. Guyon, author of a medical treatise.

[16]Francis Bacon, 1561–1626, English statesman, essayist, and philosopher.

is that baths should be composed of materials whose substances are similar to those of the flesh and the body, and which can sustain and nourish the interior.' Such an expectation was fanciful, obviously, and simply added new variations to the theme of infiltration.

Times of plague strengthened the impression of bodily frontiers which could be penetrated, of bodies open to poison. Such rapid and terrible contagion suggested that an active element could infiltrate both breath and skin. The bodies most at risk must be the most porous. Their systems, succumbing within hours, must obviously be the most penetrable. This seemed to be the real danger. The plague thus established this disquieting vision, which flourished. Fear of bathing outlasted times of plague, and the permeability of the skin became a permanent source of anxiety. It was in Héroard's[17] mind when he confined the infant Louis XIII to his room after having him take two baths in 1611. It was why Guy Patin,[18] though occasionally mentioning bathing in his medical texts, omitted it entirely from his treatise on health. The mechanical effects, with their therapeutic ambivalence, were dominant. R. Bonnard's[19] engraving 'Une dame qui va entrer au bain,' might wrongly suggest the contrary. The scene appears familiar, even though the setting is sumptuous. Neither doctor nor drugs are to be seen. A maidservant busies herself round a decorated bathtub, covered with lace, surrounded by hangings, and standing on a dias. Two carved taps set into the wall supply the water. A woman clothed in silk takes a flower offered by an elegant gentleman. The extreme refinement of the occasion renders it almost allegoric. The bath will be a gracious activity, and possibly amorous. But the caption reveals the meaning as a rule to be observed. 'A bath taken at the right time acts on me like medicine, and damps down the fire about to consume me.' Despite the sexual ambiguity, cleanliness was not explicitly at issue. It was a matter of the restoration of lost equilibrium, and of knowing when it was right to bathe. Water in itself only upset the balance....

The new attention paid to childhood in the sixteenth century, for example, and the emphasis placed on its frailty, rapidly confirmed such ideas. The theme of infiltration was again all-pervasive from the sixteenth century on. It was because the bodies of new-born babies were thought to be completely porous that a technique of massage developed which employed both the hand and the warmth of water. The bath was intended both to cleanse the skin of the blood and mucous substances of birth, and at the same time to allow the limbs to be moulded to the desired physical form. Midwives used the water to facilitate this sort of massage. Immersion was intended, amongst other things, to correct the shape. 'Remember, too, while the bones

[17] Jean Héroard, 1551–1628, physician to the dauphin and then King Louis XIII (1610–1643), and author of a celebrated medical diary of Louis.

[18] Physician and letter writer, 1601–1672.

[19] Robert Bonnard (1652–1729), painter and engraver.

of the limbs are softened by the heat of the bath in which they have just been washed, to give each limb, by gentle manipulation, the form and the straightness that is required to produce complete perfection.' This bath in the first few days had several purposes, amongst which cleanliness did not yet figure. It involved manipulation precisely because it permeated the flesh. It helped 'to adjust the limbs to the proper shape.' For the same reason the skin of the nurse, most fragile of all, had to be permanently clogged up. 'To strengthen the skin and equip it to withstand external accidents, which might damage and harm it as a result of its weakness, it should be spread with the ash of mussels which can be found all over in rivers and marshes, or with ash made from calves' horns, or with the ash of lead well pulverised and mixed with wine.' The most diverse substances could be used to saturate the skin. Salt, oil and wax, in particular, would all serve to stop up the pores. The body was even coated as if it were a glossy and protected object. 'Children, once out of the womb, should be wrapped in roses crushed with salt to strengthen the limbs.'

The swaddling clothes which enveloped skin treated in this way, and imprisoned limbs previously 'anointed with oil of roses or bilberries... to close the pores,' had a specifically protective role. It was for the same reason, too, that baths were strictly limited in childhood. There was a risk that they would prolong softness in systems already too moist. The slow drying out of the body which accompanied growth might be impeded. The clay would remain too soft. Once the new-born child 'appeared nice and dry, ruddy and rosy all over,' further bathing seemed almost to tempt fate. The legs of the Dauphin, the future Louis XIII, were never washed before he reached the age of six. Their first immersion, with the exception of a very brief one immediately after birth, took place when he was seven.

On the basis of this same image of fragile pores, anxieties proliferated and fed each other. Hot water attacked a passive body which it permeated and left open. Where children were concerned, there was added a whole range of comparisons with substances which were flexible and malleable; thus it was tempting to mould their docile limbs. The problem was to balance the dangers of bathing against freeing the skin.

... All these fears and contrivances produced a logic quite other than the precautions of today. They supposed a frame of reference for bodily functions quite alien to ours. Though they seem to be marginal to hygiene, they could, in fact, affect it. That such influence is possible is hardly open to doubt. When, for example, sixteenth-century books on health refer to certain bodily smells, they also refer to the need to remove them. But they assume friction and perfume, not washing, to achieve this. The skin should be rubbed with scented linen. 'To cure the goat-like stench of armpits, it is useful to press and rub the skin with a compound of roses,' that is, to wipe vigorously, applying perfume, but not actually to wash.

Rules for polite behaviour are equally significant in this connection. It was these which, from the sixteenth century, dictated good manners and good taste at court. They constituted an inventory of 'noble' behaviour in its most humdrum aspects, real-life, commonplace situations, private or public, but always envisaged from the point of view of manners. The texts refer repeatedly to the 'cleanliness of the body.' They ignored bathing, but that is not what is most important in this connection. They focused attention on the parts which were visible—the hands and the face. 'Washing the face in the morning in cold water is both clean and healthy.' They sometimes equate correct behaviour and hygiene even more pointedly: 'It is a point of cleanliness and of health to wash the hands and face as soon as one rises.'

Caution with regard to water is also visible in this type of text. Water, from the seventeenth century in particular, became more disquieting as the face became more fragile. Great care was taken in seventeenth-century books of etiquette to ensure that the face was wiped rather than washed. 'Children should clean their face and their eyes with a white cloth, which cleanses and leaves the complexion and colour in their natural state. Washing with water is bad for the sight, causes toothache and catarrh, makes the face pale, and renders it more susceptible to cold in winter and sun in summer.' The same fears applied here as with bathing, and affected both actions and their context. Actual washing was no longer involved, though cleansing persisted, and even, in a sense, became more precise. One action gave way to another; splashing with water was replaced by wiping. The influence of the image of the body is clear to see; skins which had been infiltrated were susceptible to every ill.

As early as the beginning of the seventeenth century, Jean du Chesne, describing, as a scrupulous hygienist, all the actions which followed getting up, emphasized wiping and rubbing. Water was not involved. Cleanliness was achieved by wiping. The toilet was both 'dry' and active. 'Having opened his bowels, he should as his first act comb his hair and rub his head, always from front to back, right to the neck, with suitable cloths or sponges, for some little time, so that the head is well cleansed of all dirt; while the head is being rubbed, he might well walk about, so that the legs and arms are gradually exercised.' Next comes cleaning the ears and teeth, with water used only to wash the hands and the mouth. Lastly, the very frequently described act of Louis XIV, washing his hands in the morning in a mixture of water and spirits of wine, poured from a rich ewer into a silver saucer, does not imply washing the face. The mirror held at a distance by a valet emphasises that there was, in any case, 'no toilet-table nearby.'

On a more everyday plane, some seventeenth-century school rules institutionalized wiping. The pupils of both Jacqueline Pascal[20] and the Ursulines[21] washed their hands and mouth when they got up. On the other hand, they only wiped their faces. Their toilet also involved attending to their hair, the older children combing that of the younger ones. Water was

---

[20] 1625–1661; cloistered nun, educator, and sister of the philosopher Blaise Pascal.

[21] The oldest teaching order of women in the Roman Catholic Church.

hardly used. Only when they were dressed, and various items had been tidied away, did the pupils of the Ursulines splash water on their hands and face. 'When dressed, after having neatly folded away their things, they wash their mouth and hands.' In the case of Jacqueline Pascal, who described in great detail a veritable orchestration of the process of rising, water was mixed with wine to give it acidity, but was still not used on the face. 'While they made their beds, one of them brought breakfast and what was needed to wash their hands, and wine and water for washing the mouth.' In the eighteenth century, the rules of Jean-Baptiste de La Salle[22] perpetuated these instructions unchanged; the fears were sufficiently strong to persist. 'It is correct to clean the face every morning by using a white cloth to cleanse it. It is less good to wash with water, because it renders the face susceptible to cold in winter and sun in summer.' Rétif[23] carried out these same actions at the choir school of the Centre Hospitalier de Bicêtre,[24] which he attended in 1746. Water still had a precise and limited use. 'Not a moment was lost; prayers in the morning: after getting up, one rinsed one's mouth with water and vinegar; one took breakfast.' These examples of cleansing are all the more interesting in that the rejection of water does not rule out the practice of cleanliness. A norm existed, with specific utensils and methods, but it involved minimal washing.

A rapid reading of successive texts can give an impression of a distinct reduction in the requirements of hygiene dating from the sixteenth century. Water, after all, to some extent disappeared. Closer reading suggests rather a change; the insistence on wiping, on the whiteness of linen, and on the fragility and the colour of the skin are in fact evidence of increased attention. Texts are longer and more specific, as if concern was stronger. In treatises on manners, for example, most themes were more developed with the passage of time. The standards were more rigorous in the manual of Jean-Baptiste de La Salle in 1736 than in that of Erasmus[25] in 1530, even though the latter mentions washing the face. La Salle dwells on the care of the hair, which is to be cut and combed, and should have the grease regularly removed by the use of powder and bran (without washing); he dwells on the care of the mouth, which is to be washed every morning, and the teeth briskly rubbed; he describes in detail the care of the nails, which are to 'be cut every week.' The same concerns are present in Erasmus, but are described more allusively, and less distinctly. In Erasmus, rapid images and advice follow in quick succession, and he is briefer. The use of the comb, for example, is in comparison described more elliptically. 'It is remiss not to comb your hair, but though you must be proper, you should not titivate yourself like

---

[22] Author of *The Rules of Christian Decorum* (1736).

[23] Nicolas Rétif de la Bretonne, French novelist and chronicler of society, 1734–1806.

[24] The Bicêtre hospital had been established in Paris in the seventeenth century for old and insane men.

[25] Desiderius Erasmus (1466–1536), Christian humanist and author of a book of manners, *On Civility in Children* (1530).

a girl.' On the same subject, La Salle covers methods of care and frequency of actions, and he specifies and discusses the procedures. His explanations become additions and reinforcement. It is the same with the face. The use of water is reduced, but in favour of a care and an attention to detail which maintains and even strengthens the norm. Wiping, as described here, can even constitute a new demand. Acts of cleanliness were not abolished, but altered. They were affected by the image of the body. To understand this, all reference to the criteria of today has to be put aside and the existence of a cleanliness which assumed other methods than washing accepted.

The problem is, however, more complex. Two specific practices, public and private bathing, which had once existed, both disappeared almost completely between the sixteenth and seventeenth centuries, at the very period when the particular horror of the plague was being formulated. It is as if the image of the body had had a determining effect. These practices merit particular attention; they were the principal victims of the rejection of water. And it is their widespread disappearance which can give the impression of a lowering of standards of hygiene.

The Family in Renaissance Italy

DAVID HERLIHY

During the fourteenth and fifteenth centuries, a cultural flowering known as the Renaissance took place in Italy. David Herlihy studies primarily Florence, the center of the Renaissance and a leading city in Europe, in order to understand the nature of the family in Renaissance Italy. He finds that three factors—demography, environment, and wealth—affected the long-term development of the family.

Population trends, especially after the Black Death, shifted during the Renaissance. How did those changes influence the size of households and the number of servants? Note that Herlihy is very careful to make comparisons whenever possible between urban and rural families. In other words, environment influenced the structure of the family and the functions it performed. Families in cities differed from their counterparts in the countryside, not only in size, but also in the establishment of new families, remarriage, and the very functions the family performed. Wealth likewise shaped the family in determining whom to marry, household size, and age at marriage. What does Herlihy mean when he argues that demography, environment, and wealth led to a crisis of the Renaissance family?

Herlihy next discusses the composition of the Italian household, particularly in regard to marriage and children. Age at marriage seems to provide much information about family structure. Why was there such a disparity in Florence between the age of first marriage for women and for men? Why did the situation differ in rural areas? Why did some men and women remain unmarried? What was their fate?

Why did some women prefer to remain widows rather than remarry?
How did marriage patterns affect the prevalence of prostitution and homosexuality?
Children were very important to the Renaissance family, though the relationship
between mother and child was unlike that between father and child. The fathers cared
for their children's future, especially their sons', often leaving some posthumous
instructions specifying their upbringing. Mothers, closer in age to their offspring
and tending to survive their husbands, influenced their children in areas of
special concern to women. In this way, Herlihy believes that the character of the
Renaissance was determined considerably by female education of the young. Thus
he accords singular importance to the family and holds its peculiar structure
responsible in large part for the cultural awakening of the Renaissance.

...Sociologists and historians once assumed that the typical family in traditional Europe (that is, in Europe before the Industrial Revolution) was large,
stable and extended, in the sense that it included other relatives besides the
direct descendants and ascendants of the head and his wife. The sources of
Renaissance Italy rather show that there is no such thing as a traditional
family, or, in different terms, a family with unchanging characteristics. The
family in ca. 1400 was perceptibly different from what it had been in ca. 1300,
and was to be different again in the sixteenth century. Moreover, the rural
family varied in marked respects from the city household, and the poor—can
this be surprising?—lived differently from the rich. How precisely did the
times, location and wealth affect the Renaissance household?

In Italy as everywhere in Europe, the population between the thirteenth
and the sixteenth centuries experienced powerful, even violent, fluctuations.
These directly affected the households in their average size and internal
structure. The history of population movements in late medieval and Renaissance Italy may be divided into four periods, with distinctive characteristics:
(1) stability in numbers at very high levels, from some point in the thirteenth
century until ca. 1340; (2) violent contraction, from ca. 1340 to ca. 1410, to
which the terrible Black Death of 1348 made a major but not exclusive contribution; (3) stability at very low levels, from approximately 1410 to 1460;
(4) renewed expansion, which brought the Italian population to another peak
in the middle sixteenth century.

To judge from Tuscan evidence, the population in our second period (ca.
1340 to ca. 1410) fell by approximately two-thirds. A city of probably 120,000
persons in 1338, Florence itself counted less than 40,000 in 1427. In some
remote areas of Tuscany, such as the countryside of San Gimignano, losses
over the same period surpassed 70 percent. The region of San Gimignano
was in fact more densely settled in the thirteenth century than it is today.

It is difficult for a modern reader even to grasp the dimensions of these
losses; for every three persons living in ca. 1300, there was only one to
be found alive in ca. 1410, in many if not most Italian regions. And the
population, stable at low levels from approximately 1410, shows no signs
of vigorous growth until after 1460. The subsequent expansion of the late

fifteenth and early sixteenth centuries was particularly notable on the fertile plain of the Po river in Northern Italy and in the Veneto (the region of Venice). Verona, near Venice, for example, had fewer than 15,000 inhabitants in 1425, but reached 42,000 by 1502, nearly tripling in size. Venice itself reached approximately 170,000 persons by 1563; it was not to reach that size again until the twentieth century. Rome and Naples were also gaining rapidly in population. Florence too was growing, but at a moderate rate. In 1562 Florence counted slightly fewer than 60,000 inhabitants, which made the city only a third larger than it had been in 1427. Florence, in sum, even in this period of growth, was losing relative position among the major cities of Italy.

Inevitably, the collapse in population, subsequent stability, then growth affected the average size of the households. At Prato, for example, a small region and city 20 miles west of Florence, the average size of the rural household was 5.6 persons in 1298, and only 5 in 1427. Within the city of Prato, average household size similarly fell from 4.1 persons in 1298 to only 3.7 in 1427. By the late fourteenth and fifteenth centuries, the urban household widely across northern Italy was extremely small: 3.8 persons per household at Florence in 1427; 3.6 at Pistoia in the same year; 3.5 at Bologna in 1395; and 3.7 at Verona in 1425.

The acute population fall and the ensuing period of demographic stability at low levels (to ca. 1460) also affected the internal structure of the households. The demographic catastrophes, especially the plagues and famines, left within the community large numbers of incomplete or truncated households—those which lacked a married couple and included only widowers, widows, bachelors or orphaned children. At Florence in 1427, the most common of all household types found within the city counted only a single person; these one-member households represented some 20 percent of all urban households. The numerous, small, severely truncated and biologically inactive families (in the sense that they could produce no children) may be regarded as the social debris, which the devastating plagues and famines of the epoch left in their wake.

The renewed demographic expansion from about 1460 in turn affected average size and the internal structure of the household. Average household size at Verona, only 3.7 persons in 1425, reached 5.2 persons only thirty years later, in 1456, and was 5.9 persons in 1502. Within the city of Florence, average household size gained from 3.8 persons in 1427 to 4.8 persons in 1458 to 5.2 persons in 1480, and reached 5.7 members in 1552. Within the Florentine countryside, average household size similarly grew from 4.8 persons in 1427, to 5.3 in 1470, to 5.8 in 1552.

Several factors explain this increase in average household size in both city and countryside, during this period of demographic growth after 1460. As the plague and famine lost their virulence, the numbers of very small, highly truncated and biologically inactive families diminished within the community. Families were also producing larger numbers of children (perhaps we should say, of surviving children). Paradoxically, however, the large households of the late fifteenth and sixteenth centuries also indicate an effort to slow the rate of population growth. In a rapidly growing community, average household size tends to remain relatively low, as sons and daughters leave the paternal home at an early age to marry, and the community contains many young, hence small, families. But no community can allow its population to grow without limit, and in traditional society the principal means of slowing or stopping growth was to prevent young persons from marrying, or marrying young. These young persons remained in their parents' house for long periods, thus increasing average household size. Many of them, especially males, remained unmarried even after the death of their parents, living as bachelors in households headed by an older, married brother. Within the city of Florence, for example, in 1427 some 17.1 percent of the households included a brother or sister of the household head, but 26.1 percent did so in 1480. We have no exact figures from the sixteenth century, but the percentage was doubtlessly even larger. The Florentine household, in other words, was much more laterally extended in the sixteenth century than it had been in 1427. The effort to slow or stop population growth, more than the growth itself, accounts for the larger size and more complex structure of the Italian household in the late fifteenth and sixteenth centuries.

Another factor which contributed to these shifts in average household size was the changing servant population. The drastic fall in the population in the late fourteenth century made labor scarce and forced wages upward, and this meant that households before 1460 could afford to support comparatively few servants. At Verona in 1425, for example, some 7 percent of the urban population were employed as household servants. After 1460, as the population once more was growing, wages tended to decline, and households could afford to support larger numbers of retainers. By 1502 at Verona, servants constituted 12.3 percent of the urban population. The numbers of servants grew especially large in the city of Florence, where, by 1552, 16.7 percent of the urban population were employed in household service; nearly half the urban households (42 percent) had at least one domestic, and one Florentine citizen employed no fewer than 57 servants. This growth in the number of servants has great social and cultural importance. It meant that the Italian urban family of some means could live with considerably greater comfort and elegance in ca. 1500—during the height of the Renaissance—than had been possible a hundred years before.

By the sixteenth century, the typical Italian household was large in size and complex in structure; it included numerous children, servants, and lateral relatives of the head. Sociologists and historians used to consider this extended household characteristic of traditional European society. Today, we can discern that this type of household was characteristic only of particular periods and circumstances in the varied history of the Italian family.

The location of the household, its surroundings or environment, also exerted a powerful influence upon its internal structure. Unlike the long-term demographic trend, this factor exerted a largely uniform influence over time. In most periods and places, the rural household was larger than its urban counterpart. At Prato in 1298, the average household size was 5.6 in rural areas and 4.1 in the city; at Florence in 1427, the comparable figures are 4.8 in the countryside and 3.8 in the city. However, the changes we have already considered—particularly the great growth in the number of servants, which was more characteristic of the cities than of rural areas—tended to reduce these contrasts in the sixteenth century. In 1552, the average size of the urban household at Florence was 5.7 persons; it was 5.8 in the countryside.

Average household size, however, reveals very little about the internal character of the family. No matter what their relative size, the households of the countryside remained fundamentally different from those of the city. Perhaps the most evident contrast was this: almost invariably, the rural household contained at least one married couple; households headed by a bachelor, widow, widower or orphans were rarely found in rural areas. In the cities, on the other hand, bachelors and widows frequently appeared at the head of households at all periods. Households which lacked sexually active partners were therefore common in the city, but rare in the countryside. So also, the number of children supported in urban households tended to be below the number found in rural homes. . . .

These contrasts point to fundamental differences in the functions of the family in the countryside and the city. In the countryside, the family fulfilled both biological and economic functions: the procreation and rearing of children, and the maintenance of a productive enterprise, the family farm. In Italy, as everywhere in medieval Europe, a peasant economy dominated the countryside. In the peasant economy, the basic unit of labor was not so much the individual but the family. A single man or woman did not have the capacity to work an entire farm, but needed the help of a spouse and eventually children. The young peasant who wished to secure his own economic independence consequently had to marry. For the same reason, if a peasant or his wife were widowed, he or she tended to remarry quickly, unless a young married couple was already present in the household, for the farm could be successfully worked only through family labor. In rural areas there were consequently very few truncated households, that is, those which did not contain at least one married couple. The rural environment encouraged marriage, not only for biological but for economic reasons. Conversely, those residents of the countryside who did not wish to marry or remarry were strongly drawn to the cities.

Within the cities, the family of course continued to perform its biological functions of rearing children, but its economic functions were very different. The young man seeking to make his fortune in most urban trades or professions often found a wife more of a burden than a help. He frequently had to serve long years at low pay as an apprentice. He had to accumulate diligently his earnings and profits; capital alone permitted him one day to pursue his trade in his own right and name. Such a man could not usually contemplate marriage until his mature years, when he was economically established; even then, the urban family was not cemented, as was the rural household, by close participation in a common economic enterprise.

The urban environment, in other words, tended to be hostile to the formation of new households, and added little to their inner strength. Moreover, at the death of a spouse, his or her partner was not under the same pressures to remarry, as was the rural widower or widow who needed help in farming. Urban communities consequently contained far greater numbers of adult bachelors and widows than could be found in the rural villages. The urban environment was often hostile to the very survival of lineages. Both inside and outside of Italy, the city frequently proved to be the graveyard of family lines. . . .

The third factor which strongly influenced the character of the household was wealth or social position, but this influence was exerted in complex ways. In some respects, wealth reinforced the environmental influences reviewed above. Thus, in the cities, rich young men tended to approach marriage even more cautiously than their poorer neighbors. Marriage among the wealthy involved the conveyance of substantial sums of money through the dowry. Marriage also called for the sealing of family alliances, which affected the political and social position of all parties involved. The high stakes associated with marriage frequently led the wealthy young man (or his family) to search long for a suitable bride, and to protract the negotiations when she was found. Marriage, in other words, was not lightly regarded, or hastily contracted, among the rich. Moreover, if death should dissolve the marriage, the surviving partner, particularly the widow, usually controlled enough wealth in her own name to resist pressures to remarry. Bachelors and widows were therefore especially numerous among the wealthy. The poorer families of the city, in approaching marriage, had less reason for caution and restraint.

In the countryside, on the other hand, the wealthy peasant usually owned a large farm, which could only be worked with the aid of a wife and family. The rich inhabitant of the city looked upon marriage in the light of future advantages—the dowry and the family connections it would bring him; the substantial peasant needed family labor to make himself rich in harvests as well as land. Among the rural rich there were consequently few families headed by a bachelor or widow. Poorer inhabitants of the countryside—peasants who possessed less than an entire farm and who worked primarily as agricultural laborers—were less eager to take a wife, who, with children, might excessively tax already scant resources. Wealth, in sum, facilitated marriage in rural areas, while obstructing it within the city.

We must note, however, that there are important exceptions to the rule we have just enounced. In Tuscany, and widely in central Italy, there existed large numbers of sharecroppers, called *mezzadri*, who leased and worked entire farms in return for half the harvest. The owner of the farm provided his *mezzadro* with most of the capital he needed—cattle, tools, seed, fertilizer and the like. With few possessions of his own, the sharecropper usually appeared in the tax rolls as very poor, but he still required a wife and family to help him in his labors. In other words, the need to recruit a family of workers, rather than wealth itself, was the critical factor in encouraging marriages among the peasants.

Besides reinforcing environmental influences, wealth had another effect upon households, which was common to both cities and countryside. In both environments, almost invariably, rich households tended to be larger than poor households. And they were more abundantly supplied with all types of members: they supported relatively more children, more servants and more lateral relatives of the head. For example, if we consider only those households in the city of Florence in 1427 with a male head between age 43 and 47, the average size for the richer half of the urban households was 6.16 persons; it was 4.57 among the poorer half. In rural areas too, and in other periods, wealth exerted a similar, strong influence upon the size and complexity of households. It was as if the family head of the Renaissance, in both city and countryside, equipped himself with as large a household as his resources could reasonably support.

The marked influence of wealth upon household size had some paradoxical effects. Considerations of property . . . prompted rich young men in the city to marry late, and some did not marry at all; but once married, the rich were prolific in producing children. . . . The urban poor were far less hesitant in entering marriage, but the poor urban family was also far less successful than the rich in rearing children. Probably the children of the deprived fell victim, in greater relative numbers than the children of the privileged, to the rampant diseases of the age. Poor parents certainly had strong reasons for exercising restraint in procreating children, and they probably limited the number of their offspring in other ways—through primitive methods of birth control and through the abandonment of babies they could not support. In the countryside, on the other hand, wealth tended to encourage both early marriage and high fertility among those who married.

Our consideration of these three factors—the long-term demographic trend, environment and wealth—which strongly influenced the Renaissance family brings us to the following conclusion. The huge losses and slow recovery in the population in the late Middle Ages precipitated a major crisis within the Italian household, as it did in many other social institutions. Frequent deaths undermined the durability and stability of the basic familial relations—between husband and wife, and parents and children. High mortalities threatened the very survival of numerous family lines. The crisis was especially acute within the city, the environment of which was already basically hostile to the formation of households and to their cohesiveness. . . .

This grave crisis did, however, increase awareness of the family and its problems. Writers of the age were led to examine, and at times to idealize, familial relationships and the roles which father, mother and children played within the household. They sought to determine when young men should marry, how brides should be chosen, and how children should be trained, in order to assure the happiness and especially the survival of the family....

Against this background, we can now look in more detail at the Renaissance household. Specifically, we shall examine what sociologists call the "developmental cycle" of the household—how it was formed through marriage, grew primarily through births, and was dissolved or transformed through deaths.

Perhaps the most distinctive feature of the Renaissance marriage was the great age difference which separated the groom from his bride. At Florence in 1427–28, in 55 marriages reported in the *Catasto*,[1] the average age difference between the bride and groom was 13.6 years. Demographers can also estimate age of first marriage from the proportions of the population remaining single at the various age levels, through somewhat complicated calculations we need not rehearse here. By this method, the average age of first marriage for women in the city of Florence in 1427 can be estimated at 17.9 years; for men it is 29.9 years.

In this, the city of Florence presents an extreme example of a common pattern. In the Florentine countryside in 1427, the estimated age of first marriage for women, based on the proportions remaining single, was 18.3 years, and for men 25.6 years. The age difference between the spouses, 7.3 years, was less than in the city, but still considerable. In the city of Verona in 1425, the age difference was also smaller—7 years—but still extended.

The three factors of environment, wealth and long-term demographic trend affected the formation of new households and inevitably therefore the age of first marriage. However, the age of first marriage for men was far more sensitive to all these influences than the marriage age for women. The typical bride was never much older than 20 years, and was usually much younger. The age of first marriage for men varied over a much wider range of years, from 25 to 35 and at times perhaps to 40. According to a Florentine domestic chronicler writing in the early 1400's, Giovanni Morelli, his male ancestors in the thirteenth century were prone to postpone their first marriage until age 40.... In the period before the devastating plagues,[2] when the mean duration of life was relatively extended, men would be forced to wait long before they would be allowed to marry. The medieval community had already reached extraordinary size in the thirteenth century and could ill support continued, rapid growth.

It is at all events certain that the great plagues and famines of the fourteenth century lowered the average age at which men first entered marriage. Thus, in 1427 in the city of Florence, the average age of first marriage for men was approximately 30 years, which compared to Morelli's estimate of 40 years for the thirteenth century. Subsequently, as the plagues

---

[1] 1427 census in Florence.

[2] That is, before 1348.

grew less virulent, and lives became longer, the age of first marriage for men again moved upward. In 1458, for example, the estimated age of first marriage for Florentine men was 30.5 years, and it was 31.4 years in 1480.

The age of first marriage for women moved upward and downward in the same direction as that of men, but, as we have mentioned, over a shorter range of years. (The estimated age of first marriage for Florentine women was 17.9 years in 1427, 19.5 in 1458 and 20.8 in 1480.) The reasons for this relative inelasticity in marriage age for women seem to have been preeminently cultural: Italian grooms of the Renaissance, under almost all circumstances, no matter what their own age, preferred brides no older than 20.

So also, between city and countryside, the differences in age of first marriage for men (29.9 and 25.6 years respectively in 1427) were much greater than the differences in age of first marriage for women (17.9 and 18.3 years respectively). Women were slightly older at first marriage in rural areas, perhaps because the agricultural labors they were to perform required physical maturity. Again within the city, the richest Florentine males in 1427, from households with an assessment of over 400 florins, entered marriage for the first time at an estimated age of 31.2 years; their poorest neighbors, from households with no taxable assets, were considerably younger at first marriage—only 27.8 years. But rich girls and poor girls married for the first time at nearly the same ages—17.9 and 18.4 years respectively. Rich girls tended to be slightly younger, perhaps because their worried fathers wanted to settle their fate as quickly as possible. But almost all Florentine brides, in every corner of society, were remarkably young, at least by modern standards.

We should further note that in those segments of society where men married late (that is, in the towns, and particularly among the wealthy) many men, perhaps 10 percent, did not marry at all, but remained as bachelors, usually in the households of married relatives. On the other hand, girls who did not marry either entered domestic service—an option not open to girls from well-to-do households—or joined a religious order. There were almost no lay spinsters in urban society, apart from servants.

How does this pattern of marriage compare with modern practices? Sociologists now identify what they call a "west European marriage pattern," which is apparently found in no other, non-Western society. This pattern is distinguished by late marriages for both men and women, and by the presence in the population of many adult men and women who do not marry at all. How "modern" were the men and women of the Renaissance? Clearly, within the cities, male behavior already corresponded closely to this modern pattern; men married late and some did not marry at all, especially among the wealthy. The women of the Renaissance, on the other hand, even within the cities, were far from modern in their marital behavior; they married young and those who did not marry rarely remained in the lay world. Renaissance Italy, in other words, was not the birthplace of the modern marriage pattern, at least not for women.

The long span of years, which separated the groom from his bride, had distinctive effects upon both the character of the Renaissance household and upon the larger society. The young girl had little voice in selecting her mate, and usually no competence to choose. The first weeks of marriage must have been traumatic for these child brides.... But the position and status of these young matrons thereafter improved, for several reasons. The husbands were older, occupied men; many were already past the prime of their years. The brides, themselves only reaching maturity, rapidly assumed chief responsibility for the management of their households.... For many women, ultimate liberation would come with the deaths of their much older husbands. At the death of the husband, the dowry returned to the widow; the large sum of money which had taxed her family's resources at her marriage now could make her a woman of means, independent enough to resist a second marriage if she did not want it. As a widow with some property, she was free from male domination in a way she had never been as a child and a wife. The years of childhood, of service as a wife, were hard but often abbreviated for the lady of the Renaissance; and time worked in her favor.

Within the larger society, especially within the cities, the tendency for males to postpone marriage meant that the community would contain large numbers of unattached young men, who were denied legitimate sexual outlets for as long as two decades after puberty. Erotic tensions thus ran high within the city, and the situation inevitably promoted both prostitution and sodomy, for which the Renaissance cities enjoyed a merited reputation. The typical triad of many contemporary stories and dramas—the aged husband, beautiful young wife, and clever young man intent on seducing her—reflects a common domestic situation. These restless young men, uninhibited by responsibilities for a wife and family, were also quick to participate in the factional and family feuds and battles which were frequent occurrences in Renaissance social history....

Delayed marriage for men inevitably affected the treatment and the fate of girls. Because of high mortalities and the inevitable shrinking of the age pyramid, there were fewer eligible and willing grooms, at approximately age 30, than prospective brides, girls between 15 and 20. The girls, or rather their families, had to enter a desperate competition for grooms, and this drove up the value of dowries to ruinous levels.... Since prospective brides outnumbered available grooms, many girls had no statistical chance of finding a husband. For most of them, there would be no alternative but the convent. A great saint of the fifteenth century, Bernardino of Siena, once described these unhappy girls, placed in convents because they were too poor, too homely, or too unhealthy to be married, as the "scum and vomit of the world."

The acts by which the marriage was contracted were several. The formal engagement usually involved the redaction of a notarial contract, which stipulated when the marriage should occur and how the dowry should be paid. The promise of marriage would often be repeated solemnly in church.

On the wedding day, the bride and groom would often attend a special Mass, at which they received the Church's blessing. But that blessing, or even the presence of a priest, was not required for a legitimate marriage until the Council of Trent[3] in the sixteenth century made it obligatory for Catholics. The central act in the wedding ceremony was a procession, in which the groom led his bride from her father's house to his own. Through this public display, society recognized that this man and this woman would henceforth live together as husband and wife. The groom then usually gave as lavish a feast as his resources would allow, which sometimes lasted for days.

... Given the character of the marriage, the typical baby was received by a very young mother and a much older father. Within the city of Florence in 1427, the mean age of motherhood was approximately 26.5 years...; the mean age of fatherhood was 39.8 years. The age differences between mothers and fathers were again, less extreme in the countryside or in other Italian towns, but still must be considered extended.

The great differences in the average ages of fathers and mothers affected the atmosphere of the home and the training of children The mature, if not aged, fathers would have difficulty communicating with their children, and many would not live to see their children reach adulthood. One reason the male heads of family placed moral exhortations in their *ricordi*[4] is that they feared that they would not survive long enough to give much advice... to the younger generation.

This distinctive situation placed the wife and mother in a critical position between the old generation of fathers and the children. Much younger and more vigorous than her husband, usually destined for longer and more intimate contact with her children, she became a prime mediator in passing on social values from old to young. Understandably, many of the educational tracts, which proliferate in Italy from the early fifteenth century, are directed at women. One of the first of them, Dominici's *Governance and Care of the Family*, ... beautifully describes both what Florentine mothers did, and what the author, a Dominican friar, wished them to do. Mothers, according to the friar, spent the days pampering and playing with their young children, fondling and licking them, spoiling them with beautiful toys, dressing them in elegant clothes, and teaching them how to sing and dance. An effeminizing influence seems evident here, which was not balanced by a strong masculine presence within the home. The friar recommends that the mothers rather impart spiritual values to their children; in telling them how to do this, he shows the new fifteenth-century awareness of the psychology of children. The home should contain a play altar, at which the young could act out the liturgy, and pictures of Christ and St. John represented as playful children, to whom real children will feel immediate rapport. Clearly, Dominici did not

---

[3]Church council, 1545–1563.
[4]Diaries.

regard the child simply as a miniature adult, without a mind and psychology of his own.

Two conclusions seem appropriate here. The Renaissance household, with an aged, occupied and often absent husband and a young wife, was not ideally equipped to give balanced training to its children. But this deficiency seems to have increased the concern for the proper education of children.... [W]omen continued to dominate the training of young children, and inevitably they inculcated in them qualities which they admired—a taste for refined manners and elegant dress, and a high esthetic sensibility. In the sixteenth century, a character in the *Book of the Courtier*, by Baldassare Castiglione, then the most popular handbook of good manners, attributes all gracious exercises—music, dancing and poetry—to the influence of women. The gentleman of the Renaissance was fashioned to the tastes of women; so also was much of the culture of the age.

Births also helped shape the total society. Here, an important factor was the differences in relative fertility among the various segments of the community. The rural population, as we have mentioned, tended to be more prolific than the urban, and the rich, while slow to marry, still reproduced themselves more successfully than the poor. Differences in fertility rates inevitably generated flows of people from some parts of society to others. Thus, differential fertility between city and countryside assured that there would be constant immigration from rural areas into the towns.... This immigration had important social effects. It appears to have been selective, as the city especially attracted the skilled and the highly motivated. At Florence, many of the cultural leaders of the Renaissance ... were of rural or small-town origins. The urban need for people promoted the careers of these gifted men. On the other hand, by introducing them into a milieu which made their own reproduction difficult, immigration also tended over the long run to extirpate the lines of creative individuals. It was not an unmixed blessing.

Within the cities, the wealthier families, in spite of the male reluctance to enter marriage, still tended to produce more children than the poor. Many of these children would be placed in convents or enter careers in the Church, but some would face a difficult decision. Either they would have to accept a social position lower than their parents, or they would have to seek to make their fortunes outside of their native city, even outside of Italy.... Many were forced therefore to wander through the world in search of fortune. Demographic pressures, in other words, required that even the sons of the wealthy adopt an entrepreneurial stance. This helps explain the ambitions and high energy of the Florentines and other Italians, and the prominence they achieved all over Europe, in many fields, in the Renaissance period.

The final event in the history of a marriage was death, and we can deal with death more briefly, as we have already referred to its central role in the social history of the epoch. Death was everywhere present during the Renaissance, and the ravages it perpetrated were at the root of the crisis of the family, which was most severe in the late fourteenth and early fifteenth centuries. Here, we shall note only the distinctive reactions of the surviving partner in a marriage to the death of a spouse. For reasons already discussed, in the countryside it was typical for both widows and widowers quickly to remarry, if they were of suitable age. But in the city, the behavior of widowed men and women was quite different. The urban widower, who as a young man had usually waited long before entering his first marriage, quickly sought out a new wife. The widow, on the other hand, who as a young girl had been rushed into wedlock, delayed remarriage, and many widows did not remarry at all. The cities of the Renaissance consequently contained numerous male bachelors and widows, but very few spinsters and widowers. The mature male, who once had married, found it difficult to live without the continuing companionship of a woman. But the woman, after she had lost a husband, felt little compulsion to remarry....

The Effects of the Black Death on North Africa and Europe

M. E. COMBS-SCHILLING

The plagues known as the Black Death constituted the greatest catastrophe in European history, killing perhaps twenty-five million people. Periodic outbreaks recurred from the mid-fourteenth through the mid-eighteenth century. The plagues had profound social, economic, and psychological consequences in Europe, yet, as M. E. Combs-Schilling shows, plagues had even more devastating effects on the Islamic world and on the shaping of European world hegemony.

What specifically were the plagues' dissimilar consequences in Europe and North Africa? Why did the social structure and economy of Europe recover quickly, while society and economy crumbled in North Africa? How did the different religions—Christianity and Islam—work to define and understand the plagues? How did Christians and Muslims react to the plagues? How did these reactions affect Christian and Muslim responses in the aftermath of the plagues?

Combs-Schilling focuses on Morocco and Iberia. Arab converts to Islam had conquered North Africa in the seventh century, and by 711 they, with the help of the Berbers, had overrun Spain. Throughout the Middle Ages, the Islamic world flourished intellectually and economically and was certainly more advanced than Christiandom. How did the plagues contribute to the shifting of Western hegemony that enabled the Christians' complete reconquest of Spain in 1492? What changes in Europe enabled Portugal to proceed with a military and economic assault on Morocco? How did European religion, technology, and economy each encourage Christian advance at Muslim expense?

> *At the end of the Roman Empire, western Europe had suffered the invasions of Germanic tribes, while in the eighth, ninth, and tenth centuries, Muslims, Vikings, and Magyars had attacked from the south, north, and east. Beginning in the late eleventh century, Crusades to the Middle East and North Africa attempted and ultimately failed to establish a European presence in the "Holy Land." The Crusades did, nevertheless, represent the new vitality of the European population, economy, and society in the eleventh through the thirteenth centuries. On the other hand, plague contributed to the Spanish attack on Muslims and the Portugese advance in Morocco and down the west coast of Africa in the fourteenth and fifteenth centuries. Why did these successful crusades of the Spanish and Portugese result in part from the aftermath of plague, whereas the earlier crusades had been driven by socioeconomic advance? To what extent did the failure of the earlier crusades and the success of the Iberian crusades have to do with the religion of Islam itself and the withering repercussions of the fourteenth-century plague?*

Earthly power is fickle. In part, it must be seized. In part, it is bestowed by processes of history that lie beyond the ability of any given powerholder to control. In the 600s (the first century after the hijra),[1] the cluster of variables that made for domination came to rest with the Muslim world, which then experienced seven hundred years of political, economic, and cultural hegemony. But by the 1400s (A.H.[2] 800s), the foundations of world power were shifting, and the countries to the north of the Mediterranean were coming into their age of glory.... The shifts in power were particularly dramatic in the western Mediterranean, where Christian Iberia's gain was Islamic Morocco's loss. Two factors were crucial in the transformations: the differing impact of the bubonic plague upon the economies of the two regions, and the switch in international commerce from overland to oversea.

In the fourteenth century, after six hundred years of prosperity, Morocco's economy crashed. Previous declines had been short-term, but the 1350 (A.H. 750/51) plummet was systemic. One factor overrides all others: the bubonic plague, which first struck in 1347–1348 (A.H. 748–749). The initial wave of the "new" pestilence was devastating to the population, which had no resistance to it. Along trade and pilgrimage routes it traveled, leaving a gruesome path of death in its wake—dead people, dead camels, dead birds. As much as half of the Moroccan population perished.

If the plague had not struck, the Berber[3] model of rule might have endured for some time. After all, it had brought Morocco its age of brilliance. But it did strike, and the world changed....

---

[1] Also spelled hegira or hejira. The flight of the prophet Muhammad (the founder of Islam) from Mecca, his native city, to Medina in 632.

[2] After the hijra. Muslims date their calendar from the first day of the lunar year in which the hijra occurred.

[3] People native to North Africa before the Muslim conquest of the seventh century. The Berbers today comprise much of the population of Morocco, Libya, and Algeria.

CONTRAST: EUROPE AND NORTH AFRICA

The plague hit Europe as well as North Africa and the Middle East, and the short-term effects were much the same throughout the Mediterranean—death of one-third to one-half of the population, the disruption of economic, social, and political life, and the questioning of world views. Yet the long-term effects were exactly the opposite in Europe as compared with North Africa and the Middle East. One can convincingly argue that the long-term effects of the plague on Europe were basically beneficial, that they spurred the transformations in agriculture, commerce, and social organization that enabled Europe to embark on its road to world domination; whereas for North Africa and the Middle East, the long-term effects of the plague were unequivocally negative, destroying the foundations of what had been a world dominating system. . . .

The differing impacts were a function of the differing kinds of economic systems that operated in the two regions. Those of the Muslim world were highly developed, dynamic, and lucrative, and depended on a complex infrastructure that had taken centuries to build. The very prosperity and intricacy of the North African and Middle Eastern economic systems made them vulnerable to the plague's damage. There were more levels at which the plague's destruction could strike, more dimensions that could be ravaged, making it harder to rebuild.

In contrast, when the plague struck Christian Europe, its economic order was less developed and was in need of and already in the process of transformation, and the plague's destruction cleared the way for a new, more complicated economic reality. In North Africa and the Middle East, the plague undid world hegemony. In Europe, the plague helped set the context for hegemony's creation.

Plague and Christian Europe

When the plague struck in 1350 (A.H. 750/51), Europe was still something of a backwater. The manor system of agriculture still dominated production, and the countryside was overpopulated. . . . The plague reduced the European population to more "reasonable proportions" and speeded up beneficial processes of change already in motion. "The moment . . . was one of great fluidity. . . . The Black Death did not initiate any major social or economic trend, but it accelerated and modified—sometimes drastically—those which already existed". . . .

The plague pushed the disintegration of the manor system, freeing land and labor for new forms of economic and political life: "the Black Death introduced a situation in which land was plentiful and labor scarce. The scales were tipped against the landowner". . . . The reduction in population left those who remained in an immeasurably stronger position to bargain with their employers and to acquire land. As agricultural production became a burden for large-scale landowners, manors broke up and peasants took over who with their own labor began to produce significant surpluses. European peasants here had an advantage over their North African and Middle Eastern counterparts in the relative ease with which land—taken out of production with the plague—could be put back in production in the plague's aftermath. Europe's rainfall was the critical factor. If peasants had land and seeds, they could begin production, whereas in North Africa and the Middle East, more complex support systems, such as irrigation, were needed.

In the plague's European aftermath, pay for urban workers rose and a new skilled class of workers came into being. The plague left the available capital and medium of exchanges intact, hastening the transition from a system of barter to a system of cash exchange, all necessary transformations if Europe was to experience the economic "takeoff"....

Plague and Muslim North Africa

The long-term effects of the plague on the economies of North Africa and the Middle East were exactly the opposite.... Their infrastructural elaboration made them vulnerable. Sugar production and long-distance commerce are intricate systems with multiple interconnected links; the plague struck at each connection.

Sugar Production. The sugar production in which the Islamic world, particularly Morocco, excelled was a labor and capital intensive process. In the Mediterranean, a large body of skilled labor is needed to build and maintain irrigation systems, oversee the watering, carry out the fertilization, reap the crops, and manufacture and distribute the cones. The plague wreaked havoc with each aspect of production and made the overarching system almost impossible to rebuild. With the wave of death, expert knowledge was lost, skills vanished, irrigation systems fell apart, crops died, and the land was left fallow. There was little sugar cane left to refine, and the manufacturing industry and the distribution networks collapsed.

The decline in population was a disaster for the sugar economy because sugar cane is a labor intensive crop. Labor became scarce and costly; this undercut the economic incentives for rebuilding the labor intensive system. Exacerbating the problem of overall population decline was the flight of the rural peoples to the urban areas. Sugar cane is a rural crop. In contrast to what occurred in Europe, when the plague hit North Africa and the Middle East, the population fled the cities in order to receive medical care. The Muslim world had a well-organized system of medicine, which included hospitals, trained doctors, nurses, and medications. It was urban based. (European medical care was remedial in comparison.)

The bottom dropped out of sugar production in each of the four main Muslim centers—Morocco, Egypt, Palestine, and Syria. Some of the best statistics come from Egypt, where the most archaeological work has been done. In 1324 (A.H. 724/25), sixty-six sugar refineries operated full-scale in

Old Cairo. A hundred years later, after the plague, only nineteen still existed, and none operated at previous capacities. . . .

From the mid-1300s (A.H. 750s) to the mid-1400s (A.H. 850s), Morocco went from being the producer of vast quantities of what many considered the finest refined white sugar in the Mediterranean to producing only small quantities of the raw, dark product. . . . In 1470 (A.H. 875), Morocco began, for the first time in history, to export raw or only partially refined sugar to Europe for refinement there, first to Venice and Bologna, then to Antwerp and Holland. The move was significant because of the future it augured. North Africa was being transformed from a center of manufacturing into a center of raw materials production for a European-based manufacturing center. The change carried the familiar cluster of characteristics: "It transferred employment in the industry from producer to importer; it reduced the producer's interest in making fine quality sugar, and it made the producer subservient to the importer. The development of refining in Europe placed the producer in a dependent or 'colonial' relationship with the manufacturer. . . . In the late 1400s (A.H. 800s), European economic imperialism had achieved its first foothold in North Africa.

By the mid to late 1400s (A.H. 800s), the Muslim world, the center of Mediterranean sugar production for five hundred years, had to import refined sugar to meet its needs. Trade deficits mounted. The sugar pillar of Muslim economic supremacy was lost.

Agriculture. The plague wreaked havoc on the whole of agricultural production in North Africa and the Middle East—not on sugar production alone. The disintegration of irrigation systems brought about general crop failure and famine. Famine led to yet more deaths and a higher cost of labor, and the downward cycle continued. The problems caused by the plague were exacerbated when an animal murrain hit North Africa's work animals at about the same time that the plague struck its human population, reducing the stock of plow and work animals, which further devastated agriculture. . . . In North Africa and the Middle East, the plague did not simply destroy crops and change the basis of land ownership: it destroyed the infrastructure upon which crop production depended. Many lands were transferred to less intensive forms of cultivation, while others fell out of the productive cycle.

Long-Distance Trade. The black plague also devastated the other pillar of Muslim economic prosperity, the trans-Saharan commerce, especially in gold. That trade depended on an intricate banking, information, and transportation network that was built upon trust and personal connections that took years to develop. The plague collapsed these networks because so many of the merchants died simultaneously. When the plague finally subsided, newcomers could began to buy and sell, but the elaborate network of relationships upon which sophisticated commercial exchange depended could not easily be rebuilt.

Plague and Dominion. When the plague struck, Morocco had known centuries of economic, political, and cultural domination. Its economic wealth lay in an intricate system of international commercial exchange in which prosperity depended upon the constance of gold and silver prices, the steady production of manufacturing goods for export (e.g., refined sugar, paper products), the free flow of overland trade, and the availability of basic agricultural commodities. The plague struck at each of the mainstays and sent the system as a whole spiraling downward.

CHRISTIAN MILITARY ASSAULT

The plague turned the Moroccan countryside into political and economic turmoil. When the last great Berber monarch died in 1358 (A.H. 759/60), numerous contenders for power arose. Former advisors, subdivisions of the dynasty, and subsections of the militia vied for power.... The central administration disintegrated, education was damaged, and the legal system had difficulty functioning even at the lowest levels.

But the worst had not yet struck. It was soon to come: Christian military attack followed the plague's devastation. The first attack came in 1399 (A.H. 801/02) when Henry III[4] of Castille crossed the Mediterranean and invaded the port of Tetouan, slaughtering half of the inhabitants and reducing the other half to slavery before abandoning the city and returning home. The second attack was no more lethal, but it was more ominous because the attacker did not leave: in 1415 (A.H. 818/19), the Portugese invaded Sabta (Ceuta), the northern terminus of the Moroccan gold route. They successfully captured the port and left a garrison of 2,500 men to secure it for posterity. The age of European colonialism had begun. The lines of south-north military invasion were reversing.

Why the Iberians Sailed

A Muslim state had lain to Iberia's south for seven hundred years, and boats capable of crossing the Mediterranean had existed for several thousand. Why the Iberian sailing and the Moroccan attack at this time? The convergence of three variables was responsible: economic need, Inquisition fervor, and technological advance.

Economic Need. Iberia was not only politically occupied by Muslims during much of the 700-to-1500 era (A.H. 100–900); like much of the rest of Europe in the Middle Ages, Iberia depended upon the hard currency and the luxury goods that the Muslim and Byzantine worlds provided.... For Iberia, Morocco was the most important supplier. Iberia required Moroccan gold, silver, silk, sugar, dyes, and spices. As of the late 1300s (A.H. 700s),

[4]1390–1406.

these goods were scarce because of the damage the plague had brought to North Africa's systems of production and exchange. Iberia was experiencing a "desperate shortage of hard currency, the demand for which had increased forty-fold during the previous four centuries".... In search of these goods, Spain and Portugal sailed south, and Sabta was a natural target. It was the northern terminus for Morocco's river of gold, the Sijilmasa trade route.

Inquisition Fervor. Cultural factors also played a part in the southern sailing, for the plague had sent shock waves through Iberians' constructions of the world. The cosmic crisis appears to have been more severe for Christians, for whom a dominant interpretation was that God had intentionally wrought the plague's havoc upon them because of lack of faith. Self-blame and guilt dominated the Christian response.

The Muslim interpretation, on the other hand, was less inwardly focused and more circumspect. The plague caused self-searching, but Muslims were less ridden by self-doubt. They tended to interpret it not as a direct attack on themselves, but rather as one of those inexplicable crises that regularly strike humanity—like drought, famine, and locusts—the ultimate purpose of which only God knows.

The divergent Christian and Muslim interpretations created alternative perspectives on how to deal with the world in plague's aftermath. Many Muslims apparently went about trying to reconstruct the world in which they had formerly lived, while many Christians, especially those of Iberia, set about trying to change themselves and their world. They began by trying to prove themselves in God's eyes—and in their own eyes—by demolishing the Muslim and Jewish Other at home and abroad.

The Catholic Inquisition[5] was officially instituted in Rome in 1184 (A.H. 580/81) and introduced into Iberia in 1237 (A.H. 635/36), yet it never really functioned until the plague's aftermath. Not until the 1400s (A.H. 800s) were the laws on the books regularly implemented in the day-to-day; not until then were they used to strike out against Jews and Muslims within the Iberian Peninsula and outside it....

In Iberia, the plague's shaking of the cultural foundations resulted in an age of untold Inquisition fervor, a true holy war. Economic need and religious world view coalesced to fuel an unrestrained drive for inward purity and outward expansion, a drive that utilitarian goals alone could never have impelled, especially since utilitarian benefits were slow in coming. In the interim, holy rage filled the gap.

Inquisition within the Peninsula. The Christian reconquest of the Iberian Peninsula proceeded with haste. The Inquisition provided the necessary tools: terrorism, confiscation of property, and propaganda. Remaining Muslim political strongholds within the Peninsula were overthrown. In 1492, a banner year for western Europe, Granada—the last seat of Muslim power in

---

[5]Tribunal designed to seek out and suppress heresy.

Iberia—fell. Seven centuries of Muslim rule were finished. Individual Jews and Muslims were pressured into converting, and even after they converted, their professions of faith were often held suspect. After 1480 (A.H. 885/86), Jewish and Muslim "converts" began to be burned at the stake, and the flight of Jews and Muslims from the Peninsula began in earnest.

In 1492 (A.H. 897/98), on the very day the Columbus sailed west in pursuit of economic riches, all remaining Jews in Spain "were given four months either to convert to Catholicism or leave the country.... In 1502 a royal decree gave all Muslims the same alternative.... baptism or exile".... After these rulings, the practice of any allegedly "non-Catholic" behavior was sufficient to bring a person before a tribunal that could lead to death. Evidence of continuing "alliance" with Judaism included the wearing of purportedly cleaner clothes on Saturday, the Jewish Sabbath, and the washing of a dead person's body in warm water.... Evidence of continuing Islamic affiliation included the practice of taking too many baths.... In those days Christians associated cleanliness with ungodliness.

Beyond the Peninsula. The Iberian conquest beyond the Peninsula was spearheaded by Prince Henry the Navigator,[6] of Portugal, a remarkable man—adventurer, pragmatist, and devout Catholic. Prince Henry wanted to dominate the gold route that flowed through Morocco, an economic aim that was given impetus by his fervent desire to spread the true faith. "If we must choose a dominant theme in Prince Henry's plans, it was probably the destruction of Islam in Africa. The conquest of Ceuta [Sabta] seemed to open the way to a great enterprise which should reverse the Muslim invasion of the Peninsula in 711"....

Prince Henry had a twofold strategy of attack. The first was direct: to take hold of Morocco's commerce and destroy the Muslim state by seizing Morocco's ports, the northern termini of trans-Saharan trade. Hence the attack on and occupation of Sabta (the Mediterranean port for the Sijilmasa/Fas trade route). Yet the occupation did not accomplish what the Portugese wanted; neither gold nor converts came their way. The Moroccan population viewed the invading Christians as the oppositional Other and remained avidly opposed to the occupation. Moroccan merchants instituted a trade embargo, taking their commerce elsewhere, when possible, rather than acceding to Portugese control. Military assaults against the Portugese were led by local authorities and waged by local populations. Raids were mounted from as far away as the Sus, 400 miles to Sabta's south....

The vigor of Moroccan resistance turned Prince Henry to his second line of attack—a long shot, but one that Henry thought worthy of attempt: to discover sea routes that would allow Portugal to bypass Morocco's middleman position and seize the sources of supply. The enterprise seemed unlikely to succeed. Most Europeans were persuaded that no ship could sail beyond

[6]1394–1460.

Cape Bojador, a small promontory on Morocco's southern coastline. Many thought that dragons inhabited the distant waters and swallowed the ships that ventured therein; no one had ever returned from those waters to offer a different interpretation.... Yet Prince Henry was not a man to be easily discouraged—especially since someone else would be doing the sailing—and searched for a man willing to attempt the feat. Prince Henry found him in Gomes Eanes, who in 1434 (A.H. 837/38) boldly set sail into the untraversed waters to the south of Morocco. Remarkedly, Eanes succeeded. He reached Cape Bojador and sailed beyond, docking on the African coast. To prove his triumph, he plucked a sprig of rosemary and sailed home.

Prince Henry was elated with Eanes' success. The first obstacle had been surmounted: ships could sail south around Morocco. But could they bring back gold? That was another issue. Henry continued to pursue both of his strategies—to try to control the flow of gold across Morocco's mainlands, and to try to discover alternative sea routes to the sources of gold that would allow him to bypass Morocco entirely.

In 1437 (A.H. 840/41), Prince Henry's land strategy was dealt a serious blow. Henry had persuaded his brother, King Duarte,[7] to mount an attack on Tanja (Tangier). The Portugese forces invaded the port and were soundly defeated by the Moroccans. The defeat was particularly painful for King Duarte and Prince Henry because their younger brother was captured in the fighting and died in captivity before they could manage to ransom him....

The defeat at Tanja turned Prince Henry's and Portugal's attention to the sea, and official state policy was altered so that the sea search became the primary goal.... The altered focus paid off. Just three years later, in 1440 (A.H. 843/44), Portugal succeeded in producing a new type of vessel that could sail the seas in a new way, a form of sailing that would alter the course of history.

Technological Advances, Seafaring, and European Dominance. Technology was the third factor in the success of Portugal's outward expansion. Europe is a series of peninsulas. Its extensive coastline could be turned to its advantage only when the seas were opened for regular transport. That required the technology to sail the open seas and the ships to carry heavy loads across them.... Those inventions did not occur until the 1400s and 1500s (A.H. 800s and 900s), when they became the technological foundations upon which Europe's outward expansion and economic takeoff were built. Before that, Europe's cold climate and its circuitous coastline had left it a relative backwater in an international commercial network whose central arteries passed through the warm and sandy lands of North Africa and the Middle East.

---

[7]King of Portugal, 1433–1438.

The new Portugese ship was a crucial step in the right direction:

> In 1440, a new type of vessel of Portugese contrivance was put into use. The older ships, the *varinel,* combining oars and sails and therefore low and heavily manned, and the *barca,* slow and difficult to handle, were replaced by the *caravel,* light, long, and high. The necessity of coasting was now eliminated and full advantage of prevailing winds was gained by ... [traveling] over the open sea. . . .

The caravel enabled sailors to leave the coast and take advantage of the open seas, unlocking a new era in world transportation. The swift caravel replaced the plodding camel as the carrier of trade, and Muslim dominance of international transport was undone.

Other technological advances followed. Europeans began to alter their riggings. They put their square rigging on the foremast and Arab lateen riggings on the main and mizzen masts, which gave the newly outfitted ships an advantage when sailing close-hauled as well as when running.

Another important innovation came in the early 1500s (A.H. 900s) when European shipbuilders began to install guns, not only on the caste and upper decks, but also on the main deck by cutting gun ports into the ship's hull. The result was the galleon—half-warship and half-merchantman—by which Europe came to rule the seas. . . .

> The prizes in naval war no longer went to the captain who rammed or boarded his opponent, but to the naval artilleryman who knew how to maneuver his ship into position and to fire broadside. Thus at Diu, in 1509, Albuquerque[8] destroyed the joint Egyptian Mamluk and Gujarati fleet [both Muslim] and opened the sea routes of the southern seas to Portugese expansion. . . .

Economic and cultural factors impelled Europe to take to the seas, but the technology to sail them in new ways and to build new ships to carry heavy cargo account for Europe's post-1500 (A.H. 800s) hegemony. Like the Arab traversing of the desert, the European traversing of the seas fundamentally altered human interactions and made possible new lines of communication, commerce, and exploitation. Those who controlled the pathways could, to a certain extent, control the world. Trans-Saharan trade belonged to the Muslims and transoceanic trade belonged to Christians; those modes of transport partially account for their respective ages of domination.

Success by Sea and Land. With the invention of the caravel, Portugal began to penetrate West African waters and, in 1455 (A.H. 859/60), accomplished part of what it was after. It established maritime trade in gold with the people of West Africa, bypassing Morocco's overland routes. . . .

The trade in gold whetted Prince Henry's appetite, as did the 1459 map by the Venetian Fra Mauro[9] that came into Prince Henry's hands. According

---

[8] Afonso d'Albuquerque (1453–1515), Portugese admiral.
[9] Famous for his 1459 world map.

to this map, the Orient could be reached by sailing south to the tip of Africa, then east around it, and then due north. If such a route existed, it would allow Europeans to bypass the Muslim dominance of Asian trade as well as African trade. Henry threw himself into the task. The first step was completed in 1487 (A.H. 892/93), when Bartholomeu Dias[10] sailed around the Cape of Good Hope. Ten years later the Orient was reached....

In the meantime, Portugal had not entirely forgotten Morocco's ports and its wealth. In 1471 (A.H. 875/75), thirty-four years after its defeat at Tanja, Portugal launched a second attack on the city. This time Portugal won, and not only captured Tanja, but took the nearby port of Asila as well. Portugal still sought to dominate Morocco's ports and products. Even for its transoceanic trade with West Africa—the purpose of which was to bypass Morocco—it needed Moroccan goods for exchange. Africans wanted Moroccan horses, grain, gold coins, and their brightly colored woolen cloths....

Iberia in the 1490s. The 1490s (A.H. 896/905) were a momentous decade for Christian Iberians, the culmination of a century of conquest at home and abroad. In 1492 (A.H. 897/98), Granada fell, and thousands of Jews and Muslims fled to North Africa for safety. (Morocco, Algeria, Tunisia, and Egypt received major influxes of Muslim and Jewish Iberians during this era.) In that same year Christopher Columbus, flying a Spanish flag, thought he had discovered a water route to the Far East when in fact he had happened upon the Americas. Iberian Christians regained the Old World, and although they did not know it, discovered the New World, a discovery that in time would bring Iberia more hard currency, especially in silver, than its economies could handle....

Iberia's self-confidence soared, and in 1494 (A.H. 899/900), Portugal and Spain divided the world between them in the formal Treaty of Tordeiseillas; the Catholic Pope added his blessing. An imaginary line running from north to south was drawn 370 leagues west of Cape Verde Islands, located in the Atlantic Ocean off the western coast of Africa. Spain was "granted" dominion over all lands discovered to the west of the boundary, while Portugal was "granted" dominion over all land "discovered" to the east.... This was the first of a series of European treaties that would divide the world, just as arbitrarily and just as audaciously.

Three years after signing the treaty, Portugal completed the last leg of the water route to the east. With an Arab navigator at the ship's helm, Vasco de Gama[11] sailed around the Cape of Good Hope and continued all the way to Calcutta. The eastern water route to the Orient stood open. The seas were ready for war and commerce, and the world's hinterlands began to feel the weight of the sailing.

[10]c.1450–1500.

[11]c.1469–1525.

Consequences of Iberia's Outward Expansion for Morocco

Iberia's outward expansion was disastrous for Morocco. It exacerbated problems already set in motion by the plague and created a host of new ones. The occupation of the Moroccan ports did not bring Portugal its economic and cultural goals, but it kept Morocco from realizing its own. The 1415 capture of Sabta delivered the lethal blow to the last Berber dynasty, the Banu Marin, whose authority had been seriously undermined by the consequences of the plague. What power and credibility remained with them vanished with the Christian invasion. Not only had they failed to spread Islam abroad, they could no longer protect the faithful at home. In 1420 (A.H. 823/24), five years after the Portugese took Sabta, the last Berber dynasty collapsed; the centralized organization of collective existence—the administrative, military, educational, judicial, and economic systems—came undone.

A cultural crisis was also at hand. The kind of crisis that Iberian Christians experienced with the plague now struck Moroccan Muslims as they tried to make sense of why Christians successfully occupied their ports. Questioning and introspection led to self-doubt: perhaps Moroccans had not been sufficiently faithful; perhaps they had taken the wrong path.

The central structures of collective existence collapsed; the logistics of daily life came to be handled on local and regional levels—for example, the selection of political authorities and the settlement of disputes. Others simply fell by the wayside—such as the upkeep of the irrigation systems, the manufacture of sugar, and the structural integration of the educational system. Others came to be addressed in a patchwork fashion—for instance, long-distance trade was accomplished as traveling merchants made personal alliances with local and regional powerholders.

Even military opposition to the Portugese was locally and regionally organized. Fueled by long-established cultural perceptions, Moroccans avidly resisted the Portugese occupation. Yet popular resistance lacked a central focus. Instead, a series of local and regional leaders mounted short-term assaults, after which they and their men returned home to their camels and their crops. These attacks were irritating to the Portugese, but not sufficiently broad-based to pose a real threat. Portugal expanded its dominion, and Morocco spiraled downward.

The Jews of Spain and the Expulsion of 1492

NORMAN ROTH

The late Middle Ages and early modern Europe differed from the preceding eras, on the one hand, and the eighteenth and nineteenth centuries, on the other hand, by the intensive persecution of different groups. At various times and places, from approximately the twelfth century to the end of the seventeenth, Europeans victimized heretics, lepers, Jews, homosexuals, and supposed witches (who were usually women).

Spain has its legacy of persecution. The key year was 1492, when Spain conquered the Muslim kingdom of Granada, ending the 800-year presence of Islam in the Iberian Peninsula. In that same year Columbus sailed on his first voyage to the New World intent not only on riches and his own social ambitions but also on Christianizing all he met. With Columbus and the Spaniards who followed him, the Spanish concern for purity of blood and of thought (religion) translated into purity of race, to the detriment of Indians and later of African slaves.

Finally, in 1492, Spain expelled those Jews who would not convert to Catholicism. Jews had lived and prospered in Spain for over fifteen hundred years, and Christians and Jews had had cordial bonds for centuries. What circumstances in the Middle Ages led to the deterioration in Christian-Jewish relations? Why did Spain act in 1492 against the Jews, loyal subjects who had contributed greatly to Spain's economy and culture? Does Norman Roth hold King Fernando (Ferdinand) and Queen Isabel responsible? Did the populace welcome the expulsion of the Jews? What was the role of the Inquisition?

Thousands of Jews had already converted to Catholicism. What motivated them to convert? How does Roth explain the demoralization of Jewish communities? Were people's attitudes toward converted Jews (conversos) different from their feelings toward those who chose to remain Jewish? How did the doctrine of purity of blood affect anti-Semitism? What was the effect of the expulsion of the Jews on Spain?

Spain was home to Jews longer than any other country, including even the Jewish homeland of ancient Palestine. Although it is not known when Jews first arrived in Spain, there is definite proof of significant Jewish settlement by at least 300 C.E. and undoubtedly much earlier. Documentary sources from that time already demonstrate that cordial interaction existed between Jews and Christians. However, that situation soon changed when invading Visigoths established their theocratic government. Following their conversion to Roman Christianity (Catholicism), they began to impose ever more severe restrictions on Jews aimed at their compulsory baptism.

The possible end of the Jewish presence on the Iberian Peninsula was prevented by the Muslim invasion of North African Berber tribes in 711.

The Jews, used by the small invading Muslim forces to garrison conquered cities, soon became integrated into Muslim society. Increased immigration of both Muslims and Jews from Islamic lands rapidly built Spain into a major political and cultural center, from Andalusia in the south to Barcelona in the north. Muslims established an independent caliphate[1] at Córdoba, where Jews played a key role in the cultural renaissance that followed. From government service to the marketplace, Jews and Muslims interacted with little or no tension.

The situation took a turn for the worse with the Almohad invasion of Andalusia at the end of the twelfth century, although claims by modern historians of the total liquidation of Jewish settlements and the compulsory conversion of all Jews and Christians to Islam are greatly exaggerated. Nevertheless, many Jews and Christians were converted to Islam, while the great scholar Maimonides (b. 1135–d. 1204) and his family fled the country never to return. However, Maimonides continued to be proud of his Spanish origins, like many other Jewish exiles, and always referred to himself as *ha-Sefardi* (the Spaniard).

During the centuries prior to and after the Almohad occupation, Christian immigration from France and elsewhere enabled the gradual development of Christian kingdoms in northern Spain. Jews also lived in these areas and their numbers were augmented by a steady migration of Jews from Almohad-controlled provinces. Jews in Christian Spain were completely integrated into normal daily society not only as merchants, but also in agriculture and crafts. Jews brought a sophisticated culture and valuable knowledge of science and technology as well as literacy in Hebrew, Arabic, and Spanish, which was almost nonexistent among the general Christian population. They also rose to important positions in Christian governments.

As the Reconquest of Muslim Spain by the Christians began in earnest in the twelfth century and continued throughout the thirteenth, Jews served not only in administrative and diplomatic positions, but in large numbers as soldiers fighting in both Muslim and Christian armies. Along with Christians, Jews were rewarded with substantial grants of lands and houses in reconquered areas such as Seville, Jerez, and elsewhere.

The law codes (*fueros*) enacted by towns and cities, as well as privileges of settlement throughout the lands of Christian Spain, demonstrate a total equality of all citizens—Jews, Christians, and often Muslims. Frequently, Jews attained a favored subject status, marked by special exemptions from taxes and from service to overlord or king. In civil cases between Christians and Jews, both Jewish and Christian witnesses were required and judges from both communities were required to hear the case. Christian law granted full judicial rights to Jews, including the ability to testify and even serve as attorneys on behalf of Christians as well as Jews. Even kings, in their capacity

---

[1]The rulership of Islamic society.

as court of final appeal, were required to know Jewish law or to be informed by Jewish advisors.

With the completion of the Reconquest of all but the Muslim kingdom of Granada, Christian Spain was firmly established in its various if somewhat confusing and complicated kingdoms. Jews lived not only in the major cities but in literally every village and town in Spain, with sometimes as few as two or three families living in a village populated by Christians. There were no separate Jewish quarters, although in larger cities Jews often lived together in specific neighborhoods, which testifies more to the necessity to live within walking distance of a synagogue on the Sabbath than to any tension with Christians.

Although it is impossible to detail the complex history of Jewish-Christian relations in medieval Spain, to say nothing of Jewish contributions to political life or the developments of Jewish culture, relations between Christians and Jews remained generally cordial. In the reign of Alfonso X of Castile, from 1252 to 1284, Jewish scholars in Toledo translated Arabic scientific works and composed many more original treatises in Spanish, many of which were incorporated into a body of writing that became the first such collection in the vernacular and served for some time as Europe's chief source of astronomical and scientific information. Christian scholars from abroad were attracted to Toledo, as earlier scholars had been to Barcelona and elsewhere in Catalonia, to work together with Jewish scholars translating other Arabic books.

Jewish culture in Spain flourished. There was a profoundly important renaissance of the Hebrew language. The result was the first development of a secular literature of Hebrew poetry and novels that were added to legal sources and commentaries on the Talmud[2] as Spain's Jewish scholars became the most prominent in the world. Hardly less significant were Jewish contributions to Spanish culture; the first examples of written Spanish were early translations of the Bible that Jewish scholars did for Christians.

The Jewish role in science and medicine continued to grow in importance. Physicians served not only the royal and noble families, but frequently appeared on city payrolls as official physicians treating the general population. There is a vast amount of documentation on this subject that serves as important source material for the historian. Jewish government officials played an increasingly important role in the administration of the government, but not only or even chiefly in the farming of taxes.

The Spanish term *convivencia* describes the cultural interdependency and the positive relations that were maintained between Christian and Jewish communities. This word is untranslatable, but means much more than "living together," since it implies mutual exchange and goodwill, if not exactly tolerance as understood in the modern sense.

Uninformed scholars mistakenly believe that what caused the break in *convivencia* was the attack on Jews in 1391. The laws promulgated by Alfonso

---

[2]The compilation of the Jewish oral law along with commentary by rabbis.

XI (b. 1311–d. 1350) in Alcalá in 1348, which culminated earlier attempts to restrict Jews, were the most serious signs of impending trouble. Europe's Black Death had little impact in Castile, but more in Aragón and Catalonia. The Jews in Spain were not blamed for causing the plague nor were they subject to attacks as was the case in Europe generally.

The increasing role of the missionary campaign of the Dominican and Franciscan orders[3] was also important. From the early thirteenth century, these friars intensified efforts to convert Muslims and Jews by preaching and through writing polemical works. The friars' incorporation even of some Muslim ideas attacking the Jewish faith was strengthened by the hostility of Jewish converts to Christianity. Polemics were not confined to Christians, but Jewish polemics against Christianity have received practically no attention. The first two public disputations between Christians and Jews in Spain were held in Barcelona during the thirteenth century, both involving Jewish converts to Christianity. One of the Jewish participants at one of these was the famous Moses Nahman (Nahmanides) (b. 1194–d. 1270), an important Jewish authority and communal leader. The Jews lost such debates and Nahmanides left Spain for Palestine.

Jewish conversion to Christianity became a flood in the late fourteenth century. In the summer of 1391, inspired by the anti-Jewish propaganda of a minor archdeacon in Seville, mobs of lower-class peasants attacked and robbed Jews throughout Spain. Few Jews were actually killed: in many communities they were protected by their Christian neighbors and by officials; the kings severly punished all perpetrators. Nevertheless, immense damage had been done. Frightened and demoralized, thousands of Jews spontaneously converted and in a few cases were forcibly baptized. Compulsory baptism had been prohibited by Pope Gregory I (b. 540–d. 604) and that prohibition was an official part of canon law. Nevertheless, once baptized, a convert had to remain a Christian. However, secular authorities were seldom bound by canon law, especially in Spain. The kings indicated their willingness to ignore such compulsory baptisms, but few converted Jews—forced or otherwise—returned to their former faith.

A further source of demoralization for the Jewish communities was added to this catastrophe. Prior to the events of 1391, Solomon ha-Levy, an important rabbi in Burgos, had converted along with his entire family. Under the patronage of Benedict XIII (b. 1328–d. 1423), the anti-pope[4] who was recognized throughout Spain, he soon became the bishop of Burgos, one of the chief cities of Castile. Furthermore, he not only wrote an important anti-Jewish polemical work that had lasting influence but also encouraged

---

[3]St. Francis (c.1182–1226) established the Franciscan friars in 1223. St. Dominic (c.1170–1221) founded the Dominicans (the Order of Preachers) in 1216 to combat heresy.

[4]During the Great Schism (1378–1417), when there were two and sometimes three popes. The Roman Catholic Church considers those popes elected by cardinals at Rome to be true popes and those chosen by the other cardinals to be illegitimate, or anti-popes. Benedict XIII was anti-pope from 1394 to 1423.

the conversion of a former student and brilliant scholar, Joshua al-Lorqi, who took the name Jerónimo de Santa Fe and wrote an even more damaging attack on the Talmud. In 1414–15, Jerónimo joined with Benedict in organizing a disputation in Tortosa, to which all Jewish communities of Aragón-Catalonia were ordered to send representatives. Jerónimo was the chief Christian spokesman and the Jews again lost the debate. This time many of the Jewish participants converted to Christianity and more soon followed throughout the kingdom.

From 1410, the foremost preacher of the era, Vicente Ferrer (b. 1350–d. 1419), a Franciscan friar, conducted a combined campaign of religious reform and missionary activity throughout Spain. Increasing religious fervor and penitential movements swept the land as additional thousands of Jews and, in some cases, entire Jewish communities converted to Christianity. In Castile the child king, Juan II, was under the control of the regent, Fernando de Antequera, an aging war hero who was a compromise candidate chosen to be king of Aragón. Ferrer, the personal preacher to the elderly queen mother, Catherine of Lancaster (who had previously shown herself favorable to the Jews) and to Fernando, convinced them to enact a series of anti-Jewish laws at the capital city of Valladolid. Although not enforced, these laws further demoralized the Jewish community. Fernando's rule of Aragón, from 1412 to 1416, was marked by hostility to Jews.

A massive population of Jews who had converted to Christianity (*conversos*) had been created by the middle of the fifteenth century. Weakened by the decline in numbers, demoralized by the conversion of relatives and friends, and intimidated by the religious fervor of the age, the remaining Jews saw themselves for the first time as embattled. The most important rabbinical leaders fled Spain for North Africa after the events of 1391. Although they continued to direct responses to the legal and social problems of various Jewish communities in Spain, the Jews were in effect left leaderless.

Nevertheless, there is no evidence of increased hostility toward Jews on the part of ordinary Christians throughout the fifteenth century. Life went on as before. Jews continued to play an important role in business and trade, but to a lesser extent in agriculture, medicine, and government service (again probably due to the loss of Jewish population). Churches, convents, and monasteries continued to rely on Jewish administrators of estates, as did the nobility. Jews still collected various taxes and borrowed and loaned money on a regular basis. From king to commoner, substantial personal friendships prevailed between Jews and Christians, including bishops and archbishops. The existence of contracts between Christian and Jewish families to apprentice their minor children to live with each other for periods of ten years or more to learn a trade is a corrective to prevailing misconceptions about the supposed persecutions of Jews in fifteenth-century Spain.

The nature of the *conversos* in Spain is important to understanding the events that led to the Expulsion of the Jews in 1492. The prevailing myth has long been, and continues to be, that *conversos* were crypto-Jews, that is, their conversion was insincere and that they secretly professed Jewish beliefs. In the 1960s, a prominent Jewish historian wrote a book that successfully demolished this myth. Jewish and other sources clearly demonstrate that the *conversos* in fifteenth-century Spain converted of their own free will, not under any compulsion, and that most *conversos* were the descendants of those who had already converted. In any case, *conversos* were complete and willing Christians.

Jews saw *conversos* not merely as having changed their faith, but as having changed their identity. In the telling words of rabbinical authorities, the *conversos* had "gone out of the peoplehood of Israel and become another people." Thus, there was no hope of their return to Judaism. It was frequently noted that *conversos* had every opportunity to leave Spain and go to Muslim Granada, North Africa, or Portugal, where they could live as Jews if they so desired, since there was never any prohibition against *conversos* leaving the country, but they chose not to do so. Many "old Christians" went to Granada to embrace Islam during this period. One rabbi living in Muslim Granada wrote confirming that few if any *conversos* came to Granada to return to Judaism. Such Jewish hostility toward the *conversos* was already prevalent by the fourteenth century.

Not all Jews who converted did so purely from religious motivations. Many Jews converted to Christianity as a result of the anti-Jewish polemics of *converso* writers, the preaching of the Franciscans or Dominicans, or their own doubts about the ever-increasing duration of the exile and the apparent failure of the messiah to appear. But more Jews converted to Christianity to enhance their social and economic standing. By the middle of the fifteenth century, a substantial *converso* class had been created. All doors were open to them as Christians, including those of the Church. The *converso* Pablo de Santa María became bishop of Burgos and his son, Alfonso, became bishop of Cartagena and then followed his father in the Burgos see. Other members of the family became Church officials, as did many other *conversos*. Some monastic orders, such as the important order of San Jerónimo,[5] were filled with *converso* members. In both kingdoms, but especially in Aragón-Catalonia, *conversos* reached the highest government posts.

This aroused increasing resentment and hostility among elements of the general Christian population. As early as the 1430s, there were repeated petitions to the papacy by *conversos* to redress their grievances arising from mistreatment and attempts to bar them from obtaining further ecclesiastical and secular offices. The popes responded vigorously to what they rightly saw as unwarranted discrimination among Christians. Such *conversos* as Alfonso

[5] Established in Spain in the fourteenth century, the Jeronimites (the order of Saint Jerome), forbade after 1485 the entry into the order of *conversos* or their descendants.

de Cartagena and others came to the aid of their brethren and many eminent ecclesiastical and secular authorities also defended the *conversos*.

On the other side was the animosity of those who feared the growing power of the *conversos*. Alonso de Oropesa, master of the Order of San Jerónimo and an old Christian, gave vent to his anti-Jewish hatred generated by fears of possible Inquisition activity against his order. He wrote that Jews were members of the "synagogue of Satan" (Revelation 3:2, 2:9), "and therefore must be avoided with the greatest care" by Christians: the latter should "converse with them with great caution as we would do with servants and sons of Satan, to whom they are subject."

The valuable defenses of the *conversos*, to which hitherto little or no scholarly attention has been given, reveal that numerous leading noble families had *converso* members by marriage, including such powerful families as the Manriques, Mendozas, and Rojas. Noble ties to *conversos*, confirmed by other sources, added to the intense *converso*-phobia. Even royal families had *converso* members. Don Alonso Enríquez, the admiral of Castile, was descended on one side from Alfonso XI and Enrique II (b. 1333–d. 1379) and on the other from Jews. This meant that Fernando of Aragón (b. 1452–d. 1516), the ruler of Spain, was of direct Jewish ancestry.

Failing in their efforts to enforce a legal distinction between old and new Christians, *converso*-phobes evolved the first medieval example of true anti-Semitism, as opposed to anti-Jewish sentiment based on objections to Jewish religious tradition. According to the notorious doctrine of *limpieza de sangre* (purity of blood), Jews and Jewish converts to Christianity constituted a race. Jewish blood irreconcilably corrupted its possessor down to the fourth generation, despite intermarriage with old Christians. This doctrine removed the sincerity of converts and their descendents from consideration and made opposition to Jews a biological issue. Since "Jewish blood" remained to the fourth generation, such people were to be barred from holding public or ecclesiastical office or from studying in universities. The first of such laws was passed at the college of San Bartolomé of Salamanca in 1414.

There was a clear obsession with purity in fifteenth-century Spain that is evident in how the word was used in chronicles, biographies, and literary works. It was a short step from this doctrine to the belief that it was necessary to purify any Christian tainted by heresy, especially the hated *conversos* themselves. To achieve this end the Inquisition was instituted in Spain.

In 1462, the Castilian monarch Enrique IV (b. 1425–d. 1474) petitioned the Pope to establish an Inquisition in Castile. The growing animosity toward *conversos* among some old Christian elements that had erupted into riots during the reign of his father, Juan II, continued and worsened during Enrique's reign. The king, an ineffective ruler with little concern for spiritual matters, much less purity, was acting at the demand of increasingly hostile anti-*converso* elements. The Pope died before he could respond to the request. There were further riots against *conversos* in Toledo and especially in

Córdoba in 1473 that spread to other areas of Andalusia. Castile's *condestable mayor* (chief governor) was murdered for his defense of the *conversos* while in church. Large forces of *converso* militia and cavalry fought pitched battles against old Christian forces. The whole story of these events, which include an ambitious project to convert Gibraltar into a separate *converso* state, reads like some fantastic novel.

Ironically, the *conversos* themselves were at least partly responsible for the Inquisition. Alonso de Cartagena, the *converso* bishop and head of the Spanish delegation to the Council of Basel in 1434, obtained a bull allowing the Inquisition to investigate heresy among the *conversos*. Although nothing came of this, he suggested the establishment of a separate Inquisition in Castile. Although the Pope agreed, this move was forestalled by the downfall and execution of the powerful Alvaro de Luna, whose bitter struggle with prominent *conversos* had been its main motivation.

Isabel (b. 1451–d. 1504), Enrique's sister, had been waiting not so patiently in the wings for her chance to come to the Castilian throne. Since she had been supported by *conversos* in the open civil war with her brother, she began her reign in 1474 surrounded by *converso* friends and officials. Her secret marriage in 1479 to Fernando of Aragón involved *converso* messengers and arrangers on both sides. It is uncertain if Fernando's knowledge that his maternal grandmother was Jewish played a role in his constant use of *converso* officials. Upon the death of his father, when Fernando became king of Aragón (then united into one kingdom of Spain under the joint rule of the Catholic monarchs) the entire administration of his kingdom was in the hands of *conversos*.

The early years of the reign of Fernando and Isabel were beset by a rebellion of many of the nobles of Castile and by a war with Portugal, so the young monarchs needed to stop the riots and warfare involving *conversos*. They were not inspired by any supposed religious fanaticism, but were determined to bring peace and order to their kingdom. A less fanatical person than Isabel would have been hard to find in fifteenth-century Spain. The young queen requested authority from the Pope to establish an Inquisition in Castile, which he granted in 1478. However, it was not put in place until 1480.

From the outset, the Pope made it clear that the Inquisition was to be under the supervision of bishops; no more than two or three Inquisitors, masters of canon law, were to be appointed. The Inquisition was to follow strict rules of procedure. None of this was followed because of Tomás de Torquemada (b. 1420–d. 1498), the confessor of the young Isabel who had enormous influence over her. Under Torquemada an enormous, independent bureaucracy appeared without any semblance of episcopal control. Although sermons were preached and an opportunity for heretics to recant was given, secret accusations were actually solicited and the accused were simply thrown into prison to await trial. In the meantime, they were expected not only to confess their own crimes but to implicate others in turn. The Inquisition began in Seville, spread quickly throughout Andalusia and finally all of Castile into Aragón and Catalonia....

Contrary to yet another popular myth, the Inquisition had authority only over Christian heretics, not Jews. Thus, its activities are of no importance to Jewish history except as they relate to the question of Jewish conflicts with *conversos*. By the time of the establishment of the Inquisition in Spain, there were third- or fourth-generation *conversos* who, with the exception of a few recent converts, had been born and reared as Christians. Most were no better or no worse than old Christians. Why, therefore, were they accused of heresy?

The answer lies in the intense hostility of many old Christians toward *conversos*. Under the guise of purifying, the opportunity existed to eradicate them. For this purpose, the truth or falseness of the charges against the *conversos* was hardly of concern. Manuals were drawn up for the Inquisition, usually by trustworthy *conversos*, to present a litany of charges to be used. These included such obvious absurdities as the failure to light a fire in the house on the Jewish Sabbath in a climate so warm that a fire would be unbearable, or the failure to recite the Trinitarian formula before reading the Psalms aloud. Such charges can be found in the Inquisition records as proof of the supposed "crypto-Judaism" of the accused. Rarely was there any originality in the claimed observances.

The entire purpose of the Inquisition was to arrest, to intimidate by imprisonment or torture, and to kill as many *conversos* as possible, but this goal was secondary to what many regard as its chief motive, the seizure of property. Indeed, property was confiscated and, as the implication of this source of wealth became increasingly apparent, blanket preventive seizures were made whereby all the property of *conversos* was taken on the general supposition of heresy even before they were accused. Nevertheless, far more important was the burning of thousands of the despised *conversos*.

Although Jews were not the subject of Inquisitional activity, they did testify in substantial numbers against accused *conversos*, often against members of their own family. They did this knowing that their testimony was false and knowing what fate awaited the accused. In instances were the king and queen had proof of such false testimony, the Jewish witnesses were punished. Jews willingly gave such testimony because they, too, saw *conversos* as their worst enemies. Not only had the increasingly sharp anti-Jewish polemics written by *conversos* become a major problem, but the continued apostasy and abandonment of their people by the *conversos* made them the target of any abuse, including murder when possible, by the Jews. Not one Jewish source discussing the Inquisition shows any particular horror and expresses real criticism of this. Historians should not write, as some have, of cordiality between Jews and *conversos* throughout Castile, although in Aragón there were still some exceptions.

Of all the cases tried by the Inquisition, only one appears to have possibly involved Jews—the notorious ritual murder case of the "holy child of La Guardia" in 1490. Among those arrested and accused of the supposed murder, including old Christians and *conversos*, was at least one person who appears to have been Jewish. The entire case against the latter rested on the patently false testimony of one man. Able lawyers were appointed by the Inquisitional courts to defend the accused. In 1491, the Jews of Ávila, where the trials were being held, petitioned the monarchs that the trial was scandalizing the Jewish community. Fernando and Isabel agreed and immediately put the Jews under their protection so that they would not be molested in any way. This also indicated, incidentally, that the monarchs probably knew or suspected the falseness of the charges. Nevertheless, under torture, the accused confessed. All were burned at the stake. As to the murder, no such child was ever reported missing and no body was ever found. Although this case did demoralize both *converso* and Jewish communities, its almost total lack of repercussions for the Spanish Jews does not justify the hysterical reporting that has taken place in modern histories.

Although the Inquisition in Aragón has been studied less, it is more important than the Inquisition in Castile. In Zaragoza, Aragón's capital, the Inquisition had been introduced and suspended in 1482 and then reintroduced in 1484. One of the first and most notorious cases involved accusations against Alfonso de la Caballería, the vice-chancellor of the realm, and his father. The case dragged on until April 1492, which indicates that the true motive behind the Inquisition was the removal of the hated *conversos* from positions of power and influence. The assassination of Inquisitor Pedro Arbués by prominent *conversos* in 1484 in Zaragoza sealed their fate and provided fuel for the Inquisition to proceed despite strong papal and local opposition. Once the Inquisition was established and under way, further conversion of Jews came virtually to a halt. Whatever incentives may earlier have attracted such converts were now far outweighed by the obvious danger. Another motivation for the Inquisition may have been to halt further conversion of Jews to Christianity.

Contrary to popular mythology, . . . Fernando and Isabel were universally received with great joy and ceremony by Jews wherever they appeared. Very little throughout their reign shows unjust treatment, much less hostility, to the Jews. One exception was the Cortes[6] of Madrigal (1476), its restrictions being enacted mostly against usury. These were no different than similar laws enacted by Cortes of previous rulers. However, the Spanish parliament was a democratic body where laws were proposed and then merely ratified by the rulers. Thus, the monarchs should not be blamed for such legislation.

A more serious example of anti-Jewish legislation came from the Cortes of Toledo (1480), which required Jews and Muslims to move into specified

[6]Parliament.

areas in each major city. Those living outside such areas had to sell their homes and relocate. Although every effort was made to ensure fair prices in such sales, this did not always work in practice. Jews complained of having to live in crowded conditions in the newly assigned quarters. The moving force behind this legislation was Torquemada, not Fernando and Isabel.

Throughout this period, the monarchs continued to extend their protection to Jewish communities and to individual Jews whenever there were signs of disturbances or acts against them. Fernando and Isabel showed repeated, scrupulous concern for the just treatment of Jews and for redressing their grievances.

Life continued normally for Jews in the last decades of the fifteenth century. They served as tax officials for towns and cities. For example, in the late 1480s and early 1490s, there were still Jews in charge of collecting taxes on religious objects in the diocese of Toledo and administering monastery and convent estates. They continued to sue in court and win cases against Christians. Jews owned property and businesses as usual in partnership with Christians up until the very eve of the Expulsion. At the same time certain danger signs began to manifest themselves. In such cities as Plasencia and Ávila, some knights and others attacked Jews and Jewish property. That these incidents are known is due entirely to the monarchs' immediate efforts to deal with them. Although there are isolated examples of some friars stirring up trouble in Zamora and Segovia, church officials appear to have played no role in arousing anti-Jewish sentiment.

Another unrecognized but important factor is the major role *converso* writers played in the growing eschatological fervor of a united Christian Spain. *Conversos* saw the monarchs, especially Isabel, whom they glorified as a reincarnation of the Virgin Mary, as model Christian rulers. Spain, under the glorious rule of Fernando and Isabel, was to have a role unparalleled in Christian history that was to include perhaps the defeat of the entire Muslim world. That campaign had to begin with the conquest of the last Muslim stronghold in Spain itself, the kingdom of Granada. This was part of the general campaign being urged by the real fanatics in the kingdom, such as Torquemada.

Although it is well-known that Jews were taxed for the war, other facts are less well-known or simply ignored. In 1484, Jewish leaders gathered in Toledo and voluntarily contributed to the war effort. That same year, the monarchs imposed compulsory taxes on the Jews through their elected parliamentary delegates. Abraham Seneor, the powerful court-appointed "rabbi" (actually tax official and judge) of all Spanish Jews, was given broad powers to force any reticent Jews to comply with the taxation. However, Jews had not been singled out, since Christians also paid annual war taxes.

In addition to taxes, Isabel personally borrowed large sums of money both from individual Jews and from Jewish communities to pay for the war. In the years 1489–1492, these loans were repaid almost entirely, but some loans were repaid to Jews exiled from Spain after the Expulsion. From

Isaac Abravanel, a financial official of the monarchs, Isabel borrowed the huge sum of 1,500,000 *maravedis*[7] for the war (almost identical to the sum provided by the *converso* treasurer and other *converso* officials to finance Christopher Columbus' voyage). This sum was also repaid.

The Edict of Expulsion in 1492 noted that the monarchs could be content with the Jews leaving Andalusia. This enigmatic statement refers to the apparent decision, again, the direct responsibility of the Inquisition, to expel Jews from certain cities of Andalusia in 1483. Apparently this affected only the Jews of Seville and Jerez. In 1485, there were still Jewish communities in Córdoba and other cities, despite some evidence that many of Córdoba's Jews had been expelled. More serious was the decision of Fernando, in his separate capacity as kind of Aragón, to expel all Jews from Zaragoza. This was done because Jews had violated certain privileges granted them, but once again it was carried out at the instigation of the Inquisition. The expulsion document notes the danger of Christian heresy from constant conversation between Jews and *conversos*. The expulsion from Zaragoza was not permanent, for an important Jewish community soon reappeared in the city.

The monarchs' repeated reappointment of Jews to government posts through the years 1492–94 proves that they did not intend to expel the Jews entirely from Spain. They would not have made such appointments if they had intended to expel Jews. Among such appointments were those of Abraham Seneor and his relative Meir Melamed, both of whom converted when the edict of Expulsion was proclaimed.

The edict was proclaimed in Granada on 31 March 1492, giving the Jews three months from the date of the edict to leave Spain. Within a month, Jews, who had not yet received word of this, continued to buy and sell property and conduct normal business relations with Christians. In an important letter by the monarchs on the date the Edict was proclaimed, the Inquisitors were specified as the ones who had decided to expel Jews. In fact, it was Torquemada himself who demanded this. However, Fernando and Isabel continued their policy of scrupulous justice with regard to the rights of Jews. On 26 April and again on 20 May, the monarchs ordered the further repayment of loans to various Jewish communities and individuals, some of which had been made before they began to rule.

Despite the myths concerning the fanaticism of the Catholic monarchs, Jews were not banned from taking money and personal property with them, nor was their property seized as was the case in the expulsion of Jews from England and in their repeated expulsions from France. Spanish Jews were also permitted to sell all personal real property. These sales were legitimate, with the payment of just prices. Fernando issued an order in May that the Jews of Aragón-Catalonia were under his personal protection and that they and their goods were under royal protection when they left the kingdom. He ordered officials to provide the troops to guard the Jews and their

[7]Gold coins.

property. Yet, the Inquisitors of Zaragoza countermanded Fernando's orders there, prohibiting Jews from taking goods with them. That prohibition was ultimately rescinded. Only such communal property as schools, synagogues, cemeteries and hospitals could not be sold and was acquired by the Crown. Many of these properties were later sold to cities or individuals.

When some Jews complained that they owed money to Muslims and Christians who also owed them money that they could neither pay nor collect, the monarchs appointed special judges to arrange the speedy payment of such debts. There was continued concern on the part of the monarchs that all outstanding debts to Jews be paid. On 30 May orders went throughout the kingdom that special officials should immediately arrange these repayments by Christians and Muslims. Even individual Jews, some from small towns, were able to petition the monarchs to intervene in such matters as outstanding payments owed them for their community work. Some Jews took not only their considerable personal wealth, but even their enormous libraries. For example, Judah Bienveniste went to Salonika and established there the first library of any kind in the Ottoman Empire.

Following the Expulsion, the monarchs continued to ensure that fair treatment had been accorded to the Jews in repayment of debts and sales of property. Commissions were appointed in July to conduct local investigations into these matters. Since there were cases of Jews engaged in complicated business partnerships and other affairs that could not be quickly liquidated, officials were chosen to handle these matters and make payment to Jews *after* the Expulsion. Many Jews chose baptism rather than face expulsion from their homeland. Most of the large Jewish population of Ávila converted.

Many expelled Jews returned to Spain and were baptized, unable or unwilling to face the perils of an uncertain destiny abroad. However, most of the Jews of Castile who left simply went by foot across the border into Portugal and upon payment of bribes and "entry fees," lived there for a short period in peace until they were again compelled to convert or face another exile. The evidence points to the overwhelming majority of Jews still in Spain in 1492 choosing conversion rather than exile.

Contrary to myth, the economy of Spain was neither bankrupted nor even slightly affected by the Expulsion of the Jews. Spain was culturally diminished, however, and its reputation tarnished for centuries to come. The glorious history of tolerance and of harmonious cultural and social symbiosis that characterized Spain for nine centuries had come to an end.

IV

EARLY MODERN EUROPE

In one sense, history is the solving of problems. Two of the classic problems have been the difficulty of defining "modern" and, following from that, the difficulty of determining when the modern world began. Wrangling over these problems persists, with little agreement. The Italians of the Renaissance were the first to broach the subject, seeing themselves, with no little immodesty, as the first modern people, more closely akin to the ancient world than to their immediate ancestors, whom they called Gothic and barbaric. Renaissance Italy saw the centuries after the fall of Roman civilization as the Middle Ages, a period between the classical world of Greece and Rome and fifteenth-century Italy. In the nineteenth century, historians began a debate over whether Renaissance Italy was modern, protomodern, or perhaps still essentially medieval. The debate continues today, part of the larger problem of periodization. Are there periods in history, or do historians arbitrarily classify certain centuries as periods, distinct eras?

As a way out of the dilemma, the term "early modern Europe" has come frequently to be favored, possibly because its chronological boundaries are so nebulous that historians can include within it very different cultures. Sometimes the early modern period in Europe refers to 1400–1789, thus encompassing Renaissance Italy, or 1500–1789, omitting both the Renaissance and the French Revolution. On the other hand, all categories of early modern Europe contain the sixteenth and seventeenth centuries, the period that the following selections describe.

These were the centuries when Italian humanism spread beyond the Alps, becoming Northern or Christian humanism. This is the era of the Protestant Reformation, Catholic Counter-Reformation, European exploration overseas, and the beginnings of political absolutism. It is the age of Michelangelo, Cervantes, Shakespeare, and Milton. But this was also a premodern society, characterized by tradition, relative immobility, and privilege. This society was still predominantly rural, though urban centers increased in size. Capitalism likewise grew, though this was surely not its heyday. Monarchy remained the political ideal and reality, though there were some calls for socialist or republican governments. The religion was Christian, though Christianity changed dramatically. In sum, the early modern era in Europe was a period of the confluence of old and new, a period of rapid change in some areas, but not a period of desire for or expectation of change, as the modern Western world is. Some historians refer to this as an age of crisis, because so much was called into question and so many institutions, beliefs, and conventions were shaken.

The following selections show dramatically a life that could be described in the words of the English philosopher Thomas Hobbes as "poor, nasty, brutish, and short." Condemned to hunger and cold, wracked by diseases, intensely religious if not fanatical, often violent, subject to increasing supervision by church and state, sixteenth- and seventeenth-century Europeans could, moreover, expect a lifespan less than half that of ours today.

The Early History of Syphilis: A Reappraisal

ALFRED W. CROSBY, JR.

Too often historians have described the voyages of Columbus and their aftermath in terms of how Europeans affected the Americas through exploration and settlement. In his important book, The Columbian Exchange: Biological and Cultural Consequences of 1492, *Alfred W. Crosby, Jr., offers a more balanced perspective by showing that the opening up of the Western Hemisphere affected life—human, animal, and plant—on both sides of the Atlantic. Although the balance sheet is mixed, Crosby believes that the bad outnumbered the good. Thus, maize, manioc, and potatoes increased the amount of food, improved the diet, and so led to a rise in the population of Europe. On the other hand, smallpox and measles decimated the American Indians, and the Spaniards began the breakdown of ecological stability in the New World.*

In this selection, Crosby discusses syphilis, the New World's revenge on the Old World. Against those who argue that syphilis had been present in Europe before Columbus, Crosby maintains that it first came to Europe in the 1490s. What arguments does the author make to support this claim? How did syphilis spread in Europe once it had arrived? In other words, what groups of people were primarily responsible for infecting others with that loathsome disease?

What exactly did syphilis do to people physically? Crosby stresses that the disease changed over time. How did people cope with it? What cures were available? Syphilis affected social relations even as it infected bodies. How did the relations of men and women—how did lovemaking—change as a result of this new virus? Bedeviled by herpes and AIDS, our own age might seem analogous to the sixteenth century.

The New World gave much in return for what it received from the Old World. In the writings of Desiderius Erasmus,[1] one can find mention of nearly every significant figure, event, crusade, fad, folly, and misery of the decades around 1500. Of all the miseries visited upon Europe in his lifetime, Erasmus judged few more horrible than the French disease, or syphilis. He reckoned no malady more contagious, more terrible for its victims, or more difficult to cure . . . or more fashionable! . . .

The men and women of Erasmus's generation were the first Europeans to know syphilis or so they said, at least. The pox, as the English called it, had struck like a thunderbolt in the very last years of the fifteenth century. But unlike most diseases that appear with such abruptness, it did not fill up the graveyards and then go away, to come again some other day or

[1]Dutch humanist, c.1466–1536.

perhaps never. Syphilis settled down and became a permanent factor in human existence.

Syphilis has a special fascination for the historian because, of all mankind's most important maladies, it is the most uniquely "historical." The beginnings of most diseases lie beyond man's earliest rememberings. Syphilis, on the other hand, has a beginning. Many men, since the last decade of the fifteenth century, have insisted that they knew almost exactly when syphilis appeared on the world stage, and even where it came from. "In the yere of Chryst 1493 or there aboute," wrote Ulrich von Hutten,[2] one of Erasmus's correspondents, "this most foule and most grevous dysease beganne to sprede amonge the people." Another contemporary, Ruy Dáz de Isla,[3] agreed that 1493 was the year and went on to say that "the disease had its origin and birth from always in the island which is now named Española."[4] Columbus had brought it back, along with samples of maize and other American curiosities.

. . . In fact, the matter of the origin of syphilis is doubtlessly the most controversial subject in all medical historiography. . . .

Until the most recent decades there were only two widely accepted views of the provenance of syphilis: the Columbian theory and its antithesis, which stated that syphilis was present in the Old World long before 1493. Now the Unitarian theory has appeared, which postulates that venereal syphilis is but one syndrome of a multi-faceted world-wide disease, treponematosis. But before we examine this newest challenge to the veracity of Ulrich von Hutten and Dáz de Isla and the other Columbians, let us deal with the older argument: was venereal syphilis present on both sides of the Atlantic in 1492 or only on the American?

The documentary evidence for the Old World seems clear. No unequivocal description of syphilis in any pre-Columbian literature of the Old World has ever been discovered. . . .

The physicians, surgeons, and laymen of the Old World who wrote about venereal syphilis in the sixteenth century recorded, with few exceptions, that it was a new malady; and we have no reason to believe they were all mistaken. . . . Spaniards, Germans, Italians, Egyptians, Persians, Indians, Chinese, and Japanese . . . agreed that they had never seen the pox before. It is very unlikely that they were all mistaken on the same subject at the same time.

. . . The variety of names given it and the fact that they almost always indicate that it was thought of as a foreign import are strong evidence for its newness. Italians called it the French disease, which proved to be the most popular title; the French called it the disease of Naples; the English called it the French disease, the Bordeaux disease, or the Spanish disease; Poles called

---

[2]German humanist, 1488–1523.

[3]Sixteenth-century writer of medical books.

[4]Currently Hispaniola, divided between Haiti and the Dominican Republic.

it the German disease; Russians called it the Polish disease; and so on. Middle Easterners called it the European pustules; Indians called it the disease of the Franks (western Europeans). Chinese called it the ulcer of Canton, that port being their chief point of contact with the west. The Japanese called it Tang sore, Tang referring to China; or, more to the point, the disease of the Portuguese.... [I]t was not until the nineteenth century that... "syphilis," minted in the 1520s, became standard throughout the world.

Another indication of the abrupt appearance of the pox is the malignancy of the disease in the years immediately after its initial recognition in Europe. The classic course of a new disease is rapid spread and extreme virulence, followed by a lessening of the malady's deadliness. The most susceptible members of the human population are eliminated by death, as are the most virulent strains of the germ, in that they kill off their hosts before transmission to other hosts occurs. The records of the late fifteenth and early sixteenth centuries are full of lamentations on the rapid spread of syphilis and the horrible effects of the malady, which often occurred within a short time after the initial infection: widespread rashes and ulcers, often extending into the mouth and throat; severe fevers and bone pains; and often early death. The latter is a very rare phenomenon in the initial stages of the disease today, and most who do die of syphilis have resisted the disease successfully for many years. Ulrich von Hutten's description of syphilis in the first years after its appearance indicates a marked contrast between its nature then and its "mildness" today:

> There were byles, sharpe, and standing out, hauying the similitude and quantite of acornes, from which came so foule humours, and so great stenche, that who so ever ones smelled it, thought hym selfe to be enfect. The colour of these pusshes [pustules] was derke grene, and the slight therof was more grevous unto the pacient then the peyne it selfe: and yet their peynes were as thoughe they hadde lyen in fire.

... The most convincing of all evidence for the abrupt arrival of the French disease in the Old World in approximately 1500 is the physical remains, the bones of the long dead. No one has ever unearthed pre-Columbian bones in the Old World which display unequivocal signs of syphilitic damage....

Several anti-Columbian theorists have brushed aside all the above arguments by hypothesizing that syphilis had existed in the Old World prior to the 1490s, but in a *mild* form. Then, in the 1490s the causative organism mutated into the deadly *Treponema pallidum*, and syphilis began to affect the deep body structures and became a killer. This hypothesis cannot be disproved and it comfortably fits all the facts, but it cannot be proved, either....

Where did syphilis come from? If it came from America, then we may be nearly certain that it came in 1493 or shortly after. Let us consider the physical evidence first. Is there a contrast here between the Old and New Worlds? The answer becomes more and more unequivocally affirmative as the archeologists and paleopathologists disinter from American soil an increasing number of pre-Columbian human bones displaying what is almost surely syphilitic damage....

The documentary evidence for the Columbian provenance of venereal syphilis is obviously shaky. We cannot say, moreover, that the evidence provided by the paleopathologists is utterly decisive, but when the two are combined—when archivists and gravediggers join hands to claim that America is the homeland of *Treponema pallidum*—it becomes very difficult to reject the Columbian theory....

Is venereal syphilis a separate and distinct disease, once endemic to only one part of the world, or is it merely a syndrome of a disease which has always been worldwide, but happens to have different symptoms and names in different areas? Those who accept the Unitarian theory, as it is called, claim that that which is called syphilis, when transmitted venereally, is really the same malady as the nonvenereal illnesses called yaws in the tropics, bejel in the Middle East, pinta in Central America, irkinja in Australia, and so on. The manner in which this ubiquitous disease, named "treponematosis" by the Unitarians, manifests itself in man is somewhat different in different areas, because of climatic and cultural differences, but it is all one disease. If this is true, then all the squabble about deformation of forehead bones here and not there, ulcers on the sex organs now and not then, and on and on, is completely irrelevant. As E. H. Hudson, the foremost champion of the Unitarian theory, puts it, "Since treponematosis was globally distributed in prehistoric times, it . . . is idle to speak of Columbus' sailors bringing syphilis to a syphilis-free Europe in 1493." . . .

In fact, such is the paucity of evidence from the fifteenth and sixteenth centuries that the Unitarian theory is no more satisfactory than the Columbian. We simply do not know much, and may never know much about the world distribution of the treponemas in the 1490s. . . .

There are only two things of which we can be sure. One, the only pre-Columbian bones clearly displaying the lesions of treponematosis or one of that family of disease are American. . . . Two, several contemporaries did record the return of venereal syphilis with Columbus. . . .

The Columbian theory is still viable. Even if it is unequivocally proved that all the treponematoses are one, the Columbians can simply claim that treponematosis was exclusively American in 1492. There is no unquestionable evidence that any of the treponematoses existed in the Old World in 1492. . . .

It is not impossible that the organisms causing treponematosis arrived from America in the 1490s in mild or deadly form, and, breeding in the entirely new and very salubrious environment of European, Asian, and African bodies, evolved into both venereal and nonvenereal syphilis and yaws. If this is true, then Columbus ranks as a villain with the serpent of the Garden of Eden.

A less presumptuous theory is that the treponematoses were one single disease many thousands of years ago. Then, as man changed his environment and habits, and especially when he crossed the Bering Straits into the isolation of the Americas, the differing ecological conditions produced different types of treponematosis and, in time, closely related but different diseases....

...It seems logical to believe that if deadly diseases crossed the Atlantic from east to west, then there must have also been a similar countercurrent. The most likely candidate for the role of America's answer to the Old World's smallpox is venereal syphilis. The theory of the origin of the treponematoses offered in this chapter squares with all Darwin tells us about evolution, and allows the American Indians and Columbus the dubious honor of incubating and transporting venereal syphilis. It is this hypothesis which, in the current state of medical and historical research, seems to hold the most promise as a vehicle for future inquiry and speculation.

Having finished with the polemics of syphilis, let us turn to the first century of its recorded history. By the fifteenth century, treponematosis had evolved into several related maladies in the desert-isolated jungles, isolated plateaus, different islands, and continents of the world. Then came one of the greatest technological advances: European innovations in shipbuilding, seamanship and navigation.... A great mixing of peoples, cultural influences, and diseases began.

The various treponematoses spread out from their hearthlands, mixing and changing under new ecological conditions in a way that will probably always confound medical historians. The evidence that comes down to us from that time is sparse and confused....

Europeans drew the world together by means of ocean voyages.... The epidemiology of syphilis has a special characteristic: it is usually transmitted by sexual contact and spreads when a society's or a group's allegiance to marital fidelity fails. Sailors, by the nature of their profession, are men without women, and therefore men of many women. If we may assume that the nature of sailors in the sixteenth century was not radically different than in the twentieth, then we can imagine no group of the former century more perfectly suited for guaranteeing that venereal syphilis would have worldwide distribution.... European sailors carried it to every continent but Antartica and Australia before Columbus was in his grave.

Venereal syphilis arrived in Barcelona in 1493, according to Diáz de Isla, but we have no other news of it in Spain for several years. Why? First, because of the paucity of documentation. Second, because syphilis spreads by venereal contact, and not by touch, breath, or insect vectors, as do the traditional epidemic diseases of smallpox, typhus, plague, and so on. In a stable society its spread will be steady but not extremely fast.... Imagine 1,000 people, one of whom is syphilitic. He infects two others, who infect two others each, in turn. The number of the diseased goes up steadily: 1, 2, 4, 8, 16, 32, and so on. In the early stages the disease's advance is rapid, but the victims are few and below the threshold of society's attention. The disease's spread does not accelerate, it is passed on from one to another no more rapidly than before, but 32 becomes 64, 64 leads to 128, 128 is suddenly 256—and society abruptly decides that its existence is threatened by epidemic, long after the initial arrival of syphilis.

Venereal syphilis will only spread with the rapidity of plague or typhus when a society is in such chaos that sexual morality breaks down. Such a sad state of affairs is usually the product of war. Women are without protection or food, and have only their bodies to sell. The men of the armies have a monopoly of force, most of the wealth and food—and no women.

The first recorded epidemic of syphilis took place in Italy in the mid-1490s. In 1494 Charles VIII of France,[5] in pursuit of his claims to the throne of Naples, crossed the Alps into Italy with an army of about 50,000 soldiers of French, Italian, Swiss, German, and other origins. The campaign was not one marked by full-scale battles, but the army, trailing its column of the usual camp followers, engaged in the usual practices of rape and sack anyway. The Neapolitans, retreating toward their city, laid the countryside to waste. Charles, once ensconced in Naples, discovered that the Italians, appalled by his success, were putting aside their personal conflicts and forming a coalition against him. Ferdinand[6] and Isabella,[7] anxious to prevent the establishment of French hegemony in Italy, were sending Spanish troops. Charles packed his bags and marched back to France, and the whole process of battle, rape, and sack was repeated in reverse.

Syphilis, hitherto spreading slowly and quietly across Europe, flared into epidemic in Italy during this invasion, just as the epidemiology of the malady would lead one to expect. It is probable that there was also a rapid spread of typhus, another traditional camp follower. It was in Italy that the truth of Voltaire's[8] epigram was first demonstrated: "Depend upon it, when 30,000 men engage in pitched battle against an equal number of the enemy, about 20,000 on each side have the pox."

Charles arrived back at Lyon in November 1495, where he disbanded his army; and its members, with billions of treponemas in their blood streams, scattered back to their homes in a dozen lands or off to new wars. With the dispersal of that army, the lightning advance of syphilis across Europe and the rest of the Old World became inevitable.

Syphilis had already appeared in Germany by the summer of 1495, for in August Emperor Maximilian[9] of the Holy Roman Empire issued a mandate at Worms calling it the "evil pocks" and blaming it on the sin of blasphemy.

---

[5]King of France, 1483–1498.

[6]Ferdinand V, the Catholic King of Castille and Léon (1474–1504, ruling jointly with his wife, Isabella I). As Ferdinand II, King of Aragon (1479–1516) and as Ferdinand III, King of Naples (1504–1516).

[7]Isabella I, the Catholic Queen of Castile and Léon (1474–1504), Queen of Aragon (1479–1504), and wife of Ferdinand V.

[8]French author, 1694–1778.

[9]1493–1519.

In the same year Swiss and Frenchmen recorded its arrival with horror. The pox reached Holland and England no later than 1496. Greece knew it in the same year, and Hungary and Russia in 1499. . . .

The epidemic rolled on into Africa, where "If any Barbarie be infected with the disease commonly called the Frenche pox, they die thereof for the most part, and are seldom cured"; and appeared in the Middle East as early as 1498, with a similar result. The Portuguese, among the earliest to receive the infection, probably carried it farthest, around the Cape of Good Hope. It appeared in India in 1498 and sped on ahead of the Portuguese to Canton by 1505. In a decade it advanced from the Caribbean to the China Sea, at once a tribute to man's nautical genius and social idiocy.

We are lucky in our attempt to trace the early history of syphilis in that shame was not attached to the disease at the beginning. . . . As if to illustrate the frankness of the age, Ulrich von Hutten, the great humanist, wrote a gruesomely detailed tract on his own sufferings, gratuitously mentioning that his father had the same disease, and dedicated the whole to a cardinal! . . .

The plentiful documentation enables the venerologist of an antiquarian bent to trace not only the history of the epidemic but the history of its remedies and of the character of the disease itself. The best analysis of the latter is by Jean Astruc.[10] . . . He breaks down the early history into five stages.

1. 1494–1516. In this period the first sign of the disease in a patient was small genital ulcers, followed by a widespread rash of various character . . . As the disease spread through the victim's body, palate, uvula, jaw, and tonsils were often destroyed. Large gummy tumors were common, and the victim suffered agonizing pains in muscles and nerves, especially at night. General physical deterioration followed and often culminated in early death.

2. During the period 1516 to 1526 two new symptoms were added to the syphilis syndrome: bone inflammation, characterized by severe pain and eventual corruption of the bone and marrow; and the appearance in some sufferers of hard genital pustules, resembling warts or corns.

3. A general abatement of the malignancy of the disease marked the period 1526 to 1540. The number of pustules per sufferer decreased, and we hear more of gummy tumors. Inflamed swelling of the lymph gland in the groin became common. Loss of hair and teeth became common, but this may have been caused by mercury poisoning, mercury having been used as a remedy.

4. From 1540 to 1560 the diminution of the more spectacular symptoms of the malady continued. Gonorrhea, which by this time and for centuries afterward was confused with syphilis, became "the most common, if not perpetual symptom" in the early states of syphilis.

5. Between 1560 and 1610 the deadliness of the malady continued to decline, and only one new symptom was added: noise in the ears.

[10]Eighteenth-century venerologist.

By the seventeenth century syphilis was as we know it today: a very dangerous infection, but not one that could be called explosive in the nature of its attack on the victim....

If one wished to create a disease to encourage the proliferation of quacks and quack remedies, one could do no better than syphilis; and this was particularly true in the sixteenth century. The disease was new and no traditional remedies for it existed. Its symptoms were hideous, persuading sufferers to try any and all cures. Syphilis is a malady characterized by periods of remission and latency...and so if the quack does not kill with his cure, he can often claim success—for a time, at least. The quacks cured by searing the pustules with hot irons, and prescribed an unbelievable assortment of medicines to swallow and to apply, the latter including even boiled ants' nest, along with the ants....

The two most popular remedies for syphilis in the sixteenth century were mercury and guaiacum. The first came into use very soon after the appearance of the pox, both in Europe and Asia....[I]t proved to be the only generally effective means of arresting syphilis for the next four hundred years. Before the middle of the sixteenth century, mercury was being rubbed on, applied to the body in plasters and swallowed in pills.

Unfortunately, mercury was overused, and in many cases the cure was successful but the patient died of it. The humoral theory of disease, which dominated European thinking at the time, taught that illness came as the result of an imbalance among the four humors. Syphilis could be cured if the body could be obliged to bleed, defecate, sweat out, and spit out the excess of the offending humor: phlegm, in this case. The most obvious symptom of mercury poisoning is the constant dribbling of saliva, even to the amount of several pints a day. What, thought the sixteenth-century physician, could be more desirable? The body is purging itself of that which is making it sick. Out came the offending excess, often along with gums, teeth, and assorted interior fragments of the body....

...Many other remedies were tried in its place—China root, sassafras, sarsaparilla, and so on—but only one displaced mercury as the cure, if only for a time. This was guaiacum, a decoction of the wood of a tree of the West Indies, which became the most popular panacea of the 1520s. The wood had much to recommend it. It came from America, as did the disease; and this is, of course, the way a thoughtful God would arrange things. It was a very impressive wood, extremely hard and so heavy that "the leaste pece of its caste into water, synketh streyght to the bottom," which indicated that it must have additional miraculous properties. A decoction of it caused the patient to perspire freely, a very desirable effect, according to humoral theory....

The prevalence of syphilis and the wood's effectiveness not only against it but also against "goute in the feete, the stone, palsey, lepre, dropsy, fallying evyll, and other diseases," drove its price to dizzy heights. Like a poor man's soup bone, the sawdust of guaiacum was boiled up again and again for those not lucky enough or wealthy enough to buy the first decoction. Counterfeit guaiacum flooded the market and pieces of the wood were hung in churches to be prayed to by the most impecunious syphilitics....

...Murmurs, soon rising to shouts, of the wood's ineffectiveness began to be voiced in the 1530s....The fad of the Holy Wood from the New World returned a few generations later, and the use of it never quite died out—it was not removed from the British Pharmacopoeia until 1932—but its reputation as *the cure* had evaporated. Europe returned to China root, sassafras, prayer, and, especially, mercury....

...In an age in which the Pope had to rescind an order expelling all prostitutes from Rome because of the loss of public revenue that resulted, the new venereal disease inevitably spread to every cranny of Europe and became, like smallpox or consumption, one of the permanently resident killers. The English doctor, William Clowes, stated in the 1580s that one out of every two he had treated in the House of St. Bartholomew had been syphilitic, and that "except the people of this land do speedily repent their most ungodly life and leave this odious sin, it cannot be but the whole land will shortly be poisoned with this most noisome sickness."

However, *Treponema pallidum* brought some good in its train, though those who benefited from it were few. Physicians, surgeons and quacks found a source of wealth in the pox....

...When man is both helpless and foolish in the presence of horror, as is often the case in matters pertaining to venereal disease, he finds solace in jokes. There was a great deal of joking about the French disease in the sixteenth century....

Erasmus mentions syphilis a number of times. In one of his *Colloquies* he announces to the world that "unless you're a good dicer, an infamous whoremonger, a heavy drinker, a reckless spendthrift, a wastrel and heavily in debt, decorated with the French pox, hardly anyone will believe you're a knight."...

To most, however, the pox was no subject for laughter, but an unmitigated disaster. It was no respecter of rank, and thus had a direct and dismal effect on political and church history....Two dynasties whose members were not noted for monogamous behavior died out in that age, the House of Valois[11] and the House of Tudor.[12] As usual, little can be proved, but the inability of queens to give birth to living children makes one suspect that syphilis played a role in the demise of these families, and thus in the political turmoil of their realms. There is little doubt that Francis I,[13] famous for having "lost all save

[11] Royal dynasty in France, 1328–1589.
[12] Royal dynasty in England, 1485–1603.
[13] King of France, 1515–1547.

life and honor" in the battle of Pavia, lost both in the end to the pox. And there is little doubt that one and possibly two of the husbands of Mary Queen of Scots,[14] and, therefore, possibly the woman herself, had the disease. . . .

The pox's full impact, however, can never be measured if we restrict ourselves to economics, literature, politics, and religion. *Treponema pallidum* was chiefly a social villain, one of the most evil of the whole age of Erasmus, Shakespeare, and Francis I. The fear of infection tended to erode the bonds of respect and trust that bound men and women together. The prostitute's chance of Christian forgiveness faded. "If I were judge," roared Luther,[15] "I would have such venemous syphilitic whores broken on the wheel and flayed because one cannot estimate the harm such filthy whores do to young men." And those less obviously offensive suffered, also, from the terror engendered by the new plague. The sick and the stranger found closed doors where once they had found hospitality. Friendships were altered by a new coolness, as men began in some degree to limit their contacts with any who might conceivably have been touched by the pox.

We find little bits of information indicating the change. Public baths went out of style, for it was widely realized that many as innocent of promiscuity as newborn babes had contracted the French disease in such places. The use of the common drinking cup fell out of style. The kiss, a customary gesture of affection between friends as well as lovers, came under suspicion. . . .

What was the effect of syphilis on general human contact? Consider that one of the crimes—false or no—of which Cardinal Woolsey[16] was accused in his arraignment before Parliament in 1529 was that he, "knowing himself to have the foul and contagious disease of the great pox . . . came daily to your grace [Henry VIII],[17] rowning in your ear, and blowing upon your most noble grace with his perilous and infectious breath, to the marvellous danger of your highness." . . .

It is obvious that in no area did syphilis wreak more havoc than in relations between men and women. No civilization has ever satisfactorily solved the problem of sex. Even if there were no such thing as venereal disease, the sex relationship would still produce distrust, fear, and pain, as well as confidence, love, and comfort. Add to the normal emotional difficulties of the sex relationship not just the possibility of the pains of gonorrhea but the danger of a horrible and often fatal disease, syphilis. Where there must be trust, there must now also be suspicion. Where there must be a surrender of self, there must now also be a shrewd consideration of future health. . . .

---

[14]Mary Stuart, Queen of Scotland, 1542–1567.

[15]Martin Luther, German Protestant reformer, 1483–1546.

[16]Lord Chancellor of England, 1515–1529.

[17]King of England, 1509–1547.

Gabriello Falloppio, in his book of syphilis, *De Morbo Gallico*[18] (1564), suggested that after sexual intercourse a man should carefully wash and dry his genitals. The age of the canny lover had arrived.

Nuns, Wives, and Mothers: Women and the Reformation in Germany

MERRY WIESNER

In a famous essay, a historian argued that there had been no Renaissance for women. That is, examined from the perspective of gender, the cultural flowering in the fourteenth and fifteenth centuries celebrated as the Italian Renaissance in fact scarcely affected the daily lives of women. Humanism, artistic innovations, and political experimentation did not improve the status of women in law, in the home, or in the workplace. In fact it has been argued that the condition of women may even have worsened during the Renaissance. Merry Wiesner takes a similar approach to the Protestant Reformation of the sixteenth century by examing how that religious movement influenced German women. She finds that—unlike the Italian Renaissance—the German Reformation made an appreciable difference to women.

Nevertheless, on the eve of and during the Protestant Reformation, German society placed social and political restrictions on women. What were these impediments that closed possible avenues of advancement to women? Moving beyond these hindrances, Wiesner sketches neatly the impact of religious change on women according to their status in three categories: as members of female religious orders, as single and married, and as workers. Within these broad typologies, there existed different groups. It is imperative to distinguish how the religious change from Catholic to Protestant marked the lives of these various groups.

First and most clearly, the Protestants closed convents. What happened to the nuns and lay sisters who now had to fend for themselves in the larger world? What might have happened when nuns refused to renounce their cloistered lives?

Second, the Reformation altered the lives of other women, single or married. How did the Protestant reformers get their ideas across to women, many of whom could not read? What were the reformers' ideas about women? How did the reformers view marriage and the relationship of wife and husband? Were women any less subordinate in the Protestant religions than in Catholicism? How did the reformers see single women?

One thorny problem in a society that looked upon religious toleration as an evil was marriages in which each spouse belonged to a different religion. What was a Protestant wife to do when her husband, to whom she owed obedience, was Catholic?

---

[18]*Of the French Disease.*

There is a difference, to be sure, between the ideas of Protestant theologians on the nature of women, their proper place, and their duties, on the one hand, and the translation of those ideas into actual practice, on the other hand. What laws did Protestant states pass that modified the behavior of women in marriage and in religion?

Wiesner rightly stresses that women reacted to the Reformation; they were not just acted upon. How did women have an impact on the religious developments sweeping Germany? To what extent did it make a difference if a woman was an aristocrat or a commoner? In what areas of religious change could women make themselves known? Did males welcome the efforts of women to further the cause of the Reformation? How did Protestant ideas and Protestant wives sway marriages?

Third, Wiesner scrutinizes the Reformation's impact on working women. How did new religious practices affect women in various occupations?

Could one conclude that overall the Reformation was beneficial to women? Did the Reformation improve the status or situation of any groups of women?

It is in many ways anachronistic even to use the word "Germany" when discussing the sixteenth century. At that time, modern-day East and West Germany were politically part of the Holy Roman Empire, a loose confederation of several hundred states, ranging from tiny knightships through free imperial cities to large territorial states. These states theoretically owed obedience to an elected emperor, but in reality they were quite independent and often pursued policies in opposition to the emperor. Indeed, the political diversity and lack of a strong central authority were extremely important to the early success of the Protestant Reformation in Germany. Had Luther been a Frenchman or a Spaniard, his voice would probably have been quickly silenced by the powerful monarchs in those countries.

Because of this diversity, studies of the Reformation in Germany are often limited to one particular area or one particular type of government, such as the free imperial cities. This limited focus is useful when looking at the impact of the Reformation on men, for male participation and leadership in religious change varied depending on whether a territory was ruled by a city council, a nobleman, or a bishop. Male leadership in the Reformation often came from university teachers, so the presence or absence of a university in an area was also an important factor.

When exploring the impact of religious change on women, however, these political and institutional factors are not as important. Except for a few noblewomen who ruled territories while their sons were still minors, women had no formal political voice in any territory of the empire. They did not vote or serve on city councils, and even abbesses were under the direct control of a male church official. Women could not attend universities, and thus did not come into contact with religious ideas through formal theological training. Their role in the Reformation was not so determined by what may be called "public" factors—political structures, educational institutions—as was that of men.

Women's role in the Reformation and the impact of religious change on them did vary throughout Germany, but that variation was largely determined by what might be termed "personal" factors—a woman's status as a nun or laywoman, her marital status, her social and economic class, her occupation. Many of these factors, particularly social and economic class, were also important in determining men's responses to religious change, but they were often secondary to political factors whereas for women they were of prime importance.

The Protestant and Catholic reformers recognized this. Although they generally spoke about and to women as an undifferentiated group and proposed the same ideals of behavior for all women, when the reformers did address distinct groups of women they distinguished them by marital or clerical status. Nuns, single women, mothers, wives, and widows all got special attention in the same way that special treatises were directed to male princes and members of city councils—men set apart from others by their public, political role.

It is important to keep in mind that although a woman's religious actions were largely determined by her personal status, they were not regarded as a private matter, even if they took place within the confines of her own household. No one in the sixteenth century regarded religion or the family as private, as that term is used today. One's inner relationship with God was perhaps a private matter (though even that is arguable), but one's outward religious practices were a matter of great concern for political authorities. Both Protestants and Catholics saw the family as the cornerstone of society, the cornerstone on which all other institutions were constructed, and every political authority meddled in family and domestic concerns. Thus a woman's choice to serve her family meat on Friday or attend the funeral of a friend whose religion was unacceptable was not to be overlooked or regarded as trivial.

Although "personal" is not the same as "private" in Reformation Germany, grouping women by their personal status is still the best way to analyze their role in religious change. This essay thus follows "personal" lines of division and begins with an exploration of the impact of the Reformation on nuns, Beguines,[1] and other female religious. It then looks at single and married women, including a special group of married women, the wives of the Protestant reformers. Although the reformers did not have a special message for noblewomen, the situation of these women warrants separate consideration because their religious choices had the greatest effect on the course of the Reformation. The essay concludes with a discussion of several groups of working women whose labor was directly or indirectly affected by religious change.

Women in convents, both cloistered nuns and lay sisters, and other female religious, were the first to confront the Protestant Reformation. In

[1] Roman Catholic lay sisterhoods.

areas becoming Protestant religious change meant both the closing of their houses and a negation of the value and worth of the life they had been living. The Protestant reformers encouraged nuns and sisters to leave their houses and marry, with harsh words concerning the level of morality in the convents, comparing it to that in brothels. Some convents accepted the Protestant message and willingly gave up their houses and land to city and territorial authorities. The nuns renounced their vows, and those who were able to finds husbands married, while the others returned to their families or found ways to support themselves on their own. Others did not accept the new religion but recognized the realities of political power and gave up their holdings; these women often continued living together after the Reformation, trying to remain as a religious community, though they often had to rely on their families for support. In some cases the nuns were given a pension. There is no record, however, of what happened to most of these women. Former priests and monks could become pastors in the new Protestant churches, but former nuns had no place in the new church structure.

Many convents, particularly those with high standards of learning and morality and whose members were noblewomen or women from wealthy patrician families, fought the religious change. A good example of this is the St. Clara convent in Nuremberg, whose nuns were all from wealthy Nuremberg families and whose reputation for learning had spread throughout Germany. The abbess at the time of the Reformation was Charitas Pirckheimer, a sister of the humanist Willibald Pirckheimer and herself an accomplished Latinist. In 1525, the Nuremberg city council ordered all the cloisters to close; four of the six male houses in the city dissolved themselves immediately, but both female houses refused. The council first sent official representatives to try to persuade the nuns and then began a program of intimidation. The women, denied confessors and Catholic communion, were forced to hear Protestant sermons four times a week; their servants had difficulty buying food; people threatened to burn the convent, threw stones over the walls, and sang profane songs when they heard the nuns singing. Charitas noted in her memoirs that women often led the attacks and were the most bitter opponents of the nuns. Three families physically dragged their daughters out of the convent, a scene of crying and wailing witnessed by many Nurembergers. The council questioned each nun separately to see if she had any complaints, hoping to find some who would leave voluntarily, and finally confiscated all of the convent's land. None of these measures was successful, and the council eventually left the convent alone, although it forbade the taking in of new novices. The last nun died in 1590.

Charitas' firmness and the loyalty of the nuns to her were perhaps extraordinary, but other abbesses also publicly defended their faith. Elizabeth Gottgabs, the abbess of Oberwesel convent, published a tract against the Lutherans in 1550. Although she denigrated her own work as that of a "poor woman," she hardly held back in her language when evaluating the reformers: "The new evangelical preachers have tried to plug our ears with their abominable uproar...our gracious God will not tolerate their foolishness any longer."...

Nuns who chose to leave convents occasionally published works explaining their actions as well. Martha Elizabeth Zitterin published her letters to her mother explaining why she had left the convent at Erfurt; these were republished five times by Protestant authorities in Jena, who never mentioned that the author herself later decided to return to the convent. Even if the former nuns did not publish their stories, these accounts often became part of Protestant hagiography, particularly if the women had left the convent surreptitiously or had been threatened. Katherine von Bora and eight other nuns were smuggled out of their convent at night after they had secretly made contact with Luther. The fact that this occurred on Easter and that they left in a wagon of herring barrels added drama to the story, and Katherine's later marriage to Luther assured that it would be retold many times.

The Jesuits[2] and other leaders of the Catholic Reformation took the opposite position from the Protestants on the value of celibacy, encouraging young women to disobey their parents and enter convents to escape arranged marriages. Although they did not encourage married women to leave their husbands, the Jesuits followed the pre-Reformation tradition in urging husbands to let their wives enter convents if they wished.

The Counter-Reformation church wanted all female religious strictly cloistered, however, and provided no orders for women who wanted to carry out an active apostolate; there was no female equivalent of the Jesuits. The church also pressured Beguines, Franciscan tertiaries,[3] and other sisters who had always moved about somewhat freely or worked out in the community to adopt strict rules of cloister and place themselves under the direct control of a bishop. The women concerned did not always submit meekly, however. The Beguines in Münster, for example, refused to follow the advice of their confessors, who wanted to reform the beguinage and turn it into a cloistered house of Poor Clares.[4] The women, most of whom were members of the city's elite families, appealed to the city council for help in defending their civil rights and traditional liberties. The council appealed to the archbishop of Cologne, the cardinals, and eventually the pope, and, though the women were eventually cloistered, they were allowed to retain certain of their traditional practices. In some ways, the women were caught in the middle of a power struggle between the archbishop and the city council, but they were still able to appeal to the city's pride in its traditional privileges to argue for their own liberties and privileges. Perhaps the fact that they had not been cloistered kept them aware of the realities and symbols of political power.

[2]Members of the Society of Jesus, a Roman Catholic religious order established in 1540.

[3]A group of lay women attached to the Franciscan order, a Roman Catholic religious order founded in 1209.

[4]An order of Franciscan nuns.

Of course most of the women in sixteenth-century Germany were not nuns or other female religious but laywomen who lived in families. Their first contact with the Reformation was often shared with the male members of their families. They heard the new teachings proclaimed from a city pulpit, read or looked at broadsides attacking the pope, and listened to traveling preachers attacking celibacy and the monasteries.

The reformers communicated their ideas to women in a variety of ways. Women who could read German might have read Luther's two marriage treatises or any number of Protestant marriage manuals, the first of which was published in Augsburg in 1522. They could have read tracts against celibacy by many reformers, which varied widely in their level of vituperation and criticism of convent life. Both Protestant and Catholic authors wrote books of commonplaces and examples, which contained numerous references to proper and improper female conduct attributed to classical authors, the church fathers, and more recent commentators.

The vast majority of women could not read but received the message orally and visually. Sermons, particularly marriage sermons but also regular Sunday sermons, emphasized the benefits of marriage and the proper roles of husband and wife. Sermons at women's funerals stressed their piety, devotion to family, and trust in God through great trials and tribulations and set up models for other women to follow. Vernacular dramas about marriage replaced pre-Reformation plays about virgin martyrs suffering death rather than losing their virginity. Woodcuts depicted pious married women (their marital status was clear because married women wore their hair covered) listening to sermons or reading the Bible. Protestant pamphlets portrayed the pope with the whore of Babylon, which communicated a message about both the pope and about women. Catholic pamphlets showed Luther as a lustful glutton, driven only by his sexual and bodily needs. Popular stories about Luther's home life and harsh attitudes toward female virginity circulated by word of mouth. . . .

The Protestant reformers did not break sharply with tradition in their ideas about women. For both Luther and Calvin, women were created by God and could be saved through faith; spiritually women and men were equal. In every other respect, however, women were to be subordinate to men. Women's subjection was inherent in their very being and was present from creation—in this the reformers agreed with Aristotle[5] and the classical tradition. It was made more brutal and harsh, however, because of Eve's responsibility for the Fall—in this Luther and Calvin[6] agreed with patristic[7] tradition and with their scholastic and humanist predecessors.

There appears to be some novelty in their rejection of Catholic teachings on the merits of celibacy and championing of marriage as the proper state

[5]Greek philosopher, 384–322 B.C.

[6]John Calvin (1509–1564), French Protestant theologian, founder of Calvinism and religious leader of Geneva.

[7]Referring to the fathers, or theologians, of the early Christian Church.

for all individuals. Though they disagreed on so much else, all Protestant reformers agreed on this point; the clauses discussing marriage in the various Protestant confessions show more similarities than do any other main articles of doctrine or discipline. Even this emphasis on marriage was not that new, however. Civic and Christian humanists also thought that "God had established marriage and family life as the best means for providing spiritual and moral discipline in this world," and they "emphasized marriage and the family as the basic social and economic unit which provided the paradigm for all social relations."

The Protestant exhortation to marry was directed to both sexes, but particularly to women, for whom marriage and motherhood were a vocation as well as a living arrangement. Marriage was a woman's highest calling, the way she could fulfill God's will: in Luther's harsh words, "Let them bear children to death; they are created for that." Unmarried women were suspect, both because they were fighting their natural sex drive, which everyone in the sixteenth century believed to be much stronger than men's, and because they were upsetting the divinely imposed order, which made woman subject to man. Even a woman as prominent and respected as Margaretha Blarer, the sister of Ambrosius Blarer, a reformer in Constance, was criticized for her decision to remain unmarried. Martin Bucer[8] accused her of being "masterless." Her brother defended her decision by pointing out that she was very close to his family and took care of the poor and plague victims "as a mother."

The combination of women's spiritual equality, female subordination, and the idealization of marriage proved problematic for the reformers, for they were faced with the issue of women who converted while their husbands did not. What was to take precedence, the woman's religious convictions or her duty of obedience? Luther and Calvin were clear on this. Wives were to obey their husbands, even if they were not Christians; in Calvin's words, a woman "should not desert the partner who is hostile." Marriage was a woman's "calling," her natural state, and she was to serve God through this calling.

Wives received a particularly ambiguous message from the radical reformers.... Some radical groups allowed believers to leave their unbelieving spouses, but women who did so were expected to remarry quickly and thus come under the control of a male believer. The most radical Anabaptists were fascinated by Old Testament polygamy and accepted the statement in Revelations that the Last Judgment would only come if there were 144,000 "saints" in the world; they actually enforced polygamy for a short time at Münster, though the required number of saints were never born. In practical terms, Anabaptist women were equal only in martyrdom.

Although the leaders of the Counter Reformation continued to view celibacy as a state preferable to matrimony, they realized that most women

---

[8]German Protestant reformer, 1491–1551.

in Germany would marry and began to publish their own marriage manual to counter those published by Protestants. The ideal wives and mothers they described were, however, no different than those of the Protestants; both wanted women to be "chaste, silent, and obedient."

The ideas of the reformers did not stay simply within the realm of theory but led to political and institutional changes. Some of these changes were the direct results of Protestant doctrine, and some of them had unintended, though not unforeseeable, consequences. . . .

Every Protestant territory passed a marriage ordinance that stressed wifely obedience and proper Christian virtues and set up a new court or broadened the jurisdiction of an existing court to handle marriage and morals cases which had previously been handled by church courts. They also passed sumptuary laws that regulated weddings and baptisms, thereby trying to make these ceremonies more purely Christian by limiting the number of guests and prohibiting profane activities such as dancing and singing. Though such laws were never complete successful, the tone of these two ceremonies, which marked the two perhaps most important events in a woman's life, became much less exuberant. Religious processions, such as Corpus Christi[9] parades, which had included both men and women, and in which even a city's prostitutes took part, were prohibited. The public processions that remained were generally those of guild masters and journeymen, at which women were onlookers only. Women's participation in rituals such as funerals was limited, for Protestant leaders wanted neither professional mourners nor relatives to take part in extravagant wailing and crying. Lay female confraternities, which had provided emotional and economic assistance for their members and charity for the needy, were also forbidden, and no similar all-female groups replaced them.

The Protestant reformers attempted to do away with the veneration of Mary and the saints. This affected both men and women, because some of the strongest adherents of the cult of the Virgin had been men. For women, the loss of St. Anne, Mary's mother, was particularly hard, for she was a patron saint of pregnant women; now they were instructed to pray during labor and childbirth to Christ, a celibate male, rather than to a woman who had also been a mother. The Protestant martyrs replaced the saints to some degree, at least as models worthy of emulation, but they were not to be prayed to and they did not give their names to any days of the year. The Protestant Reformation not only downplayed women's public ceremonial role; it also stripped the calendar of celebrations honoring women and ended the power female saints and their relics were believed to have over people's lives. Women who remained Catholic still had female saints to pray to, but the number of new female saints during the Counter Reformation was far

---

[9]A Roman Catholic festival instituted in the thirteenth century to honor the Blessed Sacrament (the body of Jesus).

fewer than the number of new male saints, for two important avenues to sanctity, missionary and pastoral work, were closed to women.

Because of the importance Protestant reformers placed on Bible-reading in the vernacular, many of them advocated opening schools for girls as well as boys. The number of such schools which opened was far fewer than the reformers had originally hoped, and Luther in particular also muted his call for mass education after the turmoil of the Peasants' War.[10] The girls' schools that were opened stressed morality and decorum; in the words of the Memmingen school ordinance from 1587, the best female pupil was one noted for her "great diligence and application in learning her catechism, modesty, obedience, and excellent penmanship." These schools taught sewing as well as reading and singing, and religious instruction was often limited to memorizing the catechism.

Along with these changes that related directly to Protestant doctrine, the Reformation brought with it an extended period of war and destruction in which individuals and families were forced to move frequently from one place to another. Women whose husbands were exiled for religious reasons might also have been forced to leave. Their houses and goods were usually confiscated whether they left town or not. If allowed to stay, they often had to support a family and were still held suspect by neighbors and authorities. A woman whose husband was away fighting could go years without hearing from him and never be allowed to marry again if there was some suspicion he might still be alive.

Women were not simply passive recipients of the Reformation and the ideas and changes it brought but indeed responded to them actively. Swept up by the enthusiasm of the first years of the Reformation, single and married women often stepped beyond what were considered acceptable roles for women. Taking literally Luther's idea of a priesthood of all believers, women as well as uneducated men began to preach and challenge religious authorities. In 1524 in Nuremberg, the city council took action against a certain Frau Voglin, who had set herself up in the hospital church and was preaching. In a discussion after a Sunday sermon by a Lutheran-leaning prior, a woman in Augsburg spoke to a bishop's representative who had been sent to hear the sermon and called the bishop a brothel manager because he had a large annual income from concubinage fees. Several women in Zwickau, inspired by the preaching of Thomas Müntzer,[11] also began to preach in 1521.

All of these actions were viewed with alarm by civic authorities, who even objected to women's getting together to discuss religion. In their view, female preachers clearly disobeyed the Pauline injunction against women speaking in church and moved perilously close to claiming an

---

[10] Uprisings in central and southwest Germany, 1524–1525, inspired by the Reformation leaders' defiance of authority.

[11] Radical religious leader who led a peasant rebellion in 1524–1525.

official religious role. In 1529, the Zwickau city council banished several of the women who had gathered together and preached. In the same year, the Memmingen city council forbade maids to discuss religion while drawing water at neighborhood wells. No German government forbade women outright to read the Bible, as Henry VIII[12] of England did in 1543, but the authorities did attempt to prevent them from discussing it publicly.

After 1530, women's public witnessing of faith was more likely to be prophesying than preaching. In many ways, female prophets were much less threatening than female preachers, for the former had biblical parallels, clear biblical justification, and no permanent official function. Ursula Jost and Barbara Rebstock in Strasbourg began to have visions and revelations concerning the end of the world. When Melchior Hoffman, the Spiritualist, came to Strasbourg, they convinced him he was the prophet Elijah born again and thus one of the signs of the impending Apocalypse. He published seventy-two of Ursula's revelations, advising all Christians to read them. They were written in the style of Old Testament prophecy and became popular in the Rhineland and Netherlands. Several other female Anabaptists also had visions that were spread by word of mouth and as broadsides or small pamphlets. Though these women were illiterate, their visions were full of biblical references, which indicates that, like Lollard[13] women in England, they had memorized much of the Bible. Female prophecy was accepted in most radical sects, for they emphasized direct revelation and downplayed theological training. That these sects were small and loosely structured was also important for the continued acceptance of female revelation; in Münster, the one place where Anabaptism became the state religion, female prophecy was suppressed.

Not all female visionaries were radicals, however. Mysticism and ecstatic visions remained an acceptable path to God for Catholic women and increased in popularity in Germany after the works of Saint Theresa[14] were translated and her ideas became known. Even Lutheran women reported miracles and visions. Catherine Binder, for example, asserted that her speech had been restored after seven years when a pastor gave her a copy of the Lutheran Catechism. The Lutheran clergy were suspicious of such events, but did not reject them out of hand.

With the advent of the religious wars, female prophets began to see visions of war and destruction and to make political, as well as religious and eschatological, predictions. Susanna Rugerin had been driven far from her home by imperial armies and began to see an angel who revealed visions of

---

[12]Ruled 1509–1547

[13]Lollard was originally a name given to followers of the fourteenth-century English reformer John Wycliffe. Later the name was applied to any English religious dissenter in the fifteenth century.

[14]Spanish nun and mystic, 1515–1582.

Gustavus Adolphus.[15] The visions of Juliana von Duchnik were even more dramatic. In 1628 she brought a warning from God to Duke Wallenstein, a commander of imperial troops, telling him to leave his estate because God would no longer protect him. Though Wallenstein's wife was very upset, his supporters joked about it, commenting that the emperor got letters from only the pope, while Wallenstein got them directly from God. Von Duchnik published this and other of her visions the following year and in 1634 returned to Wallenstein's camp warning him that she had seen a vision of him trying to climb a ladder into heaven; the ladder collapsed, and he fell to earth with blood and poison pouring out of his heart. Though Wallenstein himself continued to dismiss her predictions, others around him took her seriously. Her visions in this case proved accurate, for Wallenstein was assassinated less than a month later. In general, female prophets were taken no less seriously than their male counterparts.

The most dramatic public affirmation of faith a woman could make was martyrdom. Most of the female martyrs in Germany were Anabaptists, and the law granted women no special treatment, except for occasionally delaying execution if they were pregnant. Women were more likely to be drowned than beheaded, for it was thought they would faint at the sight of the executioner's sword and make his job more difficult. Some of them were aware that this reduced the impact of their deaths and wanted a more public form of execution. A good indication of the high degree of religious understanding among many Anabaptist women comes from their interrogations. They could easily discuss the nature of Christ, the doctrine of the Real Presence, and baptism, quoting extensively from the Bible. As a woman known simply as Claesken put it, "Although I am a simple person before men, I am not unwise in the knowledge of the Lord." Her interrogators were particularly upset because she had converted many people: they commented, "Your condemnation will be greater than your husband's because you can read and have misled him."

Although most of the women who published religious works during the Reformation were either nuns or noblewomen, a few middle-class women wrote hymns, religious poetry, and some polemics. Ursula Weide published a pamphlet against the abbot of Pegau, denouncing his support of celibacy. The earliest Protestant hymnals include several works by women, often verse renditions of the Psalms or Gospels. Justitia Sanger, a blind woman from Braunschweig, published a commentary on ninety-six Psalms in 1593, dedicating it to King Frederick II of Denmark. Female hymn-writing became even more common in the seventeenth century when the language of hymns shifted from aggressive and martial to emotional and pious; it was more acceptable for a woman to write of being washed in the blood of the Lamb

---

[15]Protestant king of Sweden who defeated the Catholic imperial forces in Germany during the Thirty Years' War (1618–1648).

than of strapping on the armor of God. Not all female religious poetry from the seventeenth century was meekly pious, however. Anna Oven Hoyer was driven from place to place during the Thirty Years' War, finally finding refuge in Sweden. She praised David Joris and Caspar von Schwenkfeld[16] in her writings, which she published without submitting them for clerical approval. Some of them, including her "Spiritual Conversation between a Mother and Child about True Christianity," were later burned as heretical. In this dialogue she attacked the Lutheran clergy for laxness, greed, pride, and trust in wordly learning and largely blamed them for the horrors of the Thirty Years' War.

Seventeenth-century women often wrote religious poems, hymns, and prose meditations for private purposes as well as for publication. They wrote to celebrate weddings, baptisms, and birthdays, to console friends, to praise deceased relatives, to instruct and provide examples for their children. If a woman's works were published while she was still alive, they included profuse apologies about her unworthiness and presumption. Many such works were published posthumously by husbands or fathers and include a note from these men that writing never distracted the author from her domestic tasks but was done only in her spare time. Unfortunately, similar works by sixteenth-century German women are rare. Thus, to examine the religious convictions of the majority of women who did not preach, prophesy, publish, or become martyrs, we must look at their actions within the context of their domestic and community life.

Married women whose religious convictions matched those of their husbands often shared equally in the results of those convictions. If these convictions conflicted with local authorities and the men were banished for religious reasons, their wives were expected to follow them. Because house and goods were generally confiscated, the wives had no choice in the matter anyway. Women whose husbands were in hiding, fighting religious wars, or assisting Protestant churches elsewhere supported the family and covered for their husbands, often sending them supplies as well. Wealthy women set up endowments for pastors and teachers and provided scholarships for students at Protestant, and later Jesuit, universities.

Many married women also responded to the Protestant call to make the home, in the words of the humanist Urbanus Rhegius, "a seminary for the church." They carried out what might best be called domestic missionary activity, praying and reciting the catechism with their children and servants. Those who were literate might read some vernacular religious literature, and, because reading was done aloud in the sixteenth century, this was also a group activity. What they could read was limited by the level of their reading ability, the money available to buy books, and the effectiveness of the city censors at keeping out unwanted or questionable material. Women overcame some of the limitations on their reading material by paying for translations,

---

[16]German mystic and radical Protestant reformer, 1489–1561.

thus continuing a tradition begun before the invention of the printing press. The frequency of widowhood in the sixteenth century meant that women often carried religious ideas, and the pamphlets and books that contained them, to new households when they remarried, and a few men actually admitted to having been converted by their wives. The role of women as domestic missionaries was recognized more clearly by Catholics and English Protestants than it was by continental Protestants, who were obsessed with wifely obedience. Richard Hooker,[17] a theorist for the Anglican church, commented that the Puritans made special efforts to convert women because they were "diligent in drawing away their husbands, children, servants, friends, and allies the same way." Jesuits encouraged the students at their seminaries to urge their mothers to return to confession and begin Catholic practices in the home; in this way, an indifferent or even Lutheran father might be brought back into the fold.

There are several spectacular examples among noble families of women whose quiet pressure eventually led to their husbands' conversions and certainly many among common people that are not recorded. But what about a married woman whose efforts failed? What could a woman do whose religious convictions differed from those of her husband? In some areas, the couple simply lived together as adherents of different religions. The records for Bamberg, for example, show that in 1595 about 25 percent of the households were mixed marriages, with one spouse Catholic and the other Lutheran. Among the members of the city council the proportion was even higher—43 percent had spouses of a different religion, so this was not something which simply went unnoticed by authorities. Bamberg was one of the few cities in Germany which allowed two religions to worship freely; therefore, mixed marriages may have been only a local phenomenon. This, however, has not yet been investigated in other areas.

Continued cohabitation was more acceptable if the husband was of a religion considered acceptable in the area. In 1631, for example, the Strasbourg city council considered whether citizens should lose their citizenship if they married Calvinists. It decided that a man would not "because he can probably draw his spouse away from her false religion, and bring her on to the correct path." He would have to pay a fine, though, for "bringing an unacceptable person into the city." A woman who married a Calvinist would lose her citizenship, however, "because she would let herself easily be led into error in religion by her husband, and led astray."

As a final resort, a married woman could leave her husband (and perhaps family) and move to an area where the religion agreed with her own. This was extremely difficult for women who were not wealthy, and most of the recorded cases involve noblewomen with independent incomes and sympathetic fathers. Even if a woman might gather enough resources to support herself, she was not always welcome, despite the strength of her

[17]1554–1600, author of the *Laws of Ecclesiastical Polity* (1594).

religious convictions, for she had violated that most basic of norms, wifely obedience. Protestant city councils were suspicious of any woman who asked to be admitted to citizenship independently and questioned her intensely about her marital status. Catholic cities such as Munich were more concerned about whether the woman who wanted to immigrate had always been a good Catholic than whether or not she was married, particularly if she wished to enter a convent.

Exceptions were always made for wives of Anabaptists. A tailor's wife in Nuremberg was allowed to stay in the city and keep her house as long as she recanted her Anabaptist beliefs and stayed away from all other Anabaptists, including her husband, who had been banished. After the siege of Münster, Anabaptist women and children began to drift back into the city and were allowed to reside there if they abjured Anabaptism and swore an oath of allegiance to the bishop. Both Protestant and Catholic authorities viewed Anabaptism as a heresy and a crime so horrible it broke the most essential human bonds.

It was somewhat easier for unmarried women and widows to leave a territory for religious reasons, and in many cases persecution or war forced them out. A widow wrote to the Nuremberg city council after the city had turned Lutheran that she wanted to move there "because of the respect and love she has for the word of God, which is preached here [that is, Nuremberg] truly and purely"; after a long discussion, the council allowed her to move into the city. But women still had greater difficulties than men being accepted as residents in any city. Wealthier widows had to pay the normal citizenship fee and find male sponsors, both of which were difficult for women, who generally did not command as many financial resources or have as many contacts as men of their class. Because of this, and because innkeepers were forbidden to take in any woman traveling alone, no matter what her age or class, women's cities of refuge were often limited to those in which they had relatives.

Women who worked to support themselves generally had to make special supplications to city councils to be allowed to stay and work. Since they had not been trained in a guild in the city, the council often overrode guild objections in permitting them to make or sell small items to support themselves and was more likely to grant a woman's request if she was seen as particularly needy or if her story was especially pathetic. A woman whose husband had been killed in the Thirty Years' War asked permission in 1632 to live in Strasbourg and bake pretzels; this was granted to her and several others despite the objections of the bakers because, in the council's words, "all of the supplicants are poor people, that are particularly hard-pressed in these difficult times." Another woman was allowed to make tonic and elixirs in Strasbourg after a city pastor assured the council that "she is a pious and godly woman who left everything to follow the true word of God."

One of the most dramatic changes brought about by the Protestant Reformation was the replacement of celibate priests by married pastors with wives and families. Many of the wives of the early reformers had themselves been nuns, and they were crossing one of society's most rigid borders by marrying, becoming brides of men rather than brides of Christ. During the first few years of the Reformation, they were still likened to priests' concubines in the public mind and had to create a respectable role for themselves. They were often living demonstrations of their husbands' convictions and were expected to be models of wifely obedience and Christian charity; the reformers had particularly harsh words for pastors who could not control their wives. Pastors' wives were frequently asked to be godmothers and thereby could be "important agents in the diffusion of evangelical domesticity from the household of the clergy to the rest of the population." But they also had to bring the child a gift appropriate to its social standing from the meager pastoral treasury. The demands on pastors' wives were often exacerbated by their husbands' lack of concern for material matters. Often former priests or monks, these men had never before worried about an income and continued to leave such things in God's (or actually their wives') hands.

Pastors' wives opened up their homes to students and refugees, providing them with food, shelter and medical care. This meant buying provisions, brewing beer, hiring servants, growing fruits and vegetables, and gathering herbs for a household that could expand overnight from ten to eighty. Katherine von Bora purchased and ran an orchard, personally overseeing the care of apple and pear trees and selling the fruit to provide income for the household. She occasionally took part in the theological discussions that went on after dinner in the Luther household and was teased by her husband for her intellectual interests; he called her "Professor Katie." . . .

Other pastors' wives assisted in running city hospitals, orphanages, and infirmaries, sometimes at the suggestion of their husbands and sometimes on their own initiative. Katherine Zell, the wife of Matthias Zell[18] and a tireless worker for the Reformation in Strasbourg, inspected the local hospital and was appalled by what she found there. She demanded the hospital master be replaced because he served the patients putrid, fatty meat, "does not know the name of Christ," and mumbled the table grace "so you can't tell if it's a prayer or a fart." Wealthy women set up endowments for pastors and teachers and provided scholarships for students at Protestant, and later Jesuit, universities.

Neither the Protestant nor the Catholic reformers differentiated between noblewomen and commoners in their public advice to women; noblewomen, too, were to be "chaste, silent, and obedient." Privately, however, they recognized that such women often held a great deal of power and made special attempts to win them over. Luther corresponded regularly with a

---

[18]Katherine (c.497–1562) and Matthias Zell (1477–1548) were Protestant reformers at Strasbourg.

number of prominent noblewomen, and Calvin was even more assiduous at "courting ladies in high places."

Noblewomen, both married and unmarried, religious and lay, had the most opportunity to express their religious convictions, and the consequences of their actions were more far-reaching than those of most women. Prominent noblewomen who left convents could create quite a sensation, particularly if, like Ursula of Münsterberg, they wrote a justification of why they had left and if their actions put them in opposition to their families. Disagreements between husband and wife over matters of religion could lead to the wife being exiled, as in the case of Elisabeth of Brandenburg. They could also lead to mutual toleration, however, as they did for Elisabeth's daughter, also named Elisabeth, who married Eric, the duke of Brunswick-Calenburg. She became a Lutheran while her husband remained a Catholic, to which his comment was: "My wife does not interfere with and molest us in our faith, and therefore we will leave her undisturbed and unmolested in hers." After his death, she became regent and introduced the Reformation into Brunswick.... Several other female rulers also promoted independently the Reformation in their territories, while others convinced their husbands to do so. Later in the century noble wives and widows were also influential in opening up territories to the Jesuits.

Most of these women were following paths of action that had been laid out by male rulers and had little consciousness of themselves as women carrying out a reformation. Others as well judged their actions on the basis of their inherited status and power, for, despite John Knox's[19] bitter fulminations against "the monstrous regiment of women," female rulers were not regarded as unusual in the sixteenth century. Only if a noblewoman ventured beyond summoning and protecting a male reformer or signing church ordinances to commenting publicly on matters of theology was she open to criticism as a woman going beyond what was acceptable.

The best known example of such a noblewoman was Argula von Grumbach, who wrote to the faculty of the University of Ingolstadt in 1523 protesting the university's treatment of a young teacher accused of Lutheran leanings. She explained her reasons: "I am not unacquainted with the word of Paul that women should be silent in Church [1 Tim. 1:2] but, when no man will or can speak, I am driven by the word of the Lord when he said, 'He who confesses me on earth, him will I confess, and he who denies me, him will I deny' [Matt. 10, Luke 9] and I take comfort in the words of the prophet Isaiah [3:12, but not exact], I will send you children to be your princes and women to be your rulers."

She also wrote to the duke of Bavaria, her overlord, about the matter. Neither the university nor the duke bothered to reply but instead ordered her husband or male relatives to control her and deprived her husband of an official position and its income as a show of displeasure. Instead of

[19]c. 1505–1572, leader of the Protestant Reformation in Scotland.

having the desired effect, these actions led her to write to the city council at Ingolstadt and to both Luther and Frederick the Wise of Saxony to request a hearing at the upcoming imperial diet at Nuremberg. Her letters were published without her knowledge, provoking a student at Ingolstadt to write an anonymous satirical poem telling her to stick to spinning and hinting that she was interested in the young teacher because she was sexually frustrated. She answered with a long poem that was both satirical and serious, calling the student a coward for writing anonymously and giving numerous biblical examples of women called on to give witness. This ended her public career. ... Though she died in obscurity, her story was widely known and frequently reprinted as part of Lutheran books of witnesses and martyrs.

In the case of Argula von Grumbach, her sex was clearly more important than her noble status. Political authorities would not have ignored a man of similar status who was in contact with major reformers. Grumbach exhibited a strong sense of herself as a woman in her writings, even before her detractors dwelled on that point alone. Despite the extraordinary nature of her actions, she did not see herself as in any way unusual, commenting in her letter to the Ingolstadt city council that "if I die, a hundred women will write to you, for there are many who are more learned and adept than I am." She recognized that her religious training, which began with the German Bible her father gave her when she was ten, was shared by many other literate women and expected them to respond in the same way she did, proclaiming "the word of God as a member of the Christian church."

Like noblewomen, women engaged in various occupations did not receive any special message from the reformers. Even Luther's harsh diatribe against the prostitutes of Wittenberg was addressed to the university students who used their services. This is because in the sixteenth century, women who carried out a certain occupation were rarely thought of as a group. A woman's work identity was generally tied to her family identify.

This can best be explained with an example. For a man to become a baker, he apprenticed himself to a master baker for a certain number of years, then spent several more years as a journeyman, and finally might be allowed to make his masterpiece—a loaf of bread or a fancy cake—open his own shop, marry, and hire his own apprentices and journeymen. He was then a full-fledged member of the bakers' guild, took part in parades, festivals, and celebrations with his guild brothers, lit candles at the guild altar in Catholic cities, and perhaps participated in city government as a guild representative. He was thus a baker his entire life and had a strong sense of work identity.

For a woman to become a baker, she had to marry a baker. She was not allowed to participate in the apprenticeship system, though she could do everything in the shop her husband could. If he died, she might carry on the shop a short time as a widow, but, if she was young enough, she generally married again and took on whatever her new husband's occupation was. She had no voice in guild decisionmaking and took no part in guild festivals, though she may have actually baked more than her husband. Changes in her status were not determined by her own level of training but by changes in her marital or family status. Thus, although in terms of actual work she was as much a baker as her husband, she, and her society, viewed her as a baker's wife. Her status as wife was what was important in the eyes of sixteenth-century society, and, as we have seen, many treatises and laws were directed to wives.

Although female occupations were not directly singled out in religious theory, several were directly affected by changes in religious practices. The demand for votive candles, which were often made and sold by women, dropped dramatically, and these women were forced to find other means of support. The demand for fish declined somewhat, creating difficulties for female fishmongers, although traditional eating habits did not change immediately when fast days were no longer required. Municipal brothels were closed in the sixteenth century, a change often linked with the Protestant Reformation. This occurred in Catholic cities as well, however, and may be more closely linked with general concerns for public order and morality and obsession with women's sexuality than with any specific religion.

Charitable institutions were secularized and centralized, a process which had begun before the Reformation and was speeded up in the sixteenth century in both Protestant and Catholic territories. Many of the smaller charities were houses set up for elderly indigent women who lived off the original endowment and small fees they received for mourning or preparing bodies for burial. They had in many cases elected one of their number as head of the house but were now moved into large hospitals under the direction of a city official. The women who worked in these hospitals as cooks, nurses, maids, and cleaning women now became city, rather than church, employees. Outwardly their conditions of employment changed little, but the Protestant deemphasis on good works may have changed their conception of the value of their work, particularly given their minimal salaries and abysmal working conditions.

Midwives had long performed emergency baptisms if they or the parents believed the child would not live. This created few problems before the Reformation because Catholic doctrine taught that if there was some question about the regularity of this baptism and the child lived, the infant could be rebaptized "on the condition" it had not been baptized properly the first time; conditional baptism was also performed on foundlings. This assured the parents that their child had been baptized correctly while avoiding the snare of rebaptism, which was a crime in the Holy Roman Empire. In 1531, however, Luther rejected all baptisms "on condition" if it was known any baptism had already been carried out and called for a normal baptism in the case of foundlings. By 1540, most Lutheran areas were no longer baptizing "on condition," and those persons who still supported the practice were occasionally branded Anabaptists. This made it extremely important that midwives and other laypeople knew how to conduct correctly an emergency baptism.

Midwives were thus examined, along with pastors, church workers, and teachers, in the visitations conducted by pastors and city leaders in many cities, and "shocking irregularities" in baptismal practice were occasionally discovered. In one story, perhaps apocryphal, a pastor found one midwife confident in her reply that, yes, she certainly baptized infants in the name of the Holy Trinity—Caspar, Melchior, Balthazar! During the course of the sixteenth century, most Protestant cities included a long section on emergency baptisms in their general baptismal ordinance and even gave copies of this special section to the city's midwives. They also began to require midwives to report all illegitimate children and asked them to question any unmarried mother about who the father of the child was. If she refused to reveal his identify, midwives were to question her "when the pains of labor are greatest," for her resistance would probably be lowest at that point.

In areas of Germany where Anabaptism flourished, Anabaptist midwives were charged with claiming they had baptized babies when they really had not, so that a regular church baptism would not be required. In other areas the opposite seems to have been the case. Baptism was an important social occasion and a chance for the flaunting of wealth and social position, and parents paid the midwife to conveniently forget she had baptized a child so that the normal church ceremony could be carried out.

Despite the tremendous diversity of female experience in Germany during the Reformation, two factors are constant. First, a woman's ability to respond to the Reformation and the avenues her responses could take were determined more by her gender than by any other factor. The reformers— Catholic and Protestant, magisterial and radical—all agreed on the proper avenues for female response to their ideas. The responses judged acceptable were domestic, personal, and familial—prayer, meditation, teaching the catechism to children, singing or writing hymns, entering or leaving a convent. Public responses, either those presented publicly or those which concerned dogma or the church as a public institution, shocked and outraged authorities, even if they agreed with the ideas being expressed. A woman who backed the "wrong" religion was never as harshly criticized as a man; this was seen as simply evidence of her irrational and weak nature. One who supported the "right" religion too vigorously and vocally, however, might be censured by her male compatriots for "too much enthusiasm" and overstepping the bounds of proper female decorum. Thus, whatever a woman's status or class, her responses were judged according to both religious and sexual ideology. Since women of all classes heard this message from pamphlet and pulpit and felt its implications in laws and ordinances, it is not at all surprising that most of them accepted it.

Second, most women experienced the Reformation as individuals. Other than nuns in convents women were not a distinct social class, economic category, or occupational group; thus, they had no opportunity for group action. They passed religious ideas along the networks of their family, friends, and neighbors, but these networks had no official voice in a society that was divided according to male groups. A woman who challenged her husband or other male authorities in matters of religion was challenging basic assumptions about gender roles, and doing this alone, with no official group to support her. Even women who reformed territories did so as individual rulers. Men, on the other hand, were preached to as members of groups and responded collectively. They combined with other men in city councils, guilds, consistories, cathedral chapters, university faculties, and many other bodies to effect or halt religious change. Their own individual religious ideas were affirmed by others, whether or not they were ultimately successful in establishing the religious system they desired.

The strongest female protest against the Reformation in Germany came from the convents, where women were used to expressing themselves on religious matters and thinking of themselves as members of a spiritual group. Thus, although the Protestant reformers did champion a woman's role as wife and mother by closing the convents and forbidding female lay confraternities, they cut off women's opportunities for expressing their spirituality in an all-female context. Catholic women could still enter convents, but those convents were increasingly cut off from society. By the mid-seventeenth century, religion for all women in Germany, whether lay or clerical, had become much more closely tied to a household.

"Lost Women" in Early Modern Seville: The Politics of Prostitution

MARY ELIZABETH PERRY

In the sixteenth and for the first half of the seventeenth century, Spain was militarily the strongest country in Europe. Spain fought the Turks and the French and championed resurgent Catholicism against nascent Protestantism. Spaniards circumnavigated the world, explored distant lands, and conquered entire empires in the New World. This was Spain's "Golden Age," a period not only of political and military glory but also of brilliance in literature and art. Yet rapid socioeconomic developments during these centuries produced, in Seville at least, a golden age of prostitution.

Several topics are raised here, including the causes of prostitution, the role of the city government, and the relationship between religion and prostitution. Why in a country obsessed with religious purity—the monarch had expelled Muslims and Jews and the Inquisition strove mightily to ensure religious orthodoxy—did prostitution so flourish in Seville? What changes specifically resulted in an increase in the numbers of prostitutes in early modern Seville? How did social and economic changes affect women in their traditional roles as nuns, wives, and workers? Why did women become prostitutes?

The city government chose not to attempt to eradicate prostitution. In fact, city fathers encouraged and regulated it. Why? How did regulations support and abet the practice of prostitution? Why were the occupations of actress, streethawker, and practitioner of folk medicine of such concern to the city government?

Perry emphasizes that morality was much on the minds of the urban elite as they sought to use prostitution to preserve public order and right behavior. What were the links between prostitution, morality, and the social order? How did the powerful female symbols of the Virgin Mary, the "Painted Prostitute," and Mary Magdalene underscore the double standard between men and women and between the reality of life and the image of Christian society? Why did the city fathers see brothels as essential pillars to upholding a Christian morality and a Christian social order? What position did the Catholic Church take regarding prostitution?

In the sixteenth century a new sexually transmitted disease, syphilis, became epidemic. How did the appearance and spread of syphilis influence the world of prostitution in Seville? Prostitutes could always be shunned and feared for moral contagion; now males looked upon them as carriers of a dreadful and incomprehensible disease. Moreover, prostitutes practiced contraception, abortion, and unlicensed medicine. Despite these illicit patterns of behavior, the city government still regulated prostitution and wished no end to it. Why? Was it a matter of economics, the money to be made in various ways from prostitutes? Or did political reasons predominate in the minds of the urban elite as they watched over the practice of prostitution?

Perry concludes by saying that the "lost women" of Seville "were not lost at all." What does she mean by this?

To city fathers in early modern Seville, prostitutes were "lost women." The euphemism suggests that prostitutes were outcasts, completely outside the culture of the city. Historical evidence argues just the opposite, however, for it presents a picture of prostitutes who were an integral part of their community.

Seville offers an exciting social arena for examining prostitution in the early modern period. Thousands of people poured into the city after 1503 when the Crown of Castile placed in this inland seaport its agency to control colonization and trade with the newly discovered Americas. Seville quickly became a boom town, its streets teeming with the thousands who came to seek their fortunes. Archival documents describe many of these people and the city's attempts to control them. These sources show that the alliance of churchmen and nobles who ruled Seville reeled under the impact of rapid socioeconomic changes. Desperately trying to preserve its position, this oligarchy consciously used legislation and existing institutions to buttress the existing social order. City fathers seized upon prostitution as a commercial prop, an agency to reinforce lines of authority, and a symbol of evil. They pointed to prostitutes as diseased, disgusting, and parasitical.

They used prostitution to unite the community in their support against such evil, and they used it to justify the extension of their governmental powers.

Although historical sources provide rich descriptions of city regulation of prostitution, they contain little evidence of the numbers, ages, or social backgrounds of prostitutes in the city. Actual voices of prostitutes are heard only rarely in these sources, and then most often in the picaresque novels, plays, and ballads that they themselves did not write. For the most part, the literature, acts, medical treatises, social surveys, memoirs, and church and city documents of Seville present an official view of prostitution.

Despite these limitations, a study of "lost women" in Seville can broaden our understanding of prostitution. First, it describes sixteenth- and seventeenth-century women in a commercially active city and suggests that changes in this period disrupted traditional roles and promoted prostitution as a livelihood. Second, it demonstrates that prostitution was not only acceptable in the society of this city; it was even a pillar of the moral system that buttressed the existing social order. Finally, it suggests that any consideration of prostitution must examine its political implications, for evidence from Seville argues that prostitution thrived because it was politically useful to the ruling class.

For centuries women in Seville had found many ways to survive. As wives or nuns, many had depended for a livelihood on husbands or convents. Others worked in crafts and industry, streethawking and retail, domestic service, folk medicine, inns, and drama. Widows owned and operated the shops and dramatic companies that they had inherited. Some women were kept as concubines by the wealthier men of the community, and others earned a living as prostitutes on the streets or in the public brothels. In the early modern period, several factors combined to disrupt traditional roles of women and promote prostitution as a livelihood.

Seville thrived in the first half of the sixteenth century. Many people found instant wealth in the rich trade with the Americas, and even more benefited from the "price revolution," a sharp increase in the prices that stemmed from the influx of precious metals from the Americas and the demographic increases of this period. Nobles enriched their own families through marriage to young women of wealthy merchant families. One merchant was so eager to buy noble status that he gave to the nobleman who married his daughter a dowry of two hundred forty thousand ducats, a sum greater than an unskilled worker would make in a thousand years. Families with large land holdings married into other landholding families in order to consolidate the large blocs of land that were increasingly profitable for olive and vine cultivation.

Not everyone in Seville profited from the economic boom, however. A decline in local industry accompanied the great success of commerce, for merchants found it more profitable to ship to the Americas foreign-made products rather than locally produced merchandise. Local products were often more expensive because many wages were higher in Seville where the "price revolution" made its first impact. Some local producers failed to keep up with the improving quality and techniques of production used abroad. Seville's silk industry, for example, fell behind the French silk weavers who were able to produce in quantity the more fashionable fabrics. Convents that sustained themselves by the silk-weaving of their nuns suffered so much from foreign competition that the crown prohibited foreign-made silks in 1621, declaring that foreign producers had caused many convents to lose their livelihood. By the middle of the seventeenth century, an official of the silk masters' guild reported that of the city's three thousand silk looms, only sixty were in use. While the fortunes of merchants continued to increase, textile workers found less and less work.

Agricultural producers were also affected by this boom. The opening of markets in the New World and the increased prices of the "price revolution" encouraged larger scale agricultural production, much of it devoted to olive and vine cultivation. The government set price ceilings on wheat in an attempt to keep bread at a reasonable price, but this policy encouraged agricultural producers to turn from wheat production to olives and vines, which were more profitable in both foreign and domestic markets. Spain's wars abroad closed some foreign markets to Spanish agricultural products and increased taxes so that small agricultural producers found it increasingly difficult to pay the rising costs of production as well as the heavy taxes. By the end of the sixteenth century, viceroys reported to the crown that one-half to two-thirds of the land that had once been cultivated had been abandoned. The wealthy agricultural producers absorbed more land and prospered, but the small producers left the land to find jobs in the cities or seek their fortunes in the New World.

Government monetary policy further increased economic distress. As the crown removed precious metals from coins to enrich the royal treasury, vellon, a mixture of copper and silver, replaced gold and silver. During the first half of the seventeenth century, the government restamped or revalued coins on seven separate occasions in Seville. Monetary speculation flourished, but real purchasing power fell. While wages increased in early modern Seville, they couldn't keep up with rising prices and monetary devaluation.

These economic changes disrupted the usual roles of women of the city. Convents, for example, offered fewer women a livelihood. Fathers had traditionally placed their daughters in convents when they lacked enough money for a suitable marriage dowry....

Most convents also required a dowry, although a small amount. In some cases, the Archbishopric provided dowries so that poor girls could enter a religious order. One convent, the Monastery of the Sweet Name of Jesus, had been founded especially for reformed prostitutes, and it depended on city charity rather than dowries from its members. In 1581 this convent reported that is was the home for more than one hundred women and asked the city for more alms to support its nuns, novitiates, and lay sisters.

As prices rose and money fell in value, many convents had to increase the amount of dowry required from its members. Others simply fell into poverty. The Convent of Santa María la Real in Seville reported in 1597 that its building was in danger of collapse and its poverty was so great that it could feed its one hundred twenty members on only three days of the week. Nuns were particularly hurt by the devaluation of money because they had few ways to augment their incomes. Unlike monks, nuns could not earn fees for preaching, burying the dead, or saying Masses. In addition, they were prohibited from begging door-to-door for food.

Lacking a dowry for either marriage or convent, some women lived together in "congregations" as *beatas* (holy women). Usually widows and young unmarried women, they often lived in a house next to the parish church and considered the parish priest their director. They supported themselves by the work of their hands and by income from any property they owned, but there were generally very poor. Some priests disapproved of this spontaneous form of religious community life and tried to impose on *beatas* the control of the regular clergy.

Marriage became less likely for women in the lower income groups. In his Third Discourse, the *tratadista* (economic theorist) Martínez de Mata[1] recognized the problems resulting because marriage was discouraged for young men with no livelihood. He blamed foreign competition for taking away the jobs of many Spaniards and causing small farmers, textile workers, and artisan-producers to become vagabonds. The women who could have married them in better economic circumstances remained single and perished from hunger.

Wives were more frequently abandoned in the early modern period. Many underemployed and unemployed husbands abandoned wives and children to seek their fortunes in the Indies, a pattern noted repeatedly by the priests who surveyed the poor of the city in 1667. Rural laborers left their families and miserable existence on the land, hoping to find a better life in the cities, the army, or the Indies. Foreigners married women of Seville so they could enjoy certain economic and political privileges in the city, only to leave their wives and return to their homelands when they had earned some money. Although statistics of abandoned women are not available, this appears to have been a general pattern throughout the early modern period. The Venetian ambassador to Spain reported in 1525 that so many men had left Seville for the New World that "the city was left in the hands of women," and one hundred and fifty years later this same problem was noted in the 1667 survey of the poor.

---

[1] Francesca Martínez de Mata penned many memorials in the 1650s on the problem of Spain's decline.

Emigration, of course, was open to women as well as men, but it was regulated by the crown. A royal letter of 1604 complained that more than six hundred women had sailed from Seville for New Spain, although only fifty of them had been licensed. Women who emigrated had to have recommendations for a royal license or some money to buy passage as nonlicensed emigrants. They also had to have a certain venturesome spirit.

One emigrant in 1603 was Catalina de Crusa. A nun in Vizcaya, she had run away from her convent and arrived in Seville in 1603. Disguising herself as a young man, she went to the New World where she worked for twenty years and became a second lieutenant. A monk who knew her there said she had a string of mules in Vera Cruz that she used to bring in merchandise brought by the Spanish fleet to Mexico. Acquaintances in New Spain knew her as a young man, too tall for a woman, but lacking the stature and bearing of an arrogant youth. Her face was neither ugly nor beautiful, distinguished by shiny black wide-open eyes and a little fuzz above her upper lip. She wore her hair short like a man's, and carried a sword very well. Her step was light and elegant. Only her hands appeared rather feminine.

Catalina might have taken her secret to the grave, but in 1624 she was accused of killing a man. To save herself from the gallows, she declared that the court could not hang her because she was a woman and a nun. In great amazement, the local authorities sent her back to Spain where the king gave her five hundred ducats and the formal title of second lieutenant. She became a popular hero, treated as an awesome sensation. In 1630, the king granted her a license to dress as a man. . . .

Obviously, Catalina was an exception. For most women emigration was neither available as a means of escape nor as a catapult to fame. Marriage was favored in this society not only as a livelihood, but also as an institution to impose authority over young girls and prevent them from "losing themselves." The basic law of Castile declared that one reason for marriage was "to avoid quarrels, homicides, insolence, violence, and many other very wrongful acts which would take place on account of women if marriage did not exist." Because marriage appeared to be so crucial to social order, many benefactors provided charitable dowries so that poor girls could marry. . . .

Marriage was not always a formal arrangement in Seville, and many people took partners with neither dowry nor occupation. Poor people accepted these temporary alliances with practical cynicism, an attitude apparent in the following verse from a popular ballad:

> *A husband by night*
> *is a well-known threat:*
> *Don't believe any promises,*
> *Trust only what you can touch.*

While the men realized the inconvenience of heading a regular household, the women held no illusions about marriage.

Women who were unable to depend upon a husband for bread and shelter found their own wages increasingly inadequate and irregular. When the fleet for New Spain prepared to sail, seamstresses and silk workers worked night and day trying to fill merchants' orders. After the fleet sailed, however, demand fell off dramatically, and little money came in. Widows and women without husbands lived together to cut expenses and support one another as they tried to augment their small incomes. A report on charitable works in the city during the 1670s described the great number of widows and single women who had no other income but what they could earn with the labor of their hands. It estimated that each woman could earn only one *real* a day, while bread cost five *reales*. Unemployment, underemployement, and inadequate wages pushed many women into prostitution. For them, prostitution was a part-time occupation that could supplement their very meager incomes.

The economic and social dislocations of early modern Seville encouraged the exploitation of every possible means to survive. Traditional informal social controls no longer restrained exploitation in neighborhoods teeming with newcomers who soon moved away. Thousands of children and youths without parents appeared in Seville, overwhelming the few institutions that could provide food and shelter. People took in orphans and used them to beg money or get customers for both female and male prostitutes. Young women fortunate enough to find a job were considered fair prey by their employers.

In his report on the royal prison of Seville, the lawyer Cristóbal de Chaves described a typical pattern for young female servants. Ana was seduced by Juan de Molina, the son of her master. He gave her lessons every day in how to be a successful prostitute, and he placed her in a brothel. . . . On the days that she did not take in much money, he beat her, for he wanted the money for gambling. He taught her how to call out and get clients, and he showed her many tricks for getting money from them.

Juan developed a system to prevent Ana from cheating on him. He watched from an alleyway outside the brothel and carefully counted her clients, placing a pebble in the hood of his cape for each one. Since he had made her agree to charge each client a set price, he could easily tell if she were holding back any of her earnings by consulting the pebbles in his hood when she gave him the money.

Ana finally talked with another prostitute about her problems, and Juan was soon arrested. Sentenced to the galleys for ten years, he tried to keep his hold over her. He wrote to her from prison, reminding her that she was his "thing." He drew a picture for her that showed him, the former master, now a galley slave in chains with a chain leading from him to the hands of a woman he entitled "Ana." Between the two figures he drew a heart pierced by two arrows. The heart, he wrote, was Juan's, and the arrows were Ana's. Chaves did not indicate whether Juan and Ana saw the irony in the reversal of their roles.

Many people tried to maintain control over prostitutes who provided them with money, but others simply "pawned" women to the city brothels for a single lump sum. Fathers, brothers, boyfriends, or husbands sold women into brothels for ten or twenty ducats. A 1621 city ordinance reforming the administration of city brothels expressly prohibited the pawning of a woman to a brothel by a person to whom she owed a debt, even though she might agree to this arrangement. No woman, it asserted, should be sold into the brothels nor kept there to pay off a debt.

City regulations of the period encouraged prostitution because they made it more difficult for women to earn a living in other occupations. Streethawking, for example, was banned by city officials who suspected, with some justification, that streethawking was a cover for prostitutes and vagabonds. However, their attempts to ban street selling cut off the livelihood of many people who then turned to prostitution in earnest. One woman agreed to leave prostitution in 1572 if she could regain her place for selling fruit, which a public official had taken from her. Bartolomé Murillo, who painted saints and street people in seventeenth-century Seville, depicted streethawkers as quiet, rather serious young women trying to earn a living. City fathers, however, saw them as noisy, brazen price-gougers who threatened the peace of the city and their control of it.

The livelihood of another group of women was cut off by regulations on dramatic productions. Under pressure from clerics Philip II[2] prohibited all dramatic performances in 1598. Two years later the crown directed a group of theologians to draw up conditions for dramatic performances in Spain. Among other conditions, the theologians insisted that no women should be permitted to act in dramatic productions because "such public activity especially provokes a woman to boldness. . . . " A royal council agreed to the conditions, except that it allowed women to continue in dramatic companies so long as they were accompanied by husbands or fathers. With the licensing and limitations of dramatic companies, the reduction in the number of religious festivals, and the prohibition of certain dances in religious festivals, fortunes waned for actresses, dancers, and singers.

Sumptuary laws[3] were passed in the sixteenth and seventeenth centuries to prevent rich people from parading their wealth. Although they were aimed at the newly rich merchants and shippers who liked to dress and behave as nobles, the real victims of these laws were women workers. Prohibitions against silk and brocade fabrics reduced the jobs available for women in the silk industry and embroidery shops, while the limitation of the numbers of domestic servants meant that fewer women could earn a living as servants.

---

[2]King of Spain, 1556–1598.

[3]Sumptuary laws regulated and restrained personal extravagance, especially in dress and servants.

The Inquisition's campaign against heresy brought many folk practitioners and sorcerers to an unhappy end. The Holy Office[4] was not opposed to superstition so much as it wanted to control all uses of superstition. During the early modern period it increased its prosecution of women who challenged its monopoly. For example, a woman who was hanged in 1581 for practicing witchcraft and abortion was a Moor. As a member of this rival religious group, she challenged the Church's attempts to monopolize truth. In 1624, a twenty-two-year-old woman was burned in an *auto de fe*[5] because she claimed to have the power of knowing the future. She might have escaped notice by the Inquisition if she had been older and had quietly plied her occult gifts as a neighborhood *sabia* (wise woman). The Inquisition dealt very cautiously with madness, and it often treated people accused of witchcraft as lunatics or senile eccentrics who should be only mildly punished. Insanity could be used by the Church as a weapon to discredit its competitors, but the Church did allow it to remain as a protective shield for folk practitioners who continued their traditional profession as "María la loca"[6] or "Ana la fantastica."[7]

The practice of medicine became more tightly controlled during this period, and uneducated female practitioners suffered especially. A royal decree of 1593 required all medical practitioners to be licensed, and it prohibited women from having or dispensing medicines. In 1629 the mayor of Seville formally required that all midwives, as well as all other people practicing medicine, be examined and licensed by him within fifteen days. Noncomplying practitioners were subject to a fine of ten thousand *maravedís*. Since most midwives and folk practitioners were older women, their inability to obtain a license did not necessarily mean that they became prostitutes. However, it is very likely that they increasingly turned to the subsidiary occupations of prostitution, becoming procuresses, street bawds, and false "abbesses" who kept houses of prostitution.

Prostitution flourished in this city not only because it provided a livelihood for women who had few alternatives, but also because it was a commercial enterprise that supported a vast network of pimps, procuresses, property-owners, innkeepers, and renters of little rooms and secondhand clothing. Underworld people regarded prostitution as a business, referring to brothels as *aduanas* (customs houses) or *cambios* (exchanges). They called prostitutes *pelotas*, a word that usually means ball or toy, but a word that underworld people also used for a bag of money. Some women saw prostitution as their only means for survival, while others willingly entered prostitution

---

[4] Another term for the Inquisition.

[5] "Act of faith," a public ceremony that, after a procession, mass, and sermon, included the reading of the sentences. The Inquisition turned those sentenced for heresy over to the secular authority. The heretics were then burned at the stake.

[6] Mad Mary.

[7] Crazy Ann.

as commercial entrepreneurs. Whether women became prostitutes under duress, unable to find another livelihood and shake themselves free of an exploiting "friend," or whether they voluntarily chose this profession as offering the best livelihood in the city, the socioeconomic changes in early modern Seville disrupted traditional roles for women and encouraged increasing numbers to turn to prostitution.

One reason that Seville's social order survived the serious economic disruptions of this period was that city fathers used a widely accepted system of morality to preserve the hierarchy of authority. Prostitution itself was an integral party of the city's moral system. The connection between prostitution, morality, and social order is clearly evident in the three most popular female symbols of this period.

The Holy Virgin was elevated in the early seventeenth century through the doctrine of the Immaculate Conception[8] and stylized into the beautiful image still carried in the Holy Week processions of present-day Seville. Forever girl-like, forever grieving, with diamond teardrops on her cheeks and a dagger thrust into her breast, her head slightly bowed by the weight of the golden crown, she held out her hands for the cares and sorrows of the world.

The Virgin was a pillar of the moral order of the city. Young girls who were taught to emulate her example of chastity and modesty would be less likely to defy parental authority and run off with the wild young men of the streets. With their eyes on the Virgin, women who entered convents had a beautiful image of perfection through chastity and obedience. For married women, the Virgin also symbolized chastity and submission to authority; but in addition, she represented a curiously asexual and influential motherhood. As mother, the Virgin epitomized women who were "the pivot, the fulcrum, and hub of social relations of many, many people." Women could thus feel elevated, content with their social roles, and inspired to obedience. They would be chaste and modest, restricting sex to marriage and never endangering the social order or the system of property inheritance.

Men were considered to be much more active sexually than women, and this required another female symbol, the Painted Prostitute. Where women who emulated the Virgin were elevated above the weakness of the flesh, men were naturally expected to succomb to it, to seek sex outside marriage. If men lacked prostitutes to absorb their lust, who knew what would happen to an innocent woman walking along the street on a proper errand? The problem was to distinguish respectable women from those who served men's baser needs.

The Painted Prostitute represented depraved, sensual, commercial woman. Condemned for advertising herself in dress and manner, she was

[8]The Roman Catholic dogma holding that the Virgin Mary, from the moment of her conception, was free of original sin.

nevertheless required by law to wear a yellow hood so that she could be distinguished from the respectable women of the city. In distinction to the well-kept courtesan or flirtatious matron, she was often hungry and ill-dressed. She usually walked the city streets, unable to afford a sedan-chair or carriage. Sex to her was primarily a means of survival. She held out her hands like the Virgin, but she sought money rather than grieving hearts. She epitomized the unnatural, painting herself and publicizing her promiscuity. When syphilis appeared in Seville in the sixteenth century, she was blamed for spreading that disfiguring, often fatal, disease. This symbol, too, was a pillar for moral order, for the Painted Prostitute permitted the existence of a double standard for women and men and provided a clear example of how respectable women should not behave.

Occasionally, however, the example of the Painted Prostitute was not completely negative. Orphanage administrators and priests who tried to reform prostitutes understood that the examples of experienced pimps and prostitutes were as infectious as any diseases they might carry. The Jesuits[9] established a little house as a temporary haven for converted prostitutes, and they carefully separated those young women from the older "women of the world" who wanted to procure for them and make money from them. The Jesuits' temporary home did not solve the problem, however, and city officials continued to worry that converted prostitutes could still "infect" young girls with their examples. One administrator of a girls' orphanage wrote to the city council complaining about the city's practice of placing converted prostitutes in his institution. It was easier, he argued, for young orphan girls to follow the bad examples of these women then any good examples they might present.

Mary Magdalene, the converted prostitute in the stories of Jesus, was the third major female symbol of early modern Seville. Many clergymen taught that prostitution was an evil from which prostitutes and the entire city could be saved. They preached fervently to the prostitutes on the feast days of Mary Magdalene, and they gloried in counting their conversions. This symbol reinforced both their faith in converting sinners and their belief that extramarital, "commercial" sex was evil. In their view, unregulated sex threatened both social order and individual salvation.

A cult had grown up around the seductive figure of Mary Magdalene in the seventeenth century, perhaps a reaction to the puritanical tendencies of the sixteenth-century Counter Reformation. Mary Magdelene represented the delicious combination of sex and religion. Murillo[10] painted her as a voluptuous young woman gazing heavenward. Her expression suggests the rapture of earthy sexual delights as well as spiritual transport. She avoids looking the observer boldly in the eye, for she is an appropriately modest,

---

[9]Members of the Society of Jesus, a Roman Catholic religious order established in 1540.

[10]Bartolomé Esteban Murillo (1618–1682), Spanish painter and founder of the Academy of Seville.

but sensual, "bride of Christ." One explanation for her popularity is that she represented the love-goddess, Venus. Under the guise of pious devotion to a Church-approved saint, many people continued to venerate an ancient and traditional folk-goddess who covered sex with a cloak of religion.

The symbols of Virgin, Prostitute, and Mary Magdalene were as useful to city fathers as they were popular with all city residents. Through these symbols, city fathers demonstrated their authority to define good and evil. The image of the Holy Virgin sanctified political events and provided a single visible personification of good that was understood by the entire community. On the other hand, the Painted Prostitute personified sex outside marriage, sex without the responsibility of children and home, sex with the threat of disease. When unregulated sex threatened their society, they could point to the lessons of the Virgin, the Prostitute, and Mary Magdalene, which taught very clearly that women should be safely enveloped in a convent or marriage, obedient, chaste, and modestly accepting their places in the social hierarchy.

Some city fathers may have preferred to rely only on the Virgin to support their moral order, but the Painted Prostitute and Mary Magdalene appeared to be necessary corollaries. A social order acknowledging sexuality in men could not survive if men had to treat all women as the Virgin. Elevating women through this symbol seemed to require that they also be degraded to the status of prostitute. Sexuality in women was permitted only if it were the acknowledged evil of prostitution or the converted religious ecstasy of Mary Magdalene. Ironically, this moral system depended as much on symbols of evil as on symbols of perfection.

Francisco Farfan, a sixteenth-century cleric of Spain, recognized this upside-down morality of prostitution. In his treatise on avoiding the sins of fornication, Farfan presented an argument for the moral practicality of prostitution. He declared that the brothel was necessary to a society just as a latrine was needed in a house:

> The brothel in the city, then, is like the stable or latrine for the house. Because just as the city keeps itself clean by providing a separate place where filth and dung are gathered, etc., so, neither less nor more, assuming the dissolution of the flesh, acts the brothel: where the filth and ugliness of the flesh are gathered like the garbage and dung of the city.

To Farfan, the prohibition of prostitution was a greater evil than prostitution itself because a society without brothels encouraged homosexuality, incest, the propositioning of innocent women, and an increased number of people living together in sin. Farfan recognized the weakness of the flesh and believed that the only way to deal with it was to divert human behavior away from moral sins. In order to avoid moral sin, he argued, behavior must be controlled. Prostitution could support the moral order, but only if were closely regulated.

City fathers had long tried to control prostitution in Seville, but many nonlicensed prostitutes pursued their trade outside the confines of city-regulated brothels. These "lost women" were not lost at all geographically, for everyone in the city knew where to find them. Prostitutes gathered in several areas along the river bank, close to the port where many prospective clients entered the city. Prostitution also thrived in the poorer parts of the city that grew up along its margins and just outside its walls, such as the extramural parish of San Bernardo. Rents were undoubtedly lower in the marginal areas of the city and prostitutes could afford a room or a little shack. Since police power was less likely to invade the little alleyways on the edges of town, innkeepers here were probably less conscientious about keeping prostitutes out of their rooms. The 1568 syphilis epidemic in the city was called *"el contagio de San Gil"*[11] because it first broke out in San Gil, another parish bordering on the city's walls. Hospitals for victims of this epidemic were set up outside the city walls in the parish of San Bernardo.

Fear of disease is the major reason that the city government increased its efforts to regulate prostitution and limit it to the medically inspected, city-licensed brothels. Plagues passed from port to port in the early modern period and ravaged city populations. They posed a political threat as well as a very real physical danger, for the city in the throes of an epidemic was noted for neither law nor order. The machinery of local government frequently fell into paralysis and many officials died or disappeared. On the other hand, rumors of an epidemic so frightened city residents that they were willing for their local governments to greatly expand regulations. City fathers in Seville extended their powers when disease threatened, particularly over prostitutes who were commonly suspected of passing on plagues. Clients of prostitutes, after all, often entered the city from a ship that had arrived in port, and prostitutes could easily contract any diseases they carried and pass them on into the city. Prostitutes were more susceptible to illness, too, if they were the poorer women who were undernourished and used secondhand clothing and bedding that frequently carried disease.

Syphilis arrived in Seville in the sixteenth century, bringing death and disfigurement to thousands and frightening the city government to redouble its efforts to regulate prostitution. The city council appointed medical inspectors to examine prostitutes and recommend action against this disease. One doctor warned that the city's health was endangered by the bad condition of lettuce and deer's tongue (a plant) that were being sold in the city brothels as remedies for syphilis. A surgeon reported in 1572 that infected prostitutes dismissed from the city brothels were spreading their infection as they plied their trade in other parts of the city. He urged that Seville not merely discharge sick prostitutes from brothels, but also deliver them to hospitals for treatment. In the early seventeenth century, the administrator of city brothels countered clergymen's proposals to close public brothels. He argued that this action would not end prostitution, but merely deregulate it and damage the health and well-being of the city. If prostitutes were not

---

[11] The disease of San Gil.

confined to city-licensed and medically inspected brothels, he said, they would scatter throughout the city, free to spread disease and provoke quarrels and murders.

Seville lacked hospital space, however, to confine all its syphilitic prostitutes. Several hospitals would not accept people with any contagious disease. In the last part of the sixteenth century the *Hospital de San Cosme y San Damian* was knows as "*las Bubas*" because it was designated to treat syphilitics, or those with pustules (*bubas*) resulting from "*la mal frances.*"[12] Unfortunately, this hospital had only forty beds, and only twelve were for infected women. Patients here were treated for thirty days with... a medicinal water made with bark.

Most treatments for syphilis were ineffective, and it became a sixteenth-century successor of leprosy. It flourished despite city attempts to detect and isolate infected people. When Pedro de Leoff[13] began working with the people in the city brothels in the late sixteenth century, he found many who were ill. He described the illness as "hideous," causing great pain and many pustules. Many times it resulted in death. He also reported that a number of young boys frequented brothels. The 1621 ordinances to reform the ancient regulations on prostitution in the city prohibited the city brothels from admitting boys under the age of fourteen, adding that many "boys of a tender age" had become infected in the brothels. The infected prostitute released from city-licensed brothels could continue her trade as long as she was able to, but when her infection became so obvious that she could no longer get clients, she was as likely to die from starvation as from infection.

It is not surprising that the little houses of a brothel were sometimes called "*boticas,*" a word also used for pharmacies or little shops. Prostitutes were traditionally suspected of suing potions, herbs, ointments, and pessaries as contraceptives. In the sixteenth century they also began to use herbal preparations to treat syphilis infections, and it has been suggested that men first used contraceptive sheaths in brothels as a means to prevent venereal infection. Prostitutes and procuresses knew many other forms of contraception. They prepared pessaries and ointments from herbs and dung. They made amulets, such as a seed of sorrel enclosed in a cloth bag, which was believed to prevent contraception as long as it was carried on the left arm. They mixed alum and the yellow pulp of pomegranate to make vaginal pessaries, and they practiced some numerical magic, such as jumping backwards seven or nine times after coitus to prevent conception. Prostitutes were closely associated with the practice of abortion as well, and they and their older female companions also prepared aphrodisiacs. The brothel as pharmacy represented the evil of illicit sex supported by an unlicensed folk medicine that bordered on magic. It challenged both the Church's claim to monopolize magic and the city's presumption to license doctors. Thus

[12]The French disease, as the Spanish called syphilis.

[13]Spanish Jesuit known for his missionary work among the common people.

the brothel called even more urgently for close regulation, for churchmen and city officials feared folk customs that flourished independently of their control.

Concern with increasing public disorder also pushed city fathers into more energetic regulation of prostitution. The growing numbers of ships sailing between Seville and the New World brought increased numbers of soldiers and sailors to the city in the sixteenth and seventeenth centuries. Fights over women often ended in huge street brawls. Confining prostitutes to city-licensed brothels could prevent many quarrels, fights, and crimes. It could also get rid of the swarms of streetwalkers and children or false beggars who acted as procurers.

Closely related to the desire to keep public order was the desire to protect property. When a captain wrote the city council to complain that ships in the port were being robbed and damaged, he asserted that men were robbing the ships in order to give money to the "bad women" who lived in little houses in the area of the port. Other residents complained of property damaged in the brawls that began over women.

Confining prostitutes in licensed brothels prevented some property damage, and it also protected the interests of those who owned the property used as the city brothels.... [P]roperty used as city-licensed brothels in the last part of the sixteenth century was owned by city officials and religious corporations, including the Cathedral council. These owners leased the property to private individuals, who then rented it to various prostitutes. In 1571, owners of the houses used by the city brothel included a *veinticuatro* (one of the city's oligarchy of nobles, originally twenty-four), an official of the *Santa Hermandad* (a national law enforcement association promoted by the crown), and an *alguazil de los veynte* (one of the twenty sheriffs with major law enforcement responsibilities). In 1604 the houses of the city brothel were rented by the sheriff, Francisco Vélez, who collected a daily rent of one and one-half *reales* from each prostitute....

The city government's proprietary interest in the licensed brothels is evident in the time and money it spent administering, inspecting, and repairing them. The city government appointed "*padres*,"[14] or administrators of city-licensed brothels. In the last part of the sixteenth century, there were three *padres*, each the head of a separate house licensed by the city. The 1621 ordinances limited the number of *padres* to two and required that they swear to uphold the laws of the city. These ordinances also prohibited the *padres* from renting clothing or bedding to prostitutes and from accepting "pawned" women in the brothels, two prohibitions that were also contained in a set of 1570 royal ordinances.

Brothel administrators often requested that the city repair walls and gates that seemed to crumble rapidly in the dampness of the river air and the harshness of their use. In 1590, for example, one *padre* reported to the city

---

[14]Fathers. The word was used also for priests.

council that the gate for the brothel had been destroyed, allowing ruffians to mistreat the prostitutes, destroy the little houses of the brothel, and steal doors and other materials. Other *padres* invited the city council to send a deputation to visit the brothel and see for themselves that repairs were necessary.

City officials inspected the brothels not only to maintain the value of their real estate, but also to preserve the value of the human property contained in their brothels. Three officials accompanied the canon of the Church of San Salvador on July 22, 1620, when he visited the brothels to preach to the prostitutes and try to convert them. Immediately after the visit, the officials announced that they would bring a doctor to examine the prostitutes. They fined one *padre* twelve *reales* for receiving an unlicensed prostitute into the brothel, and she was ordered to leave under penalty of one hundred lashes. Another prostitute was ordered to leave the brothel because she appeared ill and could infect the others. A third prostitute was ordered to leave because of her age; she had been in the brothel too long. Evidently, city officials were as concerned to have attractive prostitutes in their brothels as they were to prevent epidemics of syphilis.

Prostitution made sound business sense not only to the procurers and owners of brothels, but also to the charitable benefactors who were unable to provide every poor girl of the city with a dowry or a job. As demands for charity increased in the last part of the sixteenth century, many city fathers concluded that practicality outweighed morality in the question of prostitution. They saw that it was an evil, but they agreed that it was better to accept it and regulate it than to forbid it and send converted prostitutes to seek a nonexistent livelihood. Even the optimistic and diligent Pedro de León, who worked so hard to convert women from prostitution, admitted the difficulty of finding husbands, parents, or jobs for converted prostitutes. The 1667 survey of the poor in Seville is filled with the names of young women of marriageable age unable to marry because they were too poor, unable to find work, and doomed to die from starvation. City fathers who owned brothels could thus argue that these brothels benefited the entire community because they provided a livelihood for other destitute women. It is not surprising, then, that the city council listened sympathetically to a *padre* of a brothel when he complained bitterly about "strange clergymen" and pious laymen ... who were driving women away from city-licensed brothels. To most city fathers, prostitution was not only thinkable; it was practical.

"Lost women" were not lost at all in early modern Seville. They lived within the specific social and economic conditions of their city, and prostitution was one response to these conditions. More than lost, they were used. Prostitution was commercially profitable for city fathers as well as street people. It reinforced the authority of the ruling class over unmarried women, folk-practitioners, sailors, youths, and quick-fisted dandies. Prostitution was even a form of public assistance, providing jobs for women who would otherwise starve. It strengthened moral attitudes that supported the city's hierarchy of authority, and it permitted the city oligarchy to demonstrate its authority to define and confine evil. Under the guise of public health and public order, it extended the powers of city government. If prostitution was a symptom of social disease, it was also an example of social adaptation. In Seville prostitution helped to preserve the existing social order. It became a useful, practical political tool.

Sexual Politics and Religious Reform in the Witch Hunts

JOSEPH KLAITS

During the age of the European witch hunts, which lasted from approximately 1450 to 1650, perhaps 100,000 people were executed by burning, strangulation, or hanging. Fifty thousand died in the slaughter in Germany alone. Countless others were exiled or sentenced to prison, often after having been tortured. Some were even acquitted and returned to their community to be treated as outcasts.

In the last twenty years, the witch hunts have interested a number of historians, whose research has added greatly to our knowledge of the alleged witches and those who persecuted them. But much is still not clear. For example, why did the hunts begin during the Renaissance and Scientific Revolution, supposed periods of intellectual advance? Certainly the belief in witches was not new, yet the so-called medieval "Dark Ages" witnessed no hunt for witches. Some scholars locate the origins of the hunts in folklore, theology, heresy, and changes in the law. Some look to the practice of ceremonial magic among socially prominent individuals or to the development of a fictitious stereotype of a small, secret sect of night-flying witches who met regularly and, with the aid of the devil, engaged in ritual murder, cannibalism, incest, and other antihuman activities, and strove to destroy Christian society.

The reasons for the rather sudden end of the witch hunts in the mid-seventeenth century are not clear, either. The overwhelming majority of Europeans continued to believe in the reality of the devil and witches long after courts ceased prosecuting for witchcraft. Did judges experience a crisis of conscience, unsure of their ability to determine if the person before them was a witch? Did the Scientific Revolution's conception of a universe operating through natural law convince those in control of the mechanisms of persecution that Satan's personal intervention would contradict the regularity of nature and was therefore impossible? Or did the fires of the great witch hunts run their course, with Europeans suffering burnout, exhaustion from the constant fear of witches and from each individual's fear that someday she, too, might be accused? Possibly the decline of religious intensity in post-Reformation Europe could explain the diminished concern with Satan.

In this selection, Joseph Klaits discusses first of all the relationship of sexuality to the stereotype of the witch. Why was witchcraft primarily a woman's crime?

(During this era, more women were killed for witchcraft than for all other capital crimes put together.) What were the sexual elements in the idea of the witches' sabbat? Who was the typical witch and what characteristics did she have? Does Klaits's emphasis on the role of sexuality in the hunts help to explain why approximately 80 percent of those accused as witches were women? Why, then, were males accused at all?

Second, Klaits stresses the importance of spiritual reform as a cause of the increased persecution of witches. How does he argue that the reformers of both the Protestant Reformation and the Catholic Counter Reformation share responsibility for stoking the fires of the witch hunts? How did the war on popular religion by the elite and the subsequent "Christianization" of Europe contribute to the hunt for witches? Klaits sees misogyny (woman-hating) as a significant part of the Christian tradition and argues, furthermore, that Christian misogyny increased during the sixteenth and seventeenth centuries. What sexual and misogynistic prejudices influenced judges to prosecute witches?

Finally, Klaits links the misogyny of witch hunters to the movements for religious reform. Why does he believe that spiritual reform combined with this new emphasis on sexuality helps explain the intensity of the hunts for witches?

Why did the number of witch trials in Western Europe increase greatly after about 1550? Why did the crime of witchcraft, familiar for centuries, suddenly appear so much more menacing that thousands of trials unfolded between 1550 and 1700, whereas only a few hundred seem to have occurred earlier? . . .

. . . My thesis is that changes in sexual attitudes can help explain both the metamorphosing definitions of witchcraft and the role of reforming religious ideologies in creating the environment in which witch hunting flourished.

Consider first, by way of review, the stages of evolution in the concept of witchcraft. . . . [T]he meaning of witchcraft changed around the turn of the fifteenth century. Before 1375 or so, witchcraft almost always meant sorcery, i.e., maleficent magic. In the early trials of this period, the crime was defined as harm inflicted on a victim by such magical means as spells or potions. Making an image of the victim and then breaking off a leg to cause a neighbor's lameness or inducing reciprocated affection by administering a charmed drink—these were the typical offenses of fourteenth-century witch trials. Usually in these early trials there was no mention of the devil or demons. When a demon did appear, it was generally as the servant of the witch, who had invoked demonic aid to accomplish evil magic.

After 1375, and especially during the last two-thirds of the fifteenth century, a new definition of witchcraft emerged. In some clerical treatises and torture-elicited confessions, witchcraft was pictured as a combination of traditional sorcery and a novel diabolism. The witch was no longer merely a worker of malefice. She was also a servant of the devil. Clerics explained a witch's supernatural powers as the manifestation of abilities granted her by Satan, a point of view that conformed well with Aristotelian views of causation. It seemed implausible to these writers and judges that witches could do their mischief without demonic assistance, and they cast the witch as worshiper of the devil. This new definition of the crime of witchcraft overlay the older one of the witch as sorcerer.... [I]n the initial stage of a trial, when one villager accused another, only sorcery was attributed to the witch. But, when elite authorities intervened, they introduced the issue of devil worship into the proceedings. By the 1480s, when the classic witch-hunting treatise, the *Malleus Maleficarum,*[1] was first published, the image of the witch as evildoing devil worshiper was firmly established in elite consciousness.

An analysis of Europe's witch craze can begin either at the top of society or at the bottom. One may choose to emphasize changes in the outlook of the educated elites, both clerical and secular. Or one can stress the role of popular agitation for witch trials. But these mirror-image interpretive frameworks need not be regarded as mutually exclusive. It seems entirely reasonable to expect that the witch craze, like most other complex historical episodes, cannot be explained in accord with a single theoretical model, no matter how thoughtful or sophisticated. Instead, this book argues that witch-hunting impulses both trickled down from society's leaders and rose upward on a tide of popular anxieties.

Moreover, the cultural distance between elites and populace was not at all fixed. Especially in the later stages of the witch craze, ideas and practices characteristic of society's upper echelons had penetrated deeply into village life. Thus, higher and lower cultures should be regarded not as separate compartments but as overlapping categories with many points of contact. Witch hunting was one of the most dramatic areas of overlap. In the witch trials, members of the elites and ordinary folk found a common cause.

This [selection] discusses the impulses for witch trials that came from the educated and the politically powerful. It dwells on the concerns of the elites with spiritual reform in general and sexual reform in particular. The intention here is to show the impact that changing values among the educated had on ordinary folk, who were at the receiving end of reforming religious evangelism and made up the great majority of witches and their accusers....

... After 1550, most European witch trials were of criminals who were said to be not only Satan's worshipers but his sexual slaves as well. Occasionally in the fifteenth century we read in learned treatises of witches who engage in perverse sexual practices. It was only during the witch craze itself, however, that the charge of sexual abuse became a normal component of a witchcraft indictment. As in the case of the introduction of devil worship in the fifteenth century, charges of sexual trespassing were introduced from above. They appear only rarely in the initial accusations but were raised by prosecutors predisposed to see the witch as a sex offender. A preoccupation with the sexual side of witchcraft is the feature that most clearly differentiates the witch stereotype of the sixteenth and seventeenth centuries from the earlier era of small-scale witch hunting.

[1] *The Hammer of Witches* (1486), written by Heinrich Kramer and Jakob Sprenger.

The ways in which people dealt with sexual matters had an enormous impact on witch trials. The witch craze often has been described as one of the most terrible instances of man's inhumanity to man. But more accurate is a formulation by gender, not genus: witch trials exemplify men's inhumanity to women. The sexually powerful and menacing witch figure was nearly always portrayed as a female. For example, the authors of the *Malleus Maleficarum* were convinced that the great majority of witches were women. And, like a self-fulfilling diagnosis, women comprised the overwhelming bulk of the accused during the witch craze. Evidence from about 7,500 witch trials in diverse regions of Europe and North America during the sixteenth and seventeenth centuries shows that nearly 80 percent of accused witches were female, and, in parts of England, Switzerland, and what is now Belgium, women accounted for over nine out of ten victims. This disproportion was far greater than in earlier witchcraft trials, when men had comprised close to half of the accused. Further, these numbers understate the predominance of women, because many of the accused men were implicated solely due to their connection with female suspects. Thus, in the English county of Essex, where only twenty-three of 291 accused witches were men, eleven were either husbands of an accused witch or were jointly indicted with one.

Everywhere, witchcraft was a woman's crime. Those who advocated witch trials saw nothing remarkable in this sexual imbalance. It conformed perfectly with the dominant notions of female inferiority, while it confirmed the legitimacy of woman-hatred with each new case. A circular process of great force, the dynamics of the witch trials were one expression of deep-seated misogyny in early modern times. Indeed, this [selection] will argue that the witch trials were symptomatic of a dramatic rise in fear and hatred of women during the era of the Reformation.

To illustrate the centrality of sexual imagery in the picture of the witch during the peak period of witch hunting, consider one of the most influential descriptions of a supposed witches' sabbat. This account comes from Pierre de Lancre, counselor in the Parlement[2] of Bordeaux and prosecutor, under King Henry IV's[3] commission, of hundreds of female witch suspects in the predominantly Basque region of the Labourd in southwestern France. In 1609, de Lancre sent more than eighty women to the stake in one of the largest of the French witch hunts. Three years later, he published his *Tableau de l'inconstance des mauvais anges et démons.*[4] This is a lengthy work describing the evil deeds of the Basque witches, and prominently featured in it is an extended report on the witches' sabbat.

De Lancre portrayed the sabbat as a lurid affair attended by numerous witches who flew in from considerable distances on broomsticks, shovels,

[2] A sovereign judicial court.
[3] King of France, 1589–1610.
[4] *Description of the Inconstancy of Evil Angels and Demons.*

spits, or a variety of domestic animals. Some sabbats were attended by as many as twelve thousand witches, though most meetings were of more manageable scale. The devil might appear to his congregants as a three-horned goat, a huge bronze bull, or a serpent, but, whatever his guise, de Lancre's informers rarely failed to mention his large penis and scaly testicles. A festive air prevailed, reminiscent of a wedding or court celebration. Generally, the proceedings began with the witches kissing their master's rear. Then each witch reported malefice she had carried out since the last sabbat. Those with nothing to report were whipped. The business meeting concluded, a work session followed, during which the women industriously concocted poisons and ointments out of black bread and the rendered fat of murdered infants. Having built up an appetite, they next banqueted on babies' limbs and toads, foods variously reviewed as succulent or awful-tasting. Then the devil presided over a parody of the Mass. Finally, the social hour: the naked witches danced lasciviously, back to back, until the dancing turned into a sexual orgy that continued to the dawn. Incest and homosexual intercourse were encouraged. Often the devil would climax the proceedings by copulating—painfully, it was generally reported—with every man, woman, and child in attendance, as mothers yielded to Satan before their daughters' eyes and initiated them into sexual service to the diabolical master. . . .

Such was de Lancre's account of the sabbat, boiled down from his two hundred pages of detailed description. In this portrayal the sexual elements are of course very prominent. The powerfully sexual nature of the dominant imagery begins with the broomstick ride, continues with exciting whippings, the fascinating close-up look at devilishly huge sexual organs, the baby-eating (possibly sublimated incest or infanticide?), and, finally, the frenzied orgy itself.

The important place of the sabbat in de Lancre's book and in other demonological works of the late sixteenth and early seventeenth centuries is all the more striking when we note that the witches' sabbat was not a prominent feature in earlier formulations of the witch stereotype. The sabbat does not appear, for example, in the *Malleus Maleficarum*, the most widely circulated demonological treatise of the fifteenth century, and it is encountered infrequently before 1500. Earlier, the image of the witch was that of a rather isolated individual. Witches might get together in small groups to stir their cauldrons, . . . but, until the era of the Reformation, few writers thought in terms of large prayer meetings devoted to the adoration of Satan. The *Malleus*, like other early demonological works, had discussed witches' ability to "tie the knot" and cause impotence. It also pictured witches as the sexual partners of demons in human form. In later witch-hunting treatises, sexual overtones became the leading theme of demonological imagery, and the sabbat emerged as the central focus of the witch hunters' fantasies. Not only de Lancre but nearly every continental demonologist of the era of the witch craze laid great stress on the sabbat as the occasion for witches to express their perverse sexuality.

Along similar lines, witch-hunting judges regularly warned that a sure sign of witchcraft was the presence on a woman's body of the so-called devil's mark. This was an insensible spot or anesthetic scar with which Satan branded a woman (like a slave) when initiating her into witchcraft. Related to this idea, though somewhat less common, was the belief that the witch had an extra nipple through which to suckle her familiar or incubus.[5] Any wart, mole, or other skin growth on the accused's body might be identified as a devil's mark or witch's tit. Since the devil would of course do his best to hide the evidence of his servant's fidelity, it was deemed necessary to conduct a thorough, formal search. In practice, this meant stripping and shaving the accused's entire body before meticulously examining and pricking every part of her. Such inspections were usually conducted by physicians or surgeons, but sometimes by midwives or other women, before an all-male audience. In Scotland, witch pricking was the specialty of men who made a profession of the search for the devil's mark. There, as in some other places, it was common for suspects to undergo repeated examinations until a devil's mark was discovered. The devil's mark was unknown in popular beliefs about witchcraft, and even early demonologists like the authors of the *Malleus* had never heard of it. After 1560, however, the search for the mark became an ordinary feature of witchcraft investigations, particularly in Protestant lands, where strong emphasis was placed on the witch's pact with the devil.

In the republic of Geneva, this ceremony of stripping and probing took place regularly in the more than two hundred recorded trials of women for witchcraft, although failure to find a devil's mark on the accused often sufficed to save her from a death sentence in Genevan courts. The Genevan judges' unusually high standards of proof were condemned by commentators of the time, who no doubt would have been even more critical had they known that only about one-fifth of the republic's accused witches wound up at the stake. This was one of the lowest execution ratios anywhere in Europe. Genevan witch suspects, however, were typical of their counterparts elsewhere in their preponderantly rural origins. About half of Geneva's accused witches were peasants from the city's rural dependencies, even though these hamlets accounted for only about 20 percent of the republic's total population. That an urban, reformed patriciate regularly subjected country women to the rape-like humiliation of the search for the devil's mark is an indicator of elite suspicions about rural sexual habits and of the dehumanizing consequences that such suspicions could produce, even among relatively careful and lenient judges.

Another sign of the authorities' preconceptions about female sexuality was their association of the devil's mark with women's genitals.

---

[5] A male demon who had intercourse with a woman.

Demonological experts warned judges that women often bore the devil's mark on their "shameful parts," "on the breasts or private parts." As a seventeenth-century handbook for English justices of the peace pointed out, because "these the Devil's Marks...be often in women's secretest Parts, they therefore require diligent and careful Search." One witch suspect in the Swiss canton of Fribourg contemptuously chided her judges for their naivete about female anatomy. After the prosecutors discovered what they took to be a devil's mark on her genitals, Ernni Vuffiod informed them that "if this was a sign of witchcraft, many women would be witches." The same part of the female body received careful attention from judges at the Salem witch trials. The women examiners employed by the courts reported that they found on three suspects "a preternatural excresence of flesh between the pudendum and the anus, much like teats, and not usual in women." A Scottish witch always was searched with similar thoroughness to discover "marks...between her thys and her body." ...

By about 1560, the witch stereotype had taken on all its menacing features. The witch was not only what she had been for centuries in popular imagination—a source of mischief and misfortune. Now, in the eyes of learned judges, she was much more—one of a vast number of devil worshipers who had yielded to Satan in the most repulsive ways and become his sexual servant. This newer definition of the witch as sexual servant and member of a large devil-worshiping cult became even more frightening to those in authority than the witch's power to inflict malefice. The change can be measured in the law. For example, the *Carolina*, the German imperial law code promulgated in the 1530s, punished alleged witches more severely if they could be shown to have brought harm to their neighbors. But the Saxon criminal code of the 1570s, which was widely imitated throughout Germany and Scandinavia, mandated death by fire for *any* dealing with the devil, regardless of whether the accused had brought about harm by magical means.

This reformulation of the law of witchcraft reflected the new view, frequently expressed in witch hunters' manuals published after 1560, that the real root of the witch's crime was her allegiance to Satan. The change can be dated precisely in Scotland, where the statute on witchcraft passed in 1563 defined the crime as malefice. It made no mention of dealings with Satan. But, by the 1590s, the decade of the first large Scottish witch hunts, the meaning of witchcraft had been altered. As on the continent, the offense now lay in the witch's pact with Satan and her promise of servitude. Accusations of malefice usually were not enough to condemn a suspected witch. Because evidence of the demonic pact was essential for conviction, the search for the devil's mark became an inevitable part of Scottish witch trials. ...

The triumph of this updated image of the witch as the sabbat-attending sexual servant of the devil coincided with a dramatic rise in the rate of witchcraft prosecution. For all of Europe during the last two-thirds of the fifteenth century, about three hundred witch trials have been verified.

Between 1560 and 1680 Germany alone experienced thousands of such trials. The important changes in the meaning of witchcraft and the tremendous increase in trial incidences during the era of religious reform have sometimes been played down by scholars searching for the medieval origins of witch hunting. We should remember, however, that the new stereotype of the witch current among the elites seems to have evoked far more intense fears than had earlier images of witchcraft. This redefinition set the stage for the witch craze.

It was not simply a matter of more witch trials; specifically, more women were accused of trafficking with the devil. Before 1400, when witchcraft meant sorcery, only a bare majority—50 to 60 percent—of accused witches were women. In the fifteenth century, as witchcraft became equated with diabolism, . . . the proportion of female accused rising to between 60 and 70 percent. During the witch craze itself, the preponderance of women increased still further. Over Europe as a whole in this period about 80 percent of witch suspects were women, and in some places women accounted for more than nine out of ten accused witches.

These figures suggest that originally witchcraft was not viewed specifically as a woman's crime. The stereotypical medieval sorcerer said to engage in image magic, spell casting, or the concoction of love potions was frequently perceived as a male figure learned in the arcane and dangerous science of ritual magic. As the crime was redefined in the fifteenth century to stress servitude to the devil, however, witchcraft became a gender-linked offense; women, the witch-hunting manuals repeated, were morally weaker than men and therefore were more likely to succumb to satanic temptation. The linkage thus forged became even stronger when, during the sixteenth and seventeenth centuries, lay and clerical elites came to see the witch as Satan's sexual servant. The one-fifth of witch suspects in Scotland who were men, for example, do not appear to have been accused of any sexual relationship with the devil, unlike their female counterparts. As witchcraft became identified with sexual trespasses in the minds of reforming witch hunters, its gender-linked status was greatly reinforced. . . .

The coming of the witch craze was one manifestation of the impact of spiritual reform in the sixteenth and seventeenth centuries. The twin movements of the Protestant Reformation and the Catholic Counter Reformation (referred to collectively, for convenience, as the Reformation) created a new ideology that profoundly affected all aspects of European life. The reformers—both Catholic and Protestant—saw spiritual matters as the core of human identity. In this they resembled earlier Christian leaders, but they broke decisively with the medieval past in their systematic, persistent attempts to Christianize peasants and other ordinary folk. In the reformers' ideology, Christianity was not just a matter for a few religious specialists, such as monks or priests, as had been the de facto situation in the Middle Ages. Instead, the reformers believed that each member of the community should lead a Christian life. This conviction gave all branches of reform their great stress on missionary work. As evangelists spreading the faith, the godly reformers preached and taught at all levels of European society. Their educational efforts met with considerable success, for members of the lay elites and even lower social groups adopted the values and habits required by the new doctrines of spiritual reform. In this way the ideology of the religious elite came to be a potent political and social force. Embraced by rulers, judges, and other authorities and imposed on popular classes, the ideas of godly reform penetrated deeply into European culture during the era of the witch craze. A "Christianization" of Europe in the sixteenth and seventeenth centuries was probably the major long-term result of the upsurge in spirituality that occurred during the Reformation era.

The reformers, whether Catholic or Protestant, were militants who saw the world as the scene of cosmic conflict between forces of good and evil. They were inclined to detect evidence of deviant practices everywhere. The new stereotype of the witch reflected the religious and lay authorities' concern with religious dissidents in strife-torn Reformation Europe. The witch hunters' image of collective devil worship at the sabbat undoubtedly derived in part from their knowledge of secret religious services that persecuted minorities were resorting to in many areas of Europe. Authorities predisposed to suspicions of clandestine conventicles gathering under their noses were ready to believe that large numbers of devil worshipers were also in their midst. Worth noting in this regard is the symbolism of the witches' sabbat, which reveals the authorities' belief that devil worshipers were reversing Christian ceremonial. Making an obscenity of the holy kiss, turning consecrated bread into devil's food—these, like the diabolical stigmata of the devil's mark, were the blasphemies that the orthodox expected from their heretical enemies, whether they were labeled Catholics, Protestants, or witches.

More generally, the Reformation was the occasion for renewed concern with the power of Satan in the world. Leading Protestant and Catholic reformers, continuing the tradition of late medieval Latin Christianity, laid great stress on satanic imagery. For example, in the catechism of the leading Jesuit reformer Peter Canisius, the name Satan appears sixty-seven times, four more than Jesus' name. Martin Luther believed that the devil was lord of this world; . . . he held that visible reality and all things of the flesh belonged to Satan. . . . And John Calvin,[6] who saw humans so yoked to sin that they could do nothing to save themselves, pictured human will as the captive of Satan's wiles, in most cases abandoned by God to the devil's power. . . .

Mainstream reformers and religious radicals seem to have been equally deeply concerned about Satan. John Rogers, the seventeenth-century English sectarian, admitted to seeing devils in every tree and bush. For years he slept with his hands clasped in a praying position, so that he would be ready if

[6]1509–1564, French Protestant theologian, founder of Calvinism and religious leader of Geneva.

Satan came for him during the night. As a boy Rogers was haunted by "fear of Hell and the devils, whom I thought I saw every foot in several ugly shapes and forms, according to my fancies, and sometimes with great rolling flaming eyes like saucers, having sparkling firebrands in one of their hands, and with the other reaching at me to tear me away to torments."

It may be hard to take seriously today the idea of a personal devil who brings bad weather, illness, or other misfortune, but the image was vividly real to the religious reformers and those who came under their influence....

Belief in the devil proved a psychological necessity for many people, as the intensely introspective habits and preoccupation with sin encouraged by all branches of reformed Catholic and Protestant Christianity apparently heightened feelings of inadequacy and moral responsibility. Thus, there was created powerful psychological pressure to project the resulting guilt feelings onto an external personage, the devil, if not onto the devil's human servant, a witch. Meanwhile, the Reformation era's profound political and social upheavals seemed clear proof of Satan's increased activity. Rival groups regularly cast their enemies as representatives of the devil, just as they viewed themselves as fighters on the side of God.

After 1560, clerics and other members of the elites who were influenced by reforming ideals came to interpret many folk practices as devilish and heretical. The representatives of reformed religion had little tolerance of the folklorized Christianity that had been the everyday religion of most people in the Middle Ages. Imbued with a new sense of doctrinal purity, they sought to root out all popular practices that did not flow from official teaching. Reformers labored to inculcate Christian doctrine and moral codes of behavior formerly unheard of in the European countryside. These strong missionary efforts brought the reformers into conflict with deeply traditional folk practices. In such combat the godly saw themselves fighting on one of the many fronts in the war against heresy.

Partly because elite culture laid so much stress on satanic imagery, the reformers were predisposed to find heretical dualism in the folkways of the uneducated. What they discovered in the backwoods horrified the missionaries. In Brittany, for example, peasants believed that buckwheat was not made by God but by Satan. When they harvested this grain, the staple of the poor family's diet, they threw handfuls into the ditches around the field as a thanksgiving offering to the devil. Many purifying missionaries were alarmed to discover rural folk who believed that Satan was coequal with God or that good and evil stemmed from separate forces....

... Although the Catholic church prescribed sacraments and exorcism for warding off Satan, and Protestants counseled prayer, ordinary people had invented their own remedies. The Breton peasants' buckwheat offering was typical of popular techniques for controlling evil. In general, Satan was not nearly as horrifying in folk imagery as he was in the minds of most theologians. Popular theatricals in medieval towns had featured entertaining demon-figures who danced on the scene amid exploding firecrackers. Yet these devils were defeated by Christ before the final bows. In the popular plays, even the most degenerate sinner could escape hell through a simple act of devotion to a powerful saint like the Virgin Mary.

Folklore stressed Mary's ability to cheat the devil even of his rightful prey, but to the reforming elites of the sixteenth and seventeenth centuries this was too easy a solution. Even the Catholic Counter Reformation, which, unlike Protestantism, retained the cultic veneration of saints, imagined the devil as a dreadful personage whom God permitted to operate in the world as appropriate punishment for the misdeeds of sinners. Michelangelo's depiction of the Last Judgment in the Sistine Chapel reflects the pessimistic spirit of the reformers in its representation of Christ and demons cooperating in sending the damned to hell, while Mary turns away from the doomed sinners' desperate pleas for intercession with her son. After 1560, the godly reformers labored hard to impress on the populace a much more menacing image of the devil. Popular religious plays were suppressed, and the semi-comic folk-demon of the later Middle Ages was replaced by the deadly Satan long familiar in elite culture. . . .

. . . Whether known as wizards, magicians, or cunning men, these were the leading therapeutic operatives of pre-Reformation rural Europe. . . . [T]hey were called on by peasants to heal the sick, recover stolen property, or foretell the future. In general, they functioned as protectors of the community against the invisible world of demonic evil. Magicians used herbal medicines, amulets, incantations, and elaborate rituals as their stock in trade. . . .

The existence of popular magic as a universal feature of medieval and early modern village life is testimony to the failure of institutional Christianity to penetrate into rural Europe before the Reformation era. The functions of protection and reassurance carried out by these popular practitioners paralleled certain of the functions of sacramental Christianity. Many Christian rituals were based on the invocation of God's protection for the participants, as in the priest's blessing of a maritime village's fishing fleet before the boats set out to sea. But, because the pre-Reformation clergy tended to be highly neglectful, the psychologically necessary protective role was often performed by magicians. By turning to these practitioners, the populace was in effect rejecting institutional religion. This, at any rate, was the conclusion drawn by the newly energized reforming clergy in Protestant and Catholic Europe during the sixteenth and seventeenth centuries. In this period individual magicians were regularly denounced and sometimes . . . prosecuted for sorcery. In the duchy of Lorraine, where demonologists were especially adamant about the criminality of magical healing, judges threatened and tortured witch doctors until they admitted satanic origins for their curative skills. This was one side of the war on popular religion waged during the Reformation era, as clerical and lay elites associated folk magic with libertinage, atheism, and heresy in general. Paradoxically, the authorities' campaigns against these practitioners of "white magic" may have strengthened the impulse to hunt out witches. For, if recourse to magical healers was denied, an effective technique of self-help against misfortune disappeared. Only the machinery of official witchcraft trials remained to protect the bewitched and the fearful from malefice....

The foregoing analysis may help explain the rise of a new form of the witchcraft stereotype in the environment of confessional antagonisms and revivified spirituality characteristic of the Reformation era. Yet such a line of argument is really too general to get at the issue of women and witchcraft. The problem remains: why was it generally a female who was identified as the witch? To approach this question from another angle, let us consider some of the main points of Christian tradition on the subjects of woman and sexuality.

Traditions of woman-hatred long antedate the era of the witch craze, of course. Many cultures of the ancient world regarded women as second-class members of humanity or worse, and the male fear of female domination is reflected in myths of diverse cultures. Christian traditions echoed this bias. Despite the strong emphasis placed on the equality of all Christians before God, from earliest times the Catholic church limited the priesthood to men, stressing, as Pope Paul VI reaffirmed in 1977, that the original models of Christian action, Jesus and the apostles, were all males. Although the cult of Mary developed in the Middle Ages, the church insisted that only the status of virginity and the role of motherhood could glorify the female condition. In the serious business of sanctification, even motherhood has disturbed Catholic leaders; there have been very few female saints who were not virgins throughout their lives....

In Christian ideology, antifemale bias is closely linked to fears and suspicions of sexuality. Historically, mainstream Christian teaching has been more or less hostile to the sexual side of humans. Inheriting this characteristic from the Hellenistic world in which it developed, early Christianity was greatly affected by St. Paul's emphasis on a two-sided human nature consisting of a mortal body and an immortal soul.... Christianity portrayed the body, and particularly its sexuality, as an obstacle to salvation. In St. Augustine's[7] view, which emerged as the representative Catholic teaching, sexual pleasure could be justified only by a married couple's attempt at procreation, and some medieval and early modern Catholic authorities thought sex sinful even for reproductive purposes. Although during the Reformation Protestant moralists rejected the ideal of celibacy and elevated marriage to new heights of respectability, suspicion of sexual pleasure remained a characteristic of all mainstream Christian teaching in the sixteenth and seventeenth centuries.

Jesus' warning, in the Sermon on the Mount, that lusting after a woman in the heart is an adulterous sin became, in the hands of the church fathers,[8] grounds for blaming women for their sexual attractiveness. Origen[9] allegedly

---

[7]Christian theologian, 354–430, and Bishop of Hippo in North Africa.

[8]Authoritative theologians of the early Christian Church who formulated doctrines.

[9]Early church father, 185–254.

castrated himself, an eminently logical solution. But most of the other church fathers, when they found it impossible to banish sexual desire, projected the fault on women, the forbidden objects. Thus, Jerome,[10] who has been called the patron saint of misogyny, discovered that only by studying Hebrew and working on his Bible translation could he sublimate his passion and be rid of the tormenting visions of dancing girls. He characterized woman as "the gate of the devil, the path of wickedness, the sting of the serpent, in a word a perilous object." This view was typical. Tertullian[11] told women, "you are the devil's gateway." . . . These early images established a pattern. In the Middle Ages and the Renaissance, women were consistently portrayed as the more lascivious of the sexes, forever dragging men into the sin of lust and away from the ascetic spirituality of which they might otherwise be capable. The reverse of the Victorian idea of female asexuality, the Christian tradition regarded women as quintessentially sexual beings.

Many such misogynistic ideas were compiled in the *Malleus Maleficarum* for perpetuation in subsequent witch trials. Women, wrote Kramer and Sprenger, are inferior physically, mentally, and morally. Their imperfections cause women extraordinary difficulty in warding off temptation. They have an "insatiable carnal lust," are inclined to deception, resist discipline, and lure men into sin and destruction. Such are the characteristics that make them likely targets for the devil; hence, the preponderance of females among the devil's servants. The authors of the *Malleus* rested their assertions on a jumble of historical half-truths, disfigured etymologies, and mistaken medicine. They derived the word *femina* from *fe* and *minus*, to show that women have little faith. The fall of kingdoms and of virtuous men they blamed on females. Naturally, they attributed to Eve's initiative the fall of the human race in the Garden of Eden. Adducing the accumulated wisdom of the ages, Kramer and Sprenger quoted widely from biblical and Roman sources. Only if all of these authorities were wrong could one deny the inferiority of women. And, once female biological deficiency was accepted, the foundation was set for accusations of witchcraft on the ground that women lacked the moral fortitude to resist temptation.

The antifemale prejudices of the *Malleus* were echoed repeatedly in the many demonological treatises that appeared during the age of witch trials. Nicolas Rémy, a judge who prosecuted many witches in Lorraine during the 1590s, found it "not unreasonable that this scum of humanity, i.e., witches, should be drawn chiefly from the feminine sex," for women had always been famous as sorcerers and enchanters. And King James[12] explained the disproportion of female witches by reference to Genesis: "The reason is easie, for as that sex is frailer than man is, so it is easier to be entrapped in these grosse snares of the Devile, as was over well proved to be true, by the

---

[10]Christian theologian and translator of the Bible, c.347–420.

[11]Christian theologian, c.160–231.

[12]King James VI of Scotland from 1567 and, as James I, King of England, 1603–1625.

Serpents deceiving of Eve at the Beginning," which, he thought, had given Satan ready access to women ever since. In the same vein, Henri Boguet, a witch-hunting prosecutor in the Burgundian Franche-Comté, thought it natural that witches should confess to sexual liaison with Satan. "The Devil uses them so," Boguet explained, "because he knows that women love carnal pleasures, and he means to bind them to his allegiance by such agreeable provocations; moreover, there is nothing which makes a woman more subject and loyal to a man than that he should abuse her body."

This highly unflattering image of women was not limited to a small number of enthusiastic witch hunters. The social order of the elites reflected universal and almost entirely unquestioned assumptions about the inferiority and dangerous attributes of females. The best medical opinion, like that of religious thinkers, associated women with sinful sexuality. Dr. François Rabelais gave this idea its classic Renaissance literary formulation in his *Gargantua and Pantagruel*. Expressing the standard medical view, he described the womb (*hysterus* in Greek) in graphic terms as the seat of woman's sexual passion and the dominant part of a literally hysterical female organism:

> For Nature has placed in a secret and interior place in their bodies an animal, an organ that is not present in men; and here there are sometimes engendered certain salty, nitrous, caustic, sharp, biting, stabbing, and bitterly irritating humors, by the pricking and painful itching of which—for this organ is all nerves—and sensitive feelings—their whole body is shaken, all their senses transported, all their passions indulged, and all their thoughts confused. . . .

Although by 1600 advanced medical opinion, spurred by improved understanding of female anatomy, led most leading physicians to discard this Platonic image of the migratory uterus, the female's excessive desire for coitus remained a medical truism. . . . [H]er well-known capacity for multiple orgasms prompted the belief that she habitually exhausted and ran down her mate in satisfying her carnal appetites. As physicians held that only moderate expenditure of semen was compatible with good health, female sexual demands seemed a physical as well as a moral threat to men. But, although women were seen as suffering from overwhelming sexual passion, experts on biology denied them an active role in the reproductive process. Aristotle's[13] theory that semen holds all that is necessary for generation still held sway, and the woman's part was imagined as the entirely passive one of providing a nurturing environment for the developing fetus.

Neither was there much sympathy for woman among other leaders of early modern culture. Theologians, lawyers, and philosophers were nearly unanimous in asserting her inferiority to man, even if a few legal scholars, like some physicians, seem to have been a little embarrassed about expressing antifemale opinions. . . .

[13]Greek philosopher and scientist, 384–322 B.C.

A good indicator of the notion of women that was widespread among the intellectual elites during the age of witch trials comes from Jean Bodin, the famous lawyer and political theorist who also penned a ferocious tract denouncing witches. Bodin began his masterpiece, *The Republic*, with a description of the model household. In it the wife was at the bottom. As the ultimate dependent, she came not only after her husband in the domestic order of things, but also behind the children, servants, and apprentices. Bodin's scheme may have been a bit extreme, but almost no one in the sixteenth and seventeenth centuries, not even early feminists, challenged the need for male superiority in the household. Unlike our modern democratic assumptions, the universally accepted conventional wisdom of the time was that hierarchy was necessary for every kind of social arrangement. As God presided over the universe, as humans were lords of creation, and as kings ruled their states, so it was believed that, in the family, men must be the dominant authorities and women their subordinates....

Acceptance of the principle of male superiority and its embodiment in family life, law, and all other social arrangements meant that, throughout European culture, disorder was associated with women on top. The inversion of morality that was a general feature of the witch stereotype is reflected clearly in the lack of dependency on men exhibited in supposed acts of malefice and in night riding to the sabbat. To men, the reversal in sex roles was probably among the most disconcerting elements in the image of the witch. Among theologians, lawyers, and philosophers, discussion of women was almost always linked with marriage. Thinkers seemed unable to imagine a social role for unattached females. This psychological blind spot is one way to explain why a disproportionately high number of accused witches were widows and other unmarried women not under the rule of men....

In general, the religious strife of the Reformation probably had the effect of increasing fear and hatred of women. Females had been singled out as the progenitors of heresy in medieval times, and such accusations resurfaced in the sixteenth century. In fact, earlier dissident sects, including the Cathars,[14] had encouraged women to assume active religious roles, in striking contrast to strict Catholic application of St. Paul's dictum that women must remain silent in church. And enthusiastic sects of the Reformation era regularly featured women among their leading spirits. De Lancre's horror at female participation in religious services betrayed a characteristic tendency of mainstream church and secular authorities of Reformation times to associate women with religious deviance. This association reinforced traditional Christian fears of women and helped to fuel the misogyny that underlay witch hunting.

Of course, de Lancre was not a unique case. If an argument can be made for witch trials as a manifestation of intensified misogyny in the late sixteenth

---

[14]Medieval sect in southern France and northern Italy that held that a good god had created the world of the spirit and that Satan had created the material world.

and early seventeenth centuries, the proliferation of witch-hunting godly reformers is among the most impressive kind of evidence. As we have seen, a prominent feature of all branches of reforming Christianity, Catholic and Protestant, was the evangelical impulse. In spreading Christian doctrine to the backwoods, reformers were fighting popular religious practices, including what they saw as witchcraft. The witch hunts spread with the arrival of spiritual militancy. . . .

It is important to realize, however, that this preoccupation with witchcraft and peasant religion was not limited to clerics alone. As the example of de Lancre suggests, such concerns spread to the laity as well. Many of the most active demonological writers and judges were laymen who had become imbued with the values of spiritual reform. For example, the Lorraine witch hunter Nicolas Rémy was a bitter enemy of lax priests and spoke out against the residues of pagan beliefs in Catholic folk religion. Even Jean Bodin characterized witchcraft as "superstitious religion," the same term the godly used to denounce peasant beliefs. And Bodin was far from an orthodox godly reformer in his private religious preferences and his public calls for religious toleration. The imagery of the sabbat, devil worship, and sexual servitude underlay the demonology of many other lay judges. Thus, witch hunting demonstrates the success of reforming efforts to energize the lay elites with the ideology of spiritual purification.

The sexual prejudices expressed in witch hunting are one of the best indicators of this success. The sixteenth century was the first in which it was acceptable for laymen to discuss sexual topics. Secular writers' adoption of traditional Christian ideas about women and sex suggests the considerable degree to which religiously based notions were absorbed into lay culture. Predisposed as they were to identify women with sinful sexuality, lay and clerical authorities came to express misogynistic sentiments on an unprecedented scale in their campaigns against popular religion. In the process, they gave traditional fears of women a new and sharper focus. Thus, the encounter of high and low cultures in the era of the Reformation became an occasion for transforming the ancient, conventional misogyny of the Western past into a murderous set of prejudices. The witch craze's slaughter of women was the result of the spread of woman-hatred in the spiritually reformed elites and its application in the reformers' campaigns against folk religion. . . .

That prejudice against women was based on sexual fears and guilt feelings can scarcely be doubted. Women were regularly depicted as predators, with sexuality as their weapon. . . . To twentieth-century observers, nothing could be clearer than the erotic emotions that led men, for example, to undress women publicly and minutely examine their genitals. Few people in those days thought in terms of unconscious sexual symbolism, so the possible presence of libidinous impulses in respectable judges was rarely mentioned by contemporary writers. The appeal of sexuality and violence, the mixture of pleasure and pain that we call sadism, was usually not expressed consciously at the time of the witch trials.... At least one observer in the era of witch hunting noted the prurient interests that witchcraft investigations could bring out. An astonished eyewitness at Salem recounted how the Puritan divine Cotton Mather publicly exposed and fondled the breasts of a seventeen-year-old girl as she lay writhing in a fit of ostensibly demonic possession....

To understand the predominance of women witches, then, it is not enough to cite the misogynistic sentiments of witch-hunting prosecutors. All too often earlier writers, both clerics and laymen, had given vent to traditional Christian ideas about the inferiority of women. What was new in the Reformation era was the connection of these traditional prejudices to full-fledged ideologically based movements for reform. Catholics and Protestants undertook massive campaigns to alter popular behavior, particularly sexual behavior. The relatively weak social controls characteristic of late medieval Europe were replaced by far more stringent codes and effective enforcement mechanisms.

There are many clues to the meaning of the newly enhanced sexual character of witchcraft in the clash of elite reforming impulses and popular values. As the reform of elite society progressed, many members of the upper classes came to sense a growing distance between themselves and the masses. Traditional attitudes of universal brotherhood gave way to an imagery of social cleavage built on cultural differences. By and large, the European elites grew contemptuous of popular ways and associated them with everything they had learned to despise. The manners of the upper classes, to begin with externals, were becoming notably different from those of ordinary folk. At table they used the newly invented fork instead of their fingers. It was now the mark of a gentleman to carry a handkerchief on his person at all times. In upper-class domestic architecture bedrooms were turning into private retreats for the first time, with the corridor introduced as a by-pass.

These elite expressions of individuality were founded on a sense of privacy and self-discipline that made the physically spontaneous appear dangerous and low. That which was "natural" did not seem necessarily desirable, for human nature had an animal-like side that had to be overcome in order for man to lead a moral life. Infants, therefore, were not allowed to crawl in seventeenth-century upper-class households, because this habit reminded adults of four-footed beasts. Almost inevitably, then, popular culture was associated with bestial naturalness and lack of restraint. In particular, the most subjugated groups were consistently linked with moral licentiousness. Children received hard discipline to drive out the devil in them. Blacks had a reputation for sexual potency because of their allegedly low moral status. And women were consistently tied to Satan and sex. It is not hard to see in these stereotypes projections of desires repressed by European elites ever more thoroughly imbued with the spirit of religious reform.

Here was one of the key linkages underlying the witch trials. As large segments of elite society were becoming preoccupied with self-control, physical restraint, and ascetic demeanor, the sexual aspects of popular culture caused great concern. Elite convictions that plebeian women were likely to succumb to any attractive stranger make understandable the injection of a strong dose of sex into the witchcraft recipe. Women, and particularly women of nonelite social classes, seem to have struck these judges as fundamentally immoral types who, as slaves to their sexual urges, were capable of the worst treason against man and God.

... "Whore and witch" was the standard characterization of accused women from the villages of Luxembourg, and whore meant a woman who indulged in sex for pleasure, not for money.

The accused witches ... of the fourteenth and fifteenth centuries ... were frequently males, but the proportion of men continually declined before and during the witch craze, as the crime was reformulated in strongly sex-linked terms. The one-fifth of witch suspects in Scotland who were men, for example, do not appear to have been accused of any sexual relationship with the devil, unlike their female counterparts. As witchcraft became identified with sexual trespasses in the minds of the reforming witch hunters, its sex-linked status was greatly reinforced.

This association may well be indicative of a psychological process by which women, as agents of Satan, were held responsible for male sexual inadequacy and transgressions. Symptoms of what can be termed early modern machismo include a highly patriarchal family structure, an obsession with codes of sexual honor, and the curious stress on the genital-emphasizing codpiece in dress and literary expression. All of these may betray considerable male insecurity. The purifiers' preachments about the close relationship of sin and sex surely encouraged in their audiences a sense of guilt about sexual feelings. If inability to adhere to newly generalized standards of Christian sexual behavior could be blamed on women as a consequence of satanic intervention, the male sense of guilt would be greatly reduced.

In this may be found one of the principal social and psychological foundations for witch-hunting misogyny in the age of religious reform.... [I]n the French-speaking territories of the Spanish Netherlands, the villages that experienced witch trials were the ones with parish priests who took religious reform particularly to heart. These clerics' guilt feelings about their repressed physical desires ... made them harp on sexual themes in their sermons and stress the stereotypical image of the witch as the exemplar of dangerous female sexuality. In neighboring communities with priests who behaved more like laymen, the congregants never were taught to associate women and sex with Satan, and trials for witchcraft did not occur.

Guilt feelings stemming from repressed sexuality and unrealized desires for spiritual fulfillment were not limited to men during the Reformation era. Some of the most dramatic episodes of the witch craze originated in convents, where sisters declared themselves possessed by demons and engaged in behavior regarded as lewd and indecent by scandalized observers. The nuns blamed men for their actions, claiming that they had been bewitched. Like other females who held males responsible for their bewitchment, these sisters were in effect reversing the cycle of repression, guilt, and scapegoating that the clerical establishment had burnt into the European consciousness by associating women and sex with Satan.

On the conscious level, the witch hunters and other leaders of godly reform, like the medieval inquisitors before them, saw themselves as inspired primarily by the desire to save souls. They regarded many members of their flocks as mired in sin, but the attractive Christian idea that even the worst sinner is capable of redemption and salvation spurred on the reformers. This motivation is important to remember, because the horrors of witch prosecutions can easily blind us to their judges' ideals. The art of the Catholic Counter Reformation revived the New Testament theme of the harlot redeemed by Christ, and seventeenth-century artists produced many propaganda canvases showing Mary Magdalene and others, sometimes in the dress of contemporary prostitutes. These paintings display sin as fundamentally sexual, and they associate sexuality with women. Yet also present is the theme of repentance and the ever-present possibility of salvation. In the spirit that inspired this art can be glimpsed the Christian charity that moved the godly elites, even in witch trials. The reformers' deep ideological commitment made them welcome confession and repentance. They saw such changes in behavior as a means of opening the gates of heaven to the sinner. Nevertheless, one cannot escape the conclusion that the witch hunters' identification of women with sin, sexuality, and lower-class mores, combined with their ideological zeal, led them to establish a pattern of judicial excess and gross violations of human dignity.

Ironically, the available evidence seems to indicate that, despite the cultural elites' perception of ever-increasing distance between their ethos and that of ordinary folk, plebeian behavior was in fact changing dramatically in response to pressures from above. Beginning in the mid-sixteenth century, the moderate toleration of sexual license that appears to have been the norm in the later Middle Ages was replaced by a far more repressive spirit, not only among the elites but also at lower levels of society. A few examples can illustrate the changes. For the old ways, consider the Pyrenean village of Montaillou in the fourteenth century. There casual premarital sex was accepted, and about 10 percent of the households consisted of unmarried couples living together. Meanwhile, the local priest set the pace in lechery.

Montaillou was an atypical community because of its Catharist tendencies, but a concubine-holding priesthood was standard in pre-Reformation Europe. In Bavaria, for example, only 3 to 4 percent of the parish priests of the mid-sixteenth century had *not* taken concubines. The efforts of the Catholic reformers, however, soon led to the transformation of priestly celibacy from a pious hope to an actual model for imitation. Reform-minded churchmen vigorously combated formerly widespread patterns of concubinage among the clergy and the upper classes. Those who persisted, unless they were very highborn, were subject to denunciation and eventually to excommunication. As a result, the proportion of illegitimate births attributable to concubinage fell dramatically after the sixteenth century.

Such campaigns eventually produced a marked improvement in the moral quality and educational preparation of parish priests. The spread of Protestantism in northern Europe can be understood in part as a symptom of popular revulsion against a priesthood that was badly trained and morally lax. The Protestant pastor received a systematic preparation that stressed knowledge of the Bible and methods for communicating its teaching to his congregants. One of these methods was setting a personal example of moral behavior. All over Catholic Europe, church leaders were similarly concerned with improving the quality of the local clergy. Under Jesuit leadership, the Council of Trent's[15] strictures about the training and behavior of priests gradually took hold. No longer was the local cleric just another member of the community, a good fellow who might join in a Mardi Gras dance. In reformed Europe he became a sacred figure, separated from the profane society that he was constantly trying to remake in his own new image.

Not only clerics found themselves called to higher standards of sexual behavior. As in today's ideologically motivated revolutionary regimes, the magistrates of the time developed an interest in crimes against morality. The Parlement of Rouen, for example, began to hear frequent cases of adultery, bigamy, sodomy, and incest. These kinds of crimes increased from less than 1 percent of the court's business in 1548–49 to 10 percent in 1604–06. The town fathers of the Lutheran imperial free city of Nördlingen also legislated harsher punishments for sexual offenders after the middle decades of the sixteenth century. From 1590, judges in Geneva and the Swiss Catholic canton of Fribourg, moved by exposure to reformed spiritual ideas that classified sexual deviance as heretical, regularly tried offenders accused of sodomy and bestiality. The General Assembly of the Presbyterian Church in Scotland was instrumental in prompting trials of—note the combination—"incest, adulterie, witchcraft, murther and abominable and horrible oaths." The General Assembly protested to the king in 1583 that without punishment for these offenses "daily sinne increaseth, and provoketh the wrath of God against the whole countrie." Between 1574 and 1696 the Scottish Parliament passed ten statutes condemning blasphemy and swearing and fifteen against sabbath-breaking. Adultery and incest were made capital offenses in the 1560s, at the same time that the Parliament legislated against witchcraft. After 1600, English church courts and justices of the peace also conducted many trials of fornicators. These efforts apparently were effective, to judge from

---

[15]Roman Catholic council that met intermittently between 1545 and 1563 to reform the Church, define doctrine, and roll back Protestantism.

English birth records. As late as Elizabeth's[16] reign, the rates of premarital conception and illegitimacy continued high, yet both ratios dropped by a remarkable 50 to 75 percent under Puritan influence during the first half of the seventeenth century.

The active roles taken by lay judges in these areas attest to the breakdown of traditional medieval spheres of clerical and nonclerical activities. It has often been pointed out that the state's intervention in witch trials reflects the secularization of law in early modern Europe. Equally worthy of note is the extent to which witch legislation and prosecution by state authorities responded to religious concerns. By exercising the power of the newly centralized states in cases of witchcraft and other moral offenses, lay elites showed the deep impact on them of spiritual reform.

The godly not only condemned adultery and premarital sex but also objected to strong passion in the marriage bed. "Never on Sunday" or during Lent was the standard clerical admonition, along with detailed instructions about avoiding "sinful" positions and actions while making love. The first natives to be told of the "missionary position" were the villagers of Europe. Reforming French bishops distributed detailed manuals to parish priests to help them implement approved sexual behavior among the congregants. In these handbooks, learned churchmen established an elaborate hierarchy of sexual sins and recommended appropriate penances for violations that ranged in seriousness from "unnatural" sexual positions, including women on top, to incest and sodomy. The content of this sexual advice was not particularly novel, but the vigorous, well-organized enforcement effort of reform-minded authorities was.

In all of these ways, the moral ideology of spiritual reform was given political meaning in the late sixteenth and seventeenth centuries. The emphasis on sexual repression in society made witchcraft a particularly heinous crime, especially when formulated as sexual servitude to the devil. . . .

The reformers' antipathy for popular sexual practices was merely one side of their consistent tendency to identify the folkways of ordinary people with sin and heresy. Popular recreations like dancing, gambling, and playacting were regularly condemned as immoral and in some places were suppressed. The great seasonal festivals, including Carnival, May Day, Michaelmas, and Midsummer's Eve, which were grand occasions in the life of the people, came under heavy attack by reformers, who condemned them as lewd and pagan profanations. For centuries the liberties of Mardi Gras and similar celebrations had served as a useful safety valve in the pressure-filled lives of ordinary people. But to the reformers these festivals seemed circuses of sin. Eating, drinking, sex, and violence were the chief themes of such occasions, and many of the organized activities—parades, contests, and theatricals— celebrated these basic human impulses. The carnality of Carnival implied that it was all right to give free rein to bodily pleasures, at least on some

---

[16]Queen of England, 1558–1603.

special days of the year. Heavy eating and drinking were part of the ritual, and population records show a clear rise in births nine months after festival seasons. Carnival was playtime, but to godly reformers such play appeared the height of sacrilege.

Repressive authorities were tempted to ban all types of group revelry. In Scotland the church and borough councils repeatedly prohibited large gatherings, such as the "penny bridal" weddings of poor folk who had to ask guests to bring their own refreshment. This kind of deprivation inspired the typical description of witches' sabbats in Scottish and continental trial confessions. The accounts nearly always speak of uproarious disorder—eating, drinking, music, dancing—the activities denied to ordinary people both by their poverty and by the godly elites' suspicion of festive popular gatherings.

In the imagination of the authorities, the witches' sabbat of ordinary folk naturally included unbridled, licentious celebration, because reformers were certain that their social inferiors were greatly susceptible to the enticements of bodily pleasure....

Backing for these efforts at purification came from secular rulers, who saw religious uniformity and cultural conformism as effective props for centralized absolute government. The motivation for the reform of popular culture was thus partly political. Severely traumatized by the revolutionary episodes and civil warfare that were endemic in Reformation Europe, princes were determined to suppress political and social dissidence among the lower classes. For example, secular rulers became conscious of the explosive potential of popular celebrations, for festivals sometimes sparked large-scale rioting and even full-blown rebellions. With the support of state officials, the churches moved to suppress the popular lay associations that often organized these events and substituted the parish as the main unit of urban life. An important instance was the abolition of fraternities of adolescent males, which had long been one of the central sources of community identity in European towns.

As a result, by the end of the age of witch hunting traditional forms of folk culture had either disappeared or been subdued throughout Europe.... It may be overstating the case to speak of an extinction of popular culture. Yet the wild atmosphere of Mardi Gras, the licentiousness of May Day, and the liberation from normal restraints that characterized all folk celebrations survived only in domesticated, decorous form under watchful Catholic establishments, while in most Protestant lands they were abolished as ungodly profanations. Among Catholics, formal religious processions replaced unbridled popular spectacles. In Protestant churches, Bible texts covered the walls to hide the sensual images produced by local artists in the Catholic past, and everywhere there was renewed emphasis on sermons (often stressing the horrors of hell) as the medium by which the masses were to be guided. A more rigidly controlled society emerged, organized around absolutist states and hierarchical churches that intruded into every area of community life. The witch craze was one side of this scene of generalized cultural clash.

Once sexual "deviance" was connected with witchcraft and heresy in preachers' sermons as well as in the law, the campaign against licentious behavior must surely have been easier to win. To the extent that the reformers' war against sex was successful, the elites' efforts to introduce diabolism into the stereotype of the witch were seemingly accepted by the populace. In any case, as the trials proliferated, popular culture clearly received demonic imagery as a plausible extension of the witch stereotype. Satanic stereotypes apparently did not take firm root in the folklore of witchcraft and tended to fade from popular tradition after the trials ended. But during the age of the witch hunts, ordinary people were effectively conditioned by the godly elites to accept the reality of devil worship among their neighbors. This is one measure of how thoroughly elite ideas of witchcraft were imposed on lower cultural levels....

Another indicator of the penetration of elite values into lower cultural levels was the widespread acceptance of the sexual stereotype of female witchcraft. The ancient traditions of misogyny, reinforced by a renewed preoccupation among the reformed elites with sexual sinning, were transmitted to the populace through the missionary efforts of godly reformers during the sixteenth and seventeenth centuries. Thus, bias against women, a conventional characteristic of Christian teaching, became uniquely intense during the era of religious reform. In this period alone did the West's traditional misogyny result in the execution of many thousands simply because, as women, they were automatically suspect. Sixteenth- and seventeenth-century reforming impulses found one of their most important applications in the area of sexuality. The quantum leap in witch trials during this era was one outlet for the deep stresses produced at all social levels as the godly reform of sex took hold.

In many regions of Europe, the spread of witch trials accompanied the advent of a reform-minded clergy. These men of God, trained in seminary or university, were apt to see the devil everywhere and to imagine him as the force underlying all heresy. Thus, when encountering peasant beliefs in sorcery-induced illness or crop failure, clerics and lay authorities influenced by the clerical outlook often went beyond the initial charge and began questioning the accused about devil worship and sabbats. The elites placed charges of malefice in a wider explanatory context within which they could understand the dynamics of supernatural evildoing. This kind of bicultural process, overlaying peasant beliefs with learned concepts, began in the relatively infrequent witch trials of the fifteenth century. With the coming of the Reformation and the appearance of a large, well-educated, irrepressibly evangelical clergy in Western and Central Europe, contacts between learned and popular cultures no longer were sporadic and superficial. They became a regular, permanent feature of village life. These frequent contacts made for frequent witch trials.

One way of understanding the witch craze is to see it as a part of the many-sided war on popular culture waged by reforming clerical and lay establishments in the sixteenth and seventeenth centuries. The chronology of witch hunting argues for this thesis, because the onset of large-scale witch trials corresponds almost exactly with the uneven spread of reforming impulses across Christendom. Witch hunts proliferated as the godly began to indoctrinate ordinary people with Christian theological teaching and concepts of moral behavior unknown to country dwellers of earlier generations. In Western Europe, trials for witchcraft became frequent after 1560, but in Poland and the Habsburg lands of Central Europe, where reform commenced later, such trials were rare until after 1600. As for the remote world of Orthodox Russia, Muscovy, untouched by Western spiritual movements, conducted some trials for sorcery but, lacking the concept of the devil-worshiping heretic, never knew a witch craze. Although it is far from a complete explanation of the trials, the evidence for spiritual reform as a precipitant of the witch craze is very powerful.

The Rites of Violence: Religious Riot in Sixteenth-Century France

NATALIE Z. DAVIS

Eight religious wars rocked the kingdom of France from 1562 to 1598. Spurred by the grandiose ambitions of the leading aristocratic families and fueled by the religious fervor so characteristic of the Protestant and Catholic Reformations, these civil wars became international wars as Spain sought to dismember its northern neighbor, and nearly succeeded. The devastation was enormous, as Huguenot (French Protestant) and Catholic armies crisscrossed France. Indeed, by the late 1580s, there were three competing factions: Protestant, ultra-Catholic (receiving support from Spain), and those Frenchmen who placed the state above religion. No wonder, then, that in this ungodly four decades of turmoil, violence and brutality were endemic.

    Natalie Davis explores one aspect of violent behavior in late sixteenth-century France: the religious riot. Her article is evidence of the influence of anthropology on history, for she seeks to discover the meaning of the patterns of riot behavior. Davis does not see the riots as class warfare; they drew legitimacy from religious rituals and beliefs. Most notorious of these riots was the St. Bartholomew's Day Massacre of 23–24 August 1572, when Catholics killed perhaps two to three thousand Huguenots in Paris and, later, approximately ten thousand in other parts of France. Davis goes beyond this well-known event to the dynamics of religious riots throughout the kingdom. In attempting to locate common denominators of the many outbreaks of sectarian violence during this very religious period in history, Davis raises important questions. What claims to legality did the rioters have? We are often tempted to dismiss rioters out of hand as lawbreakers, but sixteenth-century participants in crowd violence had quite another perspective. Who participated in the riots? The very poor, hoping to profit from the occasion, or better-placed social groups, committed sincerely to specific goals? What goals did rioters have? Did they simply lash out at random, unreflective as they acted? Were they organized and did they plan their acts of desecration, brutality, and death?

Davis's examination of the idea of pollution places us in the midst of the religious crowd. Sixteenth-century Catholics were certain that Protestants (who in turn believed the same about Catholics) profaned God and the community by their actions and even by their very existence. Was there not, then, an obligation, a duty to society and to God to remove the uncleanliness and profanation? How could a sincere Christian in the sixteenth century permit defilement by others who threatened to overturn society, to rupture what should be, according to both Catholics and Protestants, a society unified by the one faith and only one faith? French people did not believe in the virtue of religious toleration. In fact, religious toleration was thought to be injurious to God and to God's plan. What were the differences between Catholic and Protestant riots? How did the belief systems of each religion determine the types of violence practiced by its adherents? Finally, when did the riots most often occur?

In conclusion, we are left with great insight as to the mentality of these religious people, for we know of their greatest fears and the steps they were prepared to take to alleviate those fears. Were they justified? And was such violence extraordinary or usual in Reformation France?

These are the statutes and judgements, which ye shall observe to do in the land, which the Lord God of thy fathers giveth thee ... Ye shall utterly destroy all the places wherein the nations which he shall possess served their gods, upon the high mountains, and upon the hills, and under every green tree:

And ye shall overthrow their altars, and break their pillars and burn their groves with fire; and ye shall hew down the graven images of their gods, and destroy the names of them out of that place [Deuteronomy xii. 1–3].

Thus a Calvinist pastor to his flock in 1562.

If thy brother, the son of thy mother, or thy son, or thy daughter, or the wife of thy bosom, or thy friend, which is as thine own soul, entice thee secretly, saying Let us go serve other gods, which thou hast not known, thou, nor thy fathers ... Thou shalt not consent unto him, nor hearken unto him ... But thou shalt surely kill him; thine hand shall be first upon him to put him to death, and afterwards the hand of all the people....

If thou shalt hear say in one of thy cities, which the Lord thy God hath given thee to dwell there, saying, Certain men, the children of Belial are gone out from among you, and have withdrawn the inhabitants of their city, saying Let us go and serve other gods, which ye have not known ... Thou shalt surely smite the inhabitants of that city with the edge of the sword, destroying it utterly and all that is therein [Deuteronomy xiii. 6, 8–9, 12–13, 15].

And [Jehu] lifted up his face to the window and said, Who is on my side? Who? And there looked out to him two or three eunuchs. And he said, Throw her down. So they threw [Jezebel] down: and some of her blood was sprinkled on the wall, and on the horses: and he trode her under foot ... And they went to bury her: but they found no more of her than the skull and the feet and the palms of her hands ... And [Jehu] said, This is the word of the Lord, which he spake by his servant Elijah ... saying, In the portion of Jezreel shall dogs eat the flesh of Jezebel: and the carcase of Jezebel shall be as dung upon the face of the field [II Kings ix. 32–3, 35–7].

Thus in 1568 Parisian preachers held up to their Catholic parishioners the end of a wicked idolater. Whatever the intentions of pastors and priests, such words were among the many spurs to religious riot in sixteenth-century France. By religious riot I mean, as a preliminary definition, any violent action, with words or weapons, undertaken against religious targets by people who are not acting *officially and formally* as agents of political and ecclesiastical authority. As food rioters bring their moral indignation to bear upon the state of the grain market, so religious rioters bring their zeal to bear upon the state of men's relations to the sacred. The violence of the religious riot is distinguished, at least in principle, from the action of political authorities, who can legally silence, humiliate, demolish, punish, torture and execute; and also from the action of soldiers, who at certain times and places can legally kill and destroy. In mid sixteenth-century France, all these sources of violence were busily producing, and it is sometimes hard to tell a militia officer from a murderer and a soldier from a statue-smasher. Nevertheless, there are occasions when we can separate out for examination a violent crowd set on religious goals....

... We may see these crowds as prompted by political and moral traditions which legitimize and even prescribe their violence. We may see urban rioters not as miserable, uprooted, unstable masses, but as men and women who often have some stake in their community; who may be craftsmen or better; and who, even when poor and unskilled, may appear respectable to their everyday neighbours. Finally, we may see their violence, however cruel, not as random and limitless, but as aimed at defined targets and selected from a repertory of traditional punishments and forms of destruction....

... My first purpose is to describe the shape and structure of the religious riot in French cities and towns, especially in the 1560s and early 1570s. We will look at the goals, legitimation and occasions for riots; at the kinds of action undertaken by the crowds and the targets for their violence; and briefly at the participants in the riots and their organization. We will consider differences between Protestant and Catholic styles of crowd behaviour, but will also indicate the many ways in which they are alike....

What then can we learn of the goals of popular religious violence? What were the crowds intending to do and why did they think they must do it? Their behaviour suggests, first of all, a goal akin to preaching: the defence of true doctrine and the refutation of false doctrine through dramatic challenges and tests. "You blaspheme", shouts a woman to a Catholic preacher in Montpellier in 1558 and, having broken the decorum of the service, leads part of the congregation out of the church. "You lie", shouts a sheathmaker in the midst of the Franciscan's Easter sermon in Lyon, and his words are underscored by the gunshots of Huguenots waiting in the square. "Look", cries a weaver in Tournai, as he seizes the elevated host from the priest, "deceived people, do you believe this is the King, Jesus Christ, the true God and Saviour? Look!" And he crumbles the wafer and escapes. "Look", says a crowd of image-breakers to the people of Albiac in 1561, showing them the relics they have seized from the Carmelite monastery, "look, they are only animal bones". And the slogan of the Reformed crowds as they rush through the streets of Paris, of Toulouse, of La Rochelle, of Angoulême is "The Gospel! The Gospel! Long live the Gospel!"

Catholic crowds answer this kind of claim to truth in Angers by taking the French Bible, well-bound and gilded, seized in the home of a rich merchant, and parading it through the streets on the end of a halberd. "There's the truth hung. There's the truth of the Huguenots, the truth of all the devils". Then, throwing it into the river, "There's the truth of all the devils drowned". And if the Huguenot doctrine was true, why didn't the Lord come and save them from their killers? So a crowd of Orléans Catholic taunted its victims in 1572: "Where is your God? Where are your prayers and Psalms? Let him save you if he can". Even the dead were made to speak in Normandy and Provence, where leaves of the Protestant Bible were stuffed into the mouths and wounds of corpses. "They preached the truth of their God. Let them call him to their aid".

The same refutation was, of course, open to Protestants. A Protestant crowd corners a baker guarding the holy-wafer box in Saint Médard's Church in Paris in 1561. "Messieurs", he pleads, "do not touch it for the honour of Him who dwells here". "Does your God of paste protect you now from the pains of death?" was the Protestant answer before they killed him. True doctrine can be defended in sermon or speech, backed up by the magistrate's sword against the heretic. Here it is defended by dramatic demonstration, backed up by the violence of the crowd.

A more frequent goal of these riots, however, is that of ridding the community of dreaded pollution. The word "pollution" is often on the lips of the violent, and the concept serves well to sum up the dangers which rioters saw in the dirty and diabolic enemy. A priest brings ornaments and objects for singing the Mass into a Bordeaux jail. The Protestant prisoner smashes them all. "Do you want to blaspheme the Lord's name everywhere? Isn't it enough that the temples are defiled? Must you also profane prisons so nothing is unpolluted?" "The Calvinists have polluted their hands with every kind of sacrilege men can think of", writes a Doctor of Theology in 1562. Not long after at the Sainte Chapelle,[1] a man seizes the elevated host

---

[1] A Gothic church in Paris, built in the thirteenth century to house relics.

with his "polluted hands" and crushes it under foot. The worshippers beat him up and deliver him to the agents of Parlement.[2] ...

One does not have to listen very long to sixteenth-century voices to hear the evidence for the uncleanliness and profanation of either side. As for the Protestants, Catholics knew that, in the style of earlier heretics, they snuffed out the candles and had sexual intercourse after the voluptuous Psalmsinging of their nocturnal conventicles.... But it was not just the fleshly licence with which they lived which was unclean, but the things they said in their "pestilential" books and the things they did in hatred of the Mass, the sacraments and whole Catholic religion. As the representative of the clergy said at the Estates[3] of Orléans, the heretics intended to leave "no place in the Kingdom which was dedicated, holy and sacred to the Lord, but would only profane churches, demolish altars and break images".

The Protestants' sense of Catholic pollution also stemmed to some extent from their sexual uncleanness, here specifically of the clergy. Protestant polemic never tired of pointing to the lewdness of the clergy with their "concubines". It was rumoured that the Church of Lyon had an organization of hundreds of women, sort of temple prostitutes, at the disposition of priests and canons; and an observer pointed out with disgust how, after the First Religious War,[4] the Mass and the brothel re-entered Rouen together. One minister even claimed that the clergy were for the most part Sodomites. But more serious than the sexual abominations of the clergy was the defilement of the sacred by Catholic ritual life, from the diabolic magic of the Mass to the idolatrous worship of images. The Mass is "vile filth"; "no people pollute the House of the Lord in every way more than the clergy". Protestant converts talked of their own past lives as a time of befoulment and dreaded present "contamination" from Catholic churches and rites.

Pollution was a dangerous thing to suffer in a community, from either a Protestant or a Catholic point of view, for it would surely provoke the wrath of God. Terrible wind storms and floods were sometimes taken as signs of His impatience on this count. Catholics, moreover, had also to worry about offending Mary and the saints; and though the anxious, expiatory processions organized in the wake of Protestant sacrilege might temporarily appease them, the heretics were sure to strike again. It is not surprising, then, that so many of the acts of violence performed by Catholic and Protestant crowds have ... the character either of rites of purification or of a paradoxical desecration, intended to cut down on uncleanness by placing profane things, like chrism, back in the profane world where they belonged. ...

---

[2]The Parlement of Paris, a sovereign judicial court with jurisdiction over approximately one-half of France.

[3]The Estates in French provinces were assemblies that maintained relations with the central government and dealt with provincial affairs.

[4]1562–1563.

For Catholic zealots, the extermination of the heretical "vermin" promised the restoration of unity to the body social and the guarantee of its traditional boundaries:

> *And let us all say in unison:*
> *Long live the Catholic religion*
> *Long live the King and good parishioners,*
> *Long live faithful Parisians,*
> *And may it always come to pass*
> *That every person goes to Mass,*
> *One God, one Faith, one King.*

For Protestant zealots, the purging of the priestly "vermin" promised the creation of a new kind of unity within the body social, all the tighter because false gods and monkish sects would no longer divide it. Relations within the social order would be purer, too, for lewdness and love of gain would be limited. As was said of Lyon after its "deliverance" in 1562:

> ....
> *When this town so vain*
> *Was filled*
> *With idolatry and dealings*
> *Of usury and lewdness,*
> *It had clerics and merchants aplenty.*
>
> *But once it was purged*
> *And changed*
> *By the Word of God,*
> *That brood of vipers*
> *Could hope no more*
> *To live in so holy a place.*

Crowds might defend truth, and crowds might purify, but there was also a third aspect to the religious riot—a political one....

...When the magistrate had not used his sword to defend the faith and the true church and to punish the idolators, then the crowd would do it for him. Thus, many religious disturbances begin with the ringing of the tocsin, as in a time of civic assembly or emergency. Some riots end with the marching of the religious "wrongdoers" on the other side to jail. In 1561, for instance, Parisian Calvinists, fearing that the priests and worshippers in Saint Médard's Church were organizing an assault on their services..., first rioted in Saint Médard and then seized some fifteen Catholics as "mutinous" and led them off, "bound like galley-slaves", to the Châtelet prison.

If the Catholic killing of Huguenots has in some ways the form of a rite of purification, it also sometimes has the form of imitating the magistrate. The mass executions of Protestants at Merindol and Cabrières in Provence and at Meaux in the 1540s, duly ordered by the Parlements of Aix and of

Paris as punishment for heresy and high treason, anticipate crowd massacres of later decades. The Protestants themselves sensed this: the devil, unable to extinguish the light of the Gospel through the sentences of judges, now tried to obscure it through furious war and a murderous populace. Whereas before they were made martyrs by one executioner, now it is at the hands of "infinite numbers of them, and the swords of private persons have become the litigants, witnesses, judges, decrees and executors of the strangest cruelties".

Similarly, *official* acts of torture and *official* acts of desecration of the corpses of certain criminals anticipate some of the acts performed by riotous crowds. The public execution was, of course, a dramatic and well-attended event in the sixteenth century, and the wood-cut and engraving documented the scene far and wide. There the crowd might see the offending tongue of the blasphemer pierced or slit, the offending hands of the desecrator cut off. There the crowd could watch the traitor decapitated and disemboweled, his corpse quartered and the parts borne off for public display in different sections of the town. The body of an especially heinous criminal was dragged through the streets, attached to a horse's tail. The image of exemplary royal punishment lived on for weeks, even years, as the corpses of murderers were exposed on gallows or wheels and the heads of rebels on posts. . . . [C]rowds often took their victims to places of official execution, as in Paris in 1562, when the Protestant printer, Roc Le Frere, was dragged for burning to the Marché aux Pourceaux,[5] and in Toulouse the same year, when a merchant, slain in front of a church, was dragged for burning to the town hall. "The King salutes you", said a Catholic crowd in Orléans to a Protestant trader, then put a cord around his neck as official agents might do, and led him off to be killed.

Riots also occurred in connection with judicial cases, either to hurry the judgement along, or when verdicts in religious cases were considered too severe or too lenient by "the voice of the people". Thus in 1569 in Montpellier, a Catholic crowd forced the judge to condemn an important Huguenot prisoner to death in a hasty "trial", then seized him and hanged him in front of his house. . . . And in 1561 in Marsillargues, when prisoners for heresy were released by royal decree, a Catholic crowd "rearrested" them, and executed and burned them in the streets. . . .

The seizure of religious buildings and the destruction of images by Calvinist crowds were also accomplished with the conviction that they were taking on the rôle of the authorities. When Protestants in Montpellier occupied a church in 1561, they argued that the building belonged to them already, since its clergy had been wholly supported by merchants and burghers in the past and the property belonged to the town. . . .

To be sure, the relation of a French Calvinist crowd to the magisterial model is different from that of a French Catholic crowd. The king had not yet chastised the clergy and "put all ydolatry to ruyne and confusyon", as

[5]Pig market.

Protestants had been urging him since the early 1530s. Calvinist crowds were using his sword as the king *ought* to have been using it and as some princes and city councils outside of France had already used it. Within the kingdom before 1560 city councils had only *indicated* the right path, as they set up municipal schools, lay-controlled welfare systems or otherwise limited the sphere of action of the clergy. During the next years, as revolution and conversion created Reformed city councils and governors (such as the Queen of Navarre) within France, Calvinist crowds finally had local magistrates whose actions they could prompt or imitate.

In general, then, the crowds in religious riots in sixteenth-century France can be seen as sometimes acting out clerical rôles—defending true doctrine or ridding the community of defilement in a violent version of priest or prophet—and as sometimes acting out magisterial rôles. Clearly some riotous behaviour, such as the extensive pillaging done by both Protestants and Catholics, cannot be subsumed under these heads; but just as the prevalence of pillaging in a war does not prevent us from typing it as a holy war, so the prevalence of pillaging in a riot should not prevent us from seeing it as essentially religious. . . .

So long as rioters maintained a given religious commitment, they rarely displayed guilt or shame for their violence. By every sign, the crowds believed their actions legitimate.

One reason for this conviction is that in some, though by no means all, religious riots, clerics and political officers were active members of the crowd, though not precisely in their official capacity. In Lyon in 1562, Pastor Jean Ruffy took part in the sack of the Cathedral of Saint Jean with a sword in his hand. Catholic priests seem to have been in quite a few disturbances, as in Rouen in 1560, when priests and parishioners in a Corpus Christi parade[6] broke into the houses of Protestants who had refused to do the procession honour. . . .

On the other hand, not all religious riots could boast of officers or clergy in the crowd, and other sources of legitimation must be sought. Here we must recognize what mixed cues were given out by priests and pastors in their sermons on heresy or idolatry. . . . However much Calvin[7] and other pastors opposed such disturbances (preferring that all images and altars be removed soberly by the authorities), they nevertheless were always more ready to understand and excuse this violence than, say, that of a peasant revolt or of a journeymen's march. Perhaps, after all, the popular idol-smashing was due to "an extraordinary power (*vertu*) from God." . . .

The rôle of Catholic preachers in legitimating popular violence was even more direct. If we don't know whether to believe the Protestant claim that

---

[6]A Roman Catholic festival instituted in the thirteenth century to honor the Blessed Sacrament (the body of Jesus).

[7]John Calvin (1509–1564), French Protestant theologian, founder of Calvinism and religious leader of Geneva.

Catholic preachers at Paris were telling their congregations in 1557 that Protestants ate babies, it is surely significant that...Catholic preachers did blame the loss of the battle of Saint Quentin[8] on God's wrath at the presence of heretics in France.... And if Protestant pastors could timidly wonder if divine power were not behind the extraordinary force of the iconoclasts, priests had no doubts that certain miraculous occurrences in the wake of Catholic riots were a sign of divine approval, such as a copper cross in Troyes that began to change colour and cure people in 1561, the year of a riot in which Catholics bested Protestants....

In all likelihood, however, there are sources for the legitimation of popular religious riot that come directly out of the experience of the local groups which often formed the nucleus of a crowd—the men and women who had worshipped together in the dangerous days of the night conventicles, the men in confraternities, in festive groups, in youth gangs and militia units. It should be remembered how often conditions in sixteenth-century cities required groups of "little people" to take the law into their own hands. Royal edicts themselves enjoined any person who saw a murder, theft or other misdeed to ring the tocsin[9] and chase after the criminal. Canon law allowed certain priestly rôles to laymen in times of emergency, such as the midwife's responsibility to baptize a baby in danger of dying, while the rôle of preaching the Gospel was often assumed by Protestant laymen in the decades before the Reformed Church was set up....

...[T]he occasion for most religious violence was during the time of religious worship or ritual and in the space which one or both groups were using for sacred purposes....

Almost every type of public religious event has a disturbance associated with it. The sight of a statue of the Virgin at a crossroad or in a wall-niche provokes a Protestant group to mockery of those who reverence her. A fight ensues. Catholics hide in a house to entrap Huguenots who refuse to doff their hats to a Virgin nearby, and then rush out and beat the heretics up. Baptism: in Nemours, a Protestant family has its baby baptized on All Souls' Day[10] according to the new Reformed rite. With the help of an aunt, a group of Catholics steals it away for rebaptism. A drunkard sees the father and the godfather and other Protestants discussing the event in the streets, claps his sabots and shouts, "Here are the Huguenots who have come to massacre us". A crowd assembles, the tocsin is rung, and a three-hour battle takes place. Funeral: in Toulouse, at Easter-time, a Protestant carpenter tries to bury his Catholic wife by the new Reformed rite. A Catholic crowd seizes the corpse and buries it. The Protestants dig it up and try to rebury her. The bells are rung, and with a great noise a Catholic crowd assembles with stones and sticks. Fighting and sacking ensue.

[8]Spanish victory over the French in 1557.

[9]Bell used to sound an alarm.

[10]Commemoration of the souls of the departed, celebrated on 2 November.

Religious services: a Catholic Mass is the occasion for an attack on the Host or the interruption of a sermon, which then leads to a riot. Protestant preaching in a home attracts large Catholic crowds at the door, who stone the house or otherwise threaten the worshippers....

But these encounters are as nothing compared to the disturbances that cluster around processional life. Corpus Christi Day, with its crowds, coloured banners and great crosses, was the chance for Protestants *not* to put rugs in front of their doors; for Protestant women to sit ostentatiously in their windows spinning; for heroic individuals, like the painter Denis de Vallois in Lyon, to throw themselves on the "God of paste" so as "to destroy him in every parish in the world". Corpus Christi Day was the chance for a procession to turn into an assault on and slaughter of those who had so offended the Catholic faith, its participants shouting, as in Lyon in 1561, "For the flesh of God, we must kill all the Huguenots". A Protestant procession was a parade of armed men and women in their dark clothes, going off to services at their temple or outside the city gates, singing Psalms and spiritual songs that to Catholic ears sounded like insults against the Church and her sacraments. It was an occasion for children to throw stones, for an exchange of scandalous words—"idolaters", "devils from the Pope's purgatory", "Huguenot heretics, living like dogs"—and then finally for fighting....

The occasions which express most concisely the contrast between the two religious groups, however, are those in which a popular festive Catholicism took over the streets with dancing, masks, banners, costumes and music—"lascivious abominations", according to the Protestants....

As with liturgical rites, there were some differences between the rites of violence of Catholic and Protestant crowds....

...[T]he iconoclastic Calvinist crowds...come out as the champions in the destruction of religious property ("with more than Turkish cruelty", said a priest). This was not only because the Catholics had more physical accessories to their rite, but also because the Protestants sensed much more danger and defilment in the *wrongful use of material objects*....

In bloodshed the Catholics are the champions (remember we are talking of the actions of Catholic and Protestant crowds, not of their armies). I think this is due not only to their being in the long run the strongest party numerically in most cities, but also to their stronger sense of *the persons of heretics* as sources of danger and defilment. Thus, injury and murder were a preferred mode of purifying the body social.

Furthermore, the preferred targets for physical attack differ in the Protestant and Catholic cases. As befitting a movement intending to overthrow a thousand years of clerical "tyranny" and "pollution", the Protestants' targets were primarily priests, monks and friars. That their ecclesiastical victims were usually unarmed (as Catholic critics hastened to point out) did not make them any less harmful in Protestant eyes, or any more immune from the wrath of God. Lay people were sometimes attacked by Protestant crowds, too, such as the festive dancers who were stoned at Pamiers and Lyon, and the worshippers who were killed at Saint-Médard's Church. But there is nothing that quite resembles the style and extent of the slaughter of the 1572 massacres. The Catholic crowds were, of course, happy to catch a pastor when they could, but the death of any heretic would help in the cause of cleansing France of these perfidious sowers of disorder and disunion....

... [T]he overall picture in these urban religious riots is not one of the "people" slaying the rich. Protestant crowds expressed no preference for killing or assaulting powerful prelates over simple priests. As for Catholic crowds, contemporary listings of their victims in the 1572 massacres show that artisans, the "little people", are represented in significant numbers....

... Let us look a little further at what I have called their rites of violence. Is there any way we can order the terrible, concrete details of filth, shame and torture that are reported from both Protestant and Catholic riots? I would suggest that they can be reduced to a repertory of actions, derived from the Bible, from the liturgy, from the action of political authority, or from the traditions of popular folk justice, intended to purify the religious community and humiliate the enemy and thus make him less harmful.

The religious significance of destruction by water or fire is clear enough. The rivers which receive so many Protestant corpses are not merely convenient mass graves, they are temporarily a kind of holy water, an essential feature of Catholic rites of exorcism....

Let us take a more difficult case, the troubling case of the desecration of corpses. This is primarily an action of Catholic crowds in the sixteenth century. Protestant crowds could be very cruel indeed in torturing living priests, but paid little attention to them when they were dead. (Perhaps this is related to the Protestant rejection of Purgatory and prayers for the dead: the souls of the dead experience immediately Christ's presence or the torments of the damned, and thus the dead body is no longer so dangerous or important an object to the living.) What interested Protestants was digging up bones that were being treated as sacred objects by Catholics and perhaps burning them, after the fashion of Josiah in I Kings. The Catholics, however, were not content with burning or drowning heretical corpses. That was not cleansing enough. The bodies had to be weakened and humiliated further. To an eerie chorus of "strange whistles and hoots", they were thrown to the dogs like Jezebel, they were dragged through the streets, they had their genitalia and internal organs cut away, which were then hawked through the city in a ghoulish commerce.

Let us also take the embarrassing case of the desecration of religious objects by filthy and disgusting means. It is the Protestants ... who are concerned about objects, who are trying to show that Catholic objects of worship have no magical power. It is not enough to cleanse by swift and energetic demolition, not enough to purify by a great public burning of the images, as in Albiac, with the children of the town ceremonially reciting the Ten Commandments around the fire. The line between the sacred and the profane was also re-drawn by throwing the sacred host to the dogs, by roasting the crucifix upon a spit, by using holy oil to grease one's boots, and by leaving human excrement on holy-water basins and other religious objects.

And what of the living victims? Catholics and Protestants humiliated them by techniques borrowed from the repertory of folk justice. Catholic crowds lead Protestant women through the streets with muzzles on—a popular punishment for the shrew—or with a crown of thorns. A form of charivari[11] is used, where the noisy throng humiliates its victim by making him ride backward on an ass. . . . In Montauban, a priest was ridden backward on an ass, his chalice in one hand, his host in the other, and his missal at an end of a halberd. At the end of his ride, he must crush his host and burn his own vestments. . . .

These episodes disclose to us the underlying function of the rites of violence. As with the "games" of Christ's tormentors, which hide from them the full knowledge of what they do, so these charades and ceremonies hide from sixteenth-century rioters a full knowledge of what they are doing. Like the legitimation for religious riot . . . , they are part of the "conditions for guilt-free massacre". . . . The crucial fact that the killers must forget is that their victims are human beings. These harmful people in the community—the evil priest or hateful heretic—have already been transformed for the crowd into "vermin" or "devils". The rites of religious violence complete the process of dehumanization. So in Meaux, where Protestants were being slaughtered with butchers' cleavers, a living victim was trundled to his death in a wheelbarrow, while the crowd cried "vinegar, mustard". And the vicar of the parish of Fouquebrune in the Angoumois was attached with the oxen to a plough and died from Protestant blows as he pulled.

What kinds of people made up the crowds that performed the range of acts we have examined in this paper? First, they were not by and large the alienated rootless poor. . . . A large percentage of men in Protestant icon-oclastic riots and in the crowds of Catholic killers in 1572 were characterized as artisans. Sometimes the crowds included other men from the lower or-ders. . . . More often, the social composition of the crowds extended upward to encompass merchants, notaries and lawyers, as well as clerics. . . .

In addition, there was significant participation by two other groups of people who, though not rootless and alienated, had a more marginal relationship to political power than did lawyers, merchants or even male artisans—namely, city women and teenaged boys. . . .

Finally, as this study has already suggested, the crowds of Catholics and Protestants, including those bent on deadly tasks, were not an inchoate mass, but showed many signs of organization. Even with riots that had little or no planning behind them, the event was given some structure by the situation of worship or the procession that was the occasion for many disturbances. In

---

[11]Davis defines this elsewhere as "a noisy, masked demonstration to humiliate some wrongdoer in the community."

other cases, planning in advance led to lists of targets, and ways of identifying friends or fellow rioters.....

That such splendor and order should be put to violent uses is a disturbing fact. Disturbing, too, is the whole subject of religious violence. How does an historian talk about a massacre of the magnitude of St. Bartholomew's Day? One approach is to view extreme religious violence as an extraordinary event, the product of frenzy, of the frustrated and paranoic primitive mind of the people.

A second approach sees such violence as a more usual part of social behaviour, but explains it as a somewhat pathological product of certain kinds of child-rearing, economic deprivation or status loss. This paper has assumed that conflict is perennial in social life, though the forms and strength of the accompanying violence vary; and that religious violence is intense because it connects intimately with the fundamental values and self-definition of a community. The violence is explained not in terms of how crazy, hungry or sexually frustrated the violent people are (though they may sometimes have such characteristics), but in terms of the goals of their actions and in terms of the rôles and patterns of behaviour allowed by their culture. Religious violence is related here less to the pathological than to the normal.

Thus, in sixteenth-century France, we have seen crowds taking on the rôle of priest, pastor or magistrate to defend doctrine or purify the religious community, either to maintain its Catholic boundaries and structure, or to re-form relations within it. We have seen that popular religious violence could receive legitimation from different features of political and religious life, as well as from the group identity of the people in the crowds. The targets and character of crowd violence differed somewhat between Catholics and Protestants, depending on their perception of the source of danger and on their religious sensibility. But in both cases, religious violence had a connection in time, place and form with the life of worship, and the violent actions themselves were drawn from a store of punitive or purificatory traditions current in sixteenth-century France.

In this context, the cruelty of crowd action in the 1572 massacres was not an exceptional occurrence. St. Bartholomew was certainly a bigger affair than, say, the Saint Médard's riot, it had more explicit sanction from political authority, it had elaborate networks of communication at the top level throughout France, and it took a more terrible toll in deaths. Perhaps its most unusual feature was that the Protestants did not fight back. But on the whole, it still fits into a whole pattern of sixteenth-century religious disturbance.

This inquiry also points to a more general conclusion. Even in the extreme case of religious violence, crowds do not act in a mindless way. They will to some degree have a sense that what they are doing is legitimate, the occasions will relate somehow to the defence of their cause, and their violent behaviour will have some structure to it—here dramatic and ritual. But the rites of violence are not the rights of violence in any *absolute* sense. They simply remind us that if we try to increase safety and trust within a community, try to guarantee that the violence it generates will take less destructive and less cruel forms, then we must think less about pacifying "deviants" and more about changing the central values.

Birth and Childhood in Seventeenth-Century France

WENDY GIBSON

Historians have sometimes referred to seventeenth-century France as a zenith of French civilization, the era of absolutism in government, the Baroque in art, and classicism in literature. Yet, the regular and humble processes of birth and childhood were frightful and dangerous times for all in that century, and even more so for females.

Approximately 3 percent of births were stillborn; 25 percent of children died before their first birthday; 25 percent more died by the age of twenty. These figures varied according to social group and geographical location, but it is clear that in all circumstances the life of a child was precarious. How do you account for such a high rate of mortality? How did peasants react to the death of a child?

For girls there was an additional situation: they were as a rule unwanted, unloved, and unappreciated. It is evident from time immemorial that nearly all societies valued boys over girls, but why did seventeenth-century Frenchwomen join with males in disparaging the female sex? Aristocrats in particular bemoaned the birth of a girl. Did the nobility have better reasons than the bourgeoisie or peasants to celebrate the birth of a male infant?

Gibson traces the life of a girl from birth through adolescence. What customs at and soon after birth might have damaged the baby girl? What were the responsibilities of the midwife? Why was speed in baptism so important? Affection toward the child was lacking. Why were mothers so reluctant to nurse their own children? Nursing would have established or tightened bonds between mother and infant. How were children clothed? What games did they play? To what extent did clothes and games distinguish children from the world of adults?

How were children integrated into the life of the community through education and work? Was there children's work? Was there work deemed especially appropriate for girls? Did religion reinforce or condemn the often bestial treatment of the young? What did theologians and writers say about childhood and about girls?

In what ways do you think the French absolutist state reflected these attitudes and practices relating to childhood and to females? After all, child-rearing practices produce a new generation of adults affected by their treatment as children. Was France caught in a cycle of a lack of affection toward the young along with a

severe approach toward childhood and especially girls that led inexorably to an
authoritarian, patriarchal government and social structure?

'It's a girl!' The midwife's pronouncement was calculated to bring little joy
to the exhausted mother or her expectant relatives in seventeenth-century
France. Queen Marie de Médicis[1] 'wept loud and long' in 1602 on learning
that she had supplied France with a princess, Elisabeth, instead of a second
heir to the throne and 'could not reconcile herself to the fact'. In 1662
Louis XIV's[2] first sister-in-law Henriette d'Angleterre (Madame), having
impatiently ascertained the female sex of the child that she was in the actual
process of bearing, 'said that it would have to be thrown in the river, and
showed her extreme disappointment to everyone'. Outside the royal circle
the sense of anti-climax was equally keen. Memorialists recording the birth
of a girl into an aristocratic family speak of the 'great regret' and 'ordeal'
of the father, and of the mother's 'misfortune'. Gazette-writers and other
well-wishing versifiers stress that couples will rapidly work to correct their
mistake:

> 'But since it is only a female cherub,
> Husband and wife, redoubling their efforts,
> Will work all over again
> To produce a male cherub afterwards'.

Grandmothers for their part seek to guard against a second 'accident' by
stern injunctions to daughters not to let their unborn offspring 'become a
girl'.

The general disappointment could take on more palpable forms. When
a royal prince was born the occasion was marked by prolonged rejoicings:
cannon salvoes, bonfires, pyrotechnic displays, processions and services of
thanksgiving, free distributions of wine in the streets, and the release of
prisoners. But when, after the birth of his third daughter Henriette in 1609,
Henri IV[3] summoned the Paris Parlement[4] to make 'signs of rejoicing in the
customary manner' the First President[5] replied 'that it was not the custom to
hold any ceremonies for girls, except for the first-born one, and that no such
ceremony was registered in the rolls, in the Church of Paris, or in the Town
Hall'.

That women should accept and join in the chorus of disparaging re-
marks which greeted the arrival of a member of their own sex caused some

[1] 1573–1642, wife of King Henry IV.
[2] King of France, 1643–1715.
[3] King of France, 1589–1610.
[4] A sovereign judicial court having jurisdiction over approximately one-half of the kingdom.
[5] The highest-ranking of the presiding judges in the Parlement.

amazement to contemporaries like the Comte de Bussy-Rabutin,[6] who maliciously interpreted it as a tacit admission of male superiority. But there were other, more practical, reasons for the prevailing attitude. In a country such as France, where women were excluded from the right of succession to the throne and from effectively holding public office, and where titles and property were normally passed on from generation to generation through the eldest male, the absence of an heir could constitute a real disaster. 'The males', as Gui Patin[7] wrote, 'are the props and supports of a big family's lastingness'. Lack of them might necessitate the abandonment of rank and possessions laboriously acquired over the centuries to rival dynasties and households interested in making posterity forget to whom they owed their elevation and lustre. Expressions of chagrin over births of girls are accordingly always most pronounced amongst royalty and the aristocracy, who had most to lose by them. Lower down in the social hierarchy the bourgeoisie note the event with a noncommittal wish for the infant's future virtue:

> God give her the grace to be mindful to fear and love Him, and fill her with His gifts.

> God give her the grace to be pure white in fact as in name, before God and men.

> God give this child the grace to live and die with a holy fear and love of Him.

The reactions of the peasantry, in the absence of direct written records of their sentiments, remain still more inscrutable. But any pleasure experienced at the thought of an extra worker in the family was bound to be tempered by the awareness of an extra mouth to feed, an extra 'establishment' to provide in later life.

For the birth of a daughter meant that sooner or later a dowry would have to be handed over to a husband or to a convent, a consideration which affected every class of society. Whatever the size of the dowry it represented the cession to outsiders of cash and property which, if invested in a son's marriage or career, would either have remained within the bosom of the family or yielded appreciable returns in the form of wages, perquisites and social distinction. The unhappy father had, moreover, the invidious task of safeguarding his daughter's virginity against the stratagems of designing gallants, on pain of sullying the family name and honour.

Born into a society disposed to regard her as more of an encumbrance than a blessing, the little girl began at once a struggle for survival against the host of physical perils and superstitions that beset the seventeenth-century infant. Birth, like the other two major events of human existence,

---

[6]Roger de Rabutin, Count of Bussy (1618–1693), wit and author of a scandalous book.
[7]1602–1672, dean of the faculty of medicine at the University of Paris.

marriage and death, was surrounded by its own age-old set of rituals. Some—the custom of blowing wine into the newborn child's mouth to prevent future inebriation and epilepsy, rubbing the baby's lips with a piece of gold to ensure their redness, inducing fashionable dimples by placing peas under the cheekbones—were comparatively innocuous. Others risked causing irreparable damage. Infant heads were kneaded to give them a good shape, or tightly bound with narrow bands, producing an elongation by which Parisian children were instantly recognisable. Noses were bound, pulled and pinched to correct real or fancied deformities. A cruel operation was performed on the infant girl's breast in the belief that this would facilitate the suckling of children in later life.

Cleansed without by a mixture of water and wine, and within by means of soap suppositories, the infant had then to submit to the straitjacket of swathing bands in which it would spend the first eight or nine months of life, sometimes longer in the case of girls. The main purpose of swaddling, apart from that of providing warmth and protection, was to render the body upright and the limbs straight and to accustom the child to stand instead of crawling in an unseemly and unhealthy fashion over floors that were cold, damp and littered with human and animal droppings. In practice the reverse effect was often achieved. In their anxiety to develop a plump, well-rounded breast in their nurslings, misguided wet-nurses subjected infant thoraxes to such compression that permanent humpbacks, projecting shoulders and curvatures of the spine resulted. Constriction of the hips, impeding their proper broadening, caused serious problems when the age of child-bearing was reached. Legs emerged from their wrappings bent, twisted and chafed.

To the discomfort of cramped and sore limbs was added that of a diet calculated to extinguish rather than to sustain life. Instances of children in the upper strata of society being suckled by their natural mothers were already sufficiently rare in the sixteenth century to make Marguerite de Valois,[8] future wife of Henri IV, start at the sight of an aristocratic hostess tranquilly calling for her baby to breast-feed before guests at a feast. A powerful coalition of ignorance, vanity and selfishness militated against the performance of what indignant preachers and moralists represented as a fundamental maternal duty. Human milk was popularly supposed to be formed of blood which flowed from the womb to the breasts, where it was mysteriously whitened. Suckling, therefore, could only have a debilitating effect upon the constitution of the mother, draining her of precious life-blood. Worse still, her youthful silhouette was threatened by this messy chore, and just at a time when it was important to have the wherewithal to cajole and mollify a husband impatient for the resumption of normal conjugal services. In consequence, the infant scarcely had time to rejoice in the maternal smiles and caresses over which pedagogues waxed lyrical before being despatched to the arms

---

[8]1553–1615, daughter of King Henry II of France and Catherine de Médicis.

of a local village wet-nurse whose own frequently scanty milk was quickly supplemented with the notorious *bouillie*.[9] This glutinous concoction of flour and cow's milk worked wonders in silencing cries of hunger, sometimes permanently.

Minute prescriptions for the choice of an ideal *nourrice*[10] were listed in every gynaecological treatise of the day. The sum total of opinions was that she should be a brunette of twenty-five to thirty years and of healthy stock, with good teeth, ample but not excessive proportions, a pleasant and virtuous disposition, and clear pronunciation, the last two qualities in order that her nursling would not contract any undesirable habits or modes of speech. Sexual continence during breast-feeding, with a view to maintaining high quality milk, was a further requirement, but one which was likely to be half-heartedly obeyed and to precipitate the introduction of weaning well before the recommended stage of the appearance of teeth.

The paragon of integrity described by the specialists appears in real life to have eluded even the most earnest parental seekers of her services. For private and public journals testify to a negligence of duty on the part of the *nourrice* that caused, at best, disfigurement or crippling, at worst, death. The philosopher John Locke,[11] conversing with a physician at Orléans in 1678, learned that the lameness of the local children was due 'more to the negligence of nurses than anything else, carrying them always wrapped up and on one side, and he thinks this to be the cause, because this lameness lights more on girls that are tenderer, than boys who are stronger and sooner out of their swaddling clothes'. At the opposite end of the century Pierre de l'Estoile[12] made a grim entry in his Journal for 1608 to the effect that 'many little children' had been 'stifled by their wet-nurses', though he failed to specify whether the stifling was done deliberately or came about through the habitual accident of the wet-nurse rolling on the baby in bed. The very person, then, entrusted with the rearing and physical well-being of infants presented yet another threat to their continued existence.

Maladies of different kinds, some arising from congenital malformations and clumsy post-natal care, others contracted in insanitary homes filled to capacity with humans and livestock, and all aggravated by the bleedings and purgings which doctors ordered with gay abandon, accounted for further deaths. All sections of society had a high rate of infant mortality. The Protestant leader Henri, Duc de Rohan, managed to rear to adulthood only one of his nine children, and Henri IV's minister, Sully,[13] only four of his own ten offspring. *Livres de Raison*, diaries kept by the heads of households,

---

[9]Pap.

[10]Wet-nurse.

[11]English philosopher (1632–1704) who traveled to France from 1675 to 1679.

[12]Pierre Taisan de l'Estoile (1546–1611), a lawyer who kept a journal during the reigns of Henry III and Henry IV.

[13]Maximilien de Béthune, duc de Sully (1560–1641), first minister to Henry IV.

depress by their long casualty lists. Simon Le Marchand, a bourgeois of Caen, recorded between 1612 and 1635 the birth of twelve offspring, ten of whom were overtaken by death within a maximum of two years, and mostly within a matter of days or months. Usually the fatal occurrence is just starkly noted, an eloquent testimony to its commonplace nature. Sometimes a pious ejaculation, touching in its resignation, accompanies the entry:

God grant her peace.

May God through His grace deign to have had mercy upon her, not charging her with the sins of her father and mother, albeit that these sully her profoundly.

God has given, God has taken away, blessed be the name of the Lord. Her soul is in heaven and her body in our tomb, near that of her good mother. May it please the divine majesty that their souls be together in heaven.

Only occasionally does the note of serene acceptance waver a little, betraying a proud parent whose hopes for the future have been cruelly shattered: 'She was well taught and full of promise . . . Had considerable intelligence, knew how to read at five years and had all the good inclinations and sentiments of her late mother'.

The extreme precariousness of infant existence helps to account for the emphasis that was placed on rapid baptism. Such was the concern to avert the tragedy of a Catholic baby's soul being condemned to wander in limbo and the body confided to a specially demarcated portion of the cemetery because death had intervened before the accomplishment of this vital ceremony that provision was made for the administration of a preliminary form of baptism known as the *ondoiement* to any new-born child whose life was considered to be in imminent danger of extinction. Anyone, male or female, lay or ecclesiastic, Catholic or non-Catholic, could perform the *ondoiement*, provided that they used natural water and pronounced in whatever language they knew the formula: 'I baptise you in the name of the Father, and of the Son, and of the Holy Ghost'. It sufficed for only a part of the child to protrude from the mother's body for the emergency baptism to be legitimate, and syringes were invented for use within the womb in cases of obstructed birth.

Formal presentation of the infant at the parochial church font was generally carried out with speed, whether an *ondoiement* had already been performed or not. At eight in the evening on 8 August 1677 Ferdinand Jacque, a Parlement advocate of Dôle, hastened to church the daughter who had arrived just before two o'clock that same day. Boys and girls born into the Froissard-Broissia family, also of Franche-Comté, were rushed to the font within as little as one or two hours after birth, a practice which proved remarkably effective in weeding out the weaker scions. Usually, however, parents managed to curb their zeal sufficiently to give the newly-born twenty-four hours to gather strength before being exposed to the elements.

Fairly frequent exceptions to the rule for speedy baptism were royal and aristocratic children whose official admission to Catholicism was delayed for reasons of state or convenience. Louis XIII[14] and his sister Elisabeth, born respectively in September 1601 and November 1602, were not baptised until 14 September 1606, along with their sister Christine, who had joined the family in February of that year. The Duchesse de Montpensier, Louis's niece, received her baptism in July 1636, at the age of nine. Mlle de Béthune, a grand-daughter of Chancellor Séguier,[15] was obliged to wait fourteen years before being christened.

In the choice of godparents, a considerable amount of latitude was allowed. Children of a very young age are themselves often found acting in this capacity. The grand-daughter of the illustrious Marquise de Rambouillet[16] was allowed to be a godmother at four years because she could answer the necessary questions when interrogated by the local priest. In 1688 Racine's[17] daughter Madeleine had as godparents her elder brother and sister, despite the fact that the latter, aged seven, was unable to sign the baptismal register. Having brothers and sisters serve as godparents, a popular custom, was a useful means of reinforcing with spiritual bonds the ties of blood already existing. Respectable introductions between youngsters of the opposite sex could also be made at the baptism ceremony, forming the basis of future marriages. Just as age was taken very little into account in the selection of godparents, so was social status. The attachment and gratitude of domestics was strengthened by holding their offspring at the font and by permitting them to do likewise with the infants of their employers. The supreme gesture of piety and humility consisted in handing children for baptism to a couple of paupers, and in performing a reciprocal service for the offspring of the poor. Thus Marguerite de Valois acted as impromptu godmother to the son of an Irish beggar-woman delivered one day in her path. Not only individuals but collective bodies also could stand as godfather or godmother. Evidence of this phenomenon is more common in connection with boys, baptised under the aegis of municipal authorities or the Provincial Assemblies (*Etats Provinciaux*). But Tallemant[18] mentions a lady-love of the Duc de Guise who had the town of Marseille as godparent, while the abbess of Sainte Croix at Poitiers, Flandrine de Nassau, Princess of Orange, owed her unusual forename to the fact of being the godchild of the *Etats*[19] of Flanders.

Custom decreed that the infant be given as a first name that of the godmother or godfather, as appropriate. For the Catholic girl the name

---

[14]King of France, 1610–1643.

[15]Pierre Séguier, duc de Villemor (1588–1672), chancellor to Louis XIII and Louis XIV.

[16]Catherine de Vivonne, Marquise de Rambouillet (1588–1665), hostess of regular gatherings of the cream of Parisian society.

[17]Jean Baptiste Racine (1639–1699), playwright.

[18]Gédéon Tallemant de Réaux (c.1619–1700), author of anecdotal memoirs.

[19]The assemblies of the leading men of Flanders.

would normally be that of a saint whose virtues she might imitate and whose protection she might implore; for the Protestant girl the name of an Old Testament heroine such as Rachel[20] or Sarah[21] would be first choice. The addition of second and third names was regarded by the Church as superfluous. There were, however, few blue-blooded girls without at least a double-barrelled forename, an abuse described towards the end of the century as spreading to the *Tiers Etat*,[22] who considered that the possession of several names conferred on their infants an air of nobility....

It was not at all unusual for several children in a family to bear the same forename. When an elder child died prematurely what seems in retrospect like a pathetic attempt at resuscitation would sometimes be made by passing on the same name to the next brother or sister that came along. But a succession of living children might equally be christened alike, for religious or family reasons. The pious Ducs de Beauvillier and de Noailles bestowed the name of Marie, the former on all of his nine daughters, the latter on seven out of eleven daughters. In the Savelli household to which Mme de Rambouillet belonged the name of Lucine, a saint of the family, was added to that of all daughters on baptism. The usage was not without causing a certain amount of confusion, and was one of the reasons which prompted the authorities to insist on the regular keeping of parish baptismal records.

Baptism being essentially a solemn sacrament, the Church saw little reason for it to be accompanied by merry-making and jollification. The faithful, however, begged to differ, seeing in the occasion a glorious excuse for lavish expenditure, gastronomic indulgence and letting off steam generally. Plenty of noise was obligatory. Music from violins, fifes and tabors (or salvoes from guns in the case of the nobility) would accompany the infant to church. Guests would while away the time that it took the priest to perform the familiar ritual—exorcisms, introduction of salt into the child's mouth (a symbol of wisdom and preservation from vice), aspersion with holy water, anointment with oil, imposition of the christening bonnet..., reading from Saint John's Gospel and exhortation to the godparents—by laughing, joking, promenading and exchanging kisses. Peals of bells would signal the termination of the ceremony. At that point the new Christian was apt to be whisked away to the nearest tavern and released only when the parents gave the merry kidnappers the means to wet the baby's head. Parents of substance would seek to render the event more memorable by keeping open house over a number of days and by giving presents to the populace....

Delicate infants, perhaps born before time, or those whose mothers had made special vows in return for a safe delivery, sometimes received, in addition to baptism, an extra form of spiritual protection. This consisted in

[20]The second wife of Jacob.

[21]Wife of Abraham and mother of Isaac.

[22]Third Estate, one of the three traditional groupings of French society. The First Estate constituted the clergy, the Second the nobility, and the Third everyone else.

dedicating them to God, the Virgin Mary, or one of the saints, in honour of whom they would adopt a religious type of raiment for a number of years stipulated by their parents. Madeleine de Sourdis, a future abbess whose precarious health had caused her to be offered at six weeks of age to the Virgin 'in order that it would please her [the Virgin] to be her Protectress, and to agree to let her wear the white habit in her honour, till the age of seven', lived to be an octogenarian. Less fortunate was the prematurely-born daughter of Louis XIV, who died in December 1664, a fortnight after being taken to the Récollettes[23] in the Faubourg Saint Germain and committed to assuming the habit and scapulary of the order for the first three years of her life. White or blue were the usual colours of the garments worn by girls consecrated in this way, and a service in church commemorated the moment when they were formally exchanged for ordinary, worldly clothes.

Children were clothed, as paintings and engravings of the period show, in scarcely modified versions of the heavy dress of their elders. Aristocratic girls bowed beneath the weight of jewels and elaborate coiffures. 'She staggers under gold and jewels', wrote Mme de Maintenon[24] of the tiny young Duchesse du Maine,[25] 'and her coiffure weighs more than her whole person. She will be prevented form growing and being healthy'. To induce them to preserve an upright carriage beneath the load they had stiffening material inserted into the corsage of their dresses and wore a type of bodice similarly strengthened with bone or metal. Hunchbacks like the three daughters of the Maréchale de la Mothe were condemned from childhood onwards to life in an iron corset.

Young and not so young shared games and pastimes too. The meanest little towns boasted of a tennis court in which children outshone mothers and fathers by their precocious dexterity with a racket. Strollers in the gardens of the Tuileries were charmed by the spectacle of groups of girls playing at bowls and skittles, and engaging in jumping competitions terminated by the solemn crowning of the winner with flowers or laurel. Over in the enclosure of the Palais de Justice[26] impoverished girls who assisted the numerous merchants selling their wares there were in the habit of tossing to and fro a ball or shuttlecock while digesting their lunch. Gentlewomen did not disdain shuttlecock, since it was permitted during recreation hours at Mme de Maintenon's aristocratic boarding-school at Saint-Cyr, along with games such as spillikins, chess, draughts and *trou-madame* (played by rolling balls into holes) which the foundress of the establishment regarded as exercising the brain or the memory. Juvenile play-acting, included under the same utilitarian rubric, became as popular at Saint-Cyr as it was in

[23] A reformed branch of the Franciscans, a medieval religious order.

[24] Françoise d'Aubigné, Marquise de Maintenon (1635–1719), second wife of Louis XIV.

[25] Louise de Bourbon, duchesse de Maine (1676–1753), wife of Louis XIV's eldest son and hostess of a periodic gathering of literary and political personages.

[26] Palace of Justice, seat of the Parlement and of other law courts in Paris.

the rest of upper-class society, but it underwent an enforced eclipse after sumptuous performances of Racine's *Esther* before the court in 1689 had stirred dangerous emotions in the bosom of actresses and spectators. Mme de Maintenon continued, however, to let her girls entertain small, select audiences in conditions of strict privacy and sobriety, and did not oppose the theatrical bent of her most important charge, the Duchesse de Bourgogne,[27] whom she schooled after the ten-year-old princess's arrival at court in 1696. She even condescended to the occasional game of blind man's bluff which all the high-ranking ladies of the court had to play in order to amuse the king's effervescent grand-daughter-in-law.

Early participation by children in the social, and especially in the religious, life of the community was encouraged. It was the youngest members of the family who pronounced the benediction at mealtimes and handed round portions of the bean cake traditionally baked on New Year's Eve. Under a watchful maternal eye they distributed alms to the poor and solicited offerings from the congregation in church. Theirs were the hands trusted to select winning tickets in public lotteries. Attired in angelic or other symbolic raiment they marched in pious processions, saluted dignitaries on the occasion of a ceremonial entry into town or installation in office, and paraded at times of national rejoicing. Though contemporary recorders of such events habitually fail to specify the sex and age of the children involved, it is obvious from scattered references that young girls played their part in public ceremonies of welcome, thanksgiving and supplication. They came into their own when it was a question of greeting high-born ladies who had come to take up temporary or permanent residence in the locality.... As members of the so-called 'devout sex', girls were naturally associated with corporate demonstrations of piety. It was they who led a procession to implore the Divinity for rain to fall on their drought-stricken town of Châlons in the summer of 1624. Young daughters of upper-class families of Marseille learned an object lesson in humility when, arrayed in virginal robes, they each escorted a female from the poor-house in a procession of 1688 which ended with some of their mothers waiting upon the impoverished women at table....

It goes without saying that community life was not all play and pageantry. The sober reality of work intervened at an age which struck travellers in France by reason of its earliness: 'the smallest children are trained to work', remarked Elie Brackenhoffer of Strasbourg after a trip to Grenoble. Albert Jouvin of Rochefort made an identical observation at the arsenal of Toulon: 'You see there ... even very little children ... working'. The poverty of parents who needed every hand available, every *sou*[28] earned, in order to maintain the family bread supply was the major factor in turning children out into the fields or the forerunners of the factories as soon as

---

[27] Marie Adélaïde, duchesse de Bourgogne (1685–1712), wife of Louis XIV's grandson.

[28] A coin equivalent to twelve *deniers* (pennies).

they had sufficient intelligence and strength to be able to mind livestock and perform simple mechanical operations. Seven or eight was the age at which the exercise of reason was thought to commence. But grown-ups were impatient: children in the vicinity of Alençon were employed to manufacture pins at the ripe old age of six. Any qualms over child labour were easily stifled by the reflection that children were not worked to the point of exhaustion. Even in a poor-house like the famous La Charité at Lyons, where indigent and orphaned girls and boys were constrained from the age of seven to rise at five in the morning and busy themselves with silk-making till dark in winter and six in the evening in summer, John Locke felt that 'counting their mass and breakfast in the morning, collation in the evening and time of dinner, their work is not hard'. The idea was firmly ingrained, moreover, that the young needed to be trained and to be preserved from the evils of slothfulness. Parents who suffered no economic duress still believed in delegating household chores to their daughters at the first opportunity and in making sure that every minute of the day was fruitfully filled. 'I observed here one thing as I walked along the streets', wrote Francis Mortoft on a visit to Nantes in 1658, 'that none of the women were idle, but the gentlewomen and little girls, as they sat at their doors or walked about the streets, had their spinning work in their hands.' No devil was going to find mischief for idle young hands to do if mothers like these could help it.

Inevitably children so rapidly established in the adult roles of wage-earners and, if they were well-to-do, of marriage partners, were judged by adult criteria. Judgements were harsh. The great classical writers in general show themselves to be impervious to the charms of childhood, viewing it with some horror as an age of physical and mental weakness, essentially lacking in dignity. 'Childhood is the life of an animal' was the terse verdict of Bossuet[29] when he considered the impotence of the child's will and reason to combat the force of passions. 'Children ... are already men', that is to say, possessed of all vices, according to La Bruyère.[30] The genial La Fontaine[31] underlines their stupidity, harshness and cruelty. . . .

Manifestations of affection towards these miniature adults appear decidedly inhibited by modern standards. The few brief insights into the sentiments of the peasantry left by seventeenth-century observers attest to a certain detachment between parents and offspring, of the kind which characterises the expressions and stances of the group depicted in the painting *Famille de Paysans*,[32] attributed to Louis Le Nain,[33] where each figure seems physically withdrawn from the others and immersed in his or her

---

[29]Jacques Bénigne Bossuet (1627–1704), Bishop of Meaux, court preacher, tutor to Louis XIV's son, and author of numerous works.

[30]Jean de La Bruyère (1645–1696), author of the *Characters*.

[31]Jean de La Fontaine (1612–1695), French poet.

[32]"Peasant Family."

[33]1593–1643, painter of rustic scenes and of common people.

own private world. The ex-soldier turned moralist, Fortin de la Hoguette, cites peasant fathers and children as an example of the purely pragmatic relationship, what he calls 'a very obscure feeling of affection on the part of father towards son, son towards father...which subsists only as long as it is necessary for them to work together', that develops when parents tend their progeny like their livestock, nurturing the body at the expense of the soul. At best the generalisation would avowedly apply only to fathers and sons, leaving unsettled the question of whether peasant fathers were equally unfeeling towards daughters, and vice versa. In addition it was penned by an 'outsider' from a higher social bracket who shared with a good many of his equals the propensity for interpreting peasant behaviour in the light of that of animals. The attitude taken by some sections of fashionable society towards demonstrating love for children hardly justified feelings of superiority. Coulanges, Mme de Sévigné's[34] cousin, in a lengthy *Chanson*[35] entitled 'Avis aux Pères de Famille',[36] pleads for fathers to observe public silence about their offspring and to make sure that the latter eat apart from civilised company:

> *Know, furthermore, good people,*
> *That nothing is more intolerable*
> *Than to see your little children*
> *Strung like onions round the big table,*
> *With runny noses and greasy chins,*
> *Poking their fingers in all the dishes.*

The sight of a learned man stooping to play with his own child brought a pitying smile to the lips of Vigneul-Marville:[37]

> Learned men have their ridiculous side as well. Who would not have laughed at seeing Melancthon, the most serious and erudite of the Lutheran theologians, reading from a book held in one hand, and with the other rocking his child to sleep? I saw on one occasion the late Monsieur Esprit in a very similar posture. He was reading Plato, and from time to time he would stop reading, shake his infant's rattle, and play with this kid.

However, as this passage reveals, there *were* fathers willing to brave public ridicule and the prejudices of what were for the most part childless scholars in order to show affection for, and interest in, their young children.

Letters provide a precious testimony in this respect since, out of the public gaze, in the intimacy of a page designed only for the perusal of a

---

[34]Marie de Rabutin-Chantal, Marquise de Sévigné (1626–1696), famous letter-writer.

[35]Song.

[36]"Advice to Fathers of the Family."

[37]Pseudonym of Noël Bonaventure d'Argonne, author of a late seventeenth-century work on history and literature.

loved one or a friend, a father could abandon himself unashamedly to the promptings of paternal affection. Henri IV confides to his mistress Mme de Verneuil his pleasure in the wit, or naivety, of their four-year-old Gabrielle: 'our daughter conversed with my wife and myself and the whole company for three hours this evening, and nearly made us die laughing'. The Maréchal de La Force preoccupies himself with keeping his daughter's complexion free from sunburn in his absence, and threatens her with the ultimate sanction of no Christmas presents if she persists in talking through her nose and failing to study diligently. In the later part of the century Racine's letters are full of homely chatter about little Nanette's difficulty in cutting her teeth, the wit and intelligence of young Madelon, and his delight at receiving a bouquet for his *fête*[38] from his youngest daughters while he is busy working. But perhaps the most touching memorial to the bond between a father and his small daughter is that enshrined within the memoirs of Henri de Campion, a nobly-born military man who died in 1663. Louise-Anne entered his life on 2 May 1649, 'so beautiful and so pleasing that from the moment of her birth I loved her with a tenderness that I cannot put into words'. Scarcely had Campion time to savour the joys of paternity before death robbed him of the child on 10 May 1653:

> When I reflected that I was separated for the whole of my life from what was most dear to me, I could find no pleasure in the world, outside of which lay my happiness. I know that many will tax me with weakness and with a lack of fortitude over an accident that they will not consider one of the worst; but to that I would reply that things only affect us according to the feelings that we have for them, and that therefore one should not make blanket judgments as if we all had the same way of thinking. It is necessary to know how highly we rate things before praising the patience we show on losing them.... I confess that I would be acting like a woman if I pestered people with my laments; but always to cherish what I loved most of all, to think about her continually and to want to rejoin her, I consider that the sentiment of a man who knows what love is, and who, believing firmly in the immortality of the soul, feels that the departure of his dear daughter is a temporary absence, and not an eternal separation.

Even the fondest of fathers, it seems, was uncomfortably aware of indulging a culpable weakness in loving and grieving for his own child.

It was not, therefore, a very welcoming face that seventeenth-century society presented to the infant girl. From a physical point of view life was fraught with dangers to which her tender constitution often succumbed. From a moral point of view she suffered doubly. As a child she was an object of mistrust to theologians, moralists and certain men of letters who saw in her essentially the product of Original Sin, a wilful animal needing, they urged with some success, to be kept at a distance even from her own parents until the process of reason began to operate. As a female she was

---

[38] Name-day.

a disappointment because she was 'fragile' in all respects and inapt to maintain her family's material status. This initial burden of prejudice was to accompany her continually, and not least throughout the second major phase of existence, her education.

Insanity in Early Modern England

MICHAEL MacDONALD

Insanity, as Michael MacDonald reminds us, is not the same for all times and places, but is culturally defined. Definitions of what constitutes madness reflect the values of a society. Thus, in England, interpretations of madness and the treatment accorded the insane changed between the sixteenth-century Protestant Reformation and the eighteenth-century Industrial Revolution. What were the most significant of these changes? How do developments in English society explain the increased attention given to the mentally ill?

Many early modern Englishmen looked to family life as a cause of mental disorder. Why? Even the government held the institution of the family to be a primary concern in its efforts to deal with the insane. Thus the Court of Wards and Liveries acted rather honestly and "sanely" when it adjudicated the estates of lunatics. How did the government's behavior toward poor lunatics come to be intertwined with the problem of poverty? Just as the state had the poor locked up in workhouses, so by the eighteenth century did governments, as well as private citizens, establish asylums for the insane. Why did society now condone the confinement of these groups of people who formerly had enjoyed a measure of freedom?

There was great competition in England among those who thought they understood mental disorders. Proponents of magic, religion, and science, which interacted and overlapped in the seventeenth century, disagreed on the causes and treatment of insanity. Should we be more surprised that remedies and explanations offered by physicians did not work or that the elite of England gradually came to accept the claims of medical science? At least supernatural explanations for madness, if perhaps misguided, did not normally harm the mentally disturbed. Exorcisms and faith healing, for example, may have had therapeutic value. On the other hand, medical remedies employed techniques that were seen to be, as MacDonald says, "unpleasant, ineffective, and theoretically insupportable." Why did the ruling classes put their faith in those secular priests, the physicians? How did irrationality come to typify the attitude toward the mentally ill, cruelly treated and incarcerated, during the eighteenth-century "Age of Reason"?

Madness is the most solitary of afflictions to the people who experience it; but is the most social of maladies to those who observe its effects. Every mental disorder alienates its victims from the conventions of action, thought, and emotion that bind us together with the other members of our society. But because mental disorders manifest themselves in their victims' relationships with other men and women, they are more profoundly influenced by social and cultural conditions than any other kind of illness. For this reason the types of insanity people recognize and the significance they attach to them reflect the prevailing values of their society; the criteria for identifying mental afflictions vary between cultures and historical periods. The response to the insane, like the reaction to the sufferers of physical diseases, is also determined by the material conditions, social organization, and systems of thought that characterize a particular culture and age. The methods of caring for mentally disturbed people, the concepts that are used to explain the causes of their maladies, and the techniques that are employed to relieve their anguish are all determined more by social forces than by scientific discoveries, even today. Two central problems, therefore, confront historians of insanity. First, they must show how ideas about mental disorder and methods of responding to it were adapted to the social and intellectual environment of particular historical periods. Second, they must identify changes in the perception and management of insanity and explain how they were related to broader transformations in the society.

The history of mental disorder in early modern England is an intellectual Africa. Historians and literary scholars have mapped its most prominent features and identified some of its leading figures, but we still have very little information about the ideas and experiences of ordinary people. Both the unfortunates who actually suffered from mental afflictions and the men and women who tried to help them still inhabit *terra incognita*. Their story, the social history of insanity between the Reformation and the Industrial Revolution, falls into two distinct eras divided by the cataclysm of the English Revolution. During the late sixteenth and early seventeenth centuries, the English people became more concerned about the prevalence of madness, gloom, and self-murder than they had ever been before, and the reading public developed a strong fascination with classical medical psychology. Nevertheless, conventional beliefs about the nature and causes of mental disorders and the methods of psychological healing continued to reflect the traditional fusion of magic, science, and religion that typified the thinking of laymen of every social rank and educational background. The enormous social and psychological significance of the family shaped contemporary interpretations of insane behavior and determined the arrangements that were made to care for rich and poor lunatics alike. . . . During the century and a half following the great upheaval of the English Revolution, the governing classes embraced secular interpretations of the signs of insanity and championed medical methods of curing mental disorders. They shunned magical and religious techniques of psychological healing. Private entrepreneurs founded specialized institutions to manage mad people, and municipal officials established public madhouses. The asylum movement eventually transferred the responsibility for maintaining lunatics out of the family and into the asylum. Madmen were removed from their normal social surroundings and incarcerated with others of their kind; lunatics lost their places as members of a household and acquired new identities as the victims of mental diseases.

Interest in insanity quickened about 1580, and madmen, melancholics, and suicides became familiar literary types. Scientific writers popularized medical lore about melancholy, and clergymen wrote treatises about consoling the troubled in mind. Gentlemen and ladies proclaimed themselves melancholy; physicians worried about ways to cure the mentally ill; preachers and politicians denounced sinners and dissenters as melancholics or madmen. Anxious intellectuals claimed that self-murder was epidemical, and they argued about its medical and religious significance.... Heightened concern about the nature and prevalence of mental disorders was fostered by the increasing size and complexity of English society. Population growth and economic change increased the numbers of insane and suicidal people and overburdened the capacity of families and local communities to care for the sick and indigent. Renaissance humanism set new standards of conduct for the nobility, and the turbulent and incomplete triumph of Protestantism fragmented English society into religious groups with sharply differing views about how people ought to behave. The adequacy of traditional codes of conduct was subjected to intense criticism by learned reformers and religious zealots, and both humanist intellectuals and Puritan clergymen were naturally concerned about the causes and significance of abnormal behavior. Although they often looked to the same sources for ideas about insanity, one can say in general that religious conservatives elaborated classical medical psychology, whereas Puritan evangelists revitalized popular religious psychology and set it in a Calvinist theological framework.

In spite of the increased interest in insanity and the growing controversy about its religious implications, the perception and management of mental disorders did not change fundamentally before 1660. Contemporary ideas about the varieties of mental maladies and their characteristic signs were rooted in ancient science and medieval Christianity, and the typology of insanity was similar all over Western Europe. Within the broad framework of medical and religious thought, however, popular stereotypes of mental disorder were adapted to fit English conditions. For example, widely held beliefs about the behavior of mad and troubled people and the immediate causes of their misery reflected the psychological significance of the family in the lives of ordinary villages. Descriptions of the symptoms of violent madness placed great emphasis on irrational threats toward members of one's immediate family. Traditional legal prohibitions against suicide aimed to prevent it by emphasizing the responsibility of potential self-murders for their family's welfare. Common complaints about the causes of overwhelming anxiety and despair included unrequited love, marital strife, and bereavement. This preoccupation with the family was the consequence of its elemental importance in English society. The household was the basic social unit, and at every level of society it performed a myriad of functions. Within the walls of great houses and cottages children were reared and educated, the sick and infirm were nursed and maintained, estates were managed and goods were manufactured. Most households were very small. Except among the wealthy, whose entourages often included dozens of servants, clients and kin, households normally consisted only of a married couple, their young children, and, in many cases, a servant or apprentice. The small size of domestic groups and the high rate of geographical mobility in early seventeenth-century England greatly enhanced the part that the nuclear family played in the emotional lives of people of low and middling status.

The social importance of the family was also recognized in the arrangements for maintaining mad and troubled people. Only a handful of the insane in a nation of five million souls were cast into an asylum before the English Revolution. Bedlamites[1] swarmed through the imaginations of Jacobean playwrights and pamphleteers, but the famous asylum was in truth a tiny hovel housing fewer than thirty patients. Bethlem Hospital was the only institution of its kind, and its inmates languished there for years, living in squalid conditions without adequate medical treatment. Private institutions to house the insane did not begin to proliferate until the last half of the seventeenth century, municipal asylums to rival Bedlam were not founded in major cities for another century, and county lunatic hospitals were not established until after 1808. Tudor and Stuart governments responded to increasing concern about insanity by refurbishing traditional institutions to help families bear the burden of harboring a madman. The welfare of rich lunatics was guarded by the Court of Wards and Liveries, which exercised the crown's feudal right to manage the affairs of minors who inherited land as tenants-in-chief. Children, idiots, and lunatics were siblings in the eyes of the law, because they all lacked the capacity to reason and so could not be economically and legally responsible.

The Court of Wards was notorious for selling its favors to the highest bidder, allowing guardians who purchased wardships to ruin their charges' estates and bully them into profitable marriages. But toward lunatics the court behaved with uncharacteristic delicacy, repudiating rapacity in favor of family and legitimacy. King James[2] instructed the court to ensure that lunatics "be freely committed to their best and nearest friends, that can receive no benefit by their death, and the committees, bound to answer for...the very just value of their estates upon account, for the benefit of such lunatic (if he recover) or of the next heir." The order was obeyed. The court usually appointed relatives or friends of mad landowners to see that they were cared for and their property preserved. Naturally, there were some sordid struggles for the guardianship of rich lunatics, and sometimes men hurled false accusations of insanity at wealthy eccentrics in hopes of winning a rich wardship. But the court was unusually scrupulous about investigating

[1] Bedlamites and Gedlamites are names derived from Bethlem Hospital in London.
[2] James I, 1603–1625.

chicanery when it concerned lunatics, and abuses appear to have been rare. Before a landowner was turned over to a committee of guardians, a jury of local notables was assembled to certify that he had been too mad to manage his estates for a year and more. Such juries relied on common sense and common knowledge to establish that a person was insane, but their chief preoccupation was to discover whether he could perform the necessary economic chores to preserve the family property.

The court and the men who acted as inquisitors and guardians on its behalf behaved more virtuously toward the estates of lunatics than those of minor heirs because there was little profit in the wardship of the insane. Lunacy was regarded as a temporary state and the law decreed that when the madman recovered he should have restored to him all of his property, save the amount the guardians expended for his care. And because lunatics were unreasoning creatures, they could not contract marriages, perhaps the most valuable aspect of the wardship of minors. Legal rules and low incentive to break them effectively protected the rights of insane landowners, and when the Court of Wards was abolished during the Revolution cries were heard that lunatics were now vulnerable to the greed of unscrupulous guardians as never before. . . .

The chief concern of the crown's policy toward insane landowners was to preserve the integrity of their estates so that their lineages would not be obliterated by the economic consequences of their madness. Paupers had no property or social standing to protect, but the Tudor and Stuart state tried also to assist poor lunatics by providing financial relief for their families. After 1601 the government obliged parishes to treat impoverished madmen as "deserving poor," people who, like orphans and cripples, were unable to work through no fault of their own. . . . These allowances were paid out of the funds from local taxation for poor relief, and they were intended to prevent humble families from starvation and fragmentation because the lunatic's labor was lost. A 1658 order by Lancashire justices to provide for Isabell Breatherton illustrates the way the system worked in practice:

> It is ordered by this court that the . . . churchwardens and overseers of the poor within the parish of Wimwick shall . . . take into consideration the distracted condition of Isabell, wife of James Breatherton of Newton and provide for her or allow unto her said husband weekly or monthly allowances as her necessity requires, so as she may be kept from wandering abroad or doing any hurt or prejudice either to herself or otherwise.

As the population grew and the economy became more specialized in the sixteenth and seventeenth centuries, poverty became a major social problem. Municipal governments experimented with new kinds of institutions, such as hospitals and workhouses, in an attempt to find some solution to the increasingly alarming situation, and the crown began slowly to imitate some features of these experiments. In 1609, for example, counties were ordered to establish houses of correction to confine the able-bodied poor and train them for gainful employment; compliance was slow, but by the 1630s every shire[3] had such an institution. Lunatics were sometimes housed in these local Bridewells,[4] but it appears that incarceration was regarded as an exceptional and undesirable expedient. Lancashire officials were reluctant to confine madmen to the county's house of correction if they could avoid it, preferring to leave them in the care of their families whenever possible. For the poor as for the rich, therefore, the Tudor and early Stuart state left the care and management of the insane largely in the hands of their families and attempted to lessen the social and economic impact of lunacy by helping families either directly through the Court of Wards or indirectly through the parishes.

Early seventeenth-century methods of explaining the natural and supernatural causes of insanity and relieving the suffering of its victims were marked by a traditional mingling of magical, religious, and scientific concepts. Individual cases of mental disorder might be attributed to divine retribution, diabolical possession, witchcraft, astrological influences, humoral imbalances,[5] or to any combination of these forces. Cures were achieved (in theory) by removing the causes of the sufferer's disturbance, and the means to combat every kind of malign effect were dispensed by a bewildering array of healers. Insane men and women were treated by specialists, such as humanistic physicians, who practiced a single method of psychological healing, or they were consoled by eclectics, such as medical astrologers or clerical doctors, who combined remedies from several systems of therapy. The profusion of causal explanations for insanity and of healing methods was not simply the result of the inchoate state of the medical profession. It was also a practical manifestation of the popular confidence that magic, religion, and science could be reconciled. Medieval and Renaissance cosmology provided a systematic model for making such a reconciliation, and on a less sophisticated plane popular religious thought fused religious and magical beliefs.

Classical medical psychology became very popular among the educated classes during the sixteenth and seventeenth centuries. It was disseminated by the physicians, who were increasingly articulate and well-organized, and by humanist intellectuals, who were often clerics and medical amateurs. ...Although the remedies sanctioned by natural scientific theories were no more effective than religious or magical treatments for mental disorder, the medical approach eventually prevailed over supernatural explanations for the causes of madness. In the early seventeenth century the natural and supernatural approaches coexisted uneasily, championed by rival groups of professionals, to be sure, but not yet incompatible to many minds. Humanistic

[3]A district in England coinciding roughly with a modern county.

[4]Jails, named after the London house of correction.

[5]Physicians believed that sickness was caused by an imbalance among the four humors (yellow bile, black bile, phlegm, and blood).

physicians battled to secure a monopoly over the care of sick and insane people and to make their trade proof against the interloping of clerical doctors, apothecaries, surgeons, astrologers, and village wizards....

... Medical practice was a natural extension of ministers' duty to relieve the afflictions of their flocks, and a great many rural rectors and vicars provided various kinds of medical services for their parishioners. Medicine was an essential aspect of the astrologers' art, and occultists of every degree of rank and learning, from highly educated university graduates to illiterate village wise folk, used astrology as a tool for medical diagnosis and prognostication. The doctors could do little to prevent clergymen from practicing their craft, because the church and the universities had the power to license medical practitioners, and neither was likely to concur that learned clerks who practiced medicine were as culpable as ignorant quacks. Humanistic physicians could not possibly supply all the medical needs of the English people, and so long as clerical doctors, and indeed astrologers and cunning men and women,[6] did not slaughter their patients and garnered reputations for effective treatments, the authorities were inclined to grant them licenses to practice medicine legally. In London and its suburbs, however, the College of Physicians were empowered to fine unlicensed practitioners, and the privilege was used to harass popular astrologers and empirics.... The doctors' efforts to persuade the public that scientific medicine was the only legitimate basis for healing made little headway before the English Revolution: Professional eclecticism and therapeutic pluralism continued to characterize the treatment of physically ill and mentally disturbed people.

During the course of the seventeenth century, religious controversy and the shock of revolution accelerated the triumph of medical explanations for insanity among the governing classes. The Anglican hierarchy repudiated popular demonology for theological reasons, only to discover that Jesuits and Puritans eagerly took up the struggle against the Fiend and his minions. Radical Protestants developed new means for casting out devils and uplifting downcast hearts and used them to proselytize as well as to console. They insisted that misery, anxiety, and sadness were the emblems of sin, the normal afflictions of the unregenerate, and they taught that the surest means to overcome them was spiritual self-discipline and godly fellowship. Insanity was the epitome of conduct unguided by a pious and responsible personality.... The Puritans produced a literature of anxious gloom in which despair normally preceded conversion, and they naturally bruited about their ability to relieve such suffering. During the Revolution the sects— especially the Quakers—employed their powers of exorcism and spiritual healing to prove by miracles their divine inspiration and refute the charges of the "hireling priests." The orthodox elite seized the healer's gown in which the radicals clothed themselves and turned it inside out, calling religious

---

[6]Cunning men and women practiced so-called white witchcraft, which involved predicting the future, healing, preparing love potions, and recovering lost objects.

enthusiasm madness and branding the vexations of tender consciences religious melancholy.

These events coincided with remarkable achievements in physical science and anatomy, and they helped to accomplish the end that physicians had been unable to attain by propaganda and persecution. They prompted the ruling elite to embrace secular explanations for mental disorders and to repudiate magical and religious methods of healing them. The secularization of the elite's beliefs about insanity affected their notions about the nature of mental diseases as well as the causes of such afflictions.... The educated classes' gradual rejection of traditional religious ideas about suicide in favor of the medical theory that it was the outcome of mental disease was also fostered by orthodox hatred of religious enthusiasm. Throughout the eighteenth century dissenting sects continued to exorcise people who believed that they were possessed by the Devil. Anglican spokesmen argued that the age of miracles was long past, and the Devil rarely if ever swayed the minds and inhabited the bodies of people in modern times. This argument corroded the traditional stereotype of suicide, which depicted self-murder as a religious crime, committed at the instigation of the Devil, who often appeared personally to urge his victims on to self-destruction.

The rejection of the supernatural beliefs and thaumaturgy of the sectaries fostered scorn for religious and magical therapies. Although the methods of psychological healing practiced by the Dissenters[7] were often effective, the governing classes abandoned them in favor of medical remedies for mental disorders, techniques that were widely recognized to be unpleasant, ineffective, and theoretically insupportable. Magical remedies against supernatural harm, such as astrological amulets, charms, and exorcisms, were discarded by reputable practitioners. By the end of the seventeenth century a loose hierarchy of prestige had been established among the various types of healers who treated insanity, and at its apex were the humanistic physicians, who viewed madness and gloom as natural disorders. The dominance of secular interpretations of insanity among the eighteenth-century governing classes was embodied in the asylum movement. Beginning about 1660, scores of entrepreneurs founded private madhouses to care for the insane, and beginning about a century later, some municipal governments established receptacles for pauper lunatics. The therapeutic practices of the new asylums were based mainly on medical theories and remedies....

The governing classes' repudiation of supernatural explanations of the signs and causes of insanity and their rejection of magical and religious therapies were not readily accepted by the mass of the English people. Throughout the eighteenth century ordinary villagers continued to believe that witches and demons could drive men mad and that the Devil could possess the minds and bodies of his victims. They sought the help of a ragtag regiment of increasingly disreputable astrologers and folk magicians

---

[7]Those who rejected Anglicanism, the state religion.

to protect them against these evils. The exorcisms and religious cures of the Non-conformist sects,[8] and particularly of the Methodists, appealed to the strong popular attachment to traditional supernaturalism. The deepening abyss between elite attitudes toward insanity and popular beliefs was not simply the consequence of the enlightened scientism of the educated classes. Medical theories about mental disorders were contradictory and controversial; medical therapies were notoriously difficult to justify either theoretically or empirically. They appealed to an elite sick of sectarian enthusiasm because they lacked the subversive political implications that religious psychology and therapy had acquired during the seventeenth century. As the eighteenth century progressed, more and more people were subjected to incarceration in madhouses and to medical brutality. The abolition of family care for lunatics and the abandonment of therapeutic pluralism were the consequences of religious conflict, political strife, and social change. The lunacy reformers of the early nineteenth century drew an exaggerated, but nevertheless genuinely horrified, picture of the terrible suffering that the asylum movement and rise of medical psychology inflicted on the insane....

[8]The Dissenters from Anglicanism (Church of England).

Acknowledgments (*continued from p. iv*)

"Organized Greek Games." William J. Baker. From *Sports in the Western World.* Lanham, Maryland: Rowman and Littlefield, 1982, pp. 14–23, 25–26. Reprinted with permission of Rowman and Littlefield Publishers.

"Marriage and the Family in Athens." W. K. Lacey. Reprinted from W. K. Lacey: *The Family in Classical Greece.* Copyright © 1968 by Thames & Hudson. Used by permission of the publisher, Cornell University Press.

"Classical Greek Attitudes to Sexual Behavior." K. J. Dover. Reprinted from *Women in the Ancient World.* The Arethusa Papers, vol. 6, ed. by John Paradotto and J. P. Sullivan. 1984. Used by permission of the State University of New York Press.

"The Roman Mob." P. A. Brunt. World Copyright: The Past and Present Society, 175 Banbury Road, Oxford, England. This article is here reprinted in abridged form, and without the original footnote sequence, with the permission of the Society and the author, from *Past and Present: A Journal of Historical Studies,* no. 35 (1966).

"Roman Marriage." Suzanne Dixon. From *The Roman Family* by Suzanne Dixon. The Johns Hopkins University Press. Baltimore. London. (1992), pages 61–90, 95–97. Reprinted with permission of The Johns Hopkins University Press.

"The Motivations for St. Perpetua's Martyrdom." Mary R. Lefkowitz. From the *Journal of American Academy of Religion,* #44 (1976). Syracuse University Press, pages 417–421. Reprinted with permission of Syracuse University Press.

"Rural Economy and Country Life in the Medieval West." Georges Duby. Translated by Cynthia Postan. Reprinted by permission of the University of South Carolina Press, Columbia, South Carolina, 1968. Also with permission of Hodder Headline PLC, 338 Euston Road, London NW1 3BH.

"Medieval Children." David Herlihy. From *Essays on Medieval Civilization,* eds. Bede Karl Lackner and Kenneth Roy Philip. University of Texas Press (1978), pp. 109–130. Used by permission of the Walter Prescott Webb Memorial Lecture Committee @ Arlington.

"Vendetta and Civil Disorder in Late Medieval Ghent." David Nicholas. Copyright © 1990 by David Nicholas. Reprinted by permission of the author.

" 'Bastard Feudalism' and the Kiss: Changing Social Mores in Late Medieval and Early Modern France." J. Russell Major. From *The Journal of Interdisciplinary History* XVII (1987), 509–535. With the permission of the editors of *The Journal of Interdisciplinary History* and the MIT Press, Cambridge, Massachusetts. Copyright © 1987 by the Massachusetts Institute of Technology and the editors of *The Journal of Interdisciplinary History.*

"Concepts of Cleanliness: The Water that Infiltrated." Georges Vigarello. From *Concepts of Cleanliness: Changing Attitudes in France Since the Middle Ages.* Cambridge, England and New York: Cambridge University Press (1988) pp. 1–11. Reprinted with the permission of Cambridge University Press.

"The Family in Renaissance Italy." David Herlihy. From *The Family in Renaissance Italy* by David Herlihy, pp. 4–12. Copyright © 1974 by Forum Press, Inc. Reproduced by permission.

"The Effects of the Black Death on North Africa and Europe." M. E. Combs-Schilling. From *Sacred Performances* by M. E. Combs-Schilling. Copyright © 1989 by Columbia University Press. Reprinted with permission of the publisher.

"The Jews of Spain and the Expulsion of 1492." Norman Roth. From *The Historian* 55 (Autumn 1992), pp. 17–30.

"The Early History of Syphilis: A Reappraisal." Alfred W. Crosby, Jr. *American Anthropologist,* 71, 2 (April 1969). Reproduced by permission of the American Anthropological Association. Not for further reproduction.

"Nuns, Wives, and Mothers: Women and the Reformation in Germany." Merry Wiesner. From *Women in Reformation and Counter-Reformation Europe: Public and Private Worlds,* ed. Sherrin Marshall. Published by Indiana University Press (1989) pp. 8–26. Reprinted with permission of Indiana University Press.

" 'Lost Women' in Early Modern Seville: The Politics of Prostitution." Mary Elizabeth Perry. This article is reprinted from *Feminist Studies,* volume 4, number 1 (February 1978), 195–214, by permission of the publisher, *Feminist Studies,* Inc., c/o Women's Studies Program, University of Maryland, College Park, MD 20742.

"Sexual Politics and Religious Reform in the Witch Hunts." Joseph Klaits. From *Servants of Satan: The Age of the Witch Hunts.* Published by Indiana University Press (1985) pp. 48–53, 56–73, 76–85. Reprinted with permission of the author and Indiana University Press.

"The Rites of Violence: Religious Riot in Sixteenth-Century France." Natalie Z. Davis. The Past and Present Society, 175 Banbury Road, Oxford, England. This article is here reprinted in abridged form, with the permission of the Society and the author, from *Past and Present: A Journal of Historical Studies,* no. 59, May 1973, pp. 51–91. This article also appears in Chapter 6 of Natalie Zemon Davis's *Society and Culture in Early Modern France,* Stanford University Press, 1975.

"Birth and Childhood in Seventeenth-Century France." Wendy Gibson. Copyright © 1989 by Wendy Gibson. Macmillan Press Ltd. and St. Martin's Press, Inc. (1989), Chapter 1. Reprinted with permission of St. Martin's Press and Macmillan Press Ltd.

"Insanity in Early Modern England." Michael MacDonald. From *Mystical Bedlam: Madness, Anxiety, and Healing in Seventeenth-Century England.* Cambridge, England and New York: Cambridge University Press, 1981, pp. 1–11. Reprinted with the permission of Cambridge University Press.